Education and the Rise
of the New South

Edited by
Ronald K. Goodenow and
Arthur O. White

Education and the Rise of the New South

G.K. Hall and Co. Boston, Massachusetts

Copyright © 1981 Ronald K. Goodenow and Arthur O. White

Library of Congress Cataloging in Publication Data

Main entry under title:

Education and the rise of the new South.

Includes index.
Contents: Ex-slaves and the rise of the universal educa-
tion in the new South, 1860–1880 / James D. Anderson—
The American compromise / Jennings L. Wagoner, Jr.—
Progressivism and rural education in the deep South,
1900–1950 / Spencer J. Maxcy—[etc.]
    1. Education—Southern States—History—Addresses,
essays, lectures. I. Goodenow, Ronald K. II. White,
Arthur O., 1942–
LA230.5.S6E38   370'.975   81–2911
ISBN 0–8161–9019–4   AACR2

This publication is printed on permanent/durable acid-free paper.
MANUFACTURED IN THE UNITED STATES OF AMERICA

Contents

Foreword

Education and the Rise of the New South is intended to meet some very basic needs. It is a new book-length treatment of Southern educational history, one of the few to be made available since the 1922 publication of Edgar Knight's *Public Education in the South*. It reflects our belief that the history of education as a field should include much more work on the South. There has been valuable material produced by educational historians over the past few years on cities, reform, testing, and other topics. Most of it, however, has dealt with the North. Participation in several conferences of the Southern History of Education Society, which meets annually at Georgia State University, has convinced us that there is fortunately a new generation of scholarship on the South that fills many gaps in our knowledge as it moves conceptually into new territory. We have drawn upon this work and are confident that it will be of value to teachers, students, and researchers in the South and elsewhere.

Much of the research now being done on the South reflects shifts and changes in American historiography over the past decade which have broadened our conception of education and linked it to the social and cultural history of a growing nation undergoing complex transformations. Themes which are apparent in many of this book's essays include the nature and impact of urbanization and the emergence of the modern political economy with its stress on education for differentiated occupational and social roles. Increased professionalization and centralization in educational leadership, administration, curriculum planning, and even guidance and testing are also discussed by several of the contributors. Running through the volume is the suggestion of complexity, paradox, and the impact of competing influences. Forces of a distinctly regional character, the reader will discover, vied with those related to class relations, economic modernization, and changes of a national character.

Some of these themes are apparent in the book's first chapter. James Anderson underscores the mixed motivations which characterized the ex-slave's well-known desire for public schooling; Anderson explains that universal education was perceived as representing but one of several interests of a class and political nature. Jennings L. Wagoner, Jr., then introduces a comparative perspective on Northern and Southern views of education and class relations. Wagoner writes that the attitudes of the liberal Harvard President, Charles Eliot, are indicative of the rise of an accommodationist consensus that watered down black aspirations such as Anderson describes, thus representing an "American Compromise" and not simply flagrant Southern racism.

There were, of course, distinctly Southern qualities to the emergence of the region's educational system. But even its essentially rural nature, as Spencer Maxcy suggests, was tempered by a complex pattern of forces not unlike those which affected educational change elsewhere in the country: progressive reform impulses, bureaucracy, powerful philanthropic involvement, and a range of often conflicting professional and political interests. Blacks, moreover, were not the only members of Southern society to be relegated to an inferior status during the process of Southern educational change. Amy Friedlander provides a valuable look at the "place" of New South women against the backdrop of institutional development. Religion, a new and somewhat "liberal" curriculum, and the motives of one Atlanta college's founders and their philanthropic supporters together reinforced many traditional views and, ultimately, subtle forms of second class citizenship for highly educated females. The often paradoxical nature of the aspirations influencing the development of Southern education is further examined in Mark Bauman's essay on Warren Candler's involvement with several colleges and universities, most notably what is now Emory University. Continuity and change, tradition and innovation, as well as class and political interests with a pervasive influence on how the higher learning was to be defined, are all present in Candler's life and work.

Wayne J. Urban and Joseph W. Newman contribute fresh perspectives into the world of Southern urban education. Professor Urban's essay on curriculum change in Atlanta shows that curriculum reformers may have used the rhetoric of reformers elsewhere but that the impulses for this change were deeply rooted in Atlanta's racism and traditions. One must, this chapter suggests, be wary of the emphasis on economic determinism as expressed in recent years by radical historians. Newman's case study of Atlanta teacher unionism in the twentieth century offers a long-overdue study of the professional lives of Southern teachers caught up in the debilitating net of persistent racism. Atlanta's white teachers, he writes here, were generally successful bread-and-butter unionists who unwittingly took money from their own pockets by refusing to make short-term economic concessions to their black colleagues, a somewhat ironic outcome in view of the liberal racial policies of the American Federation of Teachers, with which they were affiliated.

The social and ideological functions of progressive reform in the New Deal years are explored by William B. Thomas, Ronald K. Goodenow, and Nancy

L. Grant. Thomas shows that many white educators viewed intelligence testing and school guidance as new tools to adjust black youths to Southern folkways and the harsh realities of racism, elitism, and unemployment. Black educators, however, underscored the contention that properly controlled testing and guidance were not only means of "modernization," as whites were apt to argue, but also, in the hands of blacks, means to improved education and social reform. Goodenow demonstrates that if the progressive education movement was indeed alive and well in the Deep South, Southern regionalism influenced both its paradoxial functions and Depression Era practices. Grant sets out new evidence that the TVA, often claimed to be regional and federal social engineering at its most liberal and equitable, sponsored inferior programs in black education.

The book's final essays offer sweeping overviews of their topics. Arthur O. White provides an analysis of how one state, Florida, developed its educational system administratively. He highlights the interplay of complex financial and professional issues and a plethora of lobby groups. The concluding historiographical chapter by Harvey Neufeldt and Clinton Anderson serves as a detailed review of research on the history of Southern education and provides valuable insights on interpretive trends and research needs.

We would like to add a few words on this volume's focus. When we instructed contributors to *Education and the Rise of the New South*, we asked that they be alert to several things. The first is the New South phenomenon, its ideological manifestations and its relationship to regional modernization and change. As a starting point, we suggested, this might replace the more traditional emphasis on race relations. We do not deny that the causes and facts of segregation, with its brutalities, inequities, and denial of basic American rights, posed serious moral and practical dilemmas to those who wanted to bring the South into a modern America. Nor do we deny the importance of focusing upon or probing many of these causes of segregation—among them class conflict and relations, Northern exploitation, the impact of the Civil War on regional politics, populism, and the exact nature of the region's agricultural political economy. We wanted to include a diversity of opinion and to avoid the pitfalls of trying to present a uniform point of view, a search for interpretive uniformity being one of the things that has too often plagued Southern scholarship and our own field, the history of American education.

It follows from these comments that we did not propose a particular model for interpreting the New South phenomenon or modernization. In searching the field for essayists, moreover, we did not limit ourselves to Southerners or individuals who teach in the South. Southern history should no more be the exclusive domain of Southerners than urban history that of people who live in cities. Many of us believe that the Southern experience is a uniquely American one that offers critical insights into our national life. In the case of schooling, it may well be that the relative lateness of educational modernization in the South provides the historian with topics for research that fall enticingly within the grasp of the contemporary scholar. Written evidence is readily accessible and many individuals who have participated in virtually all phases of public schooling in the region are still alive.

Because *Education and the Rise of the New South* is topically diverse, it cannot pretend to be the last word on its topic. We do hope, however, that it encourages more such work, for the last thing that is needed is closure. Much needs to be done. In surveying the field, for example, we found little on girls and women, the Southern family as educator, Southern cities, and the many educational networks which encouraged region-wide curricular and administrative changes in the 1920s and 1930s. Regional professionalization and the lives of teachers beg research. Not much has come to light concerning the educational experiences of Native Americans (a large Southern population), European immigrants, or even the children of Northerners who have relocated there in the years since the Second World War. While individual topics such as these have been overlooked, there also needs to be far more sophisticated study of those "cultural configurations," including the family, the media, and non-public schools and churches, given prominence in the work of Lawrence Cremin and others who urge a broad and synthetic view of the educational enterprise in regional and local settings.

At a different level there is a need and opportunity for sophisticated comparative research. After all is said and done, do we really know what makes the South distinctive? What are important differences to be found *within* the region and what is their ultimate significance? How does the study of educational history aid in this quest? Is, for example, "urbanization" and its impact on education (and vice versa) the same in Atlanta as in Dallas, Des Moines, or even Dakar? How do we get a "big picture" of the South and particularly the education of its minorities? Do paradigms which hint at neocolonialism have merit, as suggested by some recent scholarship in comparative education? Are many of the paradoxes ascribed to the region the result of contradictions imposed more by external forces than by what may properly be described as forces indigenous to the region? It may be that as historians begin to probe the post-1954 years, especially those which have witnessed the rise of the affluent Sun Belt, such paradoxes will be better understood.

We would also like to urge a far more concerted effort to teach about Southern educational history. If ever there was a need for collaborative discussion and research, it is in this area. Conferences such as those being held at Teachers College, Columbia University on urban educational history provide one model. Another may be found in a recent colloquium sponsored by the National Institute of Education on work and education. Certainly, some of the great Southern universities should encourage such gatherings.

Discussion of and research in Southern Education would nicely complement the preservation of archival and other records and would bear directly on many policy issues.

Finally, we would like to gratefully acknowledge some assistance in the preparation of this book. Charles Strickland of Emory and Vincent Franklin of Yale nominated contributors. The University of Florida made it possible for Professor Goodenow to read the paper (published here) which brought us together in Gainesville to plan our collaboration.

January 1981   RONALD K. GOODENOW
Bloomfield, Ct.

                                                          ARTHUR O. WHITE
Gainesville, Fl.

James D. Anderson

Ex-Slaves and the Rise of Universal Education in the New South, 1860-1880

This essay is devoted to the rise and expansion of black education in the South from the Civil War era through the 1880s. It focuses primarily on the persistent struggle of ex-slaves to assure universal education for their own class but also on the impact of their movement on the whole foundation of universal education in the postwar South. Ex-slaves began a region-wide campaign for universal tax-supported education in the early 1860s, and this historical development, like so many others, placed the South at odds with the rise and expansion of schooling in the rest of American society. In the Northeast, for instance, the campaign for universal schooling was initiated and sponsored by reformers from the dominant class, necessitated in substantial part by rapid industrialization and modernization and legitimized by a popular ideology of democratic capitalism. The planter class that dominated the postwar South, however, was generally opposed to tax-supported public education, particularly for the ex-slaves. Further, the planter class adhered to a set of agrarian values inconsistent with a high rate of industrialization and modernization. The massive labor needs of the cotton economy and the planters' belief in coercive labor control discouraged the education of the laboring classes. The result was a postwar South that was hostile to the social welfare institutions which characterized the New England political economy and that had little incentive to provide universal education.

Thus, the history of the American South provides fascinating challenges to the historian studying the social origins of universal schooling. The Southern movement for the public education of all social classes developed in a political economy very different from that of the rest of the nation. More importantly, the campaign for universal education in the postwar South was initiated by a distinct ex-slave working class. Indeed, during the Civil War and the years immediately following the war, schools best flourished in Southern regions where an organized ex-slave class, often backed by the Union army, the Freedmen's Bureau, and the Northern benevolent societies, countered the negative power of the planter class and fostered a combined secular and religious system of universal schooling. The ex-slaves did not foster a system of universal schooling without first organizing to advance and defend their common interests, overcoming the resistance of opposing social classes, and gaining the cooperation of other groups. Each of these developments requires analysis; the starting point, however, is the ex-slave class itself and its centrality to the rise and expansion of schooling in the postbellum South. The significance of this development is at the heart of the story told in this essay.

The Ex-Slaves' Educational Movement

The ex-slaves' educational movement has been studied by many scholars. Two central themes emerge in virtually all writings on the subject. First, historians generally agree that ex-slaves strongly desired education for their children and for themselves. Second, they argue that the Union army, Yankee school teachers, Northern benevolent societies, and the Freedmen's Bureau combined to form the central force in the ex-slaves' educational movement. There is considerable evidence for the first claim. Virtually every account by historians or contemporary observers stresses the ex-slaves' demand for universal schooling. In 1879, Harriet Beecher Stowe said of their campaign for education: "They rushed not to the grog-shop but to the schoolroom—they cried for the spelling-book as bread, and pleaded for teachers as a necessity of life." Journalist Charles Nordhoff reported that New Orleans' ex-slaves were "almost universally . . . anxious to send their children to school." Booker T. Washington, a part of this movement himself, described most vividly his people's struggle for education: "Few people who were not right in the midst of the scenes can form any exact idea of the intense desire which the people of my race showed for education. It was a whole race trying to go to school. Few were too young, and none too old, to make the attempt to learn." These accounts are sustained by the more systematic analyses of historians Edward F. Sweat, Alton Hornsby, John W. Blassingame, Henry Allen Bullock, and Herbert G. Gutman, and also by a number of recent dissertations on black education in the postbellum South.[1]

The second theme, however, that Northerners either brought schooling to the ex-slaves or modeled and transmitted the value of education to them is not well supported in the secondary literature and is at variance with a great many primary historical sources. As historian Herbert Gutman demonstrates, "A vast quantity of historical evidence contradicts explanations which attribute the schooling of ex-slaves either to Uncle Sam, to northern benevolent societies, or to a combination of the two." More importantly, such explanations omit the most significant dimension of the ex-slaves' educational movement, the sustained efforts by ex-slaves themselves. Gutman has termed the efforts "self-activity," a metaphor for lower-class behavior of all sorts. "Significant self-activity among the ex-slaves—class self-activity informed by an ethic of mutuality—also brought schools to the children of freed men and women," writes Gutman. Significantly, he does not attribute the underlying force of the ex-slaves' educational campaign to external groups, but to the culmination of a process of social class formation and development that started decades before the Civil War. "Emancipation," he contends, "transformed an established and developed subordinate class, allowing ex-slave men and women to act on a variety of class beliefs that had developed but been constrained during several generations of enslavement." Within this framework we are directed to examine the ex-slaves' educational movement in terms of their own beliefs and behavior, which suggests, among other things, that their campaign for free schooling was rooted firmly in Southern soil and not imposed by Yankee missionaries and school teachers. Indeed, this model suggests that W. E. B. DuBois may have been correct when he said, "Public education for all at public expense was, in the South, a Negro idea." This view of postwar Southern education acknowledges the important contributions of Northerners, but recognizes the ex-slaves as the principal challenge to the region's deep resistance to free schooling.[2]

Gutman's and DuBois's works are virtually the only accounts to frame the ex-slaves' educational movement in this way. Their writings naturally collide head-on with historians who believe that ex-slaves learned the rules and values of civil society from their former owners or middle-class Yankee reformers. Such an interpretation, however, would not have surprised John W. Alvord, the national superintendent of schools for the Freedmen's Bureau.

In September 1865, Alvord was appointed "inspector of schools" for the Bureau. The title was later changed to "general superintendent of schools." To assist him in compiling records on the Bureau's educational activities, he appointed a superintendent of schools for each Southern state in July 1865. Alvord had traveled through nearly all the Confederate states by December, 1865, and filed his first general report on the Freedmen's Bureau schools in January, 1866. In this document he gave special attention to the practice of "self-teaching" and "native schools" among the freed men and women. "Throughout the entire South," Alvord reported, "an effort is being made by the colored people to educate themselves." "In the absence of other teaching they are determined to be self-taught; and everywhere some elementary text-book, or the fragment of one, may be seen in the hands of negroes." Not only were individuals found teaching themselves to read and write; Alvord also discovered a system of what he chose to call "native schools," one of which he found at Goldsboro, North Carolina: "Two colored young men, who but a little time before commenced to learn themselves, had gathered 150 pupils, all quite orderly and hard at study." Further, Alvord discovered that "No white man, before me, had ever come near them." Two of Alvord's findings must be heavily emphasized. First, he found "native schools," in his own words, "throughout the entire South." Second, he discovered many of them in places which had not been visited by the Freed-men's Bureau or Northern benevolent societies. Alvord, realizing that his findings did not square with existing perceptions of "the character of the Negro," took "special pains" to ascertain the facts on "native schools." Such schools were found in "all the large places I visited," and they were "making their appearance through the *interior* of the entire South." After receiving much testimony from his field agents, "both oral and written," Alvord estimated in 1865 that there were "at least 500 schools of this de-scription . . . already in operation throughout the South." This estimate, he warned his readers, was not an "over-statement." There was little doubt in Alvord's mind as to the significance of his findings; "this educational move-ment among the freedmen has in it a self-sustaining element." This "self-sustaining" activity which Alvord observed in 1865 was rooted firmly in the slave experience and began to surface before the war's end.[3]

Before Northern benevolent societies entered the South in 1862, before President Lincoln issued the Emancipation Proclamation in 1863, and before Congress created the Bureau of Refugees, Freedmen and Abandoned Lands (Freedmen's Bureau) in 1865, slaves and free persons of color had already begun to make plans for the systematic instruction of their illiterates. Early black schools were established and supported largely as a result of the Afro-Americans' own efforts. The first of these schools, according to current historiography, opened at Fortress Monroe, Virginia, in September, 1861, under the leadership of Mary Peake, a black teacher. Primary historical sources, however, promise to demonstrate that slaves and free persons of color started schools even before the Fortress Monroe venture. In July, 1864, for instance, the black *New Orleans Union* commemorated the founding of the "Pioneer School of Freedom" that was established in New Orleans in 1860, "in the midst of danger and darkness." Some schools predated the Civil War period and simply increased their activities after the war started. A black school in Savannah, Georgia, had existed unknown to the slave regime from 1833 to 1865. Its teacher, a black woman by the name of Deveaux, quickly expanded her literacy campaign during and following the war. It was this kind of "self-sustaining" behavior that produced the "native-schools" which Alvord observed throughout the South in 1865.[4]

Herbert Gutman's pioneering work on this subject demonstrates further that the "native schools" of Fortress Monroe, Savannah, and New Orleans were not isolated developments. Such schools also started quickly among refugees in Alexandria, Virginia. A white teacher did not work with Afro-Americans in Alexandria until October 1862. By that time they had already established several schools. "In April 1863," writes Gutman, "about four hundred children attended such schools." Likewise, he documents that rural ex-slaves in northwestern South Carolina behaved in a similar fashion. In 1867, Camden blacks, largely because of their own individual and collective efforts, established twenty-two schools, and over four thousand children were instructed. Schooling also made significant progress among blacks in Sumpter, Marion, Darlington, Simmonsville, Florence, Kingstree, Cherau, Bennettsville, and Timonville, South Carolina. Ex-slaves contributed their monies and labors to help make these schools possible, and they organized responsible committees to supervise these schools.[5]

What happened in Alexandria, Virginia, before 1865 and in northeastern South Carolina in 1866 and 1867 occurred elsewhere in the South. Afro-Americans over the entire region contributed significantly to the origin and development of universal schooling. Even where the Union army and Freedmen's Bureau were heavily involved in the educational activities of refugees and ex-slaves, the long-term success of schooling depended mainly on Afro-Americans. The activities of Louisiana refugees and ex-slaves illustrate the importance of such involvement. Blacks began establishing small private schools between 1860 and 1862. Though these first schools were inadequately financed and haphazardly run, attempts were made to organize them on a systematic basis. After Union forces occupied New Orleans in 1863, however, a federal Commission of Enrollment presided over blacks' educational activities. According to historian John W. Blassingame, Major General Nathaniel P. Banks "instituted the most thorough of all systems for educating the freedmen in his Department of Gulf (Louisiana, Mississippi, Alabama and Texas)." In October, 1863, he authorized the Commission of Enrollment to take a census of Afro-Americans in the Gulf states and to establish schools for blacks in New Orleans. On March 22, 1864, he established a Board of Education to organize and govern the spread of black schools. In September, 1864, the black *New Orleans Tribune* reported that Banks's effort had already resulted in 60 schools with "eight thousand scholars and more than one hundred teachers." By December, 1864, the Board of Education was operating 95 schools with 9,571 children and 2,000 adults instructed by 162 teachers. This system of schooling extended beyond the New Orleans area. The *Tribune* reported in July, 1864, that teachers were "sent to instruct black pupils in rural areas." In 1865, the Freedmen's Bureau took control of this school system which then comprised 126 schools, 19,000 pupils, and 200 teachers.[6]

Such historical evidence has been wrongly used to attribute the ex-slaves' school movement to Yankee benevolence or federal largesse. The events that followed the Freedmen's Bureau takeover, however, underscore Gutman's observation that the ex-slaves' educational movement was rooted deeply within their own communal values. The Board of Education and later the Freedmen's Bureau maintained these schools through federal contributions and by levying a property tax to support the schools. In 1866, allegedly to reduce the financial costs to the bureau, its officials temporarily closed all black schools under their authorization and the general tax for freedmen education was suspended by military order. The effect of this change was catastrophic. Alvord, national superintendent of the Freemen's Bureau, recorded the actions of Louisiana's ex-slaves: "The consternation of the colored population was intense.... They could not consent to have their children sent away from study, and at once expressed willingness to be assessed for the whole expense." Black leaders petitioned Yankee military officers to levy an added tax upon their community to replenish the Bureau's school fund. Petitions demanding the continuation of universal schooling poured in from all over Louisiana. As Alvord recounted:

> I saw one [petition], from plantations across the river, at least 30
> feet in length, representing 10,000 negroes. It was affecting to
> examine it and note the names and marks (x) of such a long list
> of parents, ignorant themselves, but begging that their children
> might be educated, promising that from beneath their present
> burdens, and out of their extreme poverty, they would pay for it.

Such actions reveal the collective effort and shared values of the ex-slaves who built and sustained schools across the postwar South.[7]

Much more than federal largesse made free schooling a reality among Louisiana's ex-slaves. After the bureau withdrew its support, the ex-slaves took control of the educational system and transformed federal schools into local free schools. As disclosed in the *New Orleans Tribune*, as soon as the bureau's failures were recognized, educational associations "were organized in various parts of the state, at least in its principal cities, to promote the cause of education, and with the particular view of helping the children of parents in reduced circumstances to attend schools." One such association, the Louisiana Educational Relief Association, was organized by ex-slaves in June, 1866. Its primary aim was to "disseminate the principle of education, by assisting poor children whose friends are unable to do so." The board of trustees could "lease or buy such school property as may be deemed judicious, and examine and employ teachers." Louisiana's ex-slaves believed it was primarily their responsibility to provide education for their children. "Each race of men, each class in society, have [sic] to shape their own destinies themselves," wrote J. Willis Menard, secretary of the Louisiana Educational Relief Association. While acknowledging the support of the Freedmen's Bureau and Northern benevolent societies, Menard maintained that the ex-slaves' survival and development rested largely on their own shoulders: "The colored people are called today to mark out on the map of life with their *own hands* their future course or locality in the great national body politic. Other hands cannot mark for them; other tongues cannot speak for them; other eyes cannot see for them; they must see and speak for themselves, and make their own characters on the map, however crooked or illegible." That Menard was not unusual in his beliefs is revealed through the behavior of Louisana's ex-slaves from 1866 to 1868. During this period they developed a parallel system of free schools. Even when the bureau reopened its schools, private schools for black pupils continued to spring up outside the bureau's control. Enrollment in such schools grew rapidly and actually exceeded the number registered in the bureau's system. In January, 1867, there were 65 private schools in New Orleans enrolling 2,967 pupils; the bureau maintained 56 schools with 2,527 pupils enrolled. Free schooling was sustained in Louisiana largely as a result of the ex-slaves' collective efforts.[8]

The relationship between black self-activity and educational changes in the postwar South is further illustrated by the behavior of Georgia's ex-slaves. In December, 1864, a committee of Afro-American leaders in Savannah, Georgia, met with Secretary of War Edwin M. Stanton and General William T. Sherman to request support for the education of Georgia's liberated blacks. Out of this conference evolved an initial plan for establishing an organized system of free schools. In 1865, Afro-American leaders formed the Georgia Educational Association to supervise schools in districts throughout the state, to establish school policies, and to raise funds to help finance the cost of education. Freedmen's Bureau officials described the aims and structure of this association:

> To associate the efforts of the people, the prominent educators in the
> State, the agents of northern societies, and such officers of the
> government as are authorized to aid the work, and to unite in such
> a manner as shall exclude any subject at all likely to divide their
> efforts or direct them from their one great and desirable object. To
> secure this end, subordinate associations are established as far as
> practicable. By this means a thorough union is formed and a prompt
> and constant communication with the parent society is had. Con-
> nected with the State association is a State board of education,
> which . . . is a general executive committee.

Through this association Georgia's Afro-Americans sustained in full or part the operation of more than two-thirds of their schools. In the fall of 1866, they financed entirely or in part 96 of the 123 day and evening schools. They also owned 57 of the school buildings. Such accomplishments represented the primary purpose of the Georgia Educational Association, "that the freedmen shall establish schools in their own counties and neighborhoods, to be supported entirely by the colored people." In Savannah, for instance, there were 28 schools in 1866, and 16 of them, reported the black *Loyal Georgian*, were "under the control of an Educational Board of Colored Men, taught by colored teachers, and sustained by the freed people." These beliefs and behavior were consistent with the activities of ex-slaves in Virginia, South Carolina, and Louisiana.[9]

Significantly, Georgia's black educational leaders were critical of popular misconceptions which attributed the schooling of ex-slaves to Yankee benev- olence. The *Loyal Georgian,* official newspaper of the Georgia Educational Association, rejected explicitly the argument that Yankee teachers brought schooling to the ex-slaves. In February, 1866, while defending Yankee teachers against Southern white criticism, the *Loyal Georgian* also expressed its hope that missionary teachers were not in the South, "in any vain reliance on their superior gifts, either of intelligence or benevolence; or in any foolish self-confidence that they have a special call to this office, or special endow- ments to meet its demands." Ronald E. Butchart has shown that ex-slaves not only initiated and supported education for themselves and their children but also sought to control their educational institutions. In 1867, for instance, the *Freedmen's Record* complained about the tendency of ex-slaves to prefer sending their children to black-controlled private schools rather than support- ing the less expensive Northern white-dominated schools. Similarly, a white observer noted that "in all respects apart from his or her competency to teach— they will keep their children out of school, and go to work, organize and [*sic*] independent school and send their children to it." It is no wonder, then, that some missionaries complained of the ex-slaves' lack of gratitude "for the charity which Northern friends are so graciously bestowing." The ex- slaves' educational movement became a test of their capacities to restructure their lives, to establish their freedom. While they appreciated Northern support, they resisted infringements which threatened to sap their own initiative and self-reliance.[10]

In other important ways ex-slaves initiated and sustained schools whether or not Northern aid was available. The "Sabbath" school system, about which little is known, provides a particularly clear study of educational activities operated largely on the strength of the ex-slave community. Frequently, Sabbath schools were established before "free" or "public" schools. These church-sponsored schools, opened mainly in evenings and on weekends, provided basic literacy instruction. "They reached thousands not able to attend weekday schools," writes Samuel L. Horst. In January, 1866, in his first report to the Freedmen's Bureau, Alvord commented on the existence of Sabbath schools throughout the South:

> Sabbath schools among freedmen have opened throughout the
> entire South; all of them giving elementary instruction, and reaching
> thousands who cannot attend the week-day teaching. These are not
> usually included in the regular returns, but are often spoken of with
> special interest by the superintendents. Indeed, one of the most
> thrilling spectacles which he who visits the southern country now
> witnesses in cities, and often upon the plantations, is the large
> schools gathered upon the Sabbath day, sometimes of many

hundreds, dressed in clean Sunday garments, with eyes sparkling, intent upon elementary and Christian instruction. The management of some of these is admirable, after the fashion of the best Sunday schools of white children, with faithful teachers, the majority of whom it will be noticed are colored.

Some of Alvord's findings are especially worthy of emphasis. Sabbath schools were common in ex-slave communities across the South immediately following the war's end. In 1868, Alvord described the scope of Sabbath schools in North Carolina: "In all the cities of the State, in most of the smaller towns, and in many of the rural districts, Sabbath schools are established and well conducted." Although white religious societies sponsored some Sabbath schools for ex-slaves, the system was largely black-dominated, relied on local black communities for support, and generally had all-black teaching staffs. The importance of the Sabbath schools varied across states and localities. In some areas they constituted the only viable system of free instruction. T. K. Noble, Freedmen's Bureau Superintendent of Education in Kentucky, said in 1867: "The places of worship owned by the colored people are almost the only available school houses in the State."[11]

It is important, therefore, to emphasize another of Alvord's observations, that the Sabbath schools, often spoken of with special interest by the state superintendents, were not usually included in the regular bureau reports. C. E. Compton, the bureau's superintendent of education in Tennessee, reported in 1870 that "many children attend Sabbath schools at colored churches of which no report is received." The Freedmen's Bureau kept statistics from 1866 to 1870. These records include almost exclusively schools under the auspices of Northern societies. Hence, ex-slaves laid a significantly larger foundation for universal education than is accounted for in official reports and in the histories of Southern education. Historian James M. McPherson writes that "At no time were more than 10 percent of the freedmen of school age attending the [missionary] societies' schools." Historian Meyer Weinberg concludes that, in 1870, "nine out of ten black children still remained outside any school." These estimates, however accurate for schools reporting to the bureau, do not include data on the church-operated schools. In 1869, Alvord asked his field agents to estimate teachers and enrollments in Sabbath schools. These reports, admittedly conservative in their estimates, enumerated 1,512 Sabbath schools with 6,146 teachers and 107,109 pupils. Sabbath schools continued to grow in the black community long after Reconstruction. In 1868, the African Methodist Episcopal Church (AME), for example, enrolled 40,000 pupils in its Sabbath schools. By 1885, the AME church reported having "200,000 children in Sunday schools" for "intellectual and moral" instructions. These were not Sunday schools devoted entirely to Bible study. As Booker T. Washington put it, "the principal book studied in the Sunday school was the spelling book." The Sabbath schools represent yet another remarkable example of ex-slaves seeking, establishing, and supporting their own schools.[12]

From the evidence it is extremely doubtful that the Freedmen's Bureau and Northern benevolent societies combined to form the central force in the South's postwar school campaign. What is evident, on the other hand, is that the ex-slaves initiated and supported their own schools and sustained in large part the Northern-sponsored schools. That ex-slaves were the central force in the South's postwar movement for universal education has escaped the attention of all but a few historians.[13] The larger significance of ex-slave behavior, however, did not go unnoticed by Freedmen's Bureau super- intendent John Alvord, one of the most perceptive Yankee observers of postwar Southern educational changes. As early as January, 1866, Alvord noted the "self-sustaining element" in the ex-slaves educational movement. He quickly recognized the organization and discipline that underlay the school campaign. In July, 1866, he reported "that the surprising efforts of our colored population to obtain and [sic] education are not spasmodic." "They are growing to a habit," he continued, "crystalizing into a system, and each succeeding school-term shows their Organization more and more com- plete and permanent." Initially, Alvord did not know what to make of these "surprising efforts." Foreshadowing the interpretations of later historians, in January, 1866, he attributed the ex-slaves' campaign for schooling to "the natural thirst for knowledge common to all men," a desire to imitate educated whites, an attraction to the mystery of literate culture, the practical needs of business life, and the stimulating effects of freedom. By July, however, Alvord pointed to a more fundamental motive for ex-slave behavior. "They have within themselves . . . a vitality and hope, coupled with patience and willingness to struggle, which foreshadows with certainty their higher education as a people in the coming time." Universal education was certain to become a reality in black society, not because ex-slaves were motivated by childlike, irrational, and primitive drives, but because they were a respon- sible and politically self-conscious social class. Alvord, therefore, was confi- dent that the ex-slaves' educational movement would not soon fall into decline:

> Obstacles are yet to be encountered. Perhaps the most trying period
> in the freedmen's full emancipation has not yet come. But we can
> distinctly see that the incipient education universally diffused as it
> is, has given these whole four millions an impulse onward never to
> be lost. They are becoming conscious of what they can do, of what
> they ultimately *can be*. . . . Self-reliance is becoming their pride
> as it is their responsibility.

His work in the South gave him an affirmative view of the ex-slaves' capacity to restructure their lives through the establishment of constructive social institutions, especially universal schooling.[14]

Ultimately, the formation and development of the ex-slaves' beliefs and behavior regarding universal education in the postwar South will have to be understood as part of a prcoess that started decades before the Civil War. For, as Herbert Gutman has demonstrated, the choices so many freed men and women made immediately upon their emancipation, before they had substantial rights by law, had their origins in the ways their antecedents had adapted to enslavement. Hence, before the reason why Afro-Americans emerged from slavery with a particular desire for literacy can be understood, slavery and especially slave literacy await refined and detailed study. That is beyond the scope of this essay. We can, however, examine some postslavery circumstances that provided ex-slaves with compelling reasons to become literate. The uses and abuses of written labor contracts made it worthwhile to be able to read, write, and cipher. Frequently, planters designed labor contracts in order to confuse and entrap the ex-slaves. As Alvord observed, "I saw one [labor-contract] in which it was stipulated that one-third of seven-twelfths of all corn, potatoes, fodder, etc., shall go to the laborers." Hence, when a middle-aged black woman was asked why she was so determined to learn, she replied, "so that the Rebs can't cheat me." The right to vote also gave ex-slaves an impulse to become literate. "At the place of voting they look at the ballot-box and then at the printed ticket in their hands, wishing they could read it," reported Alvord in 1867. In a practical sense, education for the ex-slaves could serve as a safeguard against fraud and manipulation.[15]

More fundamentally, as Ronald Butchart maintains, "the struggle for an education was an earnest of freedom [sic]." It was an effort of an oppressed people "to put as great a distance between themselves and bondage as possible." The New Orleans Black Republican proclaimed in April, 1865: "Freedom and school books and newspapers, go hand in hand. Let us secure the freedom we have received by the intelligence that can maintain it." This proclamation was signed by prominent black leaders of New Orleans such as Thomas S. Isabelle, C. C. Antoine, S. W. Rogers, Professor P. M. Williams, and A. E. Barber. Similarly, in 1867, the black Equal Rights Association of Macon, Georgia, resolved: "That a Free school system is a great need of our state, and that we will do all in our power by voice and by vote to secure adoption of a system." That same year black leaders Henry M. Turner, T. G. Campbell, John T. Costin, and Thomas P. Beard formed the Black Republican Party of Georgia. The organization declared "that Free Schools and churches are the guardians of civil and religious liberty." Northern observers, therefore, quickly noted that education stood as "the token and pledge" of blacks' emancipation. Even adult ex-slaves, as Alvord recorded, were "earnestly seeking that instruction which will fit them for their new responsibilities." For the ex-slaves, universal schooling was a necessary function of state and civil society.[16]

Thus, ex-slaves did much more than establish a tradition of educational self-help that supported most of their schools. They also began first among native Southerners to wage a campaign for universal public education. From its small beginnings in 1860 and with the help of the Freedmen's Bureau and Northern benevolent societies, the school system was virtually complete in its institutional form by 1870. According to historian Henry Allen Bullock, 14 Southern states had established 575 schools by 1865, and these schools were employing 1,171 teachers for the 71,779 Negro and white children in regular attendance. School attendance was not uniform across cities and towns, but it was highly visible in enough places to signal a fundamental shift in Southern tradition. In 1866, Alvord reported his findings on the level of ex-slave school attendence:

> The average attendance is nearly equal to that usually found at the North. For instance, in the District of Columbia, the daily attendance at the public school is but forty-one (41) percent; while at the colored schools of the District it is seventy-five (75) percent. In the State of New York, the daily attendance at the public school averages (43) percent. At the colored schools in the city of Memphis it is seventy-two (72) percent; and in Virginia eighty-two (82) percent.

In Louisiana over 60 percent of all black children from 5 to 12 years of age were enrolled in school by 1865. The ex-slaves' school enrollment suffered a setback in 1868, rose again in 1869, and leveled off in 1870. In the whole South in 1870, about one-fourth of the school-age ex-slaves attended "public" schools. Reliable data is not available to determine Sabbath school attendance rates, but it seems probable from scattered evidence that Sabbath schools increased their enrollment throughout the 1870s and 1880s. The ex-slaves' initiative in starting schools and their remarkable attendance rates were enough to make it evident that "free" schooling was fast becoming a customary right in the postwar South. Alvord proclaimed in January 1866, "This great multitude rise up simultaneously, and ask for education. . . . They cannot well be put off." The ex-slaves' challenge to Southern tradition, however, was more than a matter of establishing universal schooling as a customary right. They also played a central role in committing Southern states to legal, tax-supported education. Indeed, the legal foundation of universal schooling in the South was established when ex-slaves achieved political power in the Reconstruction government. Constitutional conventions held throughout the South in 1867 and 1868 produced the laws that gave the South its first system of state-supported public schools. By 1870, every Southern state had created a public school system financed by a state fund. Hence, ex-slaves had moved the whole region, historically hostile to the idea of public education, to consider the role of universal schooling in the postwar political economy.[17]

The Planters' Response

Postwar Southern economic and social development, including educational reform, was very much influenced by the persistent domination of the planter class. Traditional historiography has contended that the Civil War and Emancipation brought about the downfall of the prewar planter class. The most recent historical scholarship, however, demonstrates convincingly the extent to which wealth and power in the postwar South continued to rest in the planters' hands. Historians Dwight B. Billings, Jr., Jay R. Mandle, Harold D. Woodman, Richard Sutch, Roger L. Ransom, and particularly Jonathan M. Wiener show that what actually occurred was not the downfall or destruction of the old planter class, but rather its persistence and metamorphosis. Plantation land tended to remain in the hands of its prewar owners.[18]

The persistence and tenacity of the planter class throughout the war and Reconstruction, contends Jonathan Wiener, laid the basis for its continued domination of the Southern political economy in the 1870s and 1880s. As a consequence, the South took the "Prussian road to industrial capitalism —a delayed industrialization under the auspices of a backward agrarian elite, the power of which was based on a repressive system of agricultural labor." In 1880, 75.4 percent of the South's labor force was in agriculture. Agriculture accounted for only 23.3 percent of the work force in the Northeast and 54.5 percent in the North Central region. The planters' approach to labor-control posed a formidable threat to the ex-slaves' educational movement. Elsewhere in the nation, particularly the industrial Northeast, dominant classes had already committed themselves to tax-supported public education, partly as a means to train and discipline an industrial work force. Bureau Superintendent Alvord, echoing the Northern idea of universal schooling for the lower classes, proclaimed to the South in 1866: "Popular education cannot well be opposed; free labor is found to be more contented with its privileges." But Southern planters did not share Northern ideas of free labor or popular education. Postwar planters complained that their "free" laborers were unreliable, failed to comply with the terms of their labor-contracts, and would not obey orders. Most important of all, schooling most emphatically was not the answer to Southern labor problems. "The South could not supply by schools," said one Southern writer in 1868, "the restraining, correcting, elevating influences" cultivated and maintained by slavery. When Carl Schurz toured the South in late 1865, he found the planters believing that "learning will spoil the nigger for work." Faced with the possibilities of moving toward a Northern-style system of free labor and mass literacy or remaining with their coercive mode of labor allocation and control, the planters chose the labor-repressive system which rested at least partially on working class illiteracy.[19]

Hence, at war's end the planters attempted to reestablish the plantation system with only minor modifications. With the overseer renamed "manager" or "agent," the planters tried to force ex-slaves to work the postwar plantations in antebellum-like work gangs. What the planters needed above all was a resumption of work on the part of black laborers in numbers and involving costs similar to what had prevailed in the prewar era. From the planters' viewpoint, the chief difficulty arose when ex-slaves withdrew a substantial portion of their labor power. By greatly reducing the number of days worked and the number of hours worked each day, ex-slaves created in the South a serious labor shortage. According to economic historians Ransom and Sutch, upon emancipation the supply of black labor fell to two-thirds its prewar level. This reduced labor supply had a profound impact on the ability of the South to produce cotton. It represented a severe financial blow to the planter class. On the one hand, therefore, the labor shortage gave ex-slaves some power in the labor market to insist upon social reforms of the racial caste system upon which the agrarian order had been based. On the other hand, however, planters generally favored a policy of strict labor control and discouraged the education of ex-slaves.[20]

In the immediate postwar years, ex-slaves, sometimes assisted by Northern troops, were able to use their labor power to give weight to their educational demands. In January, 1866, Bureau Superintendent Alvord noted how ex-slaves used their labor power to overcome the traditional resistance to universal education by the planter class:

> If they are to be retained as laborers in the rural districts, [educational] opportunities must be furnished on the plantations. More than one instance could be already given where a school in the interior has been started from this motive. . . . The head of one of the largest of the timber and turpentine enterprises in South Carolina told me that he formerly had hired only men, but he had now learned that he must have their families too, and that this could only be done by allowing them patches of land, treating them properly, paying them well, and *giving them schools.*

In 1866 and 1867, Freedmen's Bureau officials observed the widespread emergence of the "educational clause" in labor contracts between planters and ex-slaves. In July 1867, Frank R. Chase, the bureau's superintendent of education for Louisiana, reported: "Many of the freedmen made it a special clause of their contract this year, that they should have the benefit of schools. But the planter was only willing to have colored teachers employed, thinking that such schools would amount to little or nothing. In this they are mistaken, as many of the most prosperous schools in the State are taught by competent colored teachers." Such reports from bureau officials across the South convinced Alvord that "the educational clause in the contracts . . . is rapidly becoming universal." Hence, he continued, "Schools are everywhere springing up from the soil itself at the demand of those who til it—a state of things which localizes the benefits of education in a fixed, permanent society." Ex-slaves understood that their labor power was essential for the restoration of Southern agriculture to its prewar level of prosperity. Consequently, they demanded not only fair wages for their work but educational opportunities as well. This practice, at least for a brief period in the postwar years, enabled some plantation ex-slaves to experience the benefits of schooling. Some planters, desiring to secure and stabilize a needed supply of laborers, even shielded freedmen schools from harassment by white terrorists. Schools on the plantations were usually financed by the ex-slaves, but a few were paid for by planters.[21]

In the long run, contrary to the assertions of some historians, ex-slaves were unable to reconcile the planters to the idea of black education. Howard A. White, historian of the Freedmen's Bureau in Louisiana, contends that "the most intelligent and successful planters were usually the ones found supporting Negro education, while the bitterest opposition came from the lower classes." To be sure, the bitterest opposition did come from the lower-class whites and a few planters did accept or tolerate the idea of universal education among the ex-slaves. As a class, however, the planters reacted decisively to the ex-slaves' educational movement; they were opposed to black education in particular and showed substantial resistance to the very idea of public schooling for the lower classes. The planters' opposition to black education surfaced early. In 1864, the *New Orleans Tribune* reported that Louisiana planters were strongly opposed to the ex-slaves' educational movement. In the country parishes, white teachers were "condemned and scorned" and landlords "refused to rent buildings for school purposes, and to board the teachers." In 1867, Louisiana's superintendent of education complained that "a large majority of the planters are opposed to the education of the freedmen." An example in 1871 illustrates the point with much greater force. General Eaton, commissioner of the new Federal Bureau of Education, sent out 3,000 questionnaires to laborers and employers regarding the benefits of universal education in the South. Concerning the replies, he wrote: "A large number [of replies] have been received, and the writers were unanimous in their testimony as to the value of education to every class of laborers, with one striking exception, namely, the Southern planters; the

majority of whom did not believe in giving the Negro ary education." Planters resisted in various ways the ex-slaves' pursuit of universal schooling.
Historian Henry Allen Bullock found that Virginia planters in 1865 "were
seeking to prevent Negro parents from sending their children to school by
threatening to put them out of their houses." Alabama whites who employed
ex-slaves as domestics would terminate the employment of servants whose
children attended school. Similarly, in 1869 the Freedmen's Bureau school
superintendent for northwestern Louisiana and northern Texas discovered
that "many of the planters will not allow colored children on their places
to go to school at all, even when we have started those which are convenient." Thus, the planters, with few exceptions, viewed black education as a
distinct threat to the racial caste system upon which their agrarian order
was based.[22]

The planters' heavy use of child labor contributed significantly to their
opposition to black education. During good crop years black school terms
were so short and irregular that children hardly had time to learn to read
and write. "Owing to unusual employment of children this season in gathering crops, especially cotton, which was very abundant, many schools did
not open until December," reported John Alvord in 1870. Many parents
fought this infringement upon their children's educational opportunities,
but others conceded to the planters' interests.[23]

Despite the ex-slaves' early success in laying the foundation for universal
education in the South, planters presented severe obstacles to those who
endeavored to establish an elaborate bureaucratic system of free public
schooling. Between 1869 and 1877, the planter-dominated white South
regained control of the state governments. The moment of broad retrenchment came with the disputed presidential election of 1876 and the settlement that resulted in the Compromise of 1877. Southerners agreed to the
election of Rutherford B. Hayes, while Republicans agreed to remove the
federal troops from the South. With both state authority and extra-legal
means of control firmly in their hands, the planters, though unable to eradicate earlier gains, kept universal schooling underdeveloped. They stressed
low taxation, opposed compulsory school attendance laws, blocked the
passage of new laws that would strengthen the constitutional basis of public
education, and generally discouraged the expansion of public school opportunities. The planters' resistance virtually froze the ex-slaves' educational
campaign in its mid-1870s position. "At the beginning of the twentieth
century," wrote historian Horace Mann Bond, "the condition of the schools
for Negro children in the South was but slightly improved over their condition in 1875." Indeed, between 1880 and 1900, the number of black children
of school age increased 25 percent, but the proportion attending public
school fell.[24]

The planters gained further control over black education as they increased their supervision and control over the ex-slave laboring class. The semi-autonomous position and newly acquired economic power of ex-slaves in the labor market had buttressed their educational movement. Hence, as postwar landlords regained control over black labor, the force and autonomy of the campaign for universal schooling were severely weakened. The planters established a system of forced labor designed to reduce wages, to restrict labor mobility, to protect individual planters from the competition of other employees, and to force blacks to sign repressive labor-contracts. Historians William Cohen, Pete Daniel, and Jonathan Wiener discovered a variety of state laws and local customs aimed at helping planters to acquire, hold, and exploit black labor virtually at will. Enticement laws passed by ten Southern states from 1865 to 1867 were the most common measures aimed at controlling the black labor force. "Enticement statutes," writes Cohen, "established the proprietary claims of employers to 'their' Negroes by making it a crime to hire away a laborer under contract to another man." Many other laws facilitated the recruitment and retention of black labor. Vagrancy laws, passed by all the former Confederate states except Tennessee and Arkansas in 1865 and 1866, gave local authorities a "virtual mandate to arrest any poor man who did not have a labor contract." Such statutes enabled police to round up "idle" blacks in times of labor scarcity and, except in North Carolina, they provided for the hiring out of convicted offenders. Those jailed on charges of vagrancy could sign a "voluntary" labor-contract with their former employer or some other white man who agreed to post bond. Workers who had no surety often wound up on chain gangs and were forced to labor through the convict-lease system.

The planters favored a labor-repressive system of agricultural production. They had little incentive to use education and technology to increase efficiency and productivity or to use schooling as a means to train and discipline a more efficient work force. The postwar planters held to the beliefs and behavior of over two centuries of slavery; they did not really trust the system of "free labor." Force, rather than rational free choice, was the basis of the South's political economy. Hence, the region's slow development in education was in substantial part due to the planters' stubborn adherence to a set of values inconsistent with democracy, modernization, rapid industrialization, and free schooling. To be sure, other factors militated against rapid educational change. Fundamentally, however, the slow rate of educational development and the particular opposition to black education sprang from the clear economic and ideological interests the planters had in preserving the racial caste system upon which their regime rested. It was both race and class conflict between white planters and their black agricultural laborers.[25]

Universal Education in the New South

Even though the long-term gains in public school facilities for ex-slaves proved to be small and slow, their organized efforts and ideological imperatives laid the foundation for universal education in the South. Between 1860 and 1880 no organized challenge to the planters' interest came from the region's white middle classes or lower classes. Both groups were not only economically dependent on the planters, as were the ex-slaves, but also subservient to the planters' interests. Freedmen's Bureau officials were particularly alarmed by lower-class whites' general apathy toward public education. Bureau officials recognized that some planters were hostile to the idea of public education for poor whites. In 1869 Louisiana's superintendent observed planter opposition to "the education of freedmen and poor whites." "In the parish of Franklin," he reported, "public sentiment, as to the education of freedmen and poor whites, is very decidedly against it." Unlike the ex-slaves, however, "the whites take little or no interest in educational matters, even for their own race." Throughout the bureau's history, its officials contrasted ex-slave and lower-class white attitudes toward public education. In 1866, Alvord noted: "We make no invidious comparisons of the ignorant freedman, and the ignorant Anglo-Saxon of the South. We only say the former has most creditably won his present position; and he has done it by good conduct, and rapid improvement under that instruction we are now reporting." In 1869, a bureau state school superintendent observed: "As a class they [ex-slaves] are eager to learn, while the poor whites are indifferent." White laborers and small farmers did not challenge the planters' opposition to universal schooling until the late 1880s. Hence, historian Louis Harlan assumes wrongly that it was "the farmers [members of the Farmer's Alliance and Populist Party] who began first among native Southerners to wrestle with the problem of universal public education." Ex-slaves, or black native Southerners, had struggled for universal schooling over two decades prior to the populist campaigns of the late 1880s and 1890s. Likewise, the ex-slaves' campaign predated the organized movement for free schooling by Southern middle-class progressives. The South's white middle classes, unorganized and subservient to planter interests throughout the nineteenth century, did not begin their campaign for universal education until the dawn of the twentieth century. Hence, surrounded by planters who were hostile to public education, middle class professionals who allied themselves with planter interests, and lower class whites who were largely indifferent to mass education, ex-slaves forged ahead to commit the South to a system of universal schooling in the immediate postwar years.[26]

Clearly, the ex-slaves' educational movement had an impact that reached far beyond their own communities. Their initiative forced whites of all classes to confront the question of universal schooling. From the Freedmen's

Bureau superintendent came testimony that "the white population of the South feels the power of the [freedman] schools. The poor whites are provoked by hearing Negroes read, while they are ignorant; and it is my belief that they will now receive schools, if furnished them, as never before," wrote Alvord in 1866. Further, "The educated class are not slow to perceive that their schools must be reopened, or fall behind humiliated, and that new schools must now be organized on a more popular plan than heretofore." Mass education was necessary for white children, insisted Robert Mills Lusher, white school superintendent of Louisiana, so that they would be "properly prepared to maintain the supremacy of the white race." The ex-slaves' initiative in establishing and supporting a system of secular and Sabbath schools and in demanding free public education presented a new challenge to the dominant class whites. They were confronted with the possibility of an emerging literate black working class in the midst of a largely illiterate poor white class. This constituted a frontal assault on the racist myth of black inferiority which was so critical to the maintenance of the racial caste system upon which the planters' agrarian order was based. The planters, unable to wipe out the educational gains made by ex-slaves between 1860 and 1870, had to take a more liberal posture regarding universal education among whites of all classes. Moreover, poor whites became less indifferent toward the idea of public education. Thus, the populist demands for free schooling in the late 1880s and 1890s, as well as the middle-class educational reforms of the early twentieth century, were influenced significantly by the ex-slaves' educational movement of the 1860s and 1870s.[27]

Conclusion

In the late 1870s and early 1880s, one could already detect a slight shift in Southern white attitudes regarding universal schooling in general and particularly for black children. Southern whites began realizing the improbability of reversing the gains made by ex-slaves during the Civil War and Reconstruction Years. Hence, a growing, although small, minority of prominent Southern whites began speaking in favor of universal schooling for the region's laboring classes, including Afro-Americans. Foremost among these whites were the ones promoting limited or rapid Southern industrialization. While traditional planters continued to favor a repressive system of agricultural labor and to discourage working-class literacy, proponents of Southern industrialization increasingly viewed mass schooling as a means to produce efficient and contented labor, and as a socialization process to instill in black and white children an acceptance of the Southern racial hierarchy. In 1877, Thomas Muldrop Logan, ex-Confederate General and industrialist in Richmond, Virginia, spoke before the American Social Science Association on the question of education in the Southern states. Morgan, who became one of the South's most prominent railroad magnates, articulated a rationale for supporting working-class and Afro-American schooling that came to characterize the thinking of many dominant-class whites in the late nineteenth and early twentieth centuries. "Wherever public schools have been established," argued Morgan, "the industrial classes, becoming more intelligent, have proved more skillful and efficient; and all competing countries must likewise establish public schools, or be supplanted in the markets of the world." Morgan was well aware of the planters' argument against black schooling, "that when the freedman regards himself qualified to earn a support by mental work, he is unwilling to accept manual labor." Morgan believed, however, that a maintenance of caste distinctions and division of labor were possible through offering blacks the kind of industrial education practiced at the Hampton Normal and Agricultural Institute of Virginia. By training blacks "to perform, efficiently, their part in the social economy, this caste allotment of social duties might prove advantageous to Southern society, as a whole, on the principle of a division of labor applied to races." These views were echoed by famous and little-known Southern industrialists as they testified before a subcommittee of the United States Senate Committee on Education and Labor in 1883.[28]

This movement for universal schooling differed in social origin and purpose from the ex-slaves' campaign. Hence, the rise of universal education in the "New South" is best viewed as several educational movements by different and conflicting social classes for different social purposes. The educational campaigns by ex-slaves, populists, industrialists, and middle-class progressives demonstrate that the region's diverse and conflicting social classes, for quite different reasons, came to support a single idea, universal schooling. A major problem with the historiography on Southern education has been the failure of historians to grasp the significance of the ex-slaves' educational movement and its impact on all subsequent campaigns for universal schooling in the American South. This is due partially to the unwarranted view of the ex-slaves' struggle for education as merely an amusing little footnote to history. Traditional accounts of postwar educational reform fail to consider the ex-slaves' behavior as independent, intelligent actions, reflecting deeply rooted and commonly held beliefs in the Afro-American community. Walter L. Fleming wrote that the ex-slaves' enthusiastic response to education was motivated by a childish desire to imitate whites and to enjoy forbidden privileges. George Bently, historian of the Freedmen's Bureau, concluded that "there was almost a religious nature to the freedman's regard for schooling." The ex-slave "was eating of the fruit so long forbidden to him, and he was entering a mystery which seemed almost holy." A more recent writer judged that ex-slaves found "a certain aura of romance and mystery surround-

2. Herbert G. Gutman, "Observations on Selected Trends in American Working-Class Historiography Together with Some New Data that Might Affect Some of the Questions Asked by Historians of American Education Interested in the Relationship between 'Education and Work'" (Paper presented at the Conference on the Historiography of Education and Work, Stanford University, August 17–18, 1979). Gutman's pioneering work in this area is invaluable; the paragraphs on ex-slave activity in Virginia and South Carolina are principally an exposition of his interpretation; DuBois, *Black Reconstruction in America*, pp. 641–649.

3. John W. Alvord, *Inspector's Report of Schools and Finances*, U.S. Bureau of Refugees, Freedmen and Abandoned Lands (BRFAL), (Washington, D.C.: Government Printing Office, January 1, 1866), pp. 9–10. Ex-slave beliefs about education were established in the slave experience and particularly in the social context of slave literacy. This experience I am examining in another essay.

4. Henry Allen Bullock, *A History of Negro Education in the South: From 1619 to the Present* (New York: Praeger, 1970), p. 26; Butchart, "Educating for Freedom," pp. 2, 25; *New Orleans Union*, July 12, 1864; Gutman, "Observations and Selected Trends in American Working-Class Historiography"; John W. Alvord, *Fifth Semi-Annual Report on Schools for the Freedmen*, BRFAL (Washington, D.C.: Government Printing Office, January 1, 1868), p. 29.

5. Gutman, "Observations and Selected Trends in American Working-Class Historiography."

6. *New Orleans Union*, July 12, 1864; Blassingame, "The Union Army as an Educational Institution for Negroes, 1861–1865," p. 154; Blassingame, *Black New Orleans*, pp. 108–109; Howard Ashley White, *The Freedmen's Bureau in Louisiana* (Baton Rouge, La.: Louisiana State University Press, 1970), pp. 167, 172, 175; *New Orleans Tribune*, September 22, 1864; *New Orleans Tribune*, July 23, 1864; Alvord, *Inspector's Report* (January 1, 1866), pp. 14–15.

7. White, *Freedmen's Bureau in Louisiana*, pp. 172–175; Alvord, *Inspector's Report* (January 1, 1866), pp. 9–10, 14–15.

8. *New Orleans Tribune*, September 5, October 31, November 6, 1866; White, *Freedmen's Bureau in Louisana*, pp. 177–179; Blassingame, *Black New Orleans*, pp. 111–112.

9. C. T. Wright, "The Development of Education for Blacks in Georgia, 1865–1900," (Ph.D. diss., Boston University, 1977), pp. 71–72; (Augusta, Georgia) *Loyal Georgian*, February 3, 1866; Alvord, *Fifth Semi-Annual Report* (January 1, 1868), p. 28; John W. Alvord, *Third Semi-Annual Report on Schools for Freedmen*, BRFAL, (Washington, D.C.: Government Printing Office, January 1, 1867), p. 12.

10. *Loyal Georgian*, May 19, 1867, February 3, 1866, March 10, 1866, May 16, 1867; Butchart, "Educating for Freedom," pp. 418–423.

11. Samuel Levi Horst, "Education for Manhood: The Education of Blacks in Virginia During the Civil War" (Ph.D. diss., University of Virginia,

ing the ability to read and write." Such notions tend to place
beliefs and behavior outside the realm of historical interpreta
we need not resort to notions of mystery and romance to a
ex-slaves' educational movement any more than we would dra
models to explain the subsequent campaigns by populists,
and middle-class progressives. We can study the social origins o
educational movement as we do for other social classes in the So

In the matter of universal schooling in the South, ex-sla
issue to which all other social classes were compelled to respor
tion and development of universal education in the South we
primarily by the relative power and interest of the region's
classes. To be sure, other factors accounted significantly for
character of educational development in the postwar South.
have said consistently, given the South's economic condition
war, it was in no position to allocate resources to establish
bureaucratic system of public education. The region also lacked
native corps of teachers, since it has no prewar tradition of
public education. Still, such objective conditions do not fully ac
slow development of universal schooling in the South. It was
economic and ideological interests and the day-to-day choices
region's social classes that shaped the pace and character of un
tion in the postbellum South. Ex-slaves formed one of those cl
that is central to any history of the rise of universal educatio
South.

Notes

1. Harriet Beecher Stowe, "The Education of the Freedmen," /
can Review (June 1879), p. 128; Nordhoff quoted in John
game, Black New Orleans, 1860-1880 (Chicago, Ill.: Univei
Chicago Press, 1973), p. 108; Washington quoted in W. E. E
Black Reconstruction in America (New York: Russell & Ru
[1935] 1962), pp. 641-642; John W. Blassingame, "The U
as An Educational Institution for Negroes, 1862-1865," Jo
Negro Education 34 (Spring 1965): 152-159; Ronald Euge
"Educating for Freedom: Northern Whites and the Origins (
Education in the South, 1862-1875" (Ph.D. dissertation, S
versity of New York at Binghamton, 1976); Edward F. Swe
Notes on the Role of Negroes in the Establishment of Publi
in South Carolina," Phylon 22 (1961): 160-166; Alton Hor
"The Freedmen's Bureau Schools in Texas, 1865-1870," So
western Historical Quarterly 76 (April 1973): 397-417.

25. Cohen, "Negro Involuntary Servitude in the South, 1865–1940," pp. 31–60; Pete Daniel, *The Shadow of Slavery: Peonage in the South, 1901–1969* (Urbana, Ill.: University of Illinois, 1972); Jonathan M. Wiener, "Planter-Merchant Conflict in Reconstruction in Reconstruction Alabama," *Past and Present* 68 (August 1975): 87–89.

26. Billings, *Planters and the Making of a "New South,"* pp. 37, 206–208; Louisiana superintendent quoted in Alvord, *Seventh Semi-Annual Report on Schools for Freedmen,* BRFAL (Washington, D.C.: Government Printing Office, January 1, 1869), pp. 33–35; Alvord, *Inspector's Report* (July 1, 1866), p. 21; Louis R. Harlan, *Separate and Unequal: Public School Campaigns and Racism in the Southern Seaboard States, 1901–1915* (New York: Atheneum [1958], 1968), p. 37.

27. DuBois, *Black Reconstruction,* p. 641; Alvord, *Inspector's Report* (January 1, 1866), p. 12; Lusher quoted in Blassingame, *Black New Orleans,* p. 113; Butchart, "Educating for Freedom,": p. 461.

28. Thomas Muldrop Logan, "The Opposition in the South to the Free-School System," *Journal of Social Science,* no. 9 (January 1878), pp. 92–100; For an analysis of industrial education, see James D. Anderson, "The Hampton Model of Normal School Industrial Education, 1868–1900," in *New Perspectives on Black Educational History,* ed. Vincent P. Franklin and James D. Anderson (Boston: G. K. Hall & Co., 1978), pp. 61–96; Industrialists' views on black education are presented in James D. Anderson, "Education for Servitude: The Social Purposes of Schooling in the Black South, 1870–1930" (Ph.D. diss., University of Illinois at Champaign-Urbana, 1973), pp. 41–80; and James D. Anderson, "Education as a Vehicle for the Manipulation of Black Workers," in *Work, Technology, and Education,* ed. Walter Feinberg and Henry Rosemont, Jr. (Urbana, Ill.: University of Illinois Press, 1975), pp. 21–26; For industrialists' original testimony, see U.S. Senate Committee on Education and Labor, *Report of the Committee of the Senate Upon the Relations Between Labor and Capital and Testimony Taken by the Committee* (Washington, D.C.: Government Printing Office, 1885), vol. 4. For an analysis of the South's middle-class educational campaign, see Louis R. Harlan, *Separate and Unequal.*

29. Fleming and Bently quoted in Butchart, "Educating for Freedom," p. 427; Ann Alexander, "Black Protest in the New South: John Mitchell, Jr. (1863–1929) and the Richmond Planet" (Ph.D. diss., Duke University, 1973), p. 49.

Jennings L. Wagoner, Jr.

The American Compromise: Charles W. Eliot, Black Education, and the New South

It is generally accepted that by the beginning of the twentieth century, most Northerners, including many who in earlier decades had been zealously involved in Southern affairs, had turned their attention away from the plight of the Southern black. Reconstruction officially ended in 1877 and, as one Northern journal then announced, "Henceforth, the nation as a nation, will have nothing more to do with him [the black].[1] Although lynching reached its peak in Southern states in the 1890s and Jim Crow legislation steadily relegated blacks to a position of political, economic, and social inequality,[2] many Northerners were apparently anxious to believe that the "wisest and best" men of the South could solve the Southern race problem and that indeed, a "New South" free from the legacy of racial injustice was in fact becoming a reality.[3]

The extent to which some Northern liberals abandoned the freedmen and the cause of civil rights around the turn of the century is an issue that invites further study. David W. Southern, in *The Malignant Heritage: Yankee Progressives and the Negro Question,* strongly indicts such national political leaders as Theodore Roosevelt, William H. Taft, and Woodrow Wilson for their racial attitudes and policies during this period. Southern condemns as well a number of leading liberal intellectuals and journalists for their blindness to racial injustice during the so-called "Progressive Era."[4] Other studies[5] have added credence to the argument that progressivism was for whites only and that many Northerners who were former allies of the freedmen had, with but few exceptions, become increasingly disillusioned with the slow pace of black progress by the opening years of the new century and in consequence reconstructed their notions of equality to exclude blacks and other "colored" peoples.

James Anderson and Donald Spivey, among others, have even more pointedly argued that those Northerners who did remain involved in Southern affairs, especially in the arena of black education, did so in order to help create an educational program "deliberately calculated to fit the freedmen to a new form of servitude in the caste economy of the post-war South."[6] Northern industrialists who had economic interests in the South are especially singled out by these historians for censure. Anderson's economic analysis, for example, leads him to contend that the "main end of the Southern industrialists, Northern philanthropists, and educational reformers was to force blacks into a workable scheme of social organization that would permit the structuring of a caste economy least removed from slavery. The problem of the school was to help fit blacks into that scheme."[7]

If Anderson's analysis resounds too strongly with conspiratorial tones, one must nonetheless confront the fact that, during this period of a retreat from reconstruction, widespread support was given to the philosophy of accommodation and compromise espoused by Booker T. Washington. While it has become fashionable to portray Washington as a Judas for the stand exemplified in his Atlanta address of 1895, such a simplistic view ignores the fact that many of America's most liberal spokesmen, for a wide range of reasons, good and bad, played a vital role in legitimizing and, to a large degree, orchestrating the position to which Washington gave voice. There is more than coincidence in the fact that Washington was awarded an honorary M.A. degree from Harvard University in 1896, only months after making his famous "Atlanta Compromise" speech. Harvard's gesture was symbolic of the fact that many Northerners as well as Southerners were indeed ready to lay aside the "bloody shirt" and to move toward the new century with the myopic assurance that all had been done that could or should be done for the black man. From here on, ran the conventional wisdom, the rise from slavery would largely depend upon the black man's own initiative and ability.

In the context of the paradox presented by the rising tide of progressive reform on the one hand and the capitulation of many American liberals to the concept of a racially separate and unequal society on the other, an examination of the views of selected liberal reformers can be instructive. In this study the racial attitudes and reform prescriptions of Charles W. Eliot, president of Harvard University for forty years (1869–1909), are presented as a case study in order to portray the evolving position of a widely respected educational reformer and New England liberal. Eliot, who was sometimes characterized as the nation's "first private citizen" and "our greatest moral force as an individual,"[8] was noted for his leadership in liberal causes. He was outspoken in support of "progressive" reforms in such areas as municipal government, civil service, capital-labor relations, conservation, sex hygiene, and international peace as well as in education. His direct and authoritative manner of speaking could quickly rankle those who held contrary views, but his was a voice that demanded an audience and not infrequently provoked a response. Eliot's tendency to offer judgments on issues across the spectrum of human events caused him to become, in Ralph Barton Perry's phrase, "adviser-at-large to the American people on things-in-general."[9] Although certainly Eliot cannot be said to have represented the views of all Northern whites any more than Booker T. Washington can be pictured as a spokesman for all Southern blacks, still his posture is revealing as one strand of Northern liberal thinking on the race issue. When considered in this context, the parallels between the views of Eliot and Washington as well as the paradoxes inherent in Eliot's own "liberal" attitudes take on special significance. It becomes apparent that as Eliot and other Northern liberals added their endorsement to the "Atlanta Compromise," the solution to the "Negro problem" became more than a matter of regional accommodation. The compromise, if we must call it that, took on national proportions. It became an "American compromise."

Eliot and Washington: Paradoxes and Parallels

Clearly there was little in the backgrounds of the son of a slave and the son of a mayor of Boston to cause them to reach somewhat similar conclusions regarding the place of the black man in American society.[10] When Washington was born in a crude slave hut on a Virginia plantation in 1856, Eliot had already completed his B.A. at Harvard and was serving as tutor of mathematics at his alma mater. After Emancipation young Washington struggled to obtain snatches of schooling while also working in a salt furnace and coal mine. During the same period, Eliot achieved the rank of assistant professor at Harvard and then, from 1863–1865, observed the closing years of the Civil War from newspaper accounts and letters while traveling in Europe. In 1865 Eliot returned to the states to become professor of analytical chemistry at the newly formed Massachusetts Institute of Technology. It was from this post in 1869 that Eliot was called, at the age of thirty-five, to become president of Harvard University, a position he held until 1909. Eliot was thus beginning his third year as president of Harvard when sixteen-year-old Booker T. Washington proved himself worthy of entry into Hampton Institute by sweeping the floors to the satisfaction of the matron. And it was at Hampton that Washington mastered those principles of fidelity, honesty, persistence, and a devotion to the ideals of individualism and self-help that were so highly prized by the Puritans and their descendants, men like Charles W. Eliot.

As an educational reformer, Eliot was so involved with the internal restructuring of Harvard during the first two decades of his tenure as president that he gave only passing notice to larger social currents. Strengthening the professional schools, expanding the elective system, upgrading the quality of the faculty and the student body, reforming the curriculum—these and other immediate tasks absorbed his energies and tended to divert his attention from external matters. As far as the South was concerned, Eliot's main interest during the early phase of his administration was with wooing Southern students back to Harvard. In an address before the New York Harvard

Club in 1872, Eliot observed with noticeable pleasure that Harvard could number in its ranks thirty-three students from the former slave states, not counting Missouri. Noting that Yale had twenty students from the same states, Eliot held forth the olive branch by proclaiming that "we are beginning to welcome back again the South." Encouraged as he was by these signs, however, Eliot was nonetheless sensitive to the wounds of war and reconstruction and expressed his concern that among the casualties of the war was Harvard's loss of students from the leading Southern families. "We still miss," he lamented, "the old South Carolina, Virginia, and Louisiana names, and we may be sure that the wisdom of our legislators will not have perfectly solved the difficult problem of Southern reconstruction until the Pinckneys and Barnwells, the Middletons, Eustises and Lees go to colleges again with the Adamses and Lincolns, the Kents, Winthrops and Hoars."[11]

In part, at least, Eliot's strong desire to enroll more students from the "better" Southern families at Harvard eventually motivated him to concern himself with Southern conditions. There is little question but that Eliot's own Brahmin heritage predisposed him to view the plight of the South from the perspective of the former patrician class. At the same time, however, he was struck by the sluggish pace of progress in the South when compared with the tempo of growth and industrialization in the North. He despairingly observed in 1900 that the Southern situation was "depressing" and that "the backward condition of our Southern States is one of the saddest facts in all the world."[12] Eliot's specific desire to attract Southerners to Harvard and his more general but no less genuine wish to see the South enter the mainstream of national progress prompted him by the turn of the century to investigate more closely the problems and the prospects of the region in an effort to promote both ends.

Lessons From the South

Not a few Southerners saw themselves as capable of educating the president of Harvard as to the unique dimensions of the Southern race problem. Southerners of both races and all classes made their views known to Eliot on questions regarding the social and political ramifications of suffrage for blacks, on the advisability of a dual school system, on the efficacy of industrial education or any education at all for blacks, on the moral habits and inclinations of Southern blacks as compared with whites, and even on the appropriateness of Booker T. Washington dining with President Theodore Roosevelt.

Not all correspondents were as forthright as one writer from Louisiana, who identified himself as "of the 'poor white trash' of the South—that is to say I'm only a skilled workingman—owning neither a great plantation nor a newspaper" and whose only "'Harvard' was a log schoolhouse, and not since the age of 13 at that." Apologizing for thus not being able to "produce a finished essay on the subject," the writer nonetheless proceeded to advise Eliot that the workingmen of the South had "*no interest* whatsoever in the education of the negro" and challenged that newspapermen and politicians who said otherwise were as far from representing the correct "Southern Sentiment" on the race question as was Roosevelt from approaching greatness! Should any "Tuskegeeized" or Harvard-educated black threaten to take his job, the writer advised Eliot, his response would be to "shoot him just as soon as dark gave the better opportunity! And never be in a moment's dread of indictment by a grand jury of my neighbors!" Convinced that social equality and miscegenation were the only outcomes of political and educational equality, the writer closed his letter by asserting: "The negro must move! So long as he is here so long will there be dissension. Let him go into Old Mexico and Central America and have done with this country for all time. Then will you and I be friends and not until then."[13]

A correspondent from Savannah, rejecting the idea that blacks possessed the ability to advance at all, informed Eliot that "those portions of Africa where the negro has full sway are as much of a wilderness as they were thousands of years ago." This Southerner took strong exception to the view that the black had made substantial progress in the forty years since slavery. "A forced, hothouse 'advance' is not true progress," he reasoned. "As well might driftwood be considered as swimming while transported downstream by the current. *No other race in history has been carried along on the back of another race as has the negro*."[14]

Most of the letters that Eliot received from those anxious to inform him of the racial situation in the South were more moderate in tone, and in some cases the correspondence between the Harvard president and selected Southern advisers spanned a period of several years.[15] Moreover, Eliot's connections with Northern philanthropists such as Robert C. Ogden, William H. Baldwin, and John D. Rockefeller, Jr., exposed him to the perspectives and efforts of men who were themselves involved with Southern educators and upper-class paternalists in a campaign of Southern uplift.[16] Thus, when in 1904 Eliot ventured to speak on "The Problems of the Negro"[17] before a gathering of the Armstrong Association of Hampton Institute in New York and two years later when at Tuskegee he spoke to the topic "What Uplifts a Race and What Holds It Down,"[18] he was by no means uninformed as to Southern attitudes and opinions. Yet whatever the insights and sympathies some Southerners and their Northern allies may have aroused in Eliot, his clear and uncompromising assertions in private correspondence and his conciliatory yet forceful public addresses suggest that Eliot characteristically, if not always consistently, endeavored to reason from liberal principles. Responding, for example, to a Southern minister who interpreted Roosevelt's inviting Booker T. Washington to dinner as a deliberate insult to the South, Eliot firmly expressed his own position:

> As a rule, I select my companions and guests, not by the color of their skins, but by their social and personal quality. It would never occur to me not to invite to my house an educated Chinaman or Japanese because their skin is yellow or brownish, or to avoid asking a negro to my table if he were an intelligent, refined and interesting person. It is the intelligence, refinement and good judgment of Mr. Booker Washington which makes him an agreable guest at any table; and to many of us Northern people, the fact that nearly half his blood is African is a matter of indifference.[19]

It may well be, as Hugh Hawkins contends, that Eliot's stance in this instance was at best only "superficially tolerant" and reveals formidable standards to which others had to conform.[20] Yet it is clear that Eliot outwardly rejected race as a criterion for social intercourse. However elitist as judged by contemporary standards Eliot may appear, he was in his own day among a liberal minority who were prone to interpret racial differences as legacies of culture as well as genetics. While Eliot understood that genetically inherited traits were not immutable (short of undesirable "amalgamation"), he contended that the possibilities of cultural assimilation were vast and believed that somehow the process of assimilation could gradually qualify and "render less visible" some racial differences. At the same time, he maintained that "the diversities of race need no more be extinguished under free institutions than the diversities between human individuals." "Freedom," he proclaimed, "should encourage diversity, not extinguish it."[21] It is hardly surprising then that Eliot, who stood fast against nativism and the clamor to restrict immigration, should be singled out by one historian as an example of the "minority with faith" during the years when restrictionism was on the rise.[22]

For all of Eliot's commitment to libertarian principles and dependence upon his inner-directed moral sense, however, he proved on more than one occasion not in the least hostile to the pragmatic temper. If he was a staunch individualist, he was also sensitive to the demands of a rising corporate state and could in time speak with conviction about the necessity of individualism yielding to collectivism and the needs of the larger society.[23] And, while he can be viewed as an exponent of fair play and equality of opportunity, and as an outspoken foe of racial discrimination, he must also be seen as one who, in assessing popular sentiment, could convince himself that there could perhaps be in some contexts racial distinctions without unjust racial discrimination.[24]

What then were the solutions offered by this liberal Northern reformer to the Southern race problem? What encouragement, what direction did he give those who searched for a way up from slavery and second-class citizenship into the promise of American life? And what assurances did he give those in the South and elsewhere who were prone to reject the idea that blacks and whites could ever live as coequal citizens, socially as well as politically? It is in searching out the answers to these questions that the dimensions of the American Compromise become clear.

Shaping the American Compromise

Sharing the platform with Andrew Carnegie, Hollis B. Frissell (the white principal of Hampton Institute), and Booker T. Washington, Eliot took the occasion of an address before the Armstrong Association meeting in New York City in 1904, to give public hearing to his views on the Southern race question. Eliot, then seventy years of age, was careful to note that there were fundamental points on which Northern and Southern sentiment was identical, foremost among these being the desire to preserve racial purity. "The Northern whites hold this opinion quite as firmly as the Southern whites," Eliot stated, "and," he continued, "inasmuch as the negroes hold the same view, this supposed danger of mutual racial impairment ought not to have much influence on practial measures." Sexual vice on the part of white men accounted for the limited degree of racial mixture which already existed, Eliot claimed, and nobody "worthy of consideration" would advocate racial intermarriage as a policy.[25]

It was against the backdrop of this assurance that racial mixture was anathema to the whole of American society—blacks as well as whites, Northerners as well as Southerners—that Eliot then proceeded to speak in more specific terms about differences in the treatment accorded blacks above and below the Mason-Dixon line. Noting that in the South separate provisions were made for blacks in schools, in public conveyances, and in public facilities, Eliot discounted the difference from practice in the North as being "socially insignificant." Indeed, Eliot observed, "with regard to coming into personal contact with negroes, the adverse feeling of the Northern whites is stronger than that of the Southern whites, who are accustomed to such contacts. . . ."[26] Eliot noted further that while the North had not moved toward a dual school system, "in Northern towns where negro children are proportionally numerous there is just the same tendency and desire to separate them from the whites as there is in the South," a separation, he added, which if not effected by law may well result "by white parents procuring the transfer of their children to schools where negroes are few."[27] As Eliot thus evaluated the differences in practice between the North and South, he concluded that the underlying racial attitudes of the two regions appeared much the same. No greater feeling of brotherhood, no deeper commitment to liberalism, no fervent devotion to ideals of liberty, equality, or justice were needed or warranted in explaining differences in practice. The fundamental explanation, Eliot contended, rested with the difference in the proportions between the races. Eliot described the situation accordingly:

> Put the prosperous Northern whites into the Southern states, in immediate contact with millions of negroes, and they would promptly establish separate schools for the colored population, whatever the necessary cost. Transfer the Southern whites to the North, where the negroes form but an insignificant fraction of the population, and in a generation or two they would not care whether there were a few negro children in the public schools or not, and would therefore avoid the expense of providing separate schools for the few colored children.[28]

In setting forth these propositions, Eliot was speaking not in terms of what "ought" to be, or even necessarily what he wished were the case, but rather in terms of observed social realities in the North and his understanding, based on his secondhand knowledge of the South, of conditions and attitudes in that region. However much he might personally feel that race should not be the determining consideration in regard either to dinner guests or school-mates, he judged popular sentiment to be of a different mind. And in so judging, he gave Northern liberal endorsement to the Southern system of dual schooling.

On another matter of popular sentiment, however—at least Southern sentiment—Eliot saw less national unanimity. A real difference existed, Eliot felt, between Northern and Southern views as to the supposed connection between political equality and social equality. The "Southern view" was perhaps most directly stated by Frederic Bromberg, a Mobile attorney and frequent correspondent with Eliot on the Southern problem. According to Bromberg, Southern objection to black suffrage had nothing to do with "the ignorance of the emancipated race." Rather, Bromberg asserted:

> . . . no amount of intelligence or culture upon the part of any one with negro blood in him can overcome the objection to him as a coequal citizen. . . . [We] do not object to negro suffrage because of the negro's incapacity, but because he is a negro—because suffrage and the right to hold office are usually associated with each other, and holding office means possession of power, and possession of power means social equality, and social equality tends to miscegena-tion, and miscegenation is what we will not tolerate, and therefore oppose the beginnings. . . .[29]

In correspondence as well as in public forums, Eliot labored to undermine what he perceived as the illogic of this Southern syllogism. Citing European as well as Northern experience, Eliot argued repeatedly that possession of the ballot had never had anything to do with the social status of the individual voter. Eliot favored, as he felt most Northerners did, educational qualifications for suffrage, but he refused to accept the idea that blacks, as blacks, should be denied the ballot or right to hold office. Political rights, he maintained, were separable from social intercourse. "In Northern cities," he reasoned, ". . . the social divisions are numerous and deep; and the mere practice of political equality gives no means whatever of passing from one social set to another supposed to be higher. The social sets are determined by like education, parity of income, and similarity of occupation, and not at all by the equality of every citizen before the law."[30]

It was indeed this very logic that informed Eliot's administration of Harvard University. He frequently and fondly proclaimed that Harvard recognized among its officers and students neither class, race, caste, sect, nor political party. While in one instance denying that there was a tendency in the North "to break down the social barriers between the white race and the negro race," Eliot at the same time firmly asserted that, as far as Harvard was concerned, any person who could pass the admission examinations would be received as a student and, upon completion of his studies, would "receive the degree without the least regard to his racial quality or religious or political opinions."[31] But as far as social relations were concerned, individual preferences (indeed prejudices) superceded institutional policies. "Membership in the societies and clubs of Harvard," he wrote in 1907, "is determined entirely by social selection—this social selection being made on the basis of similar tastes, habits and ambitions." Japanese students had been admitted to some of the desirable clubs at Harvard, Eliot noted, but he could recall no instance of blacks being invited to join a social club and thought the possibility of such "extremely unlikely."[32]

Thus, on the matter of social equality, Eliot's attitude closely paralleled the public pronouncements of Booker T. Washington. In social matters, at Harvard or elsewhere in the nation, individuals or groups were free to include or exclude according to their own preferences or prejudices. But in matters political, whether it be university admission or universal suffrage, meritocratic standards only should be invoked. There need not be, Eliot insisted, any connection between political equality and social equality.[33]

Education: Separate But Equal

Access to political equality (and the way toward gaining the tastes, habits, and ambitions that might make one socially acceptable), however, depended in part upon educational opportunity. Having acknowledged the apparent necessity of separate education in the Southern states, Eliot would not yield ground to those who argued for grossly unequal education for blacks. As Eliot interpreted Southern attitudes on the type and amount of schooling black children should receive, three different opinions seemed to emerge. "Some Southern whites, educated and uneducated," Eliot said, "think that any education is an injury to the negro race, and that the negro should continue to multiply in the Southern States with access only to the lowest forms of labor." Another segment of the population, he continued, "holds that negro children should be educated, but only for manual occupations. . . . This section approves of manual training and trade schools, but takes no interest in the higher education of the negro." There was, however, a third, and to Eliot, proper attitude held by still other white Southerners, one which recognized "the obvious fact that a separate negro community must be provided with negro professional men of good quality, else neither the physical nor the moral welfare of the negro population will be thoroughly provided for."[34] Thus, to Eliot, beyond the ideal of political equality and the requirements for public safety, there existed a compelling justification for adequate provisions for higher education of blacks. "The provision of a higher education for negroes," Eliot proclaimed, "is the logical consequence of the proposition that the black and white races should both be kept pure. . . ."[35] Separate education was thus a basic requirement for the maintenance of a segregated society.

Sympathetically recognizing the "peculiar burden upon the Southern States caused by the separation between the black and the white races in the institutions of education," Eliot closed his address before the Armstrong Association by calling for federal aid to Southern education.[36] The national government, he said, should make it possible for black schools in the South to be kept open eight months of the year instead of four. Separate colleges for agriculture and the mechanical arts should be provided throughout the South and separate professional schools for blacks should be established within existing Southern universities, all made possible by national support. "It was in the supreme interest of the whole nation that the Southern States were impoverished forty years ago by a four years' blockade and the destruction of their whole industrial system," Eliot reasoned. "It is fair that the nation should help rebuild Southern prosperity in the very best way, namely, through education."[37]

Concern with fairness—even with public security and racial purity—might have little impact on a man like Mississippi's James K. Vardaman who could ask "Why squander money on his education when the only effect is to spoil a good field hand and make an insolent cook?"[38] But Eliot's appeals, like Washington's, were primarily addressed to moderates and liberals who recognized that the problems of the blacks were also the problems of the whites, Northern as well as Southern. Yet Eliot believed, as did Washington, that provision of educational opportunities was only part of the struggle up from slavery. In the final analysis, both men maintained that the place of the black man in American society depended primarily upon the use he made of available opportunities, however limited. That their own and later generations would often twist this formulation into a cruel mechanism for "blaming the victim" was a consequence these "self-made" men could hardly appreciate.

Education and the Doctrine of Self-Help

When Eliot was invited to make an address at Tuskegee in 1906, he chose as his theme, "What Uplifts a Race and What Holds It Down." Eliot identified four essentials which must be sought after by any race which hoped, as he put it, to lift itself "out of barbarism into civilization." First among the elements necessary was a commitment to steady, productive labor. Eliot stated:

> Every race that has risen from barbarism to civilization has done so
> by developing all grades of productive labor, beginning with agricul-
> tural labor, and rising through the fundamental mechanic arts, and
> mining, and quarrying, to manufacturing, elaborate transportation,
> trade, commerce, the fine arts, and professional labor. Respect
> for labor of all sorts, for the simplest as well as the most complex
> forms, will be manifested by every rising race. This respect is
> founded not only on the conviction that productive labor yields
> comfort, security, and progressive satisfactions, but also on the firm
> belief that regular labor in freedom develops the higher intellectual
> and moral qualities of the human being.[39]

Second to the uplift provided by honest labor, Eliot told the Tuskegee students, was devotion to Christian family life. "Respect for family life," he said, "fidelity in the marriage relation, and appreciation of the sacredness of childhood are sure signs that a race is rising."[40]

Education held third place in the scale of values Eliot sought to impress upon Tuskegee students. Observing that Americans in general seemed to place more faith in education as an agency for uplifting a race than any other avenue, Eliot contended that "habitual productive labor and family life must precede education; and the education of children cannot prevent the decline of any people whose habit of labor or family life has been impaired." Third in importance though it might be, education, especially education that would contribute to industrial efficiency, was heralded by Eliot as vital. In a line which must have warmed the heart of Washington, Eliot declared: "This effort to make education contribute immediately to industrial effi-ciency is thoroughly wholesome in all grades of education; and particularly it is wholesome for a race which has but lately emerged from the profound barbarism of slavery; for it unites in one uplifting process all three of the civilizing agencies I have already mentioned—productive labor, home-making, and mental and moral training."[41]

Before he proceeded into a discussion of the fourth agency of the civilizing process—respect for law—Eliot acknowledged that current educational conditions in the South were inadequate, not only for black children but for whites as well. Poorly trained teachers, short school terms, early leaving age, and limited curricula offerings all were hindrances to educational opportunity. Sounding again the theme of federal aid, Eliot declared that at least one institution like Tuskegee or Hampton should exist in every Southern state.[42]

Even though Eliot publicly praised Tuskegee and was doubtless convinced that Washington's uplift philosophy, which he endorsed, was in most respects appropriate, he observed inadequacies in the program he saw in operation. Eliot's uneasiness with the Tuskegee program was no doubt heightened by information provided him by Roscoe C. Bruce, a Harvard graduate, then a teacher at Tuskegee, who had earlier complained to Washington that industrial activities too frequently encroached upon the academic and that "the education of the pupil is largely sacrificed to the demands of productive labor." The charges Bruce, an insider, leveled against Tuskegee—that standards of scholarship were woefully inadequate, that a student's capacity for productive labor and "goodness of heart" counted more toward promotion than intellectual attainment, that the teaching staff was inferior, that students "who plan to teach school have not one minute more for academic studies than the pupils who plan to make horseshoes or to paint houses"[43]—were not lost on Eliot. Several months after his visit to Tuskegee, Eliot was moved to inform Washington of areas in which the institute needed to improve. After questioning the ability of Tuskegee to offer adequate training in nursing and the ministry and making some recommendations regarding the use of capital outlay funds, Eliot then hit the problem of academic training. He noted his impression that the manual labor dimension of the Tuskegee program threatened to overshadow the mental labor side. "Is it not important," Eliot asked, "that the graduates of Tuskegee should have acquired not only a trade or an art, but the power to read and cipher intelligently and a taste for reading?"[44]

In responding to Eliot's concerns, Washington endeavored to justify the work being done at Tuskegee with rural ministers and defended the institute's nursing program by noting that prior to Tuskegee's efforts, "there was no trained nurse within a radius of a hundred miles." "The question is," Washington stated, "whether we should turn out people who can partially relieve suffering, or wait until we, or some other institution, are in a position to turn out those who are much better equipped than our nurses are now." Promising nonetheless to lay all of Eliot's suggestions before the board of trustees, Washington spoke to Eliot's concern for the academic side of

Tuskegee by briefly noting, "We have already reorganized our course of training so that we are spending more time in strictly academic work than was true when you were here."[45]

If in these particulars the Harvard president and Tuskegee principal differed in their emphases, on most other matters of what has been termed "accommodationist philosophy" the two found grounds for common agreement. The month before Eliot made his "Uplift" speech at Tuskegee, he had solicited Washington's advice as to the treatment of certain topics. Washington seconded Eliot's call for the creation of Tuskegees in every Southern state and felt that Eliot's "placing emphasis upon the fact that there is a difference between social intermingling and political intermingling" would prove helpful. But Washington expressed reservations regarding Eliot's suggestion that he speak in specific terms as to just and unjust examples of racial separation. "There is a class of white people in the South and in the North," Washington advised, "who are always ready to insist on unreasonable and unjust separations to the extent that I very much fear that anything you might say in this direction would be twisted into an endorsement of unjust and unreasonable separation." Washington in particular cautioned Eliot against repeating the statement made before the Armstrong Association to the effect that Northern whites might feel segregation in public schools justified in areas where the Negro population is large. "I am wondering," Washington said, "whether or not the result might not be that the colored people would receive inferior opportunities for education rather than equal opportunities?" While Washington doubted that it would "be desirable or practicable on the part of either race to attempt to bring about coeducation in the South," he did not wish to see present Southern circumstances used to excuse segregation in other regions of the country. Concluding this appeal to Eliot with a slightly different twist to the theme made famous in his Atlanta Compromise speech, Washington stated: "In all things that are purely social, the colored people do not object to separation . . . but the difficulty is in the South in many cases civil privileges are confounded with social intercourse."[46]

Apparently satisfied with the merits of Washington's observations, Eliot contented himself in his Tuskegee address with only general references to proper and improper modes of racial accommodation. "The Republic desires and believes," Eliot stated, "that all competent men within its limits should enjoy political equality, the tests of competence being the same for all races." But he felt compelled to add: "Of course the Republic does not include under political equality social equality; for social equality rests on natural or instinctive likes and dislikes, affinities and repulsions, which no political institutions have ever been able to control."[47]

Eliot as Ambassador of Accommodation and Compromise

In 1909, on the eve of Eliot's retirement from the presidency of Harvard and one year after he became a member of the General Education Board, he was prevailed upon to undertake a Southern tour. Seeing the trip as a way to further cement the growing bridge between Harvard and the South, Eliot also looked upon a period of Southern travel as an opportunity to study first-hand conditions in that region as well as an occasion to spread further the doctrines of the American Compromise. With extended stops in various cities in Tennessee, Texas, Louisiana, Alabama, Georgia, and South and North Carolina, Eliot praised Southern progress, assured Southerners that their white counterparts in the North were at one with them on the matter of social separation between the races, delivered messages of "uplift" at black churches and colleges, and counseled whites to be just in their dealings with blacks. In Montgomery Eliot was quoted as saying that "the policy of the South regarding the negro is a wise one. The white people and the negroes should be kept apart in every respect." Taking direct aim at the critics of accommodationism, Eliot reportedly added: "The work being done by Booker T. Washington, I believe to be good for his race, and that done by Professor DuBois, harmful."[48]

In comforting Southerners with assurances that Northerners not only understood their problem but shared it, Eliot made yet another pronounce-ment that sparked quite a controversy in Northern, and even a few Southern newspapers. "In the North we have our race problem," Eliot declared in Memphis and elsewhere on his trip. "I do not believe," he was quoted as saying, "in the admixture of even white races. For instance, the Irish, Jews, Italians, and other European nationalities should not intermarry with Ameri-cans of English descent."[49] Newspaper accounts as to Eliot's precise wording varied, and while some publications, such as *Harper's Weekly*,[50] chose to suspend judgment until confirmation of Eliot's remarks could be obtained, other papers were less patient. The *Boston Pilot* charged that Eliot was an ancestor worshipper and editorialized that he had for too many years been "talking altogether too much on every subject."[51] Other papers wrote that Eliot deserved watching, one New York paper, *Town Topics*, venturing the opinion that perhaps Eliot had "reached the period of senility."[52] Even the *Charleston News and Courier* expressed puzzlement, arguing that surely Eliot recognized that the "American" was the product of intermarriage among stocks differing "in minor degree." The *News and Courier* resolved the riddle by asserting: "Of course, the intermarriage of the races when the term connotes peoples of different color, as Chinese, Malays, and Negroes, ought to be prohibited and that is probably all that Dr. Eliot has said."[53]

A week later the same paper editorialized enthusiastically for Eliot, saying: "He has learned a great many things in the last twenty-five years, and has displayed remarkable familiarity with the peculiar problems with which our people have had to deal all these weary years."[54]

If Eliot's overzealous concern for racial purity caused a temporary controversy in the Northern press, it was an episode that rather quickly faded away. What remained from Eliot's Southern tour was a testimony to the very ideals of goodwill, patience, responsibility—and accommodation—that formed the platform of the American Compromise. Eliot had laid out, as had Washington earlier in Atlanta, a program of self-help and "uplift" that gave vague promise of allowing the black to earn a "respectable" place for himself in a socially segregated American society. To blacks whose ambitions and frustrations led them to demand or expect "too much" immediately, and to those whites who doubted that progress on the part of the black man was ever possible, Eliot could paternalistically pass on the wisdom of one of America's leading educational reformers and liberal statesmen:

> Why, you believe that your race problem is a new one, but it has
> been experienced before, only it is intensified here [in the South].
> The negro cannot be expected to be ready for all phases of civiliza-
> tion only a few decades removed from the time when he first began
> to enjoy civilization as a free man. After 500 or 1000 years we may
> expect more substantial growth.[55]

Conclusion

If the tonic of self-help, educational endeavor, dependence upon white paternalism, and faith in the gradual process of cultural assimilation seemed at best an inappropriate placebo if not a near-fatal opiate, such a prescription must nonetheless be judged in the context of prevailing American liberal thought, not merely in the narrower context of black capitulation to Southern racism. Charles Eliot was but one in a long line of Northern liberals at the turn of the century who approached the race issue with counsel of compromise and accommodation. The strategies of accommodation tacitly agreed upon by Northern philanthropists and Southern reformers and endorsed by liberals such as Eliot were intended to dampen the appeal of racist demagogues and soften the demands of impatient freedmen, all for the sake of Southern progress and racial harmony. However, advocacy of accommodationist policies served in time to weaken the position of liberals as guardians of the interests of blacks and other minorities in the North as well as in the South. Eliot, for example, although a consistent champion of political equality and an opponent of racial bigotry, discounted the significance of social discrimination and came to accept as a matter of necessity the existence of a racially segregated society. While he advocated educational opportunity, he nonetheless gave his blessing to the system of dual schooling in areas where the black population was sizeable. And although he sincerely believed in the efficacy of the Puritan ethic, he preached the values of patience as well as hard work and calmly asserted that significant advance on the part of black Americans as a whole would result only after generations of effort.

Even though such strategies of accommodation and deferred commitments were condemned by those who assumed a more militant stand, the difference between "liberal-conservatives" such as Booker T. Washington and Charles W. Eliot and their more radical critics may well have been, as Eugene Genovese has argued, more a difference in emphasis, tactics, and public stance than one of fundamental ideology.[56] The goal of Washington no less than DuBois was the attainment by blacks of full rights of citizenship. As August Meier has noted, "The central theme in Washington's philosophy was that through thrift, industry, and Christian character Negroes would eventually attain their constitutional rights."[57] Thus, the accommodationist tactics of Washington were immediate means toward an ultimate end of racial equality and justice. In adopting tactics that won the approval of liberal and moderate whites, North and South, Washington was seeking allies in the struggle, recognizing that without white support, no amount of effort on the part of blacks would bring positive results. Similarly, it was W. E. B. DuBois in his celebrated critique of Washington who asserted that "While it is a great truth to say that the negro must strive and strive mightily to help himself, it is equally true that unless his striving be not simply seconded, but rather aroused and encouraged by the initiative of the richer and wiser environing group, he cannot hope for great success."[58] Certainly the encouragement and endorsements given by Charles Eliot, a respected member of the "richer and wiser environing group," were not the only directives he could have set forth, but his axioms were unquestionably representative of the major doctrines of what had become an American Compromise.

Notes

The author wishes to thank Professors Hugh Hawkins, Robert Bremner, Louis Harlan, and Ronald Goodenow for their helpful comments on earlier drafts.

1. *Nation,* April 5, 1877, as cited in Paul H. Buck, *The Road to Reunion, 1865-1900* (New York: Vintage Books, 1959), p. 294.
2. C. Vann Woodward, *The Strange Career of Jim Crow,* rev. ed., (New York: Oxford University Press, 1966). Cf. Woodward's *Origins of the*

New South, 1877-1913 (Baton Rouge, La.: Louisiana State University Press, 1951), p. 351, where he notes that nationally lynchings averaged 187.5 per annum between 1889 and 1899 and dropped to 92.5 during the next decade. However, the percentage of lynchings in the South increased from about 82 percent in the 1890s to about 92 percent in the 1900–1909 decade and almost 90 percent of the victims were blacks.

3. The metamorphosis from "creed" to "myth" of a "New South" based on a reconciliation of sectional differences, racial peace, and a new economic and social order based on industry and scientific, diversified agriculture is insightfully examined in Paul M. Gaston, *The New South Creed: A Study in Southern Mythmaking* (New York: Alfred A. Knopf, 1970). On the dynamics of sectional reconciliation also see Buck, *The Road to Reunion* and Stanley P. Hirshon, *Farewell to the Bloody Shirt: Northern Republicans and the Southern Negro 1877-1893* (Bloomington, Ind.: Indiana University Press, 1962).

4. David W. Southern, *The Malignant Heritage: Yankee Progressives and the Negro Question, 1901-1914* (Chicago: Loyola University Press, 1968). Southern points to the clergyman Lyman Abbott and former abolitionists Carl Schurz and Charles F. Adams, Jr., as liberals who changed their views on racial equality. Ray Stannard Baker, Herbert Baxter Adams, John R. Commons, Josiah Royce, Walter Lippmann, Herbert Croly, and Walter Weyl all in varying degrees began to consider blacks a separate caste which blighted the "promise of American life." See Chapter III, especially.

5. Charles B. Dew in "Critical Essay on Recent Works" in Woodward, *Origins*, pp. 517–628, provides an excellent survey of studies on this topic. See especially pp. 577–584. See also Arthur S. Link and Rembert W. Patrick, eds., *Writing Southern History: Essays in Historiography in Honor of Fletcher M. Green* (Baton Rouge, La.: Louisiana State University Press, 1965).

6. James Douglas Anderson, "Education for Servitude: The Social Purposes of Schooling in the Black South, 1870–1930," (Ph.D. diss., University of Illinois, 1973), p. 3; Donald Spivey, *Schooling for the New Slavery: Black Industrial Education, 1868-1915* (Westport, Conn.: Greenwood Press, 1978).

7. Anderson, "Education for Servitude," p. 4.

8. Eugen Kuehnemann, *Charles W. Eliot: President of Harvard University* (Boston: Houghton Mifflin Co., 1909), pp. 1–4, as cited in Hugh Hawkins, *Between Harvard and America: The Educational Leadership of Charles W. Eliot* (New York: Oxford University Press, 1972), p. 290.

9. Ralph Barton Perry as quoted in Hawkins, *Between Harvard and America*, p. 298.

10. Booker T. Washington, *Up From Slavery: An Autobiography* (New York: A. L. Burt, Co., 1901) is Washington's most polished account of his life. A more objective analysis is provided in Louis Harlan, *Booker T. Washington: The Making of a Black Leader* (New York:

Oxford University Press, 1972). On Washington's thought (as opposed to his biography) the standard work is still August Meier, *Negro Thought in America 1880-1915* (Ann Arbor, Mich.: University of Michigan Press, 1963). On Eliot, in addition to Hawkins cited above, see Henry James, *Charles W. Eliot: President of Harvard University, 1869-1909*, 2 vols. (New York: Houghton Mifflin, 1930).

11. Charles W. Eliot, Speech at New York Harvard Club, February 21, 1872, Charles W. Eliot Papers, Harvard University Archives, Box 334 (hereafter cited as Eliot Papers.)

12. Eliot to William G. Brown, July 26, 1900 (Eliot Papers, Letterbook 92).

13. Forrest Pope to Eliot, March 2, 1904 (Eliot Papers, Box 234).

14. Charles Kohler to Eliot, March 2, 1904 (Eliot Papers, Box 234). Emphasis in original.

15. See, for example, the series of letters from Frederick G. Bromberg to Eliot (Eliot Papers, Box 123) and William B. Watkins to Eliot (Eliot Papers, Box 234).

16. On the "Ogden Movement" and the work and racial views of the men who formed the interlocking directorate of the Southern Education Board and the General Education Board, see Charles W. Dabney, *Universal Education in the South*, 2 vols. (Chapel Hill, N.C.: University of North Carolina Press, 1936); Louis R. Harlan, *Separate and Unequal: Public School Campaigns and Racism in the Southern Seaboard States 1901-1915* (Chapel Hill, N.C.: University of North Carolina Press, 1958); and Woodward, *Origins of the New South*, especially Chapter 15, "Philanthropy and the Forgotten Man." While Eliot was not formally a part of the Southern Education Movement, he was on its fringes and after 1908 became more directly involved in Southern educational developments as a member of the General Education Board.

17. Charles W. Eliot, "The Problems of the Negro," in *The Work and Influence of Hampton*, Proceedings of a meeting held in New York City, February 12, 1904, under the direction of the Armstrong Association (Eliot Papers, Box 337).

18. Charles W. Eliot, "What Uplifts a Race and What Holds It Down," Address at Tuskegee Institute, April 1906, TS (Eliot Papers, Box 338).

19. Eliot to Rev. S. A. Steel, October 25, 1901 (Eliot Papers, Letterbook 92).

20. Hawkins, *Between Harvard and America*, p. 182.

21. Charles W. Eliot, "The Contemporary American Conception of Equality Among Men as a Social and Political Ideal," Phi Beta Kappa Oration, University of Missouri, June 2, 1909 (Eliot Papers, Box 340).

22. Barbara Miller Solomon, *Ancestors and Immigrants: A Changing New England Tradition* (Cambridge: Harvard University Press, 1956), pp. 99-102, 186-188. Cf. Hawkins, *Between Harvard and America*, pp. 182, 353. See also Eliot to Edward Lauterbach (President of National Liberal Immigration League), January 10, 1911 (Eliot Papers, Box 341).

23. See, for example, Charles W. Eliot, "Individualism vs. Collectivism,"
    Address, New England Society in City of New York, 1905 (Eliot
    Papers, Box 337) and "Address at the Second Annual Conference on
    No-License Workers of Massachusetts," October 29, 1908, TS (Eliot
    Papers, Box 339).
24. Cf. Hawkins, *Between Harvard and America*, p. 191.
25. Eliot, "The Problems of the Negro," p. 9.
26. Ibid., p. 10.
27. Ibid., p. 9.
28. Ibid.
29. Frederick G. Bromberg to Eliot, October 29, 1901 (Eliot Papers, Box
    123). Bromberg was a Harvard graduate of the class of 1858, a Unionist
    during the war, and a member of Congress during Reconstruction.
    While Eliot could not agree with Bromberg's position on suffrage
    restrictions, he nonetheless recommended him to Theodore Roosevelt
    as a suitable candidate for the office of district attorney for the
    southern district of Alabama. See Eliot to President Roosevelt, Decem-
    ber 17, 1901 (Eliot Papers, Letterbook 92).
30. Eliot, "The Problems of the Negro," p. 10. See also Eliot to Frederick G.
    Bromberg, December 6, 1901 (Eliot Papers, Letterbook 92).
31. Eliot to Bruce L. Keenan, August 9, 1907 (Eliot Papers, Letterbook 96).
32. Ibid. The number of blacks at Harvard during the Eliot years was small.
    Eliot's secretary, Jerome Greene, when asked in 1904 about the
    number of "full blooded negroes at Harvard," confessed that accurate
    statistics were not available but that estimates placed the number at
    about fifteen, or one-third of one percent of the student body. He
    guessed that there had probably been forty or fifty black students at
    Harvard during the preceding ten years. See Jerome D. Greene to
    J. N. Hazlehurst, October 24, 1904 (Eliot Papers, Box 284). See also
    W. E. B. DuBois's description of his years at Harvard in *The Auto-
    biography of W. E. B. DuBois* (New York: International Publishers,
    1968), pp. 132–153.
33. Eliot, "The Problems of the Negro," p. 11.
34. Ibid., p. 13.
35. Ibid.
36. Ibid. Eliot framed a resolution to this effect for NEA consideration in
    1905. See "Resolutions Suggested to Dr. Wm. H. Maxwell at his
    Request for the NEA Convention of 1905," TS, June 12, 1905 (Eliot
    Papers, Letterbook 95).
37. Ibid., p. 15.
38. As quoted in Roger M. Williams, "The Atlanta Compromise," *American
    History Illustrated* 3 (April 1968), p. 18. For an examination of
    Vardaman's several variations on this theme, see William F. Holmes,
    The White Chief: James Kimble Vardaman (Baton Rouge, La.:
    Louisiana University Press, 1970), especially pp. 78, 122 and
    passim.

39. Eliot, "What Uplifts a Race and What Holds It Down," pp. 1–2.
40. Ibid., p. 3.
41. Ibid., p. 3–4.
42. Ibid., p. 5–6.
43. Roscoe C. Bruce to Booker T. Washington, April 12, 1906, copy, (Eliot Papers, Box 234).
44. Eliot to Washington, September 7, 1906 (Eliot Papers, Letterbook 95).
45. Washington to Eliot, October 20, 1906 (Eliot Papers, Box 255). Bruce had earlier confirmed that "to my surprise and delight Principal Washington has already granted in modified form some of the things I have so long been asking for." Roscoe C. Bruce to Eliot, April 23, 1906 (Eliot Papers, Box 204).
46. Washington to Eliot, March 7, 1906. See also Jesse Max Barber to Washington, April 23, 1906 in Louis R. Harlan and Raymond W. Smock, eds., The Booker T. Washington Papers, vol. 8, (Urbana, Ill.: University of Illinois Press, 1979), p. 585 in which Barber states: "I am glad to have had the opportunity of reading this letter which you wrote to President Eliot. Evidently, Mr. Eliot was going to make a speech that would have done us a great deal of harm, and I am glad you influenced him not to deliver the address that he had in mind. In doing so, you have rendered the race a valuable service."
47. Eliot, "What Uplifts a Race and What Holds It Down," p. 8.
48. As quoted in The Advertiser, Montgomery, Alabama, March 9, 1909 (clipping, Eliot Papers, unnumbered box). DuBois's attack on Washington in The Souls of Black Folk (Chicago: A. C. McClurg & Co., 1904) and his leadership in the founding of the Niagara Movement had clearly marked him as Washington's chief rival. See DuBois, Autobiography, pp. 236–253.
49. Ibid.
50. Harper's Weekly, April 3, 1909 (clipping, Eliot Papers, unnumbered box).
51. "Is He an Ancestory [sic] Worshipper?", The Pilot, Boston, March 6, 1909 (clipping, Eliot Papers, unnumbered box).
52. Town Topics, New York, March 11, 1909 (clipping, Eliot Papers, unnumbered box).
53. News and Courier, Charleston, S.C., March 10, 1909 (clipping, Eliot Papers, unnumbered box).
54. As quoted in ibid., March 17, 1909.
55. Ibid. In responding to a pointed letter from William Monroe Trotter, editor of The Guardian, Eliot similarly stated: "As to the most expedient treatment of colored people who are removed by four or five generations from Africa or slavery, I am in favor of leaving that problem to the people of a hundred years hence." Eliot to W. Monroe Trotter, May 5, 1909 (Eliot Papers, Letterbook 98).

56. See Eugene D. Genovese, *In Red and Black: Marxian Explorations in Southern and Afro-American History* (New York: Random House, 1968), pp. 143–144. Cf., however, Herbert Aptheker, "Comment," *Studies on the Left*, 6 (November/December 1966): 27–35.
57. Meier, *Negro Thought in America*, p. 103.
58. DuBois, *The Souls of Black Folk*, as quoted in Genovese, *Marxian Explorations*, p. 143.

Spencer J. Maxcy

Progressivism and Rural Education in the Deep South, 1900-1950

George B. Tindall has noted in his book *The Emergence of the New South,* that the South had begun a spectacular rise by the time of the First World War. The Reconstruction Period had ended and progressive reform began sweeping the Southern states. Tindall points out that this progressivism, despite its liberal programs, rested upon conservatism, traditionalism, and individualism. Instead of looking to the future, many progressives looked back to a rural Arcadia marked by pastoral values. The small one-owner farm formed the backbone of this image of the South, with independent yeoman farmers, storekeepers, and small manufacturers filling out the scene.[1] Moreover, most Americans paid a kind of homage to "the fancied innocence of their origins," Richard Hofstader observed. This innocence made up the "agrarian myth," or the notion that life on the farm was somehow superior to urban life.[2]

Between 1900 and 1950, however, a new ideology swept the Southern states that attempted to put to rest the myth of rural Arcadia. At precisely the same time that the rural myth was being promoted, the very real plight of the farmer in the South was being accurately cataloged by progressive thinkers of another ilk. The realities of Southern farm life were shocking: A breakdown in the single-family farm lifestyle was brought about through the device of foreign tenancy. In 1880, approximately 36.2 percent of the Southern farms were operated by tenants rather than owners. This number had risen to 49.6 percent by 1920, and 55 percent by 1930.[3] Novelist Helen Glasgow wrote in *Barren Ground* in 1925:

> Oh, the curse started with the tenant system, I'll admit. The tenants used the land as a stingy man uses a horse he has hired by the month. But the other farmers, even those who own their farms, are no better now than the tenants. They've worked and starved the land to a skeleton, yet it's still alive, and it could be brought back to health....[4]

The single crop of cotton dominated economic life for Southern farmers. They were reluctant to try new methods of farming or experiment with new crops like sugar cane and rice.[5] It would require the efforts of Seaman Knapp and his agricultural demonstration workers to break this monopoly after the turn of the century.

Farm youth were leaving the rural areas for more attractive jobs in the cities. Farm population still ranged from 70 percent in Louisiana to 88.5 percent in Mississippi. Seven of the Southern states had a rural population of from 70 percent to 80 percent, while six others hovered between 80 percent and 90 percent.[6] While the exodus from the farms did not seriously dent the farm population, it was nonetheless a concern of farmers who wished to pass the family farm on to the next generation.

If agricultural life was depressed, educational conditions were in equally poor shape. Small, one-room schoolhouses covered the Southern countryside. Poorly prepared and underpaid, teachers fought to teach the three Rs without proper textbooks or materials. Schoolhouses were crude buildings without proper sanitary facilities. One teacher might instruct all eight primary grades and at times "high school subjects" as well. Local school boards exercised complete control of the schools and teachers. Salaries were not uniform, and the typical teacher stayed on the job for one year. There was no tenure law to protect teachers from political pressures. Generally female, the rural schoolteacher was "boarded around" with the parents of her pupils, receiving room and board as part of her salary.[7] It is safe to say that in 1900 there was no public school system in the Deep South and the schools were in much the same condition that Horace Mann had reacted to in Massachusetts seventy years before.

It is ironic that historians have not explored more fully the juxtaposition of the rural myth, postulating the superiority of farm life, and the emerging ideology of progressive education reform that sought to address farm conditions as they were found in the South. Moreover, it is curious that historians have not exploited the fact that the "farm problem" was somehow taken to be an educational problem in at least two senses: (1) the poor quality of rural education in the South had contributed to the farmers' plight (in fact tenancy was attributed to the fact that farmers fled the rural areas for the educational advantages found in the cities); and (2) the reform of schooling would serve to raise the rural South out of the nineteenth century and into the modern age. Progressive reformers thus connected the farm problem (variously defined as a decline in farm income, a lessening of status, decreasing population, lowering of living standards, rise of absentee landlords, etc.) with the educational conditions in the South. They reasoned that the horrible conditions in the schools would first have to be improved. Better educational facilities and practices would then allow for the re-education of farmers to the new, urban, business-like methods of farm management.

The Reform Program

Farmers had been pressing for educational reform prior to 1900. As Fred A. Shannon has argued in *The Farmer's Last Frontier,* farmers throughout the nineteenth century pushed for political remedies for their problems (low commodity prices, high interest rates, high railway freight charges, etc.). After 1877, these concerns were complemented by a substantial interest in agricultural education (especially college) as a means of bringing relief.[8] Nevertheless, reform was slow to follow and conditions remained unfavorable for Southern farmers after the turn of the century. Something more was required, and for this educators looked beyond the South.

Local schoolmen with the aid of experts from Northern philanthropic and educational agencies created models for schools to follow in the Southern states that were drawn from the Common School paradigm of New England, the industrial or trade school idea, and the unique conditions found operative in the South. The General Education Board reported in 1915:

> ... the South is struggling to educate itself and to improve its educational machinery and organization—struggling with courage and enthusiasm to overcome obstacles created by poverty and long indifference. But adequate direction is lacking. This is the most serious defect, and it is, unfortunately, a defect that the states themselves are not likely to remedy entirely at this time.[9]

Yet if the general course or direction of educational reform could be extrapolated from the reforms of the New England and Midwestern states, it was still necessary to study the Southern situation before beginning work. To this end, the General Education Board, a group operating with Rockefeller money, established "rural agents" in each of the Southern states during the first decade of the twentieth century. It was the duty of the rural school agent to assist the state department of education "in making a thorough and dispassionate survey of rural education in his state, including laws, organization, finance, equipment, teaching force and methods, etc."[10]

Once the survey was complete, the Board felt warranted in prescribing a reform program:

> In general, this program should aim to bring about a readjustment which will substitute the county for the district as the unit of organization, administration, and finance; an appointive superintendent with proper qualifications ... to take the place of the elected superintendent; local as well as state taxation ... to be made possible; consolidated schools to be favored; the one-room school to be

reorganized and developed; facilities to be provided for training
teachers for a service rendered more permanent, more attractive,
and more fruitful.[11]

It is important to note that the essentials of the progressive program had
already been arrived at before the survey was undertaken. Hence, the state
surveys were designed to merely support what was already known, i.e., that
the rural South was ready for Northern educational innovations.

Heavily weighted on the side of administrative and supervisory changes,
it was assumed that reorganization would prompt an improvement in the
delivery of educational services. Clearly this was top-down reform, for the
arguments for change began with the consolidation of small rural school
districts and ended with improved teacher training facilities. Moreover, what
Robert Wiebe has called "the search for order" is clearly evident in the plans
of the progressive reformers in the South after 1900.[12]

The Reformers and Their Values

The leaders in Southern educational reform between 1900 and 1950 were
white middle-class professionals. Clergymen, newspapermen, business leaders,
and schoolmen dominated the movement and were supported by women's
clubs, parent-teacher groups, educational associations, and farmer organizations (special interests like the 4-H Clubs, Women's Christian Temperance
Union, Farm Bureau, and others). In each Southern state a collection of
progressive reformers worked actively to fill out the reform platform: for
example, Charles W. Dabney, president of the University of Tennessee; Walter
Hines Page and Edwin A. Alderman along with Charles D. McIver and Charles
B. Aycock in North Carolina; Louisiana's Clarence Ives and T. H. Harris;
and in Arkansas, Edgar Gardner Murphy.

Some individuals worked across state lines and gained national prominence. J. L. M. Curry, for example, became nationally identified with the
"new education" in the South. But, many more, such as M. V. O'Shea, head
of Mississippi's public education system in the 1920s, worked in anonymous
posts in state departments of education or in the various school districts.
When asked in 1925 to do a study of Mississippi's public schools to determine
what changes could be made to meet the standards found in other states,
O'Shea responded that Mississippi education was ripe for reform. His final
report recommended sweeping changes and reflected the typical directions
states in the deep South were taking in school reform.[13]

O'Shea correctly discerned that the philosophy of "mental discipline"
dominated teaching methodology in the schools. This outdated approach
stressed repetition and rote memorization. O'Shea proposed that teaching

be made "functional" so that students could learn to solve problems involving hygiene, economics, race, and politics.

Next, O'Shea proposed an equalization plan whereby the state as a whole was to provide funds to each county unit for maintaining the schools. Since there were vast differences in the resources counties could generate through taxation, the state equalization idea would provide a uniform set of schools throughout the rural areas.

Parent-teacher associations were encouraged to bring the home into better relationship with the school. Here was a way in which parents could better understand changing concepts of teaching methods, curriculum, and the assessment of children's needs. O'Shea saw the schools as agents of social reform and parent groups as vehicles for the smooth dissemination of reform.

O'Shea pointed out that Mississippi was leading other Southern states in 1925 in the number of schools consolidated. However, he criticized the teachers for neglecting progressive teaching methods (such as William Kilpatrick's "project method"). Teacher training was in need of reform as well. O'Shea criticized the strictly academic courses which were remote from actual life problems. He argued that teachers should be taught about children and the relative values of different educational methods and learning styles. He suggested that every beginning teacher spend some time under expert guidance in a model or "demonstration school."

Black schooling was largely to be left to the General Education Board and the philanthropists. In sum, O'Shea held to a position combining progressive reform rhetoric and continued inferior education.

> In order to be efficient leaders, they [the teachers] must study the dominant traits of the negro race and the types of vocational, industrial, and social life which will yield the highest degree of financial prosperity and physical, social, intellectual, aesthetic, and moral well-being for negroes in relation to white people. . . .[14]

O'Shea went on to point out that the administration of education was in need of simplification and unification. The entire school network was to be placed under a single Board of Education, in cooperation with the state superintendent and the chancellor of higher education. The emphasis was to be upon a rural education which featured a new pedagogy and means of evaluation. A bureau of tests and measurements was to be created in the state department of education in Mississippi. This bureau was to study the effects of the more progressive teaching techniques.[15]

Thus, while national and Southern regional progressives outlined a program for educational transformation, implementation was left to state and local educational administrators. An example more local than O'Shea was L. J. Alleman of Lafayette Parish, Louisiana, who became parish superintendent in 1902. Alleman was the first professionally trained schoolman to be made superintendent in that parish, and as such he pushed progressive reforms, including school consolidation, with the zeal of a true disciple. Alleman was followed by other professionally trained educators assuming posts in the parishes of Louisiana, the state's objective being to staff all administrative posts with dedicated schoolmen who would give all their effort to new modes of change and reform.[16]

School Consolidation

The keystone in the bureaucratic reform of Southern education was school consolidation. The notion of an efficiently organized and centralized system of county (or parish) school districts appealed to reformers. While the idea of consolidating the small school districts into larger county units originated in New England, Southern progressives adopted the plan wholesale after 1900.

In practice, consolidation entailed two separate but related changes. First, the single-room rural schools were scrapped and replaced with new multi-classroom buildings. School "wagonettes" and later buses were utilized to transport students to these new facilities. Second, the official administrative units, called "districts" or "common school districts," were abolished and replaced by larger county administrative units. Local school board members often fought this move, but in state after state the new centralized county bureaucracies took power and replaced traditionalist board officials.

State legislatures followed the recommendations of progressive reformers with little resistance. "Upon the advice of influential educators the General Assembly [of Missouri] has, on two or three occasions, passed laws for which apparently the people were not yet making any great demand."[17] Southern educational reformers were able to transform an educational structure dominated by democratic localism into a finely-tuned bureaucracy in two decades.

North Carolina was the first Southern state to consolidate its schools. Governor Charles B. Aycock ("the education governor") sought to convince farmers of the need for rural school improvement by pointing to the failures on voter literacy tests. Better schools would mean more rural youths could vote, Aycock reasoned. In 1902, he called a conference of over forty educational leaders. The outcome was a plan in which these educational progressives would stump the countryside, giving proeducational reform speeches. The progressives called for school consolidation, local taxation, and general school improvement measures. When the Southern Education Board, made up of old pals like Charles McIver and Walter Hines Page, selected North Carolina as recipient of financial assistance to upgrade its schools, Aycock's success was assured.[18]

The pattern was repeated with variations throughout the states of the Deep South. Politicians joined forces with progressive educators, newspapermen, teacher-parent groups, and others to bring about centralization of schooling. Farmer resistance to consolidation faded and centralization became the norm. Those farmers who wanted improved roads, for example, found themselves in league with consolidationists, owing to the fact that centralized schooling meant busing students and this meant paving roads. By 1930, every Southern state had consolidated its schools and school districts. School consolidation in the South was to be one of the most successful reforms in the entire progressive reform movement.[19]

While progressives worked hard to convince farmers of the virtues of centralized schools, the traditional value of local control was clearly at stake. Reformers met with stiff opposition from rural Southerners when the latter saw their local schools being torn down and the children transported to other communities. Resistance crumbled when progressives pointed out that business techniques in agriculture were calling upon farmers to become more efficient, and school consolidation was another way rural life was to be made more economical. The notion of the businessman-farmer received support from the farm press as well as the universities and extension agents. In the end, the businessman-farmer model would replace the yeoman-farmer as the ideal in the South and with it would come school centralization.

External Forces Operating for Reform

Progressive reform in the South could only have succeeded with the financial support of Northern philanthropic organizations like the General Education Board. Founded in 1902 by John D. Rockefeller and incorporated by an act of Congress the following year, the General Education Board operated throughout the first five decades of the twentieth century, supporting progressive reforms in the South (and North). Between the years 1902 and 1947, expenditures for Southern education totalled $104,615,527. The money was spent for teachers colleges, surveys, educational experiments, child growth and development projects, and general education. The General Education Board financed teacher-training programs, state supervisory agents in rural areas, state departments of education, studies, conferences, and demonstrations. Educators were granted fellowships, scholarships, grants-in-aid, and other incentives to study the latest techniques in teaching and administration at such universities as George Peabody College for Teachers and Teachers College, Columbia University.

The Report of the Secretary of the General Education Board for 1902–1914 reveals the strategic goals to be achieved. The board called for the move to a county administrative unit for the purposes of taxation and administration, creation of single county boards of education to replace local and district boards, appointment rather than election of superintendents, hiring of full-time county superintendents paid an adequate salary to discourage moonlighting, school consolidation, and better teacher-training facilities.

In addition to the General Education Board, there were a number of other groups working for progressive educational change. The Southern Association of Colleges and Secondary Schools was created in Atlanta, Georgia, on November 6, 1895. The prime mover, Chancellor James Hampton Kirkland of Vanderbilt University, was selected the first secretary. Kirkland saw the Southern Association as a means to the end of a Southern renaissance in education. However, the Southern Association would support segregated white educational institutions until the 1930s.

Evolving urbanization provides a convenient backdrop for the emergence of evaluating agencies. The Southern Association sought to bring rural schools up to Northern urban educational standards. It is crucial to keep the urban value system in proper perspective, for without the example of Northern city school structures, rural Southern secondary schools would have continued in the quasi-free academy tradition. Accrediting agencies built upon Northern standards.[20]

One of the most serious issues facing the Southern Association at the turn of the century had to do with the relationship between the high schools and colleges in the South. Academic preparation in the high schools was viewed as mediocre at best. Colleges and universities were forced to conduct special remedial classes (called "fitting schools") for sub-freshmen to help raise entrance levels of students. In an effort to smooth this transition from high school to college, the Southern Association proposed a classical curriculum for all high school students. In addition, the Southern Association advocated replacement of the three-year degree by the four-year bachelors degree, higher standards for admission to colleges, and a general upgrading of secondary schools through the vehicle of "accreditation."[21]

A new "commission" on secondary schools met in Nashville, Tennessee, on April 4, 1912, with nine representatives from six Southern states. Dr. Joseph S. Stewart of the University of Georgia and Professor Bert E. Young of Vanderbilt were chairman and secretary respectively. The commission was told to: (1) agree upon a single report form to be used by high school principals, (2) prepare and define the unit courses of study, and (3) prepare a list of accredited schools in each Southern state.[22]

As professor Ronald Goodenow has shown,

> In the South, progressivism represented an expression of expertise through educational reform and change, regional planning and progressive pedagogy. Although it was in line with much that was liberal in Southern intellectual life and politics, there is a good deal to

suggest that its progressive rhetoric was used by whites to justify and tolerate the continuation of segregation and economic exploitation of blacks.[23]

White Southern progressives were unwilling to tear down black caste and economic barriers.

The Southern Association tended to follow the lead of Northern accrediting agencies, emphasizing by the 1930s "evaluative criteria" and uniform standards for all Southern secondary schools. Many of these criteria were similar to emerging national standards. The Cooperative Study of Secondary School Standards was financed in part by the General Education Board, the Rockefeller Foundation, and regional groups like the Southern Association.[24]

A power struggle developed between the old guard and a group of younger members of the Southern Association in the 1930s. The newer members sought to penetrate the elite decision-making bodies of the Association without success. The difficulties were exaggerated by the "Thursday evening dinners" which were attended by the old guard and their wives in full evening dress. The old guard had worked so long together that they dominated the nominating procedures and continued to elect and reelect their own. Perhaps the most serious offense revolved around the standards and the fact that older member-institutions failed to meet standards. Thus, newer members found a double standard operating in the accreditation process.[25]

Dean Clarence A. Ives of Louisiana State University led a move to rewrite the constitution of the Southern Association in 1933. This new constitution equalized the nominating procedures and effectively undercut old guard control of the association. By 1935, when the new constitution was accepted, the younger members had successfully democratized the bureacratic structure of the Southern Association.[26]

Black secondary schools and colleges were subject to the "separate but equal" ideology. A survey conducted in 1928 showed that black schools were uneven in many of the same areas as white schools. In 1929, the Southern Association's "Highsmith Committee" received $35,000 from the General Education Board and the Rockefeller Foundation to inspect black schools. Growing out of this commission, the Association of Colleges for Negro Youth was formed in 1932, to be replaced in 1934 by the Association of Colleges and Secondary Schools for Negroes. An "approved schools" list for blacks was finally abolished in 1966 as part of the integration of the Southern Association. Thus, for three decades the Southern Association had supported the separate-but-equal policy while subtly controlling the black association for accrediting schools.[27]

Another agency, the National Education Association (NEA), created an internal Department of Rural Education in 1907. The NEA Proceedings were filled with reformist speeches for the next several decades. NEA activities provided an outlet for progressive reformers from the South to gain support and ideas. This association tended to favor administrative centralization, school consolidation, uniformity of curriculum, and other progressive ideas while being dominated by administrators. Thus, the NEA proved to be a powerful ally for Southern progressive reform.

Alice A. Pierce, speaking at an annual NEA meeting, identified a number of agencies that were attempting to influence rural education in the 1930s. She named twenty-one groups, eight of which had a broad sphere of influence: Boy Scouts, Agricultural Extension, Anti-Tuberculosis Society, Parent-Teachers Association, Library Association, Nursing Service, Junior Red Cross, and the 4-H Club. The agencies tended to operate outside of the school, but their programs may be seen as efforts to redefine the traditional notion of education as mental discipline and to emphasize alternative channels of social or practical work.[28]

The Women's Christian Temperance Union exercised a remarkable degree of power in the South. Traditionally anti-drinking, Southern states yielded to the campaign against alcohol abuse via public school instruction. In 1907, Mississippi passed its first law requiring the teaching of the effects of alcohol abuse. The law was a dead letter after 1924, but in 1938 anti-wet forces succeeded in getting a second law passed. A supervisor of temperance was selected and a curriculum segment dealing with the evils of drink found its way into secondary school classes in chemistry, biology, physiology, economics, sociology, education, and safety education.[29]

Professional Reforms

Teacher-training departments, normal schools, and teachers colleges offered all types of regular programs, summer sessions, and extension education opportunities to Southern teachers and administrators after the First World War. George Peabody College for Teachers, buffered by Peabody Fund monies, and Teachers College in New York led the efforts to spread the gospel of the new education in the South. Doak Campbell and John E. Brewton, working out of Peabody's curriculum laboratory, constructed in-service programs for educators in the rural schools of the South. Beginning in 1935, they studied specific problems of teacher education (implications for teacher education in new curriculum programs, the state and its program of teacher education, current practices in teacher education, education of teachers for rural schools, etc.). Campbell and Brewton grouped their proposals around three goals for the teacher (civic responsibility, self-realization, and human relationships). In printed in-service materials, the authors called for teacher trainers to establish in-service or extension programs for local teachers. They also suggested reading institutes, reading clinics, curriculum revision programs, local study clubs, camps, workshops, conferences, discussion groups, demonstration schools, and health clinics.[30]

Alabama began training teachers through in-service extension classes in 1920. In that year, Alabama normal schools enrolled 1,320 teachers in off-campus classes. By 1924, some 5,693 teachers were enrolled. Teachers took classes in tests and measurement, civics, and rural problems. Instructors for these college level courses were given financial compensation and travel expenses. As a consequence of this extension work, teachers flocked to the summer sessions at the teacher colleges throughout the South. They were able to complete their undergraduate degrees or go on for advanced degree work.[31] The increased number of teachers produced by teacher-training institutions was a response to the need for teachers in the new high schools sprouting up all over the South.

Another pressure group that sought to change the shape of rural education in the Deep South was the farmers. Through the Farmer's Union and the farm press (e.g., *Progressive Farmer*) they advocated new high schools.

In 1906, Alabama began building public high schools with the help of the General Education Board. In the same year, the Board established a professorship of secondary education at the University of Alabama. Dr. John W. Abercrombie, president of the university, selected Professor Joel C. DuBose to fill the post. DuBose quickly moved to have the High School Act of 1907 passed by the Alabama legislature, thus creating a system of county high schools for the state. A State High School Committee was formed and charged with the responsibility of establishing such schools throughout the state. The state superintendent of schools was ordered to write a uniform course of study for the new high schools.[32]

Alabama public high schools were required to use state-adopted textbooks and state courses of study and to submit to regular inspection by representatives from the State High School Commission. In point of fact, the Commission was given almost unlimited power over the new secondary schools. The Commission controlled the various county boards of education, and, through its inspector, the selection of high school teachers. Older secondary institutions came under critical scrutiny. President Abercrombie and State Superintendent Harry Gunnels succeeded in raising the standards of the existing colleges, thus forcing some of the so-called colleges (in reality, private preparatory schools) to offer four-year high school programs or go out of business.[33]

Mississippi had one hundred fifty high schools in 1910, of which only six had full four-year curriculums. The low quality schools were often graftings upon elementary schools, taught by the principal and one or two teachers. Most of the teachers were not prepared to teach high school subjects. Mississippi progressives followed a five-step process in remaking secondary education in their state. First, a four-year course of study was mandated.

Second, a uniform course of study was developed by the new professor of secondary education. Third, a law established a "county agricultural high school system" in 1910. Fourth, an effort was made to upgrade the preparation of high school teachers. And finally, a State High School Meet was established in which youths from the high schools could come to the universities to take part in athletic and debate contests. To further advance education the Mississippi State Teacher's Association in 1914 created a department that proved to be "a helpful agency for getting progressive ideas."[34]

In 1908, the Kentucky legislature required a law that all counties create and maintain at least one high school. A county board of education was given control over all high schools in the state, while a state board of education was given the power to set teacher qualifications. There were 1,500 students in high schools in 1908, 5,000 in 1910, and 24,000 in 1920 in Kentucky.[35] Florida instituted a high school system in 1903 after the state superintendent's office formulated a bill specifying a high school system, a standard course of study, and fixed appropriations for the entire operation.[36]

A special solution to the rural problem in the Deep South centered around the "agricultural high school," a response to the demands of the farmer and his organizations for an educational plant ministering to their needs. Efforts to build such schools had succeeded in the North. In 1908, the Farmer's Union advocated agricultural high schools in Mississippi. However, a conflict arose between farmers who wished to see these agricultural high schools teach practical farming techniques plus domestic science for the girls and those conservatives who wished a classical curriculum. In his biennial report, State Superintendent of Public Education Henry L. Whitfield wrote:

> Rural high schools well-distributed in the country would have the tendency to stop the exodus of country people to the town.
> They would largely increase the facilities for the education of teachers for the country schools.
> Such schools would stimulate a larger number of our boys and girls to go to college or technical schools and would furnish the connecting link between the common schools and the State's colleges.
> These schools would create centers of social life in the county.[37]

Thus, the combined demand by farmers and the legislature for high schools resulted in the "agricultural high school" idea. These new schools were to do extension work and provide leadership in establishing cooperatives and clubs. Progressives saw them as places to train teachers as well as to prepare youth for college work. In 1910, Mississippi had fourteen agricultural high schools, Georgia had eleven, Alabama and Louisiana nine each.[38]

After 1910, however, the agricultural high schools were displaced by newer consolidated high schools. The demise of the agricultural high school may be traced to a number of factors: (1) people expected too much from the agricultural high school and it could not fulfill all the demands placed upon it; (2) legislators and farmers were never fully satisfied with the way the schools were operated or the ways in which agricultural and home economics courses were taught; (3) the consolidated high schools, supported by federal money, displaced the agricultural high schools; (4) state departments of education reimbursed consolidated schools for teaching agriculture; and (5) instead of setting up model farms on agricultural high school acreage, educators shifted farm projects to home farms.[39]

By 1930, progressive reformers in the Deep South would be attempting to make rural schools as much like Northern urban institutions as possible. The agricultural high school simply did not fit into this plan, for it singled out farmers as different. In addition, fewer young people would be remaining on farms after attending school, so a more diversified curriculum, like that offered by consolidated schools, was preferred. And finally, the ideal of the businessman-farmer would replace that of the sturdy yeoman-farmer of the agrarian myth: successful farmers were those who copied their urban cousins by adopting efficient industrial (urban) techniques. The consolidated high school became the answer to the modern farmer's prayer.

So pervasive was the belief in Southern regeneration through education that even the United States Congress came under the domination of Southern education progressives. Hoke Smith, author of the Smith-Lever Act (1914) as well as the Smith-Hughes Act (1917), led the Congress into a new age of federal involvement in education. The Smith-Lever Act helped colleges provide "extension" teachers for farmer-oriented instruction programs. Federal monies were fed to the agricultural colleges throughout the South (and the other sections of the country as well). Extension education carried the latest techniques in farming and household management to even the most remote rural areas. Coupled with the pioneer work of Seaman Knapp in "demonstration" farming, extension education swept the South as more and more farmers saw the concrete benefits of modern fertilizers and feeds.

The Smith-Hughes Act of 1917 created a vocational education program for youth fourteen years of age and older. Federal money was to be matched by state funds to help pay salaries of vocational teachers, supervisors, and directors of agricultural subjects, as well as to provide courses in home economics and the industrial trades. The preparation of vocational and agricultural teachers in the high schools was supported by this act. Research into the problems connected with the teaching of vocational and agricultural subjects was funded as well. Viewed from a long-term perspective, the role of Hoke Smith and his fellow progressives in bringing Southern rural education closer to Northern standards cannot be minimized.

Supervision

Professional administrators introduced a progressive device for reforming rural education in the Deep South: the school "supervisor." In the 1920s the Southern states systematically began to adopt state-wide programs of instructional supervision. John M. Foote, supervisor of rural and elementary schools in Louisiana, reported to the NEA in March, 1922, that his state was "now inaugurating and executing a program of instructional supervision."[40]

These new instructional supervisors in the South must be distinguished from *administrative* supervisors. The instructional supervisor was to be in charge of curriculum and teaching methods in the various rural schools. Administrative supervisors were already an accepted part of the bureaucracy that ran the schools; the instructional supervisors, however, provided a unique service to reformers by penetrating the classrooms and directly affecting subject matter taught and methods used in teaching. With the invention of the instructional supervisor, reformers took control of both the structure and the method of Southern education.

Foote pointed out that one of the goals of instructional supervision was "the maintenance of standards of instruction on a level with the best prevailing practices." Another goal was "directing the work of teachers so as to carry out the educational policies adopted by the school board and the superintendent." Instructional supervisors were to provide in-service education of teachers and the supervisor was to "interpret the course of study." Here was a blank check to do whatever was deemed necessary to reform current teaching practices. Instructional supervisors observed teachers and evaluated teacher techniques in terms of efficiency. Foote expected supervisors to purge the rural schools of the older recitation method of instruction and to replace it with the "review-assignment-study-test" method. By doing demonstration lessons, the supervisor was to illustrate the more practical methods of teaching. In short, the new instructional supervisors were to be agents of progressive change in the schools.[41]

North Carolina began a state-wide plan of rural supervision in 1910 that was typical of the programs found in the Southern states. The State Supervisor of Rural Schools authored the plan. Reform called for placing rural supervisors over teachers in every county, holding annual and group conferences, county supervisors visiting and working with local rural supervisors, and the printing of bulletins on progress made, methods of teaching, etc.[42] Claytie Bright, a first-year rural supervisor in Alabama, wrote of her experiences in 1926. She was a normal school graduate and had studied at other colleges including Peabody and Teachers College in New York. She had taught school and worked for a short time in the Alabama State Department of Education. Bright reported that rural teachers she met were inexperienced and not well trained. The primary problem which she as supervisor helped teachers to solve was organization. Some rural teachers were not using the state-approved course of study, nor were they using state-selected textbooks. She may be considered a typical rural supervisor of the time, overly concerned with efficiency, structure, and the need to make teachers conform to uniform methods and materials.[43]

State departments sent supervisors into the rural areas because local farmers could not be counted upon to produce quality schooling for their youngsters, it was argued. Most Southern states had been over-zealous in trying to maintain local control of schools, and progressives hit on curious arguments against such democratic localism. Reformers asserted that the small rural administrative districts could not afford the financial costs of giving expert leadership and services education required. They maintained that the larger administrative units would *decentralize* power by keeping a proper balance between state and local government.[44]

Rural supervision fit neatly into the administrative notion of centralized control of schooling. By 1930, eight out of eleven Southern states had adopted the county administrative arrangement (Alabama, Florida, Georgia, Kentucky, Louisiana, Maryland, North Carolina, and Virginia).[45] Hence, greater and greater power and control were lodged in central bureaucracies, and the supervisors, whether instructors or administrators, operated as functionaries for state-dominated school systems. An indication of bureaucratizaton of education is to be seen in the example of North Carolina. In 1917, a State Educational Commission was formed to survey educational conditions in the state. The commission asked for aid from the General Education Board, and the result was the recommendation that new departments be created in the state department of education, i.e., divisions of teacher training, physical education, schoolhouse planning, publication, and statistics. By 1921, earmarks of a bureaucratic and centralized administration worthy of any large corporation were to be found.[46]

In the state of Alabama by 1950 there were 126 superintendents, 78 attendance workers, 426 clerical assistants, 67 supervisors (white) in the elementary schools, 9 supervisors (white) in the high schools, 152.5 supervising principals (white) in the elementary schools, 333.5 supervising principals (white) in the junior and senior high schools. There were 47 supervisors (black) in the schools, and 126 supervising principals (black) in the elementary, junior high and high schools. This bureaucracy was required to oversee the approximately 21,611.5 teachers in the system.[47]

Blacks and Progressive Education in the South

Black rural reform rhetoric was often influenced by the principles of Booker T. Wasington. Education trends were the same for Southern blacks as for whites: school consolidation, construction of new buildings, the choosing of better teachers, improvements in curriculum, cooperation between school and demonstration work, and the institution of clubs. In practice, however, blacks rarely received equal educational appropriations or facilities. Moreover, emphasis was placed upon industrial and domestic education rather than the more classical curriculum.

The General Education Board, Rockefeller Fund, Jeanes Fund, Rosenwald Fund, and the other philanthropic agencies attempted to improve educational offerings in black schools in the South. The General Education Board offered to cooperate with state departments of education in the South between 1902 and 1915 by contributing money for state agents for rural black schools. Typically, rural agents for black schools were white males. The board attempted to aid black schools, usually by seeking matching funds from blacks and whites in the area where new schools were to be established. If the records are accurate, these patrons contributed heavily to the improvement of black schools.[48]

The Journal of Rural Education reported in 1923 that Southern states had built 1,700 "Rosenwald schools" and 49 teachers' homes at a cost of $6,257,492. While Rosenwald had contributed $1,204,478 of the money, blacks themselves contributed $1,600,667 to the schools (the balance being made up by contributions from whites and by public funds).[49] Public secondary schools for blacks appeared in North Carolina circa 1918 but developed slowly until the creation of a Division of Negro Education in 1921. Between 1923 and 1929, the number of black secondary schools increased from 26 to 111. It should not be assumed that these schools were uniform or that they were equal to white secondary schools at that time.[50] For example, gross disparities in teacher salaries were accepted.

After white schools underwent centralization and bureaucratic reform, black schools followed. There were disparities in expectations for black and white institutions. Generally, black schools and teachers were not expected to be as good as white facilities and faculty. It was not uncommon to prepare two different examinations for certifying black and white teachers. Black schools by the 1940s were still ill-equipped, their terms shorter, teachers more poorly trained, and programs of instruction inferior to their white counterparts. However, it should not be assumed that all progressive whites did not care about black education. Progressive reform crossed the color barriers in all the Southern states. In Louisiana, for example, we find dedicated whites like L. L. Kilgore, Assistant Superintendent of Schools for the state, working tirelessly for improvement in black education.[51]

By and large, blacks played a minor role in educational reform in the Deep South. Leo M. Favrot, a field agent for the General Education Board in the South, wrote of the conditions in black schools in 1929. According to Favrot, interest in black education had been steadily growing over the years. He cited the Jeanes teachers and the various philanthropic funds for their contributions to black education in the South. The 471 four-year high schools for blacks in 14 Southern states in 1929 were evidence of an interest in black education. The Rosenwald Fund had constructed 4,500 buildings for blacks between 1917 and 1929. By 1929, there were 351 counties in Southern states that had Jeanes agents and 400 counties with training schools funded by the Slater Fund.

Nevertheless, the inequalities persisted. In 14 Southern states in 1929, the average number of students assigned to the white teacher was 31, while the average class size in black schools was 44. The typical length of a school term for the white school was 159 days, whereas the black schools met for only 129 days per year. The average annual salary for white teachers was $900, and the average salary for black teachers was $458. In addition, the South continued to spend more on schooling for whites ($28.88 as opposed to $10.4 per black pupil).[52]

James Anderson, in his article "Northern Foundations and the Shaping of Southern Black Rural Education, 1902-1935," argues convincingly that Northern capitalists and Southern reformers, utilizing funds from philanthropic foundations, created an essentially industrial and agricultural educational program for Southern blacks aimed at keeping them on the farms or channelling them into industrial jobs. Through the devices of the State Supervisor of Negro Schools, Supervising Industrial Teachers (Jeanes Teachers), and the County Training School, Negro educational reform was translated into efforts "to develop an economically efficient and politically stable Southern agricultural economy by training efficient and contented black laborers while leaving the Southern racial hierarchy intact."[53]

Financing a dual system of schooling proved a tremendous burden to an already overburdened South. Many black schools in the rural sections of the South were so small and so poorly attended that progressive reforms like consolidation hardly affected them. The prime difficulty throughout this period was to encourage blacks to attend school in a society where education provided so little.

Teachers

Rural teachers in the South watched as the edifice of the educational bureaucracy rose about them. It was natural for teachers to attempt to improve their lot. Teachers had three options, given the reforms of the late nineteenth century: (1) to work to enhance their prestige, (2) to stabilize employment, and (3) to protect themselves from outside forces.[54] The first goal was translated into academic training and certification. By the First World War, the movement to require professional training of teachers was supported in all of the Southern states. However, it is important to see this movement as a result of administrative efforts and not as a grass-roots teachers' effort. State departments of education created and staffed divisions to oversee teacher preparation practices. Teachers organized into professional societies in the South only after stiffer professional requirements had been imposed upon them from the top.

The typical teacher in the rural South in the 1930s was a woman (although men did teach, especially in Florida), unmarried and twenty-three years of age. She had less than two years of professional training beyond high school. She had been teaching 3.8 years and she would teach seven different subjects and hear sixteen pupil recitations (of 20 minutes each) during the day. She would walk on the average 5.6 miles to school. Her board and room cost $21.11 per month and she had one roommate. She was paid $636.12 a year in salary.[55] As Mabel Carney pointed out in 1931, the extensive adoption of the county unit of administration plus the "aggressive leadership by state departments of education . . . has contributed greatly to higher qualifications for rural teachers."[56]

Robert Wiebe stated that "the teachers supported professionalized school administration, nonpartisan school boards, and definite procedures for promotions, all to discourage meddling by powerful outsiders. A tangle of regulations and rituals that would appall a later generation of critics meant professional self-preservation at the turn of the century."[57] However, it is important to keep in mind the fact that while the single schoolteacher in the one-room schoolhouse remained the norm in the South, she could do little alone to improve conditions; it took school consolidation, centralization of authority in larger and larger units of adminstration, and the resultant impersonalization of relations between teachers and supervisors to prompt teachers to begin to seek improvements in their job security and compensation.

Progressive reform was imposed upon teachers and was not subject to their vote. For example, as inducements to lure urban teachers to the country, Southern progressives built "teacherages" to house them. The most irritating feature of teaching in the rural areas was the traditional practice of "boarding around." Unmarried teachers were forced to live with the parents of their pupils. Room and board were provided in this way and considered part of the teacher's salary. Teachers disliked the invasion of privacy, petty gossip, poor food, and repeated dislocations that boarding provided. Reformers proposed building homes or dormitories to house teachers (in separate homes for men and women) for the consolidated schools in agrarian sections. The teacherage idea was sold to school boards and administrators on the grounds that this was an inexpensive device useful in retaining the more qualified teachers required in the consolidated schools. The teacherage could be made to pay for itself in rents, which would be extracted from teachers' salaries. The teacher's home could function as a model home for the wives of farmers in the area. The teacherage might serve as a center for rural social life. And, the teacher's home was to make a position in a rural school similar to that in an urban consolidated school by providing the same facilities as city teachers enjoyed. Most importantly, the teacherage was to provide another means of rural progressive reform. This home would introduce the farmer to the latest in plumbing and sanitary facilities, be interrelated with the model farm, support the consolidated school through home economics classes and social activities, and in general contribute to the vision of agrarian uplift. Few challenged the basic assumptions underlying the teacherage. Modelled upon the parsonage, the teacherage eleveated the teacher's status and separated her from the students' parents. Teachers accepted the teacher's home as a sign of professionalism. It was seen, not as an institutional effort to replace a home of one's own, but rather as a kind of extension of college housing, a fraternity or sorority house in the country. Teachers would reflect upon their years in the teacherage as wonderful adventures, and occasionally would hold a reunion years later to celebrate common experiences.[58]

In 1900, rural schoolteachers in the South were generally autonomous with few bureaucratic demands made upon them; however, by 1950 they found themselves almost at the bottom of a towering structure of administrative and supervisory experts. Given this growth of centralization of authority and power, teachers came to seek some protection for themselves. Of the approximately 120,866 black and white teachers in the Southern states in 1907, only about 8.2 percent were members of state teachers associations. By 1923, however, of some 199,563 teachers, 82,468 (or 41.3 percent) were members of teacher groups. By 1930, 67.3 percent (175,472 teachers) were members of state teachers associations. One earmark of a successful association is the ability of that group to support a full-time secretary. State teachers associations were able to do so in the 1920s.

Teachers associations in the South were generally divided by race. In 1930 all eleven Southern states reported separate "colored" teachers associations. While 116,131 white teachers belonged to a state teachers association, only 21,288 black teachers were members. It is not surprising to find that only 38.7 percent of black teachers sought refuge in teacher associations in the South in 1930, given the low salaries and poorer training they received.[59]

The Depression and Progressive Reform

With many progressive programs underway, the crash of 1929 and the subsequent depression served as a catalyst for further reform in the South.

Attention was focused on the schools, owing to the fact that (1) financial support for existing programs was threatened by the depression and (2) schools were looked to for possible solutions to the sorry condition of the economy.[60]

A classic scenario of Southern progressivism during this time of economic troubles was played out in Mississippi. The State Department of Education, supported by a grant from the General Education Board and in conjunction with the Division of Surveys and Field Studies of George Peabody College for Teachers, conducted a survey of the curriculum in Mississippi in 1934. The State Board of Education, the Mississippi Education Association, and the Congress of Parents and Teachers were then called upon to implement the Mississippi Program for the Improvement of Instruction which grew out of the survey.

Behind the scenes, consultants Doak Campbell and Hollis Caswell of Peabody College for Teachers met with a group of Mississippi reformers and wrote a bulletin to be used in regional conferences for school officers and teachers. The bulletin instructed the conference members to "improve instruction" via an instructional program which made more significant contributions to the welfare of the people of Mississippi. Work in the schools, they were told, must be better adjusted to the social and economic conditions of the day. Participants were instructed to read *Dare the School Build a New Social Order* by George Counts, William H. Kilpatrick's *The Educational Frontier*, Charles A. Beard's *A Charter for the Social Studies*, and *The Great Technology* by Harold Rugg. In subsequent bulletins, the participants learned that "the school should be a conscious agency for social improvement and should provide insight as to the direction of social change. . . ."[61] There were region-wide reform efforts of the Southern Association and the blacks' organization with General Education Board support in the 1930s.

It is not surprising to find that more than 10,000 teachers attended 451 conferences. These groups, it was reported, were in favor of a progressive curriculum revision for the state of Mississippi. The groups recommended that: (1) teachers adopt more democratic attitudes toward pupils, (2) teachers use a wider selection of instructional materials, (3) attention be directed toward the individual child and guidance services be provided for all children, (4) the curriculum be linked with aspects of daily life, and (5) practical subjects be developed in the schools. Interestingly, the groups made no suggestions as to structural changes or the need for additional training for teacher required by the new curriculum, and so there was a conservative side to this rhetoric which ultimately won out.[62] Teachers were happy simply to be working in the early 1930s. Severe economic depression forced rural Southern teachers to embrace any solution (even Counts's radicalism) to the problem; the schools and schoolteachers were among the first to be affected by the Depression. By 1932 every Southern state had begun cutting back on expenditures for education. The crisis reduced school programs, capital outlay, teacher salaries, school terms, and enrollments.[63] However, it was not long after that these cutbacks were eliminated. The South suffered only a temporary setback between 1929 and 1935, and progressive reforms in education had come to be the accepted way.

The effect of the Depression was to force legislation which increased entrance qualifications for those wishing to become teachers and temporarily suspended laws requiring working teachers to complete additional professional training to renew or extend certification.[64] Thus, those teachers, no matter how poorly trained, who held teaching jobs were retained, while those seeking teaching positions were forced to take more coursework to gain certificates. Legislation in effect held the doors to the profession somewhat closed during the 1930s. This control of the teaching profession was one of the outcomes of progressive reform.

Conclusions

If we compare rural schooling in 1950 with education in country schools in 1900, the depth and range of progressive reform in the South is clear. As we noted, in 1900 progressives called for a complete system of rural education, marked by good schoolhouses, a longer school term, capable and well-paid teachers, and an enriched and graded course of study. By 1950, the rural Deep South had been transformed. Complete state-wide school systems, marked by a hierarchy of school administration, county school organization, and professionally trained teachers and administrators dominated. Consolidated schools offered rich curriculums including agricultural and home economics classes. We have seen how pressure groups like the WCTU exerted influences upon curriculum and methods. The high school and the rural supervisor forced progressive reform on more teachers, even in the remotest areas. Previously, the teachers were at the bottom of the hierarchy, and black teachers were perhaps most severely handicapped. Finally, the great economic depression of the 1930s served as a means of furthering progressive reform along more radical lines.

Southern school reforms took as their model the work done in the North. Teachers College, Columbia University and George Peabody College for Teachers sent progressive missionaries into the Deep South to implement reform programs. Southern teachers and administrators travelled to Northern colleges and universities to study the latest progressive techniques in teaching and supervision. Entire faculties were transformed by professors from the North taking posts in Southern teacher colleges. Other northern influences were the accrediting agencies and philanthropic funds, like the General

Education Board and the Jeanes Fund. The interplay between North and South continued until the 1950s, by which time the full paradigm of Southern progressivism had been implemented.

Perhaps the best indicator of how much progressivism had accomplished may be seen in Kentucky's "looking to the future" in 1950. The Superintendent of Public Instruction called for further reforms in that year building upon the progressivism of the past. He wanted the state legislature to force a "minimum program" for all counties as they financed their school systems; he called for more consolidation in the face of the teacher shortages of that year; he asked for the reorganization of school districts "into efficient administrative, supervisory and attendance units"; the Department of Education was to be expanded with new supervisors in guidance and counseling, finance, music education, audio-visual education, speech and hearing, and mental retardation; he called for a nine-month school term; he requested that the state pick up the tab for school busing.[65] Plans for the future were firmly stated and took for granted the progressive gains that had been made between 1900 and 1950. Thus, by 1950 the Southern states had state-wide, centrally run and operated, professionally staffed, uniform public school systems. The structure and function of these systems differed in two respects from those found in the North or West: (1) The progressive changes in the Southern schools occurred with a far greater speed and intensity. and (2) In five decades, the South built *two* complete public and segregated school systems (one for whites and the other for blacks). Although it would never completely match schooling in other regions, the creation of such an organization must still be seen as remarkable.

Education in the South between 1900 and 1950 reflected national trends. As we have seen, however, differences in emphasis and speed of development marked the Southern progressive era. Reform was an a priori outgrowth of Northern visions as to what public schooling should be; progressives merely grafted this image upon the Southern states. Reformers exhibited the same urban values that reformers demonstrated in other sections of the United States. An example of a Northern progressive device was consolidation. In the South it came rather late and tended to run the same gamut of obstacles found in other regions. External forces operated upon Southern schools in the same vital manner as elsewhere, but the intensity of these cliques (farmers, parents, etc.) helped push the South rapidly into the urban mode. We have seen how progressives working within education (via teacher training, etc.) reformed the structure and function of public education in the South. The push for the high school and for rural supervision as an arm of progressively more forceful control of education by administrators reveals the extent to which Southerners were willing to change. Blacks were carried along in the wave of progressivism, but received only token reforms. Teachers too were affected by the progressive wave of restructuring and increased standards. The Depression accentuated the tenuous gains progressives had made in the first thirty years of reform, and the South's quick recovery from the Depression (in educational circles) reveals the extent to which the dream of a set of state systems of public schooling had been accepted.

Notes

1. George B. Tindall, *The Emergence of the New South 1913–1945* (Baton Route, La.: Louisiana State University Press, 1967), pp. 5–7.
2. Richard Hofstadter, *The Age of Reform* (New York: Vintage, 1955), Ch. 1.
3. Tindall, *Emergence of the New South*, p. 125.
4. Helen Glasgow, *Barren Ground* (Garden City, N.Y.: Doubleday, 1925), p. 111.
5. Robert H. Wiebe, *The Search for Order 1877–1920* (New York: Hill & Wang, 1967), pp. 126–127.
6. *The General Education Board: An Account of Its Activities 1902–1914* (New York: General Education Board, 1915), pp. 180–181.
7. Louis Win Rapeer, ed., *The Consolidated Rural School* (New York: C. Scribner's Sons, ca. 1920), pp. 190–191, 196–198.
8. Fred A. Shannon, *The Farmer's Last Frontier* (New York: Rinehart, 1945), p. 329.
9. *General Education Board*, pp. 186–187.
10. Ibid.
11. Ibid, pp. 187–188.
12. Wiebe, *Search for Order*.
13. M. V. O'Shea, *Public Education in Mississippi: Report of the Public Education System* (Jackson, Miss.: ca. 1925), pp. 351–360.
14. Ibid.
15. Ibid.
16. Milton Colvin Hall, "The Origins and Development of Consolidation of Schools in Sabine Parish" (Masters thesis, Louisiana State University, 1941), pp. 4, 13–14.
17. Irvin F. Coyle, "School District Consolidation in Missouri" (Doctoral diss., University of Missouri, 1936), p. 7.
18. Robert D. O'Conner, *The Life and Speeches of Charles Brantley Aycock* (Garden City, N.Y.: Doubleday, Page, 1912), pp. 235, 321–322; Oliver Hamilton Orr, *Charles Brantley Aycock* (Chapel Hill, N.C.: University of North Carolina Press, 1961), pp. 68–69.
19. Spencer J. Maxcy, "The Idea of School Consolidation in Southern Education During the Early Decades of the Twentieth Century," *Peabody Journal of Education* 53 (April 1976): 216–222.
20. Guy E. Snavely, "A Short History of the Southern Association of Colleges and Secondary Schools, *Southern Association Quarterly* 9 (November 1945): 3–4.
21. Ibid., pp. 8–11.

22. Donald Agnew, *Seventy-five Years of Educational Leadership* (Atlanta: Southern Association of Colleges and Schools, 1970), pp. 6–9.
23. Ronald K. Goodenow, "The Progressive Educator, Race and Ethnicity in the Depression Years: An Overview," *History of Education Quarterly*, 15 (Winter 1975): 365–394.
24. Agnew, *Seventy-five Years*, pp. 11–12.
25. Ibid., p. 28.
26. Ibid.
27. Ibid., pp. 29–31.
28. Alice A. Pierce, "Agencies Contributing to Rural Areas–Presentation of the Problem," *Proceedings of the National Educational Association*, 70 (1932): 426.
29. Euclid Ray Jobe, *Curriculum Development in Mississippi Public White High Schools 1900–1945* (Nashville, Tenn.: George Peabody College for Teachers, 1950), p. 135.
30. Doak Campbell and John E. Brewton, *The In-Service Programs for the Education of Teachers for Rural Schools,* vol. 5 in *Problems in Teacher Education* (Nashville, Tenn.: George Peabody College for Teachers, 1940), pp. 102–103.
31. Cassie R. Spencer, "Training Teachers in Service Through Normal School Extension Courses" *Rural School Journal*, 3 (April 1924): 352–356.
32. James S. Thomas, "Development of High Schools in Alabama," *High School Quarterly* 9 (October 1920): 10–11.
33. Ibid., pp. 10–18.
34. J. C. Fant, "High School Development in Mississippi 1910–1920," *The High School Quarterly*, 9 (October 1920): 22–30.
35. McHenry Rhoads, "High School Development in Kentucky," *High School Quarterly*, 9 (January 1921): 75–77.
36. W. S. Cawthron, "High School Development in Florida," *High School Quarterly*, 9 (January 1921): 77–83.
37. Jobe, *Curriculum Development*, p. 70.
38. Ibid., pp. 70–83.
39. Ibid., pp. 83–84.
40. John M. Foote, "A State Program of Instructional Supervision," *Journal of Rural Education*, 1 (April 1922): 337.
41. Ibid., pp. 337–341.
42. Hattie S. Parrott, "Rural School Supervision in North Carolina," *The Journal of Rural Education*, 5 (January-February 1926): 219–230.
43. Claytie Thornton Bright, "My First Year of Rural Supervision," *The Journal of Rural Education*, 5 (May-June 1926): 465–468.
44. Howard A. Dawson, "Satisfactory Local School Units," Field Study no. 7 (Nashville, Tenn.: George Peabody College for Teachers, 1934), pp. 85–118.
45. Ibid.
46. Brooks, *Public School Commission of North Carolina*, pp. x–xi.

47. State of Alabama Department of Education, *Annual Report, Bulletin 1951*, no. 2 (Wetumpka, Ala.: Wetumpka Printing Co., 1951), pp. 116–117.
48. *The General Education Board*, p. 202.
49. *The Journal of Rural Education*, 3 (September 1923): 42–43.
50. Hollis Moody Lang, *Public Secondary Education for Negroes in North Carolina* (New York: Teachers College, Columbia University, 1932), pp. 104–105.
51. Conversation with Dr. Leonard L. Kilgore, Jr., Louisiana State University, Baton Rouge, La., March 29, 1979.
52. Leo M. Favrot, "Negro Education in the South," Abstract, *National Educational Association Proceedings* (1929), pp. 472–477.
53. James Anderson, "Northern Foundations and the Shaping of Southern Black Rural Education, 1902–1935," *History of Education Quarterly*, 8 (Winter 1978): 371–396.
54. Wiebe, *Search for Order*, pp. 119–120.
55. Mabel Carney, "The Preparation of Teachers for Rural Schools," in *National Society for the Study of Education, Thirtieth Yearbook*, pt. 1, "The Status of Rural Education," (Bloomington, Ill.: N.S.S.E., 1931), pp. 157–158.
56. Ibid.
57. Wiebe, *Search for Order*, pp. 119–120.
58. Spencer J. Maxcy, "The Teacherage In American Rural Education," *JGE: Journal of General Education*, 30, no. 4 (Winter, 1979):267–274.
59. Albert Byron Crawford, "A Critical Analysis of the Present Status and Significant Trends of State Education Associations in the United States," *Bulletin of the Bureau of School Service*, University of Kentucky College of Education, 4 (June 1932): pp. 8–17.
60. Jobe, *Curriculum Development*, pp. 138–139.
61. Ibid., pp. 138–158.
62. Ibid.
63. W. S. Deffenbaugh, "Effects of the Depression Upon Public Elementary and Secondary Schools and Upon Colleges and Universities," in *The Biennial Survey of Education in the United States: 1934–1936*, vol. 1, U. S. Department of Interior Bulletin, no. 2 (Washington, D.C.: 1937), p. 1.
64. Ibid., pp. 27–29.
65. Commonwealth of Kentucky, *Report of the Superintendent of Public Instruction*, 9 (December 1951): 723–724.

Amy Friedlander

A More Perfect Christian Womanhood: Higher Learning for a New South

In July, 1889, a group of prominent citizens of Decatur, Georgia, met in the study of the Reverend Frank Henry Gaines, pastor of the Decator Presbyterian Church, to organize the Decatur Female Institute. Such private schools were common features of small Southern towns in the late nineteenth century, and these worthy gentlemen scarely imagined that their local academy would within twenty years become the first college in Georgia accredited by the Southern Association of Colleges and Secondary Schools. Renamed Agnes Scott Institute in 1890, the school evolved under the joint leadership of Gaines and a local businessman, George Washington Scott, who required only that the institute be named in honor of his mother.

It is now more than three decades since Wilbur J. Cash observed that the New South Movement of the 1880s and 1890s consisted of a socio-economic program in which Southerners tried to import two peculiarly Yankee institutions, the factory and the school.[1] Although the political and economic dimensions of the New South have come under historians' scrutiny, the social and cultural questions have remained unexplored, despite some evidence of interest in education.

The New South Movement witnessed the growth of more schooling for women. Between 1866 and 1884, Laura Haygood, sister of Methodist bishop Atticus Haygood, was active in the development of public schools for girls in Atlanta, situated six miles from downtown Decatur. She ran her own school for several years immediately after the Civil War, and, from 1872 until 1884 when she left Georgia to become a Methodist missionary in China, Haygood taught Latin, English literature, mental philosophy, and moral science in Atlanta Girls' High School. She was the school's principal from 1877 until her departure and also conducted the school's normal class, thus influencing the training of the city's schoolteachers.[2]

It was Kate Hillyer's resignation from a small private school for girls in Decatur to take a position in Atlanta's public school system which led directly to the founding of the Decatur Female Institute, the future Agnes Scott Institute.[3] In the 1880s, the citizens of Decatur supported a succession of private schools for girls in addition to the public school. At different times, the Baptist, Methodist, and Episcopal churches had run the school in question. After Hillyer resigned at the close of the 1888–1889 term, Gaines, then a newcomer to Decatur, decided that the time had come for the Presbyterians to open an academy. The Presbyterian school for girls in Rome, Georgia, had been closed from 1864 to 1871, and since 1885 it suffered from competition with the local public school. Statewide, Presbyterians lagged behind both the Methodists and Baptists in the number of institutions and in the amount of financial support that the synod provided.[4]

Although the establishment of public or common schools represented the major development in Southern education in the late nineteenth century, the founding of a series of private schools for girls is a parallel phenomenon. These institutions were virtually protegees of the small towns, and frequently they had a religious association, if not a formal affiliation. In his late nineteenth century history of higher education in South Carolina, Colyer Meriwether commented that although there had been little interest in education for women prior to the Civil War, local boosterism in the 1880s demanded that nearly every town have its own academy or so-called college.[5] A coalition of local businessmen and leading Baptists organized a seminary for young women in Florence, Alabama, in the flush 1880s, when it looked as if the city was on its way to becoming an industrial and commercial center from the production of iron and the concomitant rise in the value of real estate. Although Florence was already home to the Florence Synodical Female College and Florence State Normal School, these civic leaders did not feel that either of these institutions held the promise of becoming a prominent center of higher education.[6]

Although historians once applauded American education as an institution of democratization and progressivism, a recent revisionist movement has begun to explore the impact that society has had upon education, emphasizing, perhaps excessively, the school as a transmitter of values rather than as an instrument of social change. In recent studies, Jill Conway, Glenda Riley, and Roberta Wein have used education as a lens through which to examine the history of women in the late nineteenth century. Conway argued that women's education has been a peculiarly American concern since the founding of the republic. Republics, according to early nineteenth century social theory, lasted only as long as the virtue of the people endured. Women as the principal educators of the young and the home as the incubator of the young consequently assumed critical positions in the survival of the American experiment in republicanism. On the one hand, the theory placed women squarely in the home. Yet, as Riley demonstrated, it also called for their careful training and thus justified systematic attention to women's education. Sarah Josepha Hale and other advocates of improved education for women argued that women were natural teachers. They, in effect, expanded the proposition, extending women's association with domesticity into a justification for prying them out of the home. The limits of this rationale, however, eventually became apparent. Wein analyzed the bulletins of two leading Northern women's colleges and found that, although colleges in the late nineteenth century offered a more sophisticated academic regimen, they did not challenge women's essentially home-bound role.[7]

Agnes Scott's "success" as an educational institution represents a complex set of historical developments. Unraveling its history widens our understanding of the New South by suggesting ways in which new industrial wealth and civic pride found expression in communities across the South. This period saw the establishment of public schools in cities and counties, but the fact that Agnes Scott was a private school implies a tension between public and private education during these decades. Finally, the pronounced Protestant cast to the school introduces the question of the social function of religion in the late nineteenth century South. Tracing developments at Agnes Scott between 1889 and 1907, the year in which it was accredited, will not resolve all of these issues; it can, however, show the many factors that affected educational institutions and that influenced educational change.

Expanding Roles for Southern Women

In his two-volume survey, *A History of Women's Education in the United States*, Thomas Woody argued that the gradual transfer of the education of women from the home to schools of one sort or another coincided with the disintegration of the strict differentiation between male and female roles which had characterized nineteenth century social theory, as women slowly ventured out of the home as teachers, factory and office workers.[8] Although she did not address women's education directly, Anne Firor Scott charted a similar development in the activities of women in the South after the Civil War and Reconstruction. She argues that socio-economic pressures during these years drew women out of the home and into other occupations. For women who were not affected by these pressures, participation in an ever-increasing number of clubs, guilds, and associations like the Women's Christian Temperance Union accustomed them to a more active social role. Women led campaigns for prohibition, labor reform, public education, the prohibition of lynching, and ultimately suffrage.[9] Like other scholars working in women's history, Scott has shown that women embraced moral and humanitarian causes, which were consistent with their function within the home, in order to justify their participation beyond it.

The passage of women from the home to the world beyond did not go unnoticed by contemporaries. In 1891, Wilbur Fisk Tillett eulogized the antebellum Southern ladies who excelled in "native womanly modesty, in neatness, grace and beauty of person, in ease and freedom without boldness of manner, in refined and cultivated minds, in gifts and qualities that shone brilliantly in the social circle, in spotless purity of thought and character, in laudable pride of family and devotion to home, kindred and loved ones." Then, describing a social dynamic similar to that Woody and Scott outlined, he went on to state that in the hardship that the Civil War and Reconstruction had imposed on the South, "it was the heart, the hope, the faith of Southern womanhood that set Southern men to working when the war was over, and in this work, they led the way, filling the stronger sex with utter amazement at the readiness and power with which they began to perform tasks to which they had never been used before."[10]

Observers of the South after Reconstruction found it less usual for Southern men to support all of their dependent female relatives. Instead, impoverished Southern women went to work, frequently as teachers. This was consistent with national trends, which saw women working in increasing numbers, often out of economic necessity. Teaching, which required more years of preparation, was for women a profession of high status and was, therefore, attractive to ambitious daughters of the lower class as well as to daughters of formerly affluent families. In the last three decades of the nineteenth century, the percentage of women in the total teaching population, as measured in successive censuses, rose from 66.3 percent in 1870 to 73.4 percent in 1900. The change in the South was particularly dramatic.

Before the Civil War, women had constituted less than 25 percent of the total number of teachers in the region, and this pattern changed very little in the 1860s and 1870s.[11] This is consistent with the data presented in Claudia Goldin's study of female participation in the total labor force. Goldin found that in seven Southern cities, including Atlanta, the degree of white women's participation changed very little, growing from 16.5 percent to 18.5 percent between 1870 and 1880. The participation of single white women dropped from 26.4 percent in 1870 to 23.8 percent in 1880, and the participation of married white women grew from 4.0 percent in 1870 to 7.3 percent in 1880.[12]

The decade of the 1880s presents a marked contrast, at least as far as the composition of the teaching population is concerned. In this decade, the percentage of women grew from less than one-third of the total to nearly 60 percent, marking not only the emergence of a greater public role for more Southern women, but also the relative decline of the number of men in the teaching population. By the turn of the century, moreover, there was very little difference between the North and the South in the composition of the teaching force.[13]

The Reverend Amory Dwight Mayo, an authority well respected by Northerners and Southerners, rationalized the expanded role of Southern women by emphasizing the contribution that the values of the Southern womanly ideal made to the classroom. The entrance into the teaching force of young women from the "best" families, he believed, significantly raised the quality of education and was partly responsible for the revival in Southern education in the 1880s and 1890s. This renewed interest in education in the South consisted primarily in the establishment of graded public schools in the cities and common schools in rural areas.[14] Indirectly, it fostered higher education for young women by creating a demand for teachers and ultimately providing better-qualified applicants.

The Debate Over the Status of Women

Although Mayo managed to reconcile the Southern lady with the lady teacher, other people felt that the ideal itself impeded the cause of women's higher education. Celestia S. Parrish, a Virginian by birth, professor at Randolph-Macon Woman's College and cofounder with Elizabeth Avery Colton of the Southern Association of College Women in 1903, argued that rather than shaping society, educational institutions reflected social ideas. The ideal of the Southern lady, which consisted of traits men found attractive, did not stimulate honest work or intellectuality in women's education. "We have thought of women as a means to an end," she declared in 1900 at a meeting of the Southern Educational Association, "not as ends in themselves."[15]

Mary V. Woodward of Spartanburg, South Carolina, concurred and pointed out in an article contributed to the *Educational Review* in 1894 that the Southern ideal of womanliness, a standard defined by social and domestic virtues, emphasized marriage and family to the exclusion of other goals for young women. Women were themselves indifferent to their education, and natural conservatism gained additional strength from the conviction that a woman's "intellectual enfranchisement is indissolubly connected with her political enfranchisement, a result that seems to them at one with the disruption of society."[16] A doctrine of womanly education for women, which conformed strictly to conventions about women's "place," found many adherents in the South where President John McBryde of Sweet Briar Institute wrote in the *Sewanee Review* in 1907 that "education which fills a woman's soul with foolish notions of a glorious independence apart from man and apart from home is ... pernicious.... It can never be too strongly emphasized or too often repeated that home is the center of woman's influence and the source of her power, and the instruction in every subject of study should be directed with that important fact in view."[17] McBryde was not howling in the wind. Many parents, in fact, sent their daughters to Mary Baldwin Seminary in Virginia because they believed that the school would instill in the girls the gracious values of the antebellum Southern lady. Similarly, the Lucy Cobb Institute in Athens, Georgia, and its principal, Mildred Lewis Rutherford, devoted themselves to the training of girls in the genteel traditions of Southern womanhood.[18]

The polar opposite to McBryde's point of view was that expressed by President M. Carey Thomas of Bryn Mawr, born to a prominent Baltimore family and educated in the European universities. If there were any difference between male and female intellect, it was, Thomas concluded, "so slight that teachers of men and women students have never been able to agree as to the nature of that difference."[19] By 1900, the experience of Northeastern women's colleges had demonstrated women's mental and physical abilities to withstand the strains of the collegiate curriculum. The question then became normative; ought women pursue the same collegiate course that men did? Yes, Thomas and her followers emphatically affirmed, for "so long as men and women are to compete together and associate together in their professional life, women's preparation for the same profession cannot safely differ from men's. If men's preparation is better, women who are less well prepared, will be left behind in the race; if women's is better, men will suffer in competition with women."[20]

Thomas's vision of competition between men and women represented precisely the sort of unnatural situation that McBryde felt that women ought to avoid. Between these two extremes, Parrish forged an intellectual compromise. Like Thomas, she denied any intellectual basis for the different education of women and men, but experience convinced her that opportunities for women were not identical with those open to men. Since education reflected rather than reformed society, young girls would do well to spend their schooldays preparing themselves to find places within society as it then existed. Parrish, in effect, believed that at best education trained women to perform more efficiently those functions already open to them. Ladies of leisure enjoyed higher social status than women who worked, and Parrish hoped to raise the status of working women by raising the status of the profession in which they usually found themselves.[21] Implicitly, her argument became a justification for working women rather than a rationale for a woman's personal fulfillment in a career instead of marriage and motherhood.

The stumbling block was entrenched opposition to any measure that came between women and home. Southerners rejected state-supported education in the interest of lower taxes and because they felt that the state usurped the parent's responsibility. In the opinion of one writer to the *Atlanta Constitution* in July, 1889, who opposed the proposed state industrial school for women pending before the state legislature, were Georgia to establish such an institution, the natural father would be compelled to turn over to the state his parental obligation to his children. "Heavy, fatal blows are being struck at the very foundation of society and government," the author cautioned; "blows aimed at the family—at its relationship and mutual obligations. Blows that will drive asunder parents and children, blows that will demolish parental obligations, filial love, individual responsibility, and that will set in motion disorganizing and destructive forces that the state will be powerless to control."[22]

Private education was in principle more compatible with these sentiments than mandatory public education; no independent agency intervened between family members. Rather, parents retained choice over which institutions their children attended and exercised a measure of direct control over these academies through tuition and seats on their governing boards. The religious association, moreover, assured moral legitimacy.

Parrish attempted no assault on the citadel of domesticity but contended instead that motherhood—"the highest function possible to women"—was not accessible to all women, since "the highest development possible to any member of a class is not necessarily possible to reach."[23] Education, in any event, should not only equip girls to take their places in alternative professions but should also train them for motherhood. To the extent that this introduced differences between male and female education, then these distinctions were necessary.[24] Parrish and Thomas thus differed in their belief in the ability of educational processes to effect changes and in the desirability and content of change in the status of women. Although Thomas's opinions mellowed over the years, she continued to argue that educated men and women would become equals as either professional competitors or married comrades. Parrish, articulating a more conservative view, felt that education took its values from society and that school, at most, only enabled women to achieve greater satisfaction in their complementary feminine roles, whether these were traditional domestic roles or new ones mandated by socio-economic circumstances.

This division in views on the relationship between social change, social roles, and education continued to characterize the discussion of higher education for women. At a meeting of the Southern Association of College Women in 1913, Eleanor Lord, Dean of Goucher College, advocated equal responsibilities of both sexes to home and society and pointed proudly to more and more graduates of Goucher and Bryn Mawr who were economically independent and who accepted greater social and political responsibility.[25] At the same meeting, Edward K. Graham, Dean of the College of Liberal Arts, University of North Carolina, expressed the more conservative, more popular point of view when he assured his audience that the equal education of men and women in no way suggested that women's chief vocation was other than marriage and motherhood.[26]

Christian Principle and New South Philanthropy

In this spectrum of opinion, Agnes Scott Institute incarnated an educational philosophy equivalent to Parrish's compromise between feminism and social realities, taking its cue, however, from Gaines's religiously inspired views of the role of women. Early in his pastorate, Gaines had become convinced that the extension of Christianity was linked to the Christian education of girls. He believed that the untrained aspects of the mind inevitably governed the trained aspects and that an untrained moral nature would inevitably dominate a trained mind. Education must be, therefore, the systematic regulation of both mind and character, lest both fall prey to the "unrestrained domination of indwelling sin."[27]

By 1889, schools for white Southern women lagged financially behind schools for black women, which profited from Northern philanthropy. Northern support for schools for black women became highly visible in Atlanta after 1881. A girls' school founded by Atlanta's Friendship Baptist Church was supported partially by the Women's American Baptist Home Mission Society of New England, and during a tour through the North in 1882 the school's founders attracted the attention of John D. Rockefeller. Rockefeller and his wife contributed generously to the school in the next decade, and the institution was eventually renamed Spelman Seminary in honor of Mrs. Rockefeller's mother. In addition to support from the Rockefeller family, Spelman also benefited from contributions from the Slater Fund and other Northern philanthropic agencies.[28]

White Atlantans viewed these proceedings with mixed feelings. One woman wrote to the *Atlanta Constitution* in July 1889 to voice her support for establishing the proposed industrial college for women. She argued that the state needed for its own prosperity "that those who have been disabled by poverty or orphanage or misfortune shall be lifted to the opportunity that is now extended to the colored girls by Northern philanthropy, for which all good people are grateful." Another observer feared for the future of white supremacy if white girls continued in ignorance while black women were put in positions of "greater awareness" by virtue of better educational opportunities.[29] Southern educators, including Wilbur Fisk Tillett of Vanderbilt University and Atticus Haygood of Atlanta, joined the chorus, calling upon New South businessmen to plough back into Southern education some of the fruits of their material prosperity. Emory College, then located in Oxford, Georgia, found one such benefactor in Asa Griggs Candler and the Decatur Female Institute another in George Washington Scott.[30]

Feeling that the Lord had smiled upon his very successful fertilizer business, Scott decided to donate $40,000 to build a permanent home for the

Decatur Female Institute in the spring of 1890 on the condition that it be renamed Agnes Scott Institute in honor of his mother. After touring colleges in the North, he realized that he could not provide an adequate building for that amount, and Main Building, now Agnes Scott Hall, ultimately cost $112,250, at that time the largest gift in the history of education in Georgia.[31]

The Decatur Female Institute had initially been funded by issuing stock worth $5,350 to thirty-five leading citizens of Atlanta and Decatur. This was a common method of financing private schools in the South, and many educators felt that the practice hampered the development of education because nonprofessionals interfered with the running of the institutions. Southern schools were chronically short of funds, and for partisans of public education the problem was particularly acute. Bourbon Democrats regularly campaigned on the promise of law taxation, which, in turn, boded insufficient funding for the struggling public school systems.[32]

The Reverend Gaines obtained absolutely no encouragement for his school from the Presbyterian Synod of Georgia, but in the 1890s he convinced Scott that dependence upon people outside the institute was detrimental to its development. Scott, already the largest single shareholder, accordingly bought up the outstanding shares. He then turned the entire capital over to a self-perpetuating board of trustees, which amended the charter to stipulate that only members of the Presbyterian Church (United States) might be elected to it. Until his death in 1903, Scott made up deficits in the school's budget. Although he did not leave an income-producing endowment, his gift of buildings and land, comparable with bequests to leading Northern institutions, gave the institute the appearance of permanence. In addition, his generosity during his lifetime freed Agnes Scott from complete dependence upon students' tuition for operating expenses and enabled it to develop academically in an atmosphere of relative economic security.[33]

The Curriculum and the Faculty

Scott's benevolence enabled Gaines to apply his Christian principles and to realize an educational program that, he believed, would mold model Christian women. Gaines believed that Christian work consisted of personal activity and the use of talents and opportunities to their full extent. Women, he felt, had an ordained vocation in becoming wives and mothers. Lecturing the Christian Band of Agnes Scott Institute on the twenty-third psalm, Gaines reminded them of the "*blessedness* of being a Christian—the safety, the joy, the *gladness*, the hope."[34]

Following the example of other denominational colleges and schools, the Decatur Female Institute was evangelically Christian but not sectarian in order to broaden its base of public support. Denominational colleges depended upon students' tuition to meet their operating expenses, and since the 1880s they had resented the competition from secular, state-supported institutions. In the decade prior to the First World War, the major state universities had experimented with educational reform and, for the most part, advocated improving the quality of higher education by enhancing the traditional liberal curriculum and increasing the public's respect for education through the examples of important and well-educated alumni. These universities thus followed the reform ideas associated with Henry Tappan of the University of Michigan rather than the more democratic theories posited by Francis Wayland of Brown University, who called for adding more practical courses in response to the community's needs and demands.[35] Proponents of denominational education in the South after the war emphasized the importance of mental discipline and the old-fashioned liberal curriculum in the face of the specialization that new secular colleges and universities offered.

The ethic of mental discipline admirably served the cause of religiously oriented education. Studying academic subjects was considered training for an end; thus, Latin, Greek, moral philosophy, and mathematics, the staples of the liberal curriculum, were not ends in themselves. Christian morality was usually the content of the educational process of character-building in which the classics, philosophy, and mathematics represented sets of intellectual calisthenics. At the meeting of the Southern Educational Association in 1901, Geroge Summey, chancellor of Southwestern Presbyterian College, argued that true ethics and sociology could only be taught in a denominational college where "the sources and authority from which their principles spring, in the will of a divine law giver" could be properly studied.[36]

Reflecting this religious attitude toward women's higher education, which meshed with the conservative, secular view articulated by Parrish, Agnes Scott's *Annual Catalogue and Announcement of 1889–1890* announced that the institute's administrators believed that school, after the home, was the most important formative influence upon a young woman. The institute was founded to promote "the glory of God in the higher Christian education of young women." God had assigned to them a sphere of "inexpressible importance to the welfare of Church and State." The purpose of the institute was to educate girls to perform their divine function, and such training required the finest education, "an education which would carefully guard and promote her physical development, which would give thorough mental training and furnishing, which would give that refinement and those accomplishments which adorn womanhood, and which, above all, would form and develop the highest type of character." For its curriculum, however, the institute took as its model the "leading institutions of the land" that prescribed for young women a course of study "as liberal as that prescribed in the leading male colleges."[37] The result was a paradox. On the one hand, the institute justified its policies by promising to uphold more perfectly the woman's traditional role as wife and mother. Yet the curriculum that effected this end presumed the equality of male and female intellect and thus undermined the differentiation between the sexes that the school's rationale promised to support.

Like those who defended denominational colleges for men, Gaines associated mental discipline and a liberal curriculum with the formation of Christian character. However, unlike the small denominational colleges for men, women's denominational colleges generally had higher academic standards than their secular equivalents because they were less likely to tolerate the pretentiousness that characterized many secular colleges. Maintaining high academic standards was a constant problem for Southern schools, and local boosterism led principals to christen institutions "colleges" where there was little to substantiate the claim. The Southern Association of College Women was eventually formed to eliminate the stigma of the "so-called Southern colleges for women" by establishing a code of standards and ranking Southern institutions. The association then published its findings in an effort to influence public opinion.[38] Paradoxically, institutions like Agnes Scott and Mary Baldwin Seminary, which called themselves institutes or seminaries, were more likely to maintain high standards for both faculty and students than were the so-called colleges.[39]

The principal changes that took place at Agnes Scott Institute between 1890 and its admission to the Southern Association of Colleges and Secondary Schools in 1907 were in its organization of both students and academic subjects and in the increased size and sophistication of its faculty. In the early years, administrators did not distinguish levels of competence among the students by organizing them into the modern system of classes. Instead, students individually met the requirements of a series of schools (English, Mathematics, Natural Science, Mental and Moral Philosophy, Bible, History, and Modern Languages) in a scheme patterned on the University of Virginia. Students accumulated a sufficient number of certificates of proficiency to qualify for a degree in the Classical, Literary, Scientific or Normal courses. In 1898, however, the students were grouped into freshman, sophomore, junior, and senior classes according to their level of achievement.[40]

Changes in the composition of the faculty reflected greater diversity in the curriculum as well as Gaines's policy of adding more difficult courses and deleting elementary material each year. When the Decatur Female Institute opened in 1889, two teachers, Nannette Hopkins and Mattie Cook, divided the academic classes between them. In the following years, more teachers, both men and women, were hired to teach a wider range of courses beginning with the addition of French, Latin, and chemistry. The traditional liberal curriculum was made complete in 1897 with the introduction of Greek. Key disciplines, such as mathematics, were divided into elementary and advanced levels of instruction, and new faculty members were hired with an eye to their professional qualifications, measured by advanced degrees.

From the beginning, Gaines had employed the most highly qualified people that the school's budget could afford. These were frequently women who interrupted their own studies to teach for a year or two, hoping to save enough money to enable them to continue their own schooling elsewhere. Nannette Hopkins had graduated from Hollins Institute and planned to complete her education at Bryn Mawr. She came to Decatur in 1889 expecting to stay only one year before returning to college but remained at Agnes Scott to become the College's first Dean. Louise McKinney, who taught at Agnes Scott from 1891 to 1937, completed the course at the State Teacher College, Farmville, Virginia, which did not confer degrees. She then studied at Vassar and had planned to finish there before she came to Agnes Scott, lured by the relatively high salary of $800 a year. The increasing sophistication of the faculty brought more and more well-educated, usually Southern, women to the campus. Maud Morrow, for example, taught Greek from 1897 to 1905; she was the first woman to graduate from the University of Mississippi where she eventually took a Master's degree. Lillian Smith, the first woman on the faculty with a doctorate, arrived in 1905 to teach Greek.[41]

Students

The institute encouraged close ties between students and teachers in order to overcome parents' reluctance to send their daughters away to school. A corollary to the strict distinction between male and female roles that identified women with domesticity was the preference to keep daughters at home while their brothers went off to school. Coeducation was unpopular in the South, and, as men's universities slowly opened their doors to women, administrators maintained as much social segregation as possible. By 1892 at Vanderbilt University, women were Students by Courtesy, a status entitling them to all academic privileges and honors except formal matriculation. When Cumberland University in Lebanon, Tennessee, annexed the Lebanon College for Young Ladies, its bulletin assured patrons that the young ladies would have the full advantages of the university's faculty and curriculum but that there would be no mixing with the male university students. The University of Alabama required its female students to live with families privately and provided rooms at the university in which they might study separately. Women were admitted to the University of Tennessee by vote of the faculty in 1893 with the stipulation that they be at least seventeen years old and that the dean approve their place of residence.[42]

Insitutions solely for women had an advantage in the allaying of parental fears as they were predicated on the exclusion of male students. Agnes Scott's *Annual Catalogue and Announcement of 1891–1892* informed prospective patrons that "every effort is made to give the Institute the character of a home and to cause the pupils to feel at home," and the seal that ornamented the first diplomas conferred at Agnes Scott contained the phrase, "A Home for Young Ladies." The institute thus minimized the separation between home and school, offered spiritual security in its heavily Christian orientation, and provided social protection in its ever-vigilant faculty and its long list of rules. Prohibitions included snacking at night, wearing thin, low shoes during cold months or inclement weather, "and the too early removal of flannels or any neglect to put them on at the approach of cold weather."[43]

Parents themselves most seriously violated the institute's rules. Bulletin after bulletin requested them not to excuse their daughters from examinations or to bring them home before the end of the term. Parents living in the vicinity of Atlanta were asked not to permit their children to come home for weekends, but Gaines learned that as soon as his boarding students had settled down to study, letters would arrive asking that their girls be sent back home for a visit.[44] Finally, box after box of forbidden treats came regularly despite the bulletins' emphatic prohibition: "OUR TABLE IS ABUN-DANTLY SUPPLIED WITH WHOLESOME FOOD, AND BOXES OR EATABLES ARE FORBIDDEN. PLACING BEFORE YOUR DAUGHTER A TEMPTATION TO EAT RICH FOOD AT ALL HOURS IS A MOST EFFECTUAL MEANS OF DEFEATING ALL THE ENDS FOR WHICH THEY HAVE BEEN SENT TO US."[45]

Parental disregard for Agnes Scott's rules undermined the institute's authority over its students. Mental discipline, with the development of character as its main objective, required not only the training of the mind through the mental exercises of Greek vocabulary and algebra but also, a well-regulated extracurricular life. This was the source of the elaborate set of rules and the motivation for the teacher-directed clubs and activites, which ranged from intramural basketball teams to the embroidery club. Flouting the rules was not conducive to the formation of Christian character, but most parents, unconcerned with the effects of their indulgence and the niceties of mental discipline, preferred merely to send their daughters away for a year to be "finished" before they were married.[46]

Scott's enormous donation had attracted a great deal of attention, and the second year of operation saw a vast increase in enrollment. The turnover in the early years was rapid as a result of the relative unpopularity of the institute's rigorous academic requirements and the lack of preparation that students displayed upon their arrival at Agnes Scott. Nannette Hopkins remembered that finding students with adequate preparation was a difficult problem in the first few years and credited Gaines with the foresight and courage to maintain their somewhat unpopular policies until secondary schools began to prepare students to meet Agnes Scott's requirements.[47] Looking back on his career at Agnes Scott, Gaines himself remarked that the school had given its students high educational standards, "something real and true, not a veneer or sham."[48] Not everyone appreciated his principles; "we had an awful reputation for overworking the girls," Louise McKinney remembered. "Mothers thought we were ruining their daughters' health."[49]

In both academic subjects and extracurricular activities, collegiate life for women was very similar to that offered men at numerous small colleges. By 1900, the women published an annual for which they solicited advertisements from local merchants, and shortly thereafter they began a literary magazine. Organizing classes led to the election of class officers. The predominantly female faculty, moreover, presented them with an alternative model to that of their mothers. At Agnes Scott, educated professional women supervised their studies and activities and in the nature of the institute were the immediate executors of the policy in loco parentis. Occasionally, a graduate of the institute returned to teach there. Anna Irwin Young, for example, graduated from Agnes Scott, studied at the University of Chicago, and came back to Decatur to assist in the mathematics department in 1897. Like other teachers before her, she ultimately finished a degree at Columbia University.[50]

A "Prophesy" written for the annual in 1897 saw the institute's graduates as physicians and lawyers, missionaries and teachers, administrators and musicians. Two former companions, Lily Little and Anna Wiley, became bitter enemies while campaigning for president on the Republican ticket, but Ada Hooper defeated both as the Democrats' candidate. One classmate became a conductor on a streetcar in Atlanta, another a book agent, and one Alice Barker became mayor of Utopia.[51] In spite of the fantasy, the realistic elements—the choice of professions such as medicine, law, missionary work and education, fields in which women were beginning to succeed or had always succeeded—suggests that alternatives to motherhood were attractive possibilities.

A few graduates of Agnes Scott Institute still corresponded with the College Alumnae Association in 1923. The Annual Register that year listed a handful who were involved in church activities and in education and who had not married.[53] The college experience most likely became a bond of friendship rather than a stimulus for active careers. The Georgia Branch of the Southern Association of College Women reported in 1912, for example, that the members had spent the last year studying contemporary literature together and organizing a College Day to introduce high school girls to the idea of college. They had also sponsored the creation of a censorship bureau to review vaudeville features and collected a Christmas Fund to purchase shoes for deserving school children.[54]

This behavior was apparently not unique to Agnes Scott graduates or to Southerners, although a systematic review of the impact of college on late nineteenth century women is by no means complete. One study of the women who graduated from Smith College between 1879 and 1888 indicated that the experience of college had little or no effect on a young woman's decision to enter a profession. Family obligations frequently demanded that many alumnae go straight back home to stay "unless they could find a husband."[55] Poverty as well might preclude further study. The most popular profession was teaching, and only 37.9 percent taught at any time in their lives after college. Only 10.7 percent held a job in any of the other open professions, which included medicine, college teaching and administration, and architecture.[56] For the majority, college life was a privilege. It became, for some, a social bond; "I have finally come to the conclusion that there are no girls like college girls, after all," one Smith graduate confessed, "and have consoled myself with the three Vassar girls on this coast, since I cannot have Smith girls."[57]

College and Change

Critics had argued that utilitarian considerations impeded the development of women's higher education by channeling efforts into teacher preparation and away from the broad liberal curriculum that represented genuine education, i.e., the formation of character rather than the acquisition of skills. This position was consistent with that taken by the founders of the Northeastern women's colleges who had justified their emphasis on the liberal curriculum in order to establish the equality of male and female capabilities. By 1900, however, these advocates of higher education for women were failing to reckon with the increasing emphasis on professional skills and qualifications that had come to be a feature of higher education for young men. Undergraduate education for young women, centered on the liberal curriculum, was in the end self-defeating as an instrument for social change because it did not prepare its students to enter any professions or to challenge the conventions that restricted opportunities to the home or to careers that represented extensions of domesticity and the putative superiority of feminine morality. M. Carey Thomas's "race" between educated, qualified men and women failed to materialize.

Both the ideal of Christian motherhood and the liberal curriculum, the basis of Agnes Scott's high academic standards, were central to the institute's progress. Both discouraged planning for a career after college, except perhaps teaching. Teaching itself was fast becoming a feminine preserve to the virtual exclusion of men. A wall of prejudice, moreover, limited opportunity. "Years ago in my young enthusiasm," Parrish reflected in 1899, "I believed that women had only to demonstrate their fitness for work and place in order to obtain them. That their very excellence would prove a bar, that good men would oppose them because of their superior work, arguing that since women were born to be wives and mothers no other profession must be allowed them, seemed to be impossible. To-day, I am a wiser and sadder woman."[58]

At its founding, Agnes Scott was in the vanguard of higher education for women in the South because of its emphasis on high standards and its emulation of nationally recognized institutions in order to realize these goals. To the extent that Gaines intended to create an institution of a caliber equal to these schools, he succeeded admirably. In her analysis of seven accredited Southern women's colleges which included Agnes Scott, Elizabeth Barber Young concluded that no curricular differences set Southern institutions apart.[59] Like other similar institutions, moreover, Agnes Scott offered an outlet to women who sought a career in teaching at an advanced level.

Its gospel for women, however, did not substantially disturb traditional attitudes toward women. On the contrary, Gaines's very justification for excellence, a more perfect Christian womanhood, reinforced these values. Although Young found no difference in curriculum between Northern and Southern colleges for women, Agnes Scott and other Southern women's colleges may have differed in their overwhelmingly evangelical, Protestant orientation. This difference and the relationship between Protestantism and higher education for women in the South offer fruitful avenues for further research. Until the early 1960s, Agnes Scott College maintained a religious requirement for members of the faculty. Students are still required, unless otherwise exempted, to complete one course in biblical literature "in order to have some understanding of the Judaeo-Christian dimension of Western civilization." A subsection of the part of the current catalogue devoted to "Student Life," entitled "Religious Life," describes the students' active Christian Association and encourages students to affiliate with a local "church of their choice."[60] Although these may now represent survivals from the nineteenth century, the religious character of the institute was part of the fabric of its founding and very much a reflection of the deeply Protestant character of Southern culture.

Historians have only begun to analyze the confluence of forces and trends that were involved in the women's movement of the late nineteenth century. In the late nineteenth and early twentieth centuries education was considered an agent of progress. That we have come to see women's colleges as signs of feminist activity rather than as vehicles for change testifies not so much to the failure of these institutions as to the extent to which we have begun to discard the convictions of our grandfathers.

Notes

1. Wilbur J. Cash, *The Mind of the South* (New York: Vintage Books, Random House, 1941), pp. 179–181. Cash ridiculed the Yankee schoolmarm who came south to teach the freedmen; for a modern discussion of the Northern schoolteacher during Reconstruction, see Sandra E. Small, "The Yankee Schoolmarm in Freedmen's Schools: An Analysis of Attitudes," *Journal of Southern History*, 45 (1979): 381–402.

2. Edward T. James, ed., *Notable American Women, 1607–1950*, 3 vols. (Cambridge: Harvard University Press, 1971), 2, 167–169.

3. Frank Henry Gaines, *The Story of Agnes Scott College (1889–1921)* (Atlanta, Ga.: Agnes Scott College, n.d.), p. 6. Gaines's study is typical of the traditional, narrowly conceived histories of individual colleges. Other useful sources of information are Robert G. Gardner, *On a Hill: The Story of Shorter College* (Rome, Ga.: Shorter College, 1972); and Dorothy S. Vickery, *Hollins College, 1842-1942* (Hollins College, Va.: Hollins College, 1942). Mary Watters, *The History of Mary Baldwin College, 1842-1942* (Staunton, Va.: Mary Baldwin College, 1942) is unusual in the extent to which Watters related the history of the college to contemporary events and themes.

4. Charles Edgeworth Jones, *Education in Georgia* (Washington, D.C.: Government Printing Office, 1889), p. 84. For a modern treatment, see Dorothy Orr, *A History of Education in Georgia* (Chapel Hill, N.C.: University of North Carolina Press, 1950); for a series of essays on topics ranging from the antebellum through the New South, see R. C. Simonini, ed., *Education in the South: Institute of Southern Culture Lectures at Longwood College* (Farmville, Va.: Longwood College, 1959).

5. Colyer Meriwether, *History of Higher Education in South Carolina with a Sketch of the Free School System* (Washington, D. C.: Government Printing Office, 1889), p. 107.

6. Kenneth R. Johnson, "Florence University for Women," *Alabama Historical Quarterly*, 38 (1976): 305–306.

7. Jill K. Conway, "Perspectives on the History of Women's Education in the United States," *History of Education Quarterly*, 14 (1974): 1–14; Glenda Riley, "Origins of the Argument for Improved Female Education," Ibid. 9 (1969): 455–470; Roberta Wein, "Women's Colleges and Domesticity, 1875–1918," Ibid. 14 (1974): 31–47. A useful anthology of primary sources with selections by Catharine Beecher, Margaret Fuller, and M. Carey Thomas is Barbara M. Cross, ed., *The Educated Woman in America, Selected Writings of Catharine Beecher, Margaret Fuller and M. Carey Thomas* (New York: Teachers College, Columbia University, 1965); for a collection of essays on women in higher education colored by the emerging Affirmative Action guidelines but without a significant historical perspective, see

W. Todd Furness and Patricia Albjerg Graham, eds., *Women in Higher Education* (Washington, D.C.: American Council on Education, 1974).

8. Thomas H. Woody, *A History of Women's Education in the United States*, 2 vols. (New York: Octagon Books, Inc., [1929], 1966).

9. Anne Firor Scott, *The Southern Lady: From Pedastal to Politics, 1830–1930* (Chicago: University of Chicago Press, 1970).

10. Wilbur Fisk Tillett, "Southern Womanhood as Affected by the War," *The Century Illustrated Monthly Magazine*, 21 (1891–92): 9–10.

11. Ibid., p. 12; Atticus G. Haygood, "The South and the School Problem," *Harper's New Monthly Magazine*, 79 (1889): 227; *Atlanta* [Ga.] *Constitution*, July 4, 1889, p. 4. These statistics were compiled with the help of Dan T. Carter of Emory University; they are derived from U. S. Department of Commerce and Labor, Bureau of the Census, *Statistics of Women at Work Based on Unpublished Information Derived from the Schedules of the Twelfth Census: 1900* (Washington, D.C.: Government Printing Office, 1907), pp. 109, 113, 120; U. S. Department of Interior, *Report of the Department of Education for the Year 1903*, 1 (Washington, D.C.: Government Printing Office, 1905): 88–89; U. S. Department of Commerce and Labor, Bureau of the Census, *Special Reports, Supplemental Analysis and Derivative Tables, Twelfth Census of the U. S., 1900* (Washington, D.C.: Government Printing Office, 1907); U. S. Department of Interior, Census Office, *Compendium of the Tenth Census, June 1880* (Washington, D.C.: Government Printing Office, 1883), pp. 1640–1641. On the need for further research into the role of teachers, see Geraldine J. Clifford, "Saints, Sinners and People: A Position Paper on the Historiography of American Education," *History of Education Quarterly*, 15 (1975): 275–272. A collection of documents illustrating the career of a schoolteacher in rural Alabama is Julia L. Williard, ed., "Reflections of an Alabama Teacher, 1875–1950," *Alabama Historical Quarterly*, 38 (1976): 291–304.

12. Claudia Goldin, "Female Labor Force Participation: The Origin of Black and White Differences, 1870 to 1880," *Journal of Economic History* 37 (1977): 95.

13. Ibid.

14. Amory Dwight Mayo, *Southern Women in the Recent Educational Movement in the South*, Library of Southern Civilization Series, ed. Dan T. Carter and Amy Friedlander (Baton Rouge, La.: Louisiana State University Press, 1978), pp. 48, 127, 134–135; Haygood, "The South and the School Problem," pp. 225–231; Charles Foster Smith, "Southern Colleges and Schools," *The Atlantic Monthly* 54 (1884): 542–557.

15. Celestia S. Parrish, "The Education of Women in the South," *Journal of Proceedings and Addresses of the Tenth Annual Meeting Held at Richmond, Va., December 27–29, 1900* (n.p.: Southern Educational Association, 1901), p. 159.

16. Mary V. Woodward, "Woman's Education in the South," *Educational Review* 7 (1894): 468.

17. John M. McBryde, "Womanly Education for Woman," *Sewanee Review*, 5 (1907): 479.

18. James, *Notable American Women*, 3: 214-225.

19. M. Carey Thomas, "Should the Higher Education of Women Differ from That of Men? *Educational Review*, 21 (1901): 8.

20. Ibid., p. 4. Fears for women's health died hard; twenty years after the founding of Vassar College, the question of physical stamina still nagged the minds of educators of women in the Northeast. In 1880, Maria Mitchell, professor of astronomy at Vassar, dissuaded the "delicate girl" from attempting the regular collegiate curriculum. Her opinions, together with pieces by Alice Freeman Parker, president of Wellesley, and Lucy M. Salmon, professor of history at Vassar, are included in Anna C. Brackett, ed., *Woman and the Higher Education* (New York: Harper & Bros., 1893). For a modern discussion of the supposed biological delicacy of women, see Caroll Smith-Rosenberg and Charles Rosenberg, "The Female Animal: Medical and Biological Views of Women and Her Role in Nineteenth-Century America," *Journal of American History* 60 (1973): 332-356. For a study of the development of the Northeastern women's colleges, see Mabel L. Newcomer, *A Century of Higher Education for American Women* (New York: Harper & Bros., 1959).

21. Celestia S. Parrish, "Shall the Higher Education of Women Be the Same as That of Men?" *Educational Review* 22 (1901): 384-389.

22. *Atlanta Constitution*, July 6, 1889, p. 4.

23. Celestia S. Parrish, "Some Defects in the Education of Women in the South," *Proceedings of the Second Capon Springs Conference for Education in the South* (Raleigh, N.C.: n.p., 1899), pp. 72-73.

24. Parrish, "Education of Women in the South," p. 36.

25. Eleanor L. Lord, "What Should the Bachelor's Degree Represent?" *Proceedings in Full of the Tenth Annual Meeting of the Southern Association of College Women* (n.p., Southern Educational Association, 1901), pp. 18-19.

26. Edward K. Graham, "A Fundamental Factor in the Education of Women," Ibid., p. 14.

27. Frank H. Gaines, *Christian Education*, as quoted by V. A. Sydenstricker, "Dr. Frank Henry Gaines and Agnes Scott College," typescript in Agnes Scott Room, James Ross McCain Library, Agnes Scott College, Decatur, Ga., p. 37.

28. *Spelman College Bulletin, 1979-80,* pp. 6-8.

29. Alice Lloyd, "Education for Southern Women," *Proceedings of the Tenth Conference for Education in the South* (Pinehurst, N.C.: Executive Committee of the Conference for Education in the South, 1907), pp. 224-225; *Atlanta Constitution*, July 4, 1889, p. 4.

30. Haygood, "The South and the School Problem," p. 231; Tillett, "Southern Womanhood," p. 16.

31. Gaines, *Story of Agnes Scott College*, pp. 19–20.
32. Ibid., pp. 12–13, 26–27.
33. Ibid., p. 29.
34. Gaines, Farewell Talk to the Christian Band of Agnes Scott Institute, undated ms., Agnes Scott Room, Agnes Scott College, Decatur, Ga.
35. Jane E. Weyant, "The Debate over Higher Education in the South, 1850–1860," *Mississippi Quarterly*, 29 (1976): 539–557.
36. George Summey, "The Denominational Colleges and Higher Education," *Journal of Proceedings and Addresses*, p. 159.
37. *Second Annual Catalogue and Announcement of Agnes Scott Institute, 1889–1890*, p. 6; *Third Annual Catalogue, 1897–1898*, p. 14.
38. Marion Talbot and Lois Kimball Mathews Rosenberry, *The History of the American Association of University Women* (Boston: Houghton Mifflin Co., 1931), p. 449.
39. Mayo, *Southern Women*, p. 66.
40. Information on the evolution of Agnes Scott's curriculum was taken from descriptions of courses in the *Annual Catalogues*.
41. For information on the faculty, see *Annual Catalogues*.
42. Charles Foster Smith, "The Higher Education of Women in the South," *Educational Review* 8 (1894): 287–290.
43. *Third Annual Catalogue, 1890–1891*, p. 16.
44. Sydenstricker, "Dr. Frank Henry Gaines," pp. 17–18.
45. *Tenth Annual Catalogue, 1897–1898*, p. 89.
46. Ibid., pp. 17–18.
47. Ibid., p. 45.
48. As quoted in *Atlanta Journal*, April 15, 1923, n.p.
49. As quoted in *Atlanta Constitution*, December 20, 1961, p. 23.
50. *Ninth Annual Catalogue, 1897–1898*, n.p.; Gaines, *Story of Agnes Scott College*, p. 33.
51. "Prophecy," *Aurora* 2 (1897): 137–139.
52. As quoted in *Atlanta Constitution*, December 20, 1961, p. 23.
53. "Annual Register," *Agnes Scott Alumnae Quarterly*, 1 (1923): 19–20.
54. Southern Association of College Women, "Report from Branches," *Proceedings of the Ninth Annual Meeting* (Nashville, Tenn., April 3–5 1912), p. 36.
55. Sarah H. Gordon, "Smith College Students: The First Ten Classes, 1879–1888," *History of Education Quarterly*, 15 (1975): p. 161.
56. Ibid., pp. 163–164.
57. As quoted in Ibid., p. 161. For another example of social bonding based on college experience and of the kinds of activities that alumnae pursued in the South at the turn of the century, see "A Vassar Enterprise in Atlanta's Schools," *Southern Educational Journal*, 13 (1900): 434–435.
58. Parrish, "Some Defects in the Education of Women," pp. 71–72.
59. Elizabeth Barber Young, *A Study of the Curricula of Seven Selected Women's Colleges of the Southern States* (New York: Teachers College, Columbia University, 1932).
60. *Agnes Scott College, 1979–1980*, p. 11.

Mark K. Bauman

Confronting the New South Creed: The Genteel Conservative as Higher Educator

Introduction

The era from the Civil War through World War I was noteworthy for psychological as well as material alterations in the Southern landscape. Many individuals travelled from the countryside and small town to the city, from an agricultural to an industrial/commercial environment both literally and figuratively. The "New South Creed" supporting Southern industrialism and urbanization, whether myth or reality, was a concept with which people were forced to grapple.[1] Living through a virtual watershed in Southern history, many sensitive men and women had to deal with wrenching ideological contradictions and paradoxes. They moved to the city as they decried its immorality and impersonal nature. Nurturing commercialism, they opposed the materialistic ethic. They spoke and thought in terms of individualism and liberty, harmony and community, at the same time that their actions led to complexity, growth, and fragmentation.[2]

The thoughts and actions of Warren A. Candler (1857-1941) typify the ways in which many in the genteel class reacted to the New South forces.[3] Brought up in an "Old South" home and educated at a college steeped in the traditional philosophy in a time of change, Candler tried to merge the two. As a college president and university chancellor, he oversaw the transition by masking the introduction of specialization and professionalism in the rhetoric of conservatism. A racist of the old patrician school, he came into conflict with the industrial education model of black higher education then in vogue because he believed that all individuals should be able to develop their capabilities fully. Only with World War I, which both accelerated change and brought it into bold relief, did Candler, like many of his peers, clearly perceive the transformation that he had actually taken part in implementing. Confronted with the consequences of the New South creed, he attempted an impossible return to past values and institutions. From a broader perspective, Candler's experiences illustrate how forces outside of an individual's control and indeed counter to his desires still affect him and influence his decisions.

The Genteel Family

It is most difficult to separate an individual's personal responses to an event from considerations of his class, status, and background. For someone of Candler's milieu, the problems multiply because his generation in the South remained very conscious of its "proper place" or role in society. To understand his reactions, then, we must first explore the foundations of his personality and world view.

Both sides of Warren Candler's family had migrated to Georgia at about the time of the American Revolution and had benefited from land bounties given in payment for war service and as an inducement for settlement. They entered the planter class and dabbled in state politics. A great-grandfather became interested in education and contracted to build the Richmond Academy, the first brick structure erected as a school in Augusta. Elected to the first state legislature after the war, he supported popular education and the founding of Franklin College which later served as the nucleus of the University of Georgia. Warren Candler's parents followed these traditions. His father, Samuel, pioneered as a miner and land speculator in north Georgia. He opened a general store in the small gold center of Villa Rica, purchased slaves, and gained statewide recognition. A Union-Democrat, he nonetheless remained loyal to his region during the Civil War.

Samuel and Martha Candler worked their children hard and forced them to learn. Besides sending Warren to a series of local one-room schools, they must also have provided a tutor to train the boy in the Latin and Greek required for college admission. He became sufficiently proficient to enter Emory College with advanced standing at the age of fifteen. Warren and the other Candler children exemplified the transition of the Southern aristocracy during the Civil War and Reconstruction era. They might hold the old plantation ideal, yet they entered into law, politics, business, real estate, education, and the clergy. One brother married into a Mississippi sugar cane family before the war and became a noted attorney and legislator. Another lawyer-politician opposed populist Tom Watson in the early 1880s for his rejection of tradition and yet became a railroad reformer at the turn of the century. Like Warren, Milton believed in change, but change within the Southern heritage. Warren's younger brother became one of the leading attorneys in Georgia and served as a state supreme court judge. Another brother emerged as a millowner-merchant-banker maintaining the family's Villa Rica interests. A sister established and presided over the West End Institute, a women's finishing school in Cartersville, Georgia. The most renowned sibling was Asa Griggs Candler. Starting as a druggist, Asa purchased a little-known elixir which had helped cure his headaches but which also tasted refreshing when mixed at the fountain. A brilliant merchandizer, he made millions selling the concoction as Coca-Cola. During his early years, he assisted Warren and John with their educations. Asa increased his fortune through real estate transactions and bank holdings. He served as a business-reform mayor of Atlanta in 1917 and president of the city's chamber of commerce. When Warren entered Emory College in 1873, he intended to become an attorney. His experiences and contacts at the school, however, led him into education and the ministry.[4] Constantly in touch with his family, their activities and ideas continued to influence him as his career development paralleled theirs.

College Days at "Old Emory"

Most of the schools of the South prior to the Civil War were small, church-related institutions dominated by a minister-president. Due in part to the rudimentary level of secondary education in the region (Georgia was typical in not having a statewide public school system until the 1870s), the majority were little more than prep schools. The war further disrupted college life, forcing many schools to close their doors. In the case of institutions like Emory, some were virtually reorganized during Reconstruction. This experience was not totally negative. Although college presidents were constantly faced with financial difficulties, they could also begin the experimentation that was impossible under the conservative antebellum regime. Reconstruction thus witnessed the very gradual adoption of the innovations that had been introduced in Northern colleges beginning with the first quarter of the century. The increasingly influential New South philosophy of industrialism and progress nurtured these steps toward modernity and encouraged the Southern schools to try to keep pace with the North in the development of programs in science, technology, and business.[5] Candler's experiences first as a student and later as president of Emory College mirrored these trends and illustrate the conflicts engendered as modernity was superimposed upon the traditional ideology.

Many experiments in popular education were undertaken during the Jacksonian era. One of the more prevalent of these was the manual labor school. At these institutions students were able to help finance their educations. Experience in the fields and in building trades offered the additional "moral reward" of working with one's hands. Macon's Mercer University was begun in this fashion by the Baptists as was the state-supported Franklin College. Emory College was founded in 1834 by the Methodists as the Georgia Conference Manual Labor School. It served as a preparatory school, training its students to meet the entrance requirements of Yale and other colleges. One of its founders and its first president was Ignatius Few, Jr., grandson of a signer of the United States Constitution and second cousin of Warren Candler. It was Few who urged the expansion and transformation of the academy into Emory College in 1836. The small college in Oxford, Georgia, slowly matured under Few's administration. Its students, admitted as freshmen at fourteen years of age, studied the classics, English, philosophy, science, ancient history, and mathematics. The Bachelor of Arts was the only degree awarded. As in most of these colleges, a key element of the training was mental and moral discipline. Most of its teachers and presidents were Methodist ministers.[6]

The conditions and the classical curriculum remained intact when Warren Candler matriculated. Candler took courses in logic and rhetoric which were to help discipline his mind and prepare him for his favorite extracurricular activity—debating for the campus literary societies. These societies acted as important adjuncts to the formal program at a time when forensics was a basic criterion of merit. They developed the student's critical abilities and served as a democratic measure of status. Anyone could join and no monetary expenditure was needed for success. The topics of debate illustrated the interests of the day and the positions taken generally reflected the patrician values of the society. In 1873, for example, Candler spoke on the affirmative side of the resolution, "That the annexation of Cuba would be beneficial to the United States." He also debated the righteousness of the salary grab (a salary increase the senators voted themselves), the benefits of the Civil Rights Act to the Negro, and the relation of education to church and state. As president of Phi Gamma Society, he decided the question, "What has been more destructive to mankind, intemperance or war?" on behalf of the former. Victorian morality was stretched in the arguments over "Has religious sex done more to advance or retard the cause of religion?" The historian of the literary society concluded that the interest in these organizations had declined in 1876.[7] Yet, when Candler returned to Emory as president in 1888, they enjoyed renewed vigor. During his tenure, the societies discussed the tariff, free coinage of silver, suffrage, and the restriction of Chinese immigration—all controversial topics typical of regional as well as national concerns. There was little, if any, faculty involvement in these organizations and the debates obviously were not censured.

Candler graduated from Emory with honors in three years, and, like so many other graduates, entered the ministry. He road circuit and ministered to congregations in Sparta and Atlanta and acted as presiding elder of Dahlonega District before going to St. John's Church in Augusta. Sparta had been the home of Bishop George Foster Pierce and Candler became Pierce's protégè. A former president of Emory, the latter had become interested in the creation of a college for Afro-Americans.

An Inter-Racial Experiment in Higher Education

Considerable racial adjustment took place in the South after Emancipation. Blacks, long oppressed and controlled, set about establishing their own institutions. Second only to the wish for their own churches, perhaps their most pressing desire was for schools. During congressional Reconstruction, many Southern legislatures with black and white representatives initiated public school systems in which blacks were allowed to attend school for the first time. Black colleges were also begun. Yet the general poverty of the region and the rural, dispersed nature of the population proved to be almost insurmountable handicaps. With Redemption [the return of Southern white Democrats to power], much of the funding ended, especially for the black colleges. By the end of the century a system of segregation had been widely implemented and the percentage of state funding for black schools in relation to that for white schools declined.

Aid to black education from Northern philanthropists and missionary societies started to flow into the South during the Civil War. From the late 1860s, most black colleges were begun and/or supported from these sources. Philanthropic educational organizations like the Slater Fund, the Jeanes Fund, and, after 1900, the Southern Education Board and the General Education Board, funded largely by financiers and industrialists, placed great emphasis on industrial/technological training. This dovetailed with the Tuskegee idea associated with Booker T. Washington. It could be also accepted by the Southern white college presidents who helped administer the funds. Such education was supposed to integrate blacks into the industrial system and help prepare them for citizenship and advancement. It was also to provide the cheap labor required for the industrial revolution and agricultural modernization. As has been shown by Louis Harlan and others, this system was based upon patronizing, if not racist, assumptions, and contributed to the creation of the separate but unequal conditions of the Jim Crow era.[8]

Not all Southern blacks and whites aligned themselves with these policies. Atticus G. Haygood, a graduate of Emory and its president just prior to Candler's entrance into the school, emerged as one of the foremost Southern white advocates of black higher education during the 1880s. In *Our Brother in Black* (1881), Haygood provided a manifesto for equal justice and fair treatment for blacks. The book was a motivating force behind the educational efforts of Pierce and Candler. But Haygood was also a leading spokesman of the New South creed. He combined his interests by serving as agent of the Slater Fund, a Northern agency which contributed to Southern black education, particularly of the Tuskegee variety. Candler, who looked to Haygood as one of his mentors and friends, selectively borrowed from the older man. Unwilling to accept the materialistic ethos of the New South,

he espoused a benevolent paternalist position without the industrial emphasis. Like many members of his class, he believed that everyone had his or her
place in a hierarchical order and that people should be allowed to develop
their potential to fulfill the responsibilities of their position. Thus, blacks,
although possessing lesser innate ability, should still be encouraged to improve
themselves within their social class. They, too, should be exposed to the
classical curriculum so that leaders—teachers and preachers—would be better
able to guide their race. An indigenous venture had a special appeal to an
individual who, like Candler, had a strong sense of regional pride that was
injured by the condescending attitude of Northerners.[9]

Many blacks also believed that they had a stake in the South and that they
could create a place for themselves, possibly with the assistance of friendly
Southern whites. Rather than organizing their churches under Northern
white denominations after the Civil War, some of these individuals formed
branches under the Southern churches. The Colored Methodist Episcopal
Church, South, was created in this manner. The efforts of the leaders of this
body from 1870 to 1882 to build colleges met with failure, primarily because
of a lack of funds. Possibly encouraged by the publication of Haygood's
book, Bishop Lucius H. Holsey proposed a joint endeavor between his church
and the parent Methodist Episcopal Church, South. In 1882 the General
Conference of the white organization considered his proposal and established
a commission under Bishop George F. Pierce's chairmanship "for the purpose
of determining what may be done." The conference authorized fund raising
and the creation of a board of education to supervise the funds, but Pierce
assumed the power to establish a school as well.[10]

When Pierce sent Candler to St. John's Church, he intended the young
minister to be a part of this experiment. Candler became one of the seven
petitioners to the Superior Court of Richmond County requesting the incor-
poration of Paine Institute. He served on its board of trustees in various
capacities for thirty years and has been widely regarded as one of the pillars
of this interracial undertaking.

Candler's actions with regard to Paine illustrate the implementation of
his educational philosophy across racial lines. First of all, it was Candler
who made the motion to integrate the faculty at the board meeting held in
his office in 1888. This was a very unpopular action resulting in the resignation of a white instructor and much negative publicity. Secondly, he fought
to maintain the original purpose of the institution amidst growing black and
white sentiment in favor of industrial education for the black people. That
purpose was to train black teachers and preachers to better lead their people.
The curriculum of the school was to be the classical liberal arts. Finally,
when Paine was in financial difficulty during its first decade and several
trustees wanted to request assistance from the Carnegie and Rockefeller
Boards, Candler effectively opposed the move because he recognized that

provisos for the money would have included the transformation of the curriculum, the loss of church affiliation, and the acceptance of outside interference. To conservative, albeit benevolent, racist Warren Candler, education was to be separate *and* equal–a combination that these bureaucrats would not have allowed. An Old South theoretician, Candler wanted people to maintain their position in society, but not in a society dominated by the factory.

A Transitional Presidency of Emory College

Candler's interest in Paine overlapped his tenure as president of Emory College (1888–1898). His immediate predecessors, Atticus Haygood and Isaac Hopkins, advocated technological innovations in the curriculum. Haygood initiated Emory's first courses in toolcraft, design, and telegraphy. Hopkins taught the course in toolcraft. When Haygood resigned from Emory to work for the Slater Fund and Hopkins was elected to succeed him, course offerings were expanded to coincide with the new president's hobbies of woodcraft and ironwork. Hopkins envisioned a self-sufficient practical arts program similar to the old manual labor school. While his desire remained unfulfilled at Emory, it led to his appointment as the first president of the Georgia School of Technology (later Georgia Institute of Technology), an appointment and an institutional development which coincided with the ideas of New South advocate Henry Grady and the *Atlanta Constitution*. [11]

Candler completely reversed the trend, running counter to the vocational-utilitarian movement of higher education in the 1880s and 1890s. For him, the development of minds capable of making decisions and adjusting to any employment situation was more significant than training craftsmen for an industrializing America of which he was not at all sure that he approved. The technology building was put to use as a gymnasium and a drive was launched to expand the liberal arts broadly. At Candler's suggestion, an alumni chair of history and political science was inaugurated. The English faculty expanded. Law department additions included courses in civics and parliamentary law. Through his efforts in the state legislature, Emory law graduates received the same privileges as graduates of the University of Georgia's Lumpkin School of Law when entering the bar. Bachelor of Science and Philosophy degrees were added to the traditional Bachelor of Arts, thereby deemphasizing the classical Latin and Greek requirements and giving students more freedom of choice. Individual course requirements became more stringent. The student newspaper reported in October, 1888, that "A general changing about had been made in regard to the hours of recitation. The Seniors now go to Dr. Candler every day at 9 o'clock. They have four French lessons a week, and other things in the same ratio of increase." [12]

The sciences were also improved. In his second annual report, Candler recommended the expansion of the physics department "in this time of daily advance in the Physical Sciences. . . ."[13] Through the years, he suggested the addition of an adjunct professor of natural science, the establishment of a chair of biology with the teacher also offering courses in geology, and the creation of a department of applied mathematics. Members of the natural science faculty were sent to the most prestigious schools in the country for summer sessions to gain familiarity with recent discoveries. Facilities were expanded with a new building and the acquisition of a gas machine, microscopes, mineral cabinets, a museum, and a globe for the study of astronomy. Candler's aim for his students was a sound foundation of knowledge and the ability to use this knowledge in whatever pursuit they would enter.

In his dual concern for improving the sciences and liberal arts while rejecting the more practical business and technology courses, Candler was a transitional figure at Emory and, indeed, in national education. Candler ushered in the innovations of more advanced institutions in his expansion of course offerings and degree options. Yet he allowed his successor, C. E. Dowman, the distinction of initiating the more radical elective system. Stow Persons states that the ideal of the nineteenth century was the "gentleman scholar" and that this image was displaced by the scientific investigator of the twentieth century. In Candler's Emory, a balance was attempted. His students would be gentlemen scholars capable of scientific exploration.[14]

In the area of college finances, Candler proved to be the businessman of his upbringing and era. He started by organizing a formal records system. He wrote extensively to former presidents Haygood and Hopkins to determine the exact amount of debts owed to and by the school. He also kept close supervision over the school's investments, mostly in railroad stocks, and made certain that buildings were insured against fire losses. Subsequently, several fires on campus allowed the school to rebuild rather than incurring financial losses. Next, Candler attempted to collect unredeemed pledges and notes and to repay the college's $5,000 debt. By the end of his administration, Candler could claim credit for paying all debts, establishing a student loan fund of $20,000, and collecting endowments of $93,000 with additional promises of almost $16,000, a total increase equal to the entire endowment of 1887. Candler also doubled the number of volumes in the library and added a building to house them. Candler had collected almost $175,000 above normal operating expenses, even though a depression intermittently hindered fundraising from 1893 to 1897. Enrollment increased in these years from 229 to 325 with a corresponding rise in faculty. These were substantial achievements for the period, especially in the South. They insured Emory's continued growth and stability.

To Candler, colleges were not to be elite institutions. They were "established for the extension of opportunity lower and lower into the ranks of society."[15] Education was as much a necessity as a duty. "Popular education is an indispensible safeguard of popular government, and many believe it is the only safeguard to republican institutions."[16] During his Emory years he implemented his ideas with very real programs. An Educational Loan Fund was established to aid the poor. It assisted thirty-one students during its first year of operation. In his second year in office, he recommended school calendar changes so that "the limits of the vacation would . . . be better adopted to the needs of that large and honorable class of young men who work their way through college."[17] The Candlers boarded as many as twenty-three students in their home at one time. Taking in boarders was not unusual for Emory faculty or presidents. It served the multiple purposes of providing supplementary incomes, maintaining intimate faculty-student relations, and offering students a cheaper way of getting through school. Here was an additional buffer against too rapid change.

Another aspect of this democratic notion of education was Candler's position on intercollegiate athletics—an attitude which was mirrored by leading Northern educators and which he maintained into the 1930s. Intercollegiate athletics were relatively young when Candler became president of Emory, but he quickly decided that they were not suitable. He argued that they destroyed the proper value system of college life by "so minifying mind and magnifying muscle that serious study [was] subordinated to exciting games." They bred a "materialistic psychology" in which "important matters of mind and morality [were] ignored."[18] Schools reverted to commercialism and advertising to attract more students when good students required an entirely different atmosphere. Support for the games and these institutions came from gamblers who bet on the events, transportation companies who desired patronage, and newspapers wanting exciting news. Finally, those who most required physical development could not even participate. Only a few were allowed to join teams and those only who were already exceptionally fit.

This last disadvantage was most significant. Candler was not denouncing sports programs per se, just those played on an intercollegiate basis. He favored physical education and what he considered wholesome athletics for everyone. During the 1890s Emory held field days, had a bicycle association, and organized teams in football, tennis, and boxing. By the end of Candler's Oxford years, an instructor had been employed and a two-hour compulsory exercise program implemented. Basketball was added as were the pentathlon and relay races. Emory was in the midst of founding one of the first intramural athletic programs in the country. This democratic program became a hallmark for the "Athletics for All" philosophy of mid-twentieth century America.

Interpersonal relations were quite significant to Candler. He knew all of the students by name. In conjunction with the faculty, he assumed responsibility for student discipline. Problems arose concerning student drinking and general misbehavior. In 1888, four students expelled for drinking had their sentences commuted to one-week suspensions upon consideration of a student body petition. A student suspended for one month for another offense returned to an awaiting president who told him, "You are a man and I welcome you back to Emory." Perhaps a student article best summarizes the president-student relationship. "Tommie" wrote to "his girl":

> Our president is the biggest man in America or any other state. He jist rules these boys like they was babies. When they cuts up any devilment he calls 'em up and sentences 'em like a jidge sentences prisoners. When a feller is told to leave college, he explains it to the rest of us by saying' that his father has sent for him. But we always know better. We know Dr. Candler has been interviewin' him. The Seniors say Dr. Candler is a little dogmatic. I don't know what that is, and they don't teach dictionary in sub-fresh but I reckon the Seniors is right. They know lots more than anybody else, and nobody thinks about disputin' with them. But Dr. Candler is mighty good to me. He hasn't talked to me but once, the other day when he told me to study harder or pa'd be throwing away money on me. It was good advice, and I'm goin' to do as he says.

Candler, it would seem, mixed authority with compassion, or at least "Tommie" thought so.[19]

One final controversy which took place during Candler's presidency is of interest. This was his opposition to state funding for institutions of higher learning. He supported denominational rather than state schools for several reasons. He thought that parents should have a larger measure of control over their children's education. Most people who wanted to educate their children were religious, he argued, and would therefore prefer religious institutions. The parents believed, in particular, that science should be taught with a positive correlation to religion. Furthermore, church schools were more attuned to the needs of the average person. "The atmosphere of state universities is for the most part stimulating to aristocratic pretensions and extravagance," wrote the Emory president.[20] Finally, he stated that the poor should not be taxed to support free tuition for the rich.

In an address before the state general assembly supported by the president of Mercer and in a speech and subsequent article requested by the Putnam County Farmers' Alliance,[21] Candler lashed out against state funding for the University of Georgia. The support allowed the school to be tuition-free and thereby offered unfair competition with private schools at taxpayers' expense. Candler claimed that operating the state university cost more per capita than running a private college. The university was sufficiently old and well-endowed to care for itself. The best means for improving education in the state would be by working with the lower grades: improve the common schools by extending the school year, increase salaries to attract more talented teachers, and build better facilities with more modern equipment. Improved higher education would follow from the more prepared students the universities would receive. Candler emphasized his egalitarian educational philosophy in 1893 when he spoke before the Southern Education Association meeting in Louisville, Kentucky. The main problem facing Southern education was the rural environment. The scattered population of the region required more schools and teachers. Georgia's problems were harder to solve than, for example, those of Massachusetts, because of the comparative demographic situation. The latter's compact population was easier to serve than the former state's far-flung populace. He likened the struggle for popular education in the South to the Civil War and continued to work for harmony amidst growing dissension.

Candler's experiences at Emory were not unique. His close friend, John C. Kilgo, had many of the same problems and fought for the same causes. Kilgo was president of Trinity College (later Duke University) shortly after Candler held office at Emory. He, too, opposed state support for higher education while promoting the denominational college. Kilgo's efforts at Duke paralleled those of Candler. He increased the endowment, retired the debt, procured a new library and laboratory equipment, improved the faculty, raised the standards of legal education, and fought professionalism in intercollegiate athletics. Both men defended the academic freedom of their faculties and of key donors whose support they nurtured. Kilgo obtained the patronage of the Dukes and championed their interests against antitobacco strictures and trust allegations; Candler cultivated the philanthropic interests of his brother Asa and became a barb for the critics of Coca-Cola. Even the social and racial thought of the two appears to have coincided. The parallels are so impressive that one is forced to conclude that neither was exceptional, that their actions and ideals were closely attuned to their milieu.[22]

Vanderbilt University, the Northern "Conspiracy," and the Founding of Emory University

Upon his election to the episcopacy in 1898, Candler resigned the presidency of Emory College although he continued to serve on its board of directors. As a bishop, he also assumed the responsibilities of an ex officio member of the Vanderbilt University board. In this capacity he became entangled with the chancellor of Vanderbilt, James Kirkland, and was involved in the eventual break of the school from the Methodist Episcopal Church, South.

Vanderbilt had been founded in 1872 by Bishop Holland McTyiere with the backing of his brother-in-law, Commodore Vanderbilt, under the auspices of three Methodist conferences. Later the conferences transferred their authority to the denominational General Conference. Kirkland appears to have chafed under episcopal control exerted over issues like appointments. Apparently, he was attempting to move the school away from ecclesiasticism toward professional specialization. Neither the chancellor nor the bishops were very flexible and the matter came to a head in the state court of Tennessee as a question of the right of the church to elect trustees and control the university.

In 1910, while the case was before the court, Andrew Carnegie's Foundation for the Advancement of Teaching offered the school $1,000,000 for a medical school with the stipulation that the institution not be bound by denominational ties. This gift with its proviso transformed the matter in Candler's mind and drew his ire. "The plan of the Carnegie Fund will work a revolution in behalf of secularism if our schools accept its bribe to sever their relations with the Church,"[23] Candler wrote to James Cannon, Jr. The Vanderbilt issue became a matter of Carnegie millions and a purely secular education versus a Christian education under denominational authority. Here was an issue which brooked no compromise. When the Tennessee Supreme Court decided unfavorably for the church, Candler's wrath "knew no bounds."[24]

Candler's experience with Vanderbilt University and Carnegie colored his outlook toward the intentions of Northern philanthropy and secular influence on education. Previously, he had praised Carnegie and Rockefeller for their efforts to lift the South educationally, but now his attitude altered dramatically. The bishop began to envision a great conspiracy on the part of the General Education Board, the Southern Education Board, and the Carnegie Foundation. As Louis Harlan has shown, Robert C. Ogden was a prime example of interlocking authority, serving as he did on the directorates of all of these organizations. Candler believed that the aim of the conspiracy was subversion of ecclesiastical influence and the ultimate reconstruction of the South in the image of the industrial North. Candler's opinions of the organizations' goals were well-grounded and proved correct.

He saw the Northern-dominated boards as using several methods to achieve their ends. They utilized their money to break college ties to church and state. The creation of the teachers' pension fund by the Carnegie Foundation was a case in point. The boards created a centralized authority unresponsive to parents or other traditional groups. This was education dictated by a self-proclaimed elite. President Henry S. Pritchett of the Carnegie Foundation, for example, had published the famous Flexner report evaluating the utility of specific medical schools. Candler questioned Pritchett's authority and objectivity. It was not high standards and the need for improvement which Candler abhorred but the interference of an outside agency establishing its own standards and goals. The Rockefeller Board demanded the right to inspect college records and control the funds given by other philanthropies, although its contribution might be only a small fraction of the total endowment. The organizations demanded "mass production" in education "such as the founders of these Boards have become accustomed to use in their business enterprises." Candler also rejected the effort by the Carnegie people to standardize education through a system of accreditation and "Carnegie units." These attempts were anathema to creativity because "mental powers and intellectual attainments could [not] be measured by ounces or pint cups."[25] Further, "it is the mark of men of genius that they are different adventurous spirits, reaching results by new ways, rebellious to mental convention, strangers to uniformity."[26] The Carnegie unit system would close smaller local schools unable to meet the criteria. Thus, travel or living away from home would be required—a necessity leading to more inequality since people of "small means" would be barred from such educational opportunity. If any standardization need be imposed, the government, not Carnegie or Rockefeller, should do it.

Candler was not simply an obstructionist; he acted upon his ideas. In 1914 an education commission was established by the Southern Methodist Church to explore the possibilities of creating two schools of theology east and west of the Mississippi River. It was Warren Candler who was chosen chairman of the commission. Dallas was the logical choice for the western location since it was a central site and a Methodist institution already planned was available as a nucleus. Thus, Southern Methodist University was begun. For the eastern enterprise, Atlanta was chosen as a location with Emory College forming the core. The college was to be moved to the Druid Hills section of the city donated by Warren's brother Asa, the Coca-Cola magnate. Asa also donated $1,000,000. Wesley Memorial Hospital, founded earlier by the brothers, became the foundation of the medical school. Warren, Asa, William Danner Thomson (Coca-Cola attorney and partner of brother John), and John C. Kilgo (Warren's best friend), dominated the commission and the newly established board of trustees. Warren was elected first chancellor.[27]

Warren Candler rightly deserves the title of father of Emory University. He participated in virtually all of the major decisions involved in its establishment and headed the enterprise until 1921. To show that the church could develop an outstanding institution without outside interference, he made sure that the school of medicine obtained a class "A" rating, as did the law school. The theology school faculty, like those of other programs, was composed of individuals with graduate degrees from the top schools of Europe and America. He was accepting the professors and high standards that would be part of the New South, but on his own terms.

Typically, Candler did not remove himself from his students. To him they were the purpose of the school's existence. A letter from one Chinese alumnus of the medical school presenting the bishop with a piece of embroidered silk expressed "thanks and appreciation" for aid given while at Emory. After two years in China, this student had risen to the rank of professor of internal medicine at Kwong Wah Medical College. "Without your financial help," the young doctor recalled, "I doubt whether I could have completed my medical course."[28]

One of Candler's extended efforts at Emory met with scant support. He pressed for the founding of a great teachers' college. "The South," he maintained, "needs most of all a great college for teaching teachers such as the Teachers Colleges connected with Harvard, Columbia and Chicago Universities."[29] Without such a school, the North would continue to determine what was taught in the South by instructing its teachers. Candler went further, "Next to the education of a strong ministry for our churches is the training of these teachers for the common schools."[30]

Confrontation with Change

The period of World War I was difficult for Emory. Students and teachers were drafted or enlisted. Enrollment and income declined. Candler tried to use his influence behind the scenes to have medical students exempted from conscription but to no avail. The finance committee of the board of trustees suggested the solicitation of $500,000 from the General Education Board for the medical school in 1918. Although the board agreed to the recommendation with the stipulation that no conditions be placed on the grant, Candler voiced vehement opposition. He "wish[ed] to be recorded as opposed to asking the Rockefeller Foundation for any appropriation for Emory University and to any department of the institution."[31] Again in 1921 a similar proposal passed over the chancellor's protest.

The urban-industrial expansion and secularism resulting from the First World War troubled Candler. The individual seemed to be overwhelmed with bigness in all areas of life, and, being overwhelmed, lost much of his liberty. The cities were the geographical illustration of the New South creed. They offered the labor, markets, and sites of industry and commerce as well as the opportunity for change. But to Old South philosophers as well as to progressive conservative reformers, the cities were also the hotbeds of immorality, crime, and corruption. They contained the slums and the slum dwellers. It was essential that the "better sort" in society work to overcome these faults. Conservatives and advocates of the Social Gospel saw these difficulties compounded by low church participation among urbanites. Conservatives attempted to meet the needs of the city population by improving the environment, Social Gospel advocates by condemning sin and removing temptation. Before World War I these spokesmen of genteel morality and middle-class control optimistically pursued their separate solutions. After the war and with decades of seemingly unsuccessful efforts behind them, they were far less certain of victory.[32] Still, many of the universities like Emory, which the Candlers had helped move to Atlanta in 1915, were urban institutions.

Progressive education, as Lawrence Cremin and Laurence Veysey have shown, was in great measure an adjustment of the conservative concepts to the forces of urbanization and industrialism.[33] In the South the progressive educator faced particular problems. Burdened with the dual school system resulting from segregation and relatively poor in relation to the rest of the country, the Southern state legislatures and the local school boards could not finance the buildings, competitive teachers' salaries, longer school terms, and equipment requisite for adequate instruction. Even if they could have, they might have been unwilling to do so. The dominant ideology rejected higher taxes and the expansion of government involvement. This philosophy continued, at least until the Depression, when New Deal largesse gradually acted against the section's strong sense of individualism and independence. The Southern reticence to experiment and accept Northern innovations also acted as an effective deterrent to the adoption of progressive educational methodology.[34]

Candler, like many influential Southerners involved in education, was effected by the forces of change even as he adamantly rejected them. Initially, he fought federal encroachment into education. He considered state control of the German education system a primary cause of World War I. It had excluded "religious instruction and classical learning." It tended toward temporal, therefore material, concerns to the neglect of the "the things eternal."[35] Thus, the individuals it had trained lacked moral discernment. Since the 1880s various bills had been brought before Congress advocating the establishment of a national university. During the progressive era, a new series of proposals were recommended by Carnegie, the National Education Association, and many leaders of higher education, including Charles W. Eliot of Harvard and Nicholas Murray Butler of Columbia. Candler called these measures unconstitutional, citing the lack of need. With other opponents, he feared that the school would institute government control and censorship over economic and political learning. Neither religion nor morality could be taught. Candler also opposed repeated efforts to create a department of education and to increase federal assistance to states for education. These bills were intended to equalize the facilities and finances available throughout the country and would have helped the South. But government, Candler averred, was assuming parental control and thus destroying the integrity of the family and the rights of parents. This excessive authority, in short, would tend to the deification of the state as it had done in Germany. A federal department of education would interfere with on-going efforts of the states and inevitably lead to "antagonisms and irritations."[36] Such interference was neither required nor desirable. Moreover, the specter arose of the larger foundations gaining undue influence for personal benefit and for the subversion of educational goals for materialistic ends. The teaching profession would be undermined as conditions regulating subject matter were placed on large monetary grants on a national scale.

During the postwar years, education, reflecting the hedonism of the times, was becoming too permissive for those educated in the colleges according to prewar standards. Progressive educators emphasized an educational climate pleasantly conducive to learning. Candler held that discipline and control were the core of teaching. Progressive methods, to his mind, promoted self-indulgence. They "proceed[ed] on the false theory that everything hard must be taken out of the tasks of students, and that their pursuit of knowledge must be made a pursuit of pleasure." According to the exponents of this view, wrote Candler, "children must be amused while being taught so that they will learn without knowing and find themselves educated before they know it." Candler scoffed. Such education would weaken their will and enfeeble their intellect. They were learning to avoid hardship and "to put pleasure above duty."[37] Later in life they would reject service for personal gain. To promote this misplaced theory and to increase enrollments, colleges submitted to students' demands for intercollegiate athletics and "parasitic growths," generally known as "Student Activities." Candler thought a better term might be "student distractions."[38] Colleges also incorporated "the vicious elective system" under which "a callow youth, whose ignorance professedly requires an educational cure, is permitted to choose for himself what he will or will not study."[39] This was "immeasurable folly," breeding an exaggerated sense of liberty and self-indulgence in later walks of life.[40] Candler's was a battle between two generations. The innovations he had encouraged while president of Emory were now established. The next cycle of experimentation had begun. Yet few new concepts totally sweep away the former procedures or win the field without opposition. Continuity and change, confrontation and adaptation always coexist, usually to the benefit of both.

During the 1920s, a widespread protest against the large secular universities with their perceived emphasis on specialization, technology, and science took root which climaxed only during the 1960s and 1970s. The growing size of schools, it was believed, created an impersonal feeling and separated the instructor and the president from the most important part of the institution—the student. "School officials, superintendents and teachers [were] striving for the *MASS* instead of the individual," lamented the bishop. There was too much "mass production" while the quality of education was neglected. Candler even perceived these forces at his Emory.[41]

Warren Candler, who had organized an urban mission in Atlanta as a young minister, was one of the people who tried to counteract what were seen as faults in the educational system and in the environment with the development of a relatively new model, the junior college. Candler argued that junior colleges were "a wise remedy to arrest excessive enrollments." They were usually located "in quite places, free from the distractions of large crowds of listless matriculants and the unwholesome excitement of 'games' and 'social activities.'"[42] Immature youths should be protected from the crowded colleges as well as the cities. They could obtain more personal attention. The cost, too, was less, thereby allowing poorer people to attend. Late in the 1920s, backing was obtained to transform the old site of Emory at Oxford into a junior college. The benefactors became dismayed after early difficulties and delays and withdrew their support. Candler offered to guarantee the $100,000 with interest needed to establish the new school. At age 71, he would go out and solicit funds personally. Emory at Oxford did become a two-year college which still exists as part of Emory University. Emory also added a junior institution at Valdosta. Several other two-year colleges were developed elsewhere in the state and region during the 1920s and 1930s. Once again, Candler was not acting in isolation. Rather he was working in harmony with many others in the region and nation of like minds.

An Overview

Modernization in the South, as rationalized and promoted by the New South ideology, was a very traumatic experience for men and women accustomed to and comfortable with gradual modifications in the status quo. They did not view urbanization, industrialism, and the growth of corporate life as unmixed blessings. Yet, however much these individuals opposed the elements of modernity, as has been illustrated with Warren Candler, they were influenced by them and adjusted their institutions and thoughts accordingly.

Education reflects culture as it nurtures it. When conflicts arise in society, educators frequently disagree on the questions and answers. It was thus natural that different forces, seemingly contradictory, would emerge during this era of confrontation and change from the Civil War through the 1920s. These conflicts were fundamental in their nature, and it is not surprising that our generation continues to struggle with similar alternatives today.

Notes

1. Paul M. Gaston, *The New South Creed: A Study in Southern Mythmaking* (New York: Alfred A. Knopf, 1970).

2. There is a growing literature on specialization, professionalization, and fragmentation illustrating the transformation of the "private city" and genteel tradition into the modern American lifestyle. Robert H. Wiebe, *The Search for Order: 1877–1920* (New York: Hill & Wang, 1967); Wiebe, *The Segmented Society* (New York: Oxford University Press, 1975); Henry F. May, *The End of American Innocence* (New York: Alfred A. Knopf, 1959); Burton J. Bledstein, *The Culture of Professionalism* (New York: W. W. Norton, 1976); Stow Persons, *The Decline of American Gentility* (New York: Columbia University Press, 1973).

3. Persons gives a seminal account of gentility and its demise in *Decline of American Gentility*, yet fails to recognize regional variations. As a rough rule of thumb, it is suggested that many social and intellectual trends (educational ideas are illustrative) take about a generation longer to have an impact on the south than on the North. Thus, gentility and the images of lifestyles and values which that term defines continued in vogue in the South after Persons plots their decline elsewhere.

4. For the story of Candler's life and family see Charles Howard Candler, *Asa Griggs Candler* (Atlanta, Ga.: Emory University, 1950); Allen D. Candler, *William Candler of Georgia. His Ancestry and Progeny* (Atlanta, Ga.: Foote & Davies, 1896); Alfred M. Pierce, *Giant Against the Sky* (New York: Abingdon-Cokesbury, 1948); Mark K. Bauman, "Warren Akin Candler: Conservative Amidst Change" (Ph.D. diss., Emory University, 1975). This article is based largely on the latter source to which the reader is referred for fuller citations.

5. On the state of Southern education, see C. Vann Woodward, "Origins of the New South, 1877–1913" in *A History of the South*, ed. Wendell Holmes Stephenson and E. Merton Coulter (Baton Rouge, La.: Louisiana State University Press, 1951), pp. 61–64, 436–441; on difficulties in the antebellum period, see E. Merton Coulter, *College Life in the Old South* (New York: Macmillan, 1928); Clement Eaton, *Freedom of Thought in the Old South* (New York: Peter Smith, 1957).

6. For the early history of Emory see Henry M. Bullock, *A History of Emory University* (Nashville, Tenn.: Parthenon, 1936).

7. Thomas S. Harding, *College Literary Societies: Their Contributions to Higher Education in the United States, 1815–1876* (New York: Pageant, 1971). Information on the societies at Emory was taken from school yearbooks, catalogs, newspapers, and society minutes from Special Collections, Woodruff Library, Emory University.

8. On black higher education and problems during Reconstruction through World War I see Louis R. Harlan, *Separate and Unequal* (Chapel Hill, N.C.: University of North Carolina Press, 1958) and Harlan, "The Southern Education Board and the Race Issue in Public Education," *Journal of Southern History* 23 (May 1958): 189–202; Berenice M. Fisher, *Industrial Education: American Ideals and Institutions* (Madison, Wis.: University of Wisconsin Press, 1967); Henry A. Bullock, *A History of Negro Education in the South* (Cambridge: Harvard Univer-

sity Press, 1967); Addie L. J. Butler, *The Distinctive Black College*
(Metuchen, N.J.: Scarecrow Press, 1977); John W. Storey, "The
Rhetoric of Paternalism: Southern Baptists and Negro Education in
the Latter Nineteenth Century," *Southern Humanities Review* 12
(Spring 1978), pp. 101–109; George A. Dillingham, "The University
of Nashville, a Northern Educator and a New Mission in the Post-
Reconstruction South," *Tennessee Historical Quarterly* 37 (Fall 1978),
pp. 329–338; Clarence A. Bacote, *The Story of Atlanta University*
(Atlanta, Ga.: Atlanta University, 1969); Alphonso A. McPheeters,
"The Origin and Development of Clark University and Gammon
Theological Seminary," (M.A. thesis, University of Cincinnati, 1944);
Samuel R. Spencer, Jr., *Booker T. Washington and the Negro's Place
in American Life* (Boston: Little, Brown, 1955); Edgar W. Knight,
The Influence of Reconstruction on Education (New York: Arno
Press, 1972); Howard N. Rabinowitz, *Race Relations in the Urban
South, 1865–1890* (New York: Oxford University Press, 1978).
9. Harold W. Mann, *Atticus Greene Haygood* (Athens, Ga.: University
of Georgia Press, 1965); Mark K. Bauman, "A Famous Atlantan Speaks
Out Against Lynching," *Atlanta Historical Bulletin* 20 (Spring 1976),
pp. 24–32; Bauman, "The Inherent Disposition of Racial Conscious-
ness," ibid., 21 (Fall 1977), pp. 24–31; I. A. Newby, *Jim Crow's
Defense* (Baton Rouge, La.: Louisiana State University Press, 1965);
George M. Fredrickson, *The Black Image in the White Mind* (New
York: Harper & Row, 1971).
10. General Conference *Journal*, 1882, p. 25 (quotation). On Paine College,
see William L. Graham, "Patterns of Intergroup Relations in the
Cooperative Establishment, Control, and Administration of Paine
College [Georgia] by Southern Negro and White People," (Ph.D.
diss., New York University, 1955); George E. Clary, Jr., "The Founding of Paine College—A Unique Venture in Inter-Racial Cooperation
in the New South, 1882–1903," (Ed.D. diss., University of Georgia,
1965); Alandus C. Johnson, "The Growth of Paine College," (Ph.D.
diss., University of Georgia, 1970); Willard Range, *The Rise and
Progress of Negro Colleges in Georgia, 1855–1949* (Athens, Ga.: University of Georgia Press, 1951); Paine College Board of Trustees Minutes
Paine College, Augusta, Ga.; Bauman, "Candler," ch. 3. On the relations
of Southern blacks, Southern white denominations, and education,
see Kenneth K. Bailey, "The Post Civil War Racial Separations in
Southern Protestantism: Another Look," *Church History* 46 (December 1977), pp. 453–73; Hunter Dickinson Farish, *The Circuit Rider
Dismounts* (Richmond, Va.: Dietz, 1938); John Lee Eighmy, *Churches
in Cultural Captivity* (Knoxville, Tenn.: University of Tennessee Press,
1972); Rufus B. Spain, *At Ease in Zion* (Nashville, Tenn.: Vanderbilt
University Press, 1961); David E. Harrell, Jr., *The Social Sources of
Division in the Disciples of Christ, 1865–1900* (Atlanta, Ga.: Publishing
Systems, 1973).

11. Mann, *Haygood*; Robert C. McMath, Paper delivered on the origins of the Georgia Institute of Technology, Georgia Studies Symposium, Atlanta, Ga., February 2-3, 1976; Emory College Board of Trustees Minutes; Bullock, *History of Emory*.

12. Emory *Phoenix* 3 (October 1888).

13. Emory College Board of Trustees' Minutes, 1890.

14. From a national perspective, Candler brought Emory up to date and into the mainstream without being innovative or accepting the, for then, more radical measures of Eliot, White, or Jordan. Cf. Hugh Hawkins, *Between Harvard and America* (New York: Oxford University Press, 1972); Walter P. Rogers, *Andrew D. White and the Modern University* (Ithaca, N.Y.: Cornell University Press, 1942); Orrin L. Elliott, *Stanford University* (Palo Alto, Ca.: Stanford University Press, 1937); Frederick Rudolph, *The American College and University* (New York: Alfred A. Knopf, 1965); Persons, *Decline of American Gentility*, 183, 185; Glenn C. Altschuler, Andrew A. White: *Educator, Historian, Diplomat* (Ithaca, N.Y.: Cornell University Press, 1979).

15. "Commencements Seem to Rank High," Candler Papers, p. 8.

16. Warren A. Candler, "A Dangerous and Disappointing Education," *Atlanta Journal*, January 9, 1910.

17. Emory College Board of Trustees' Minutes, 1890.

18. Warren A. Candler, "A Safe and Sane View," Candler Papers; Warren A. Candler, "Crime and Its Cure," Candler Papers.

19. Alfred M. Pierce, "W. A. Candler as President of Emory, 1888-1898," *The Emory University Quarterly* 1 (December 1945): 247 (for story of suspended student); Emory *Zodiac*, 1895, p. 170 (for Tommie's letter).

20. Warren A. Candler, *Georgia's Educational Work; What It Has Been: What It Should Be. 'Hammond's History Corrected, etc.* (Atlanta: n.d. [ca. 1882]).

21. Ibid.

22. Earl W. Porter, *Trinity and Duke, 1892-1924* (Durham, N.C.: Duke University Press, 1964); Paul N. Garber, *John Carlisle Kilgo* (Durham, N.C.: Duke University Press, 1937); also Spring Dowell, *A History of Mercer University, 1833-1953* (Macon, Ga.: Mercer University, [1958]); Anne Lide, "Five Georgia Colleges from 1850-1875," (M.A. thesis, Emory University, 1957); William S. Powell, *The First State University* (Chapel Hill, N.C.: University of North Carolina Press, 1972); Dumas Malone, *Edwin A. Alderman* (New York: Doubleday, 1946).

23. Warren A. Candler to James Cannon Jr., 24 February 1908, James Cannon Jr., Papers, Manuscript Department, William R. Perkins Library, Duke University.

24. On Vanderbilt and the founding of Emory see Candler, *Asa Candler*, pp. 389-390; Thomas H. English, *Emory University, 1915-1965* (Atlanta, Ga.: University Press, 1966); Edwin Mims, *Chancellor*

Kirkland of Vanderbilt (Nashville, Tenn.: Vanderbilt University Press, 1940); Mims, *History of Vanderbilt University* (Nashville, Tenn.: Vanderbilt University Press, 1946); John O. Gross, "The Bishops Versus Vanderbilt University," *Tennessee Historical Quarterly* 22 (March 1963), pp. 53–65; Mark K. Bauman, "The Bishop and the University," *Emory Magazine* (Winter 1977), pp. 8–13; Methodist Education Commission Minutes, Minutes of Executive Committee, Emory University Board of Trustee Minutes, and Warren A. Candler Papers, Special Collections, Woodruff Library, Emory University.

25. Warren A. Candler, "Mass Production in Education," Candler Papers; Warren A. Candler, "An Educational Censorship Black-listing Colleges," *Atlanta Journal*, 25 June 1910.

26. Warren A. Candler, "Commencements Seem to Rank High."

27. See note 24, above, and Boone M. Bowen, *The Candler School of Theology* (Atlanta, Ga.: Emory University Press, 1974); Mary Martha H. Thomas, *Southern Methodist University* (Dallas: Southern Methodist University Press, 1974).

28. Ting D. Lee to Warren D. Candler, 10 April 1928, Candler Papers.

29. Warren A. Candler, "Educational Essays," *Bulletin of Emory University* 4 (February 1918): 6–7.

30. Warren A. Candler, "Educational Essays," *Bulletin of Emory University* (February 1918); Candler, *The James H. Carlisle Teachers' College of Emory University* (Atlanta: Byrd Printing Company, n.d. [ca. 1914]); Candler, *If You Don't Love the South Don't Read This* (n.p.: n.p. [ca. 1921]); Candler, "Prussian Paganism a Peril to the World," *Atlanta Journal*, November 4, 1917). Cf. Wayne D. Brazil, "Howard W. Odum: The Building Years, 1884–1930," (Ph.D. diss., Harvard University, 1975).

31. Emory University Board of Trustees' Minutes, 1918.

32. May, *End of American Innocence*; Henry F. May, *Protestant Churches and Industrial America* (New York: Harper & Row, 1949); Aaron I. Abell, *The Urban Impact on American Protestantism, 1865–1900* (Cambridge: Harvard University Press, 1943).

33. Lawrence Cremin, *The Transformation of the School: Progressivism in American Education, 1876–1957* (New York: Alfred A. Knopf, 1961); Laurence Veysey, *The Emergence of the American University* (Chicago: University of Chicago Press, 1965).

34. George B. Tindall, *The Emergence of the New South, 1913–1945*, vol. 10 in *A History of the South*, ed. Wendell Holmes Stephenson and E. Merton Coulter (Baton Rouge, La.: Louisiana State University Press, 1967); Thomas D. Clark, *The Emerging South*, 2nd. ed., (New York: Oxford University Press, 1968).

35. Warren A. Candler, "Educational Essays."

36. Warren A. Candler, "Dangerous to the Nation and Especially to the South," Candler Papers; for background see Daniel W. Crofts, "The Black Response to the Blair Education Bill," *Journal of Southern*

History 37 (February 1971): 41–65; Allen J. Going, "The South and the Blair Bill," *Mississippi Valley Historical Review* 44 (September 1957): 267–290; David Madsen, *The National University: Enduring Dream of the USA* (Detroit: Wayne State University Press, 1966), chapter 6.

37. Warren A. Candler, "Education Without Element of Self-Sacrifice," *Atlanta Journal*, April 10, 1921.

38. Warren A. Candler, "A Reproach to American Colleges," Candler Papers.

39. Warren A. Candler, "An Education System that Breeds Lawlessness," *Atlanta Journal,* May 27, 1923.

40. Warren A. Candler, "Two Lessons from Two Hard Cases," Candler Papers.

41. Warren A. Candler, "Mass Production in Education," *Atlanta Journal*, July 6, 1930.

42. Warren A. Candler, "The Problem of the Church is Most Urgent," Candler Papers; Warren A. Candler, "Youthful Students and Colleges," *Atlanta Journal*, August 25, 1929 (quotation).

Wayne J. Urban

Educational Reform in a New South City: Atlanta 1890-1925

During the period between 1890 and 1925, the Atlanta schools experienced what appeared to be a thoroughgoing curricular transformation. The 1880s curriculum consisted of a "three Rs" elementary education in separate schools for blacks and whites and a classical course of study in two white high schools, one for boys and one for girls. By the early 1920s the schools had added to these traditional subjects courses in manual training, bookkeeping, domestic science, sewing, whittling, cooking, salesmanship, drawing, and physical culture. A research bureau which had the responsibility of testing and counseling students with regard to their curricular choices had also been established. These changes were not unique to Atlanta, but rather they were modeled on similar developments in other parts of the nation. Advocates of changes in the Atlanta schools argued that Atlantans deserved what other cities provided in their schools. For example, in 1911 supporters of commercial education in Atlanta schools argued that their city should have the same innovations adopted by "the big Commercial High Schools of the East and West, viz., the addition of the Domestic Science Department, specifically dressmaking, millinery, cooking, science of food, etc."[1]

Historians of curriculum changes, like Ellwood P. Cubberley, who wrote at the time they occurred, or Lawrence Cremin, who described such changes from the perspective of the 1950s and early 1960s, have generally treated the new subjects as a democratic attempt to meet the needs of the new populations which were attending school under the impetus of changes in the economy and altered labor and attendance laws. Since the early 1960s, however, a revisionist interpretation of these events has emerged. Historians such as Joel Spring, Clarence Karier, and Paul Violas have argued that the new courses and subjects were not democratic attempts to extend opportunity to new students, but rather devices to lure the lower classes into the schools with false promises of economic advancement. Once in the schools, the lower-class students were led into vocational curricula where they were socialized and trained to become the foot soldiers of the American industrial army. According to this interpretation, the basis of students' curricular choices was never their ability or aptitude, but rather their social class origins. The lower classes needed to be morally and technically upgraded if they were to fill the roles required of them by the captains of the new society and the new subjects of the school curriculum, along with the testing and guidance programs which channeled students into the "appropriate" slots, were the devices to accomplish this goal.[2]

Advocates of curriculum change in Atlanta, like their counterparts elsewhere, utilized arguments which appealed to both the lower class's desire for economic sufficiency and the upper class's fear of their inferiors. One proponent of industrial education for Atlanta's youth stressed the practical, economic relevance which students could expect from such curricula:

> The great mass of our school boys must from necessity be bread winners. Their poverty compels them to enter upon labor for a living early in their careers. It is right, it is wise that the school system supported by popular taxation should so train and teach the mind and heart of these boys that they enter upon bread winning when they complete the course in our schools.

Another advocate of the same alterations gave a rationale which stressed, not the interests of the students, but those of the established classes in Atlanta when he told the school board that "you can make no mistake in extending a department which tends to correct the restless, impudent, and irreverent child which is abroad in the land."[3]

Despite the similarity between the rhetoric of reformers in Atlanta and that of their counterparts in other parts of the nation, the major point to be made in this essay is that the net result in Atlanta differed significantly from that in other settings. The heart of the difference was that Atlanta's curricular additions never culminated in the thoroughgoing vocationalism that characterized the new courses of study elsewhere. For example, Marvin Lazerson's study of Massachusetts schools in the late nineteenth and early twentieth centuries describes a two-stage development in the manual training movement in that state; the movement began as a pedagogical reform suitable for all children but culminated in a "vocational" training phase in which the less academically able lower-class students were trained for jobs. In Atlanta, manual training and other innovations began similarly, but never developed into fully vocationalized studies. At the elementary level in Atlanta, success in achieving innovation was never very great. Though manual training was proposed for the elementary curriculum as early as 1885 and a serious attempt at implementation was begun in 1899, twenty years later the board was still being told of the necessity for introducing instruction in manual training and domestic science into the elementary schools.[4]

At the secondary level, though change came earlier and faster, it still never culminated in a strictly vocational approach. A business course was introduced at the Girls' High School in the 1890s which later culminated in the establishment of a separate Commercial High School. For high school boys, manual training was initially introduced as a new course of study at the Boys' High School and later formed a significant part of the course of study at the newly established Technological High School.[5]

Reformers in the World War I era, however, expessed dissatisfaction at the lack of relationship between the curricula at these high schools and the world of work as well as displeasure over the state of academic studies in all the high schools. In 1914 a school survey severely criticized the impracticality of the existing course of study at Girls' High School. The academic, college preparatory course, argued the author of the survey, ignored the needs of the ninety-five percent of the student body who did not attend college. For this group, a different course of study was recommended which would attend to the twin needs of homemaking–child-rearing and job preparation. To meet these needs, the survey advocated commercial subjects for the girls as well as the study of "Art, Science, Literature, History, Music, Elementary Economics and Sociology, and Household Arts." Eight years later, George Strayer of Teachers College, Columbia University, made similar recommendations for both girls and boys. He noted that the Technological High School was not teaching vocational subjects, as reformers had wanted for some time, but rather that its curriculum, though somewhat technical, was mainly preparing the boys for entry into the Georgia School of Technology. Strayer complained that the shopwork at Tech High "is rather of a liberal than a vocational type." A similar problem existed at Commercial High. Strayer noted that over 60 percent of the students at Commercial High's night school enrolled in academic courses in preference to a course of study which stressed the more vocational subjects of bookkeeping and stenography. Here again, the problem was that the institution served a preparatory as well as a practical purpose. In 1918 the board had approved a diploma course of study for Commercial High which combined academic and business subjects in order to "prepare graduates for admission into the universities and schools of commerce without examination or condition." As a remedy for the situation, Strayer recommended expansion of the more directly vocational work going on in all the night schools. He also proposed the addition of a vocational department at Tech High where a student could undertake a flexible curriculum that "will be designed to train young people for a single recognized trade" and the appointment of a director of vocational education who would be responsible for linking the training in the schools to the city's job requirements.[6]

A 1937 study of the city's high schools revealed, however, that the 1914 survey and the 1922 Strayer Report had gone largely unheeded. The separate high schools existed in the late 1930s that had existed in the earlier years, and the curricula at Commerical High and Tech High were still preparatory rather than vocational. At Tech High, the manual training subjects continued "to place emphasis on general technical training rather than on specialized vocational training" and at Commercial High the stated goal continued to be to offer "pupils a broad and general understanding of business" rather than specific vocational training.[7]

Thus, full-fledged vocationalism never came to Atlanta's high schools, even its technical and commercial high schools, during the period in which it carried the day in other settings. Atlantans preferred to offer separate high school curricula that were all preparatory, or what one historian has called "different pathways to liberal education," instead of directly vocational training. In Atlanta, capital of the New South, the schooling turned out to be, not an imitation of that offered in other sections, but an expanded form of traditional, academic, secondary education that did provide practical subjects for some students, but in the larger context of preparation for higher education. On reflection, it seems that this type of education allowed the city to borrow some of the ideas of reformers in other sections of the country but to adapt them to the traditional approach that Atlantans preferred to take in education, as well as in other areas. We might say that this version of New South education, like much New South activity in other realms, resembled the Old South approach as much as it did that of the East and the West. It produced a finished product that grafted the new subjects onto the curriculum of the past rather than replacing the old with the new. The end product, however, had more of the flavor of the old studies than it did of the highly differentiated vocationalism that was developing elsewhere.[8]

A full explanation of the difference between Atlanta's curricular reform experience and that in other parts of the nation should begin with an in-depth description of Atlanta's school reformers and their political orientations. Two names stand out as the prime advocates of curricular diversification in Atlanta, Hoke Smith and Robert Guinn. The links between Smith and vocationalism on the national scene are strong. As senator from Georgia, he was coauthor of both the 1914 Smith-Lever act which provided federal funds for vocational education in agriculture and the 1917 Smith-Hughes Act which provided federal funds for vocational education in industrial pursuits. Smith also played a major role in Atlanta's school affairs, serving as a school board member from 1886 to 1893, when he left for Washington and a place in Grover Cleveland's cabinet. In 1897, shortly after his return from Washington, he resumed his place on the school board and served until 1906 when he stepped down because of his election as governor of Georgia. During his terms on the board, Smith served as president for seven years. His tenure as a board member was marked by his frequent advocacy of both manual training and commercial education. The latter innovation was initially proposed by Smith in the late 1880s.[9] He sponsored the introduction of commercial subject at Girls' High School, leading to the development of a full-fledged commercial department.

Smith advocated manual training in the schools as early as 1885. Not until 1899, however, when he was president of the board, did his proposal come to fruition. In that year, Smith turned over the presidential podium to his board colleague and law associate, Hamilton Douglas, so that he (Smith) could move that manual training be introduced into the schools. At the lower elementary level, he suggested an instructor in drawing to teach drawing, clay modeling, and paper shaping. For elementary-level girls he called for an instructor of sewing while for upper elementary-level boys he proposed an instructor in manual training to teach plain woodwork. At Girls' High School, Smith proposed the hiring of an instructor in cooking and at Boys' High he advocated the introduction of a wood shop and a forge shop. Within six months of this motion, all its provisions were carried out.[10]

Of all the innovations established, the wood shop for elementary-level boys appears to have been the hardest to initiate and the least successful. In 1903 the board passed a Smith motion calling for the continuation of the entire manual training program as established in 1899 but changing the location of wood shop for seventh and eighth grade boys from Boys' High School to four geographically dispersed elementary schools. According to this motion, shopwork for seventh and eighth grade boys could now be taken as an alternative to penmanship. For Boys' High School, Smith advocated upgrading the manual subjects to the status of a separate department.[11]

Two aspects of Smith's reform activity need to be highlighted in order to illustrate the differences between Atlanta's curricular additions and those which took place in other cities. First is the nonvocational nature of his proposals. We have already described the general nature of the commercial curriculum in the high schools. With manual training as well, Smith did not advocate job training, but rather that the manual course of study at Boys' High be preparatory to further study at the Georgia School of Technology.[12] Thus, the new studies advocated by Smith can be viewed more as an expansion of the traditional course of study, which did not abandon either its preparatory goals or its general approach, rather than as a rejection of the general course in favor of vocational specialization.

Secondly, it must be noted that Smith was primarily a politician who never let reform conflict with his political goals. The curricular innovations sponsored by Smith served to enhance his political reputation as a reformer, a reputation he used in his successful statewide political campaigns. He was also quite willing to use the political patronage powers of a board member to further the personal careers of his political associates through the introduction of curricular reform. Mrs. Hamilton Douglas, wife of his law associate and fellow board member, was the first teacher of commercial subjects at Girls' High. Her yearly salary grew from the initial part-time remuneration of $300 to the $900 she was paid as a department head in 1892. Smith was simply carrying on a tradition of patronage that he and other board members in Atlanta and other cities used to enhance their personal political power. In the 1880s, while Smith was on the board, both his father and his sister were appointed to principalships in the public schools. The point is that Smith simultaneously enhanced his image as a reformer by his sponsorship of innovations in the schools while he also used traditional patronage tactics that were anathema to reformers in Northern cities. His reform proposals never included abolishing the political control that board members exercised in school affairs, though this was a cornerstone of reform platforms in New York and Chicago.[13]

According to Smith's biographer, the label of progressive reformer, which Smith sought and used successfully to advance his political career, was misleading insofar as it implied a principled consistency in reform activity. In reality, Smith's advocacy of reform was sporadic and basically opportunistic. Though he was a school reformer in the 1880s, he left Atlanta to serve as Secretary of the Interior in a conservative Democratic cabinet. On his return to Atlanta, he again took up school reform and other reform activities as part of his pursuit of office. The consistent strain in Smith's career both as school board member and politician was pursuit of office and its perquisites, not commitment to reform.[14]

Robert Guinn, who served as board president of the Atlanta schools between 1914 and 1918, continued the Smith tradition of reform advocacy with political goals. Guinn, in fact, was a Smith political ally. His proposed innovations included vocational guidance at all levels of the system, an expansion of the manual and commercial work being done in the high schools, and the introduction of manual training into the elementary schools. Guinn pinned his reform program on the ouster of the existing superintendent, W. M. Slaton, a man too conservative in educational affairs for the reform-minded board member. Controversy over the firing of Slaton allowed the political dimension hidden beneath most school activities to surface. Superintendent Slaton's brother was Governor John Slaton, a member of the conservative Democractic faction in Georgia which was the major opposition group to Hoke Smith, Robert Guinn, and their fellow "progressive" Democrats. Thus, the struggle over vocationalism in the schools was really part of a larger political struggle for control of the Democratic party in this one-party state. From the political perspective, the great amount of vocational and other reform activity in school affairs by Smith and his political protégè, Guinn, and the modest amount of success which they experienced might be seen as sufficient for their purposes. One did not necessarily need to accomplish significant change, but rather to appear to accomplish it. Thus, part of the explanation for the failure of Atlanta's advocates of vocationalism to accomplish significant alterations in the schools' curricula is that there is considerable doubt as to whether or not they really intended such a drastic outcome. Rather, what they needed to do in school politics, as in state politics, was to project an image that enabled them to differentiate themselves from the other Democratic faction, though they did not really differ substantially on most issues from that faction.[15]

Having accounted for some of the reasons for failure of the new curricula to carry the day in Atlanta by looking at the reformers themselves, the remaining specific factors which help explain the modest results they achieved are to be found by looking at the various groups in the city who opposed the reforms. The city council, which controlled the finances of Atlanta's schools throughout the early twentieth century, was one group which questioned the various curricular additions. The council's main motivation was cost control, since schools were dependent on council appropriations for all their funds. The periods of the greatest activity for new curricula, those during which Smith and Guinn were board president, were also the periods when the board, under these men, wielded some political influence of its own and thus could approach the council armed with some independent power.

Smith's dogged pursuit of manual training after his proposal for its introduction in 1899 testifies both to his own political acumen in pursuing this innovation and to the council's reluctance in funding it. After proposing manual training in both the elementary and high schools in June of 1899, Smith arranged for a committee of three members of the board, with himself as chairman, to go to the council to seek the additional appropriations which would be required to fund the new program. Despite Smith's personal appearance, the board heard at its next meeting that council had not appropriated funds for manual training. The board then proceeded to implement the innovations with existing funds, moving personnel from one school to another and assigning additional duties to several teachers and supervisors. Two years later, the board scaled down its plans for manual training, confining it to the elementary and night schools, where the staffing could be handled by using existing teachers in different ways. In 1903, Smith was back again with a proposal to establish shops in the elementary schools and Boys' High School where the manual training work could be undertaken with the proper equipment. Again the council balked because of the cost. A few months earlier, some council members had complained that manual training and other new courses were taking away scarce funds from the schools which might be better used to seat children in classrooms who could not now be accommodated because of a lack of space. Smith never responded directly to this concern, but he did indicate that it was less important to him than the new curricula, for shortly after introducing the proposal for shops, he struck a deal with the city council to finance these shops through a reduction in the appropriation for lots for new school buildings. This testified both to his political astuteness and his preference for new curricula over other educational priorities.[16]

When an innovation could be combined with a new facility, the council was much less reluctant to act. Thus, the Technological High School and the Commercial High School were both approved by the board and funded by the council. Innovations which did not result in new buildings or programs, however, were not so well accepted by the council. The board noted in 1911 that the council in the midst of a financial emergency was considering a motion to abolish the position of Director of Drawing in the elementary schools, a position created as part of Smith's manual training drive some years earlier. The council evidently felt that drawing, physical culture, and music, all areas whose directors were marked for extinction, were frills. The board responded vehemently to this contention: "These subjects are not 'frills.'" There are no 'frills' in the Atlanta Schools. They are denominated 'frills' by those who are unacquainted with their educational value. They are of equal importance to any other subjects in the curriculum. . . ."[17]

We might summarize the differences between board members and council members as analogous to those between reform politicians and traditional politicians. The board sought innovations which would add new elements to the school system while the council first sought to add new places in the system by expanding existing institutions and programs. The council also was more cost-conscious than the board, particularly when it was confronted with board innovations that added no places in the schools for new students. When the principles of innovation and new places could be combined, as in the creation of the Technological and Commercial High Schools, the board and the council worked together. It should be noted that these two new institutions were created between the Smith and Guinn eras on the board when the points of view of the board and council were quite compatible. The ideological heat between "reform" on the board and "traditionalism" on the council was highest when these two men were active on the board. As we will see shortly, neither reformer favored the separate high schools.

Tradition-oriented, cost-conscious city councilmen were not the only obstacles to the various curricular diversifications advocated by Hoke Smith, Robert Guinn, and their board colleagues. At different times during the more than three decades under study here, school staff members questioned or voiced reservations about the plans of the innovators. One source of these questions was the superintendent's office. Between 1879 and 1914, the superintendency of the schools was in the hands of the Slaton family, with W. F. Slaton serving from 1879 to 1907 and then being succeeded in office by his son, W. M. Slaton, who served until he was ousted by Robert Guinn in 1914. We have already underscored the larger political background which related to the tension between Smith-Guinn innovators and the Slatons. In addition, a difference in educational ideology should also be mentioned which was highlighted by Guinn's charge in 1914 that W. M. Slaton was not sufficiently "progressive" in his educational ideas. The superintendents Slaton, though seldom outright opponents of manual training, commercial education, and other curricular diversifications pushed by Smith and his innovation-minded board colleagues, never embraced the changes as fully as the board members who advocated them. When Hoke Smith first broached the idea of manual training in 1885, Superintendent Slaton cautioned the board that behind Smith's advocacy of this innovation was a plan to establish an industrial trade school. In August of 1903, after Smith had gained board approval for the additon of a commercial and technological course to the existing academic course at Boys' High School, he made arrangements to have himself appointed to a board committee of three to "aid the Faculty of Boys' High School in inaugurating the new courses in that school." Why the faculty needed the services of the three board members to help implement the new curricula is unknown. It seems however, to have been an unusual procedure, one that might have been necessitated by the unwillingness or at least suspicion with which the faculty greeted the plans of the board. The principal of Boys' High School at this time was W. M. Slaton, son of the then superintendent and himself future superintendent of the school system. W. M. Slaton's defenders in his 1914 battle with Robert Guinn included organized labor and two of the city's daily newspapers. They all supported the superintendent's emphasis on basic skills and on discipline in the classroom.[18]

One should not assume from these instances that there was a constant and principled clash of educational points of view, since the board and the superintendents Slaton worked together on most matters throughout the period in question. Given the political allegiances of the Slaton family and Hoke Smith and Robert Guinn, it seems fair to conclude that differences on educational innovation were to be emphasized when they could be used for larger political purposes. At least at the rhetorical level, however, the different positions represented by the superintendents and the board reformers were characterized as "traditional" and "progressive" respectively, an indication that each group sought to rally supporters around a familiar ideological label.

The teachers, particularly the elementary school teachers, formed another group of potential opponents to the curricular additions championed by Hoke Smith and Robert Guinn. Most of the new courses and subjects in the high schools called for new teachers, thus presenting no direct threat to the existing teachers of the more traditional subjects. In the lower schools, however, the new tasks would be simply added to the work of the existing teachers, who would have to learn the new skills from supervisors. The elementary teachers frequently objected to this situation. In 1896, the board recommended that a teacher in industrial drawing be hired for the business department of the Girls' High School who would also instruct "all the teachers of the grammar schools in drawing in the several normal classes which are held from week to week." Elementary teachers were never happy with this arrangement. In 1903, a group of elementary principals objected to the inroads on teacher time being made by activities and subjects supplementary to the regular curriculum such as "the preparation of specimens in manual training for exhibition." By 1907 the teachers had evidently made some progress in alleviating the situation, for the superintendent reported that the instruction of grammar school teachers in the subjects of music, drawing, and physical culture would be given in the afternoons instead of on Saturdays. This was one year after instruction in manual training had been subdivided into subjects such as penmanship and drawing, which were taught first to the grammar school teachers who in turn instructed the students.[19]

In 1911, in the same report in which the board defended itself against the city council charges that the newer subjects were "frills," it acknowledged that teachers in the lower grades had reason to be unhappy with the innovations. The board cautioned the supervisors of drawing and manual training that "the quantity of work given the teachers is too great" and that it should be curtailed in "proportion to the time alloted" to the subject in the schools. The board also directed the supervisors not to stray from the course of study in the subject as it had been approved by the board. No new innovations or additions to the teachers' work load were to be permitted. Here we should note that teacher objections were not on grounds of principled opposition to the new subjects, but rather because the new duties were simply being added to their work by the board without any diminution of existing obligations. This attitude, however, fit quite nicely with the no-frills traditionalism of the city council, the cautious approach to change of the superintendant, and the general traditionalism of the Atlanta populace.[20]

In 1914, the advent of Robert Guinn to a place of prominence on the board brought about a polarization of the interested parties in school affairs around the issue of innovation. Guinn's career on the board lasted for four years, a period in which substantial reform plans for all areas of the schools were introduced. Initial negative reaction to his plans came about when he made known his intent to remove superintendent W. M. Slaton as the first step in revamping the schools. We have already discussed the political and ecucational difference between Guinn and Slaton. What needs to be mentioned here, in addition, is the substantial support Slaton received from the white working class of the city in his battle to retain his position. Organized labor's official newspaper, the *Journal of Labor*, came to the superintendent's defense, noting its own agreement with his traditional approach to school affairs and his suspicion of "fads," such as those innovations supported by Robert Guinn. Local labor had supported the public schools for many years, but with an approach geared to adding new schools and raising teachers' salaries rather than sponsoring wholesale curricular changes advocated by Guinn. The superintendent's traditionalism also appealed to others in the

Atlanta populace, since 10,000 signatures were gathered on a petition to retain him in office. Despite the mass approval of the status quo, Guinn and his board colleagues ignored the petition and proceeded with the superintendent's dismissal in 1914.[21]

The traditionalists were thus initially defeated by Robert Guinn. Four years later, however, they would gain revenge by forcing him to resign from the school board. Guinn's pursuit of innovation was broader than that of Hoke Smith. To the industrial and commercial curricula which both he and his predecessor championed, he added other curricular and organizational innovations, most notably the consolidation of the four separate high schools into one unified high school. Consolidation was the capstone of the plan of curricular diversification for the second generation of reformers like Robert Guinn. It did not represent a repudiation of diversification as advocated by his predecessors like Hoke Smith, but rather a new stage in reform plans which paid rhetorical respects to both diversification and democratization. A comprehensive high school would allow a healthy mixing of students from the various curricula in certain core subjects like social studies and in extracurricular settings while still maintaining the separation of students in the various academic and technical curricula "appropriate" to their backgrounds and their futures. In Atlanta, where none of the high schools were vocational, one might have expected little opposition to the plan since the class issues raised by the new curricula in other cities were not present.[22]

Atlantans, however, opposed consolidation for a variety of other reasons. Parents of Boys' High students combined with alumni and students from that school to oppose consolidation on the grounds that it would dilute the identity and prestige of that institution. Girls' High parents and alumnae had similar fears. The specter of coeducation probably haunted the tradition-minded parents from both institutions, and the guardians of the girls could be expected to be especially fearful of the fate of young Southern womanhood in mixed settings like the comprehensive high school. In fact, some years earlier, in the midst of Hoke Smith's successful introduction of curricular diversification into Atlanta's high schools, his own proposal for coeducation through the combining of Boys' and Girls' Highs had been ignored. Standards and sex were not the only issues that motivated upper-class parents like those who sent their children to Boys' and Girls' Highs. Status and sectional issues were also involved in their opposition to consolidation. Rumors flooded the city that Guinn was intent on implementing the entire "Gary" [Indiana] system of education in Atlanta. Local upstanding citizens who may or may not have been familiar with the particulars of the Gary reform plan were familiar enough with the reputation of Gary or any other Northern "factory town" to know that they did not want such schooling for their children.[23]

Organized labor also opposed consolidation because it would mark the end of Tech High, an institution described in the newspaper of the Georgia Federation of Trades as "labor's univeristy." The *Journal of Labor* editorialized in defense of Tech High: "No matter who the boy, rich or poor, when he enters . . . he must give part of his time to the training of his hands; he thereby understands that the labor of the hands is quite as important as the cultivation of the mind." These sentiments clearly illustrate the allegiance of the local labor movement to the liberal, manual training curriculum at Tech High and its preference for the separate high school over a consolidated high school where the manual studies would be given a second-class status. Alumni and other supporters of Commercial High had similar negative reactions to consolidation.[24]

The opposition of affluent parents, labor, and commercial groups combined with that of conservative politicians and change-resistant school employees to force Guinn's removal from office. In addition, the opposition successfully pushed through a measure to change selection of school board members from council appointment to popular election, thereby attempting to insure that a man with such wild ideas would no longer be chosen as a manager of the public schools.[25] This resistance to consolidation was successful for a long period in Atlanta, for it was not until the 1940s that the high schools were consolidated, many years after the introduction of comprehensive high schools in most cities.

One other factor remains to be mentioned if we are to understand fully Atlanta's failure to adopt full curricular diversification in its schools. That factor was, as in so many other areas of Southern experience, race. Though Hoke Smith had proposed commercial and manual training in various Atlanta schools throughout his board tenure, he never advocated that these innovations be introduced in the separate black schools. Others on the board claimed to see value in these new studies for black students, however, and called for their addition to the curriculum in the black schools. These calls initially went unheeded, with the board claiming financial inability as the main reason for its inaction.[26] It is noteworthy that these early unsuccessful advocates of curricular innovations in the black schools used arguments about the value of such studies for black students that were similar to those given for whites.

In 1913, however, the argument shifted subtly, but importantly, and with this shift vocational curricular additions to the black schools were successfully introduced. At the November 26, 1913 meeting, the board heard that manual training should be added to the curriculum in the seventh and eighth grades of the black schools, the top two grades which then existed in the public schools for blacks. The argument for adding these studies was as follows: "We need more industrially trained workers and fewer professionals among the Negro population, and we believe this will aid in attaining the desired increase and reduction." A delegation of black citizens addressed the board and indicated the possible negative consequences of adding these subjects to the curriculum. Mr. H. H. Proctor and his fellow blacks pleaded with the board that adding manual training in the two grades of the black grammar schools not result in the curtailing of the literary studies of those schools. Proctor advocated, as an alternative to adding manual studies in the upper two grammar grades, the establishment of an Industrial High School for blacks who at that time had no publicly funded high school. Proctor's alternative would have given blacks not the second-class status desired by white proponents of industrial education for blacks, but the same kind of preparatory, liberal manual high school that whites had. It was not approved. The board chose to use manual training to keep the blacks in their place, not to offer them advancement.[27]

The board implemented its rather "special" brand of manual training for blacks when it cut the number of grades in their elementary schools to six and specified that "industrial training . . . may be substituted for a portion of the work now done in the grades. . . ." The industrial training for blacks was to be much more job-related than that offered for whites. The board specified that blacks should receive instruction in "domestic science, plain sewing, laundrying, the elements of plastering, bricklaying, carpentry, etc." All of these studies were in areas related to the jobs and skills which blacks were permitted to learn in the segregated New South, areas which were the core of Booker T. Washington's Tuskegee curriculum, and areas which were guaranteed to maintain the blacks' second-class citizenship.[28]

More job-specific training was also introduced in the non-black sectors of the Atlanta schools at this time, but not in the regular high schools. The Smith-Hughes Vocational Education Act of 1917 provided federal funding for job training and Atlanta's school officials moved quickly to make use of this funding. Smith-Hughes funds went for job training in the two night schools of the city, both black and white, but not for job training in any of the regular high schools. Smith-Hughes classes, like all Atlanta's classes, were segregated. The different races received different kinds of trade training, geared to maintain the inequalities in the existing occupational structure. While whites could receive Smith-Hughes training in areas such as "applied electricity, machine shop, machine drawing, auto shops, pipe fitting, sheet metal, and architectural drawing, printing and wood work," blacks were limited to instruction in "auto shops, sewing, and cooking."[29]

Thus, the final arrival of truly vocational education in the Atlanta schools represented little break with the existing traditions in the schools. The addition of federally funded job-training programs was not allowed to interfere with the existing school curricula. The Atlanta pattern of a liberal or general approach to manual and commercial education, instead of introducing specific, job-related vocational training, remained intact. Job training, when it existed, was either for blacks in their separate schools or for whites and blacks in racially segregated night schools.

What conclusions can be drawn from this study of curricular innovation in Atlanta's schools? First, and most obviously, the inapplicability of the revisionist, class-biased interpretation of vocationalism and curricular diversification should be stressed. Atlanta's manual training and commercial high schools were never social-class sorting grounds for the lower socioeconomic groups. Rather, they were founded and continued as preparatory schools which added manual and commercial subjects to the regular academic courses and gained support for their approach from the city's organized labor movement and its businessmen. When trade training finally came to Atlanta, it came in settings outside the regular high schools, thereby insuring that the more pedestrian pursuits would not dilute the regular high school curricula. When the race or caste issue is considered, it is clear that the multiple approaches to liberal education for whites were undertaken with the understanding that the city's black population would remain to do most of the menial chores along with any other jobs which whites did not want. Job training for these tasks might be made available to blacks in their schools if federal funds would be provided to support the programs.

Atlanta's differential development must be attributed, in large degree, to the traditionalism (buttressed by racism) which pervaded the city's political and educational affairs. "Progressivism," "reform," and "innovation" did not carry the same automatic positive rhetorical loading in this New South city that they seemed to carry in other settings. While the reformers might from time to time be successful in introducing new educational programs in Atlanta, the innovations, as shown in this essay, were tailored to the traditional ideology of this city rather than to the social engineering plans of reformers in the urban North and Midwest. Atlanta's victory of traditionalism over reform might be contrasted with Michael Katz's account of the victory of Horace Mann and other soft-line reformers over the hard-line traditionalists in mid-nineteenth century Massachusetts. Katz argues that the soft-line victory was so complete that meaningful debate on educational issues was completely stilled.[30] If this account of Atlanta's experience with innovation in the late nineteenth and early twentieth centuries is correct, the victory of the soft-line has been seriously overstated, perhaps because of the concentration of educational historians on large Northeastern and Midwestern settings and/or the domination of educational history, and even revisionist history, by the categories as defined by proreform historians like Ellwood P. Cubberley.

In fact, one wonders whether the Atlanta situation is as unique as depicted in this article. It is possible, and certainly worthy of further study, that the revisionist accounts of reform are so influenced by their battle with Cubberley that they have overlooked the existence of important traditionalist opposition to change. Only by paying attention to the opponents of reform, as well as to the reformers, can historians arrive at a full understanding of the schools in their period of greatest change. Until such study is undertaken, we must be content with the picture of Atlanta traditionalism as a pockmark on the generally reformist landscape in American education and American educational history.

Notes

1. Atlanta Board of Education Minutes, April 27, 1911 (hereafter cited as Board Minutes).
2. Ellwood P. Cubberley, *Public Education in the United States: A Study and Interpretation of American Educational History* (Boston: Houghton Mifflin, 1934) was the standard educational history from the time of its publication until the 1950s. Lawrence Cremin, *Transformation of the School: Progressivism in American Education, 1876-1957* (New York: Alfred A. Knopf, 1967) brought new and improved scholarly standards into play in the field of educational history but was as approving of educational innovations as Cubberley. Recent criticism of the intent and effects of educational reform includes Clarence J. Karier, Paul Violas, and Joel Spring, *Roots of Crisis* (Chicago: Rand McNally, 1973); Joel Spring, *Education and the Rise of the Corporate State* (Boston: Beacon Press, 1972); and Paul C. Violas, *The Training of the Urban Working Class* (Chicago: Rand McNally, 1978).
3. Board Minutes, January 1, 1908, December 26, 1901.
4. Annual Report of the Board of Education (1885) pp. 9, 17; Board Minutes, June 22, 1899, January 9, 1919.
5. Melvin W. Ecke, *From Ivy Street to Kennedy Center: Centennial History of the Atlanta Public School System* (Atlanta, Ga.: Atlanta Board of Education, 1972), pp. 41, 59-60, 75-76.
6. C. S. Parrish, *Survey of the Atlanta Public Schools* (May 1914, rpt. Atlanta Board of Education, 1973), pp. 24-26; George D. Strayer and N. L. Engelhardt, *Report of the Survey of the Public School System of Atlanta, Georgia* 2 (New York: Division of Field Studies, Institute of Educational Research, Teachers College, Columbia University, 1921-1922): 241, 246-248; Board Minutes, August 30, 1918.
7. Henry Reid Hunter, "The Development of the Public Secondary Schools of Atlanta, Georgia 1845-1937" (Ph.D. diss., George Peabody College, 1937, rpt. Atlanta Public Schools, 1974), p. 157.
8. Edward A. Krug, *The Shaping of the American High School 1880-1920* (New York: Harper & Row, 1964), p. 146. The twists and turns of economic, political, and cultural development in the New South of the late nineteenth and early twentieth centuries are brilliantly recorded

and analyzed in C. Vann Woodward, *Origins of the New South, 1877-1913* (Baton Rouge, La.: Louisiana State University Press, paperback ed., 1971). Though Woodward devotes little space to education, he turns a phrase which aptly describes Atlanta's school reform when he uses "The Divided Mind of the New South" as the title for one of his chapters.

9. Ecke, *Centennial History*, p. 41.
10. Annual Report of the Board of Education (1885), p. 17; Board Minutes, June 22, 1899.
11. Board Minutes, August 9, 1903.
12. *Atlanta Constitution,* April 30, 1903.
13. David B. Tyack, *The One Best System: A History of American Urban Education* (Cambridge: Harvard University Press, 1974), Part IV.
14. Dewey W. Grantham, Jr., *Hoke Smith and the Politics of the New South* (Baton Rouge, La.: Louisiana State University Press, 1958).
15. I have described and analyzed the Guinn board presidency in Wayne J. Urban, "Progressive Education in the Urban South: The Reform of the Atlanta Schools, 1914-1918," in *The Age of Urban Reform*, ed. Michael H. Ebner and Eugene M. Tobin (Port Washington, N.Y.: Kennikat Press, 1977), ch. 9.
16. Board Minutes, June 22, 1899, August 3, 1899, December 27, 1900, April 9, 1900, September 12, 1901, April 30, 1903, February 6, 1903. Also, see *Atlanta Journal*, July 25, 1903.
17. Board Minutes, May 25, 1911.
18. Annual Report of the Board of Education (1885), p. 17; Board Minutes, August 19, 1903; and Urban, "Progressive Education in the Urban South," p. 135.
19. Board Minutes, May 28, 1896, May 28, 1903, July 25, 1907, July 26, 1906.
20. Board Minutes, May 25, 1911.
21. *Journal of Labor* January 22, 1915; Ecke, *Centennial History*, p. 105.
22. Krug, *Shaping of the American High School*, p. 276.
23. "Evidence and Proceedings Before a Special Committee of Five, Appointed under a Resolution of City Council," (1918), pp. 152-160. My copy of this document was obtained from Professor Melvin Ecke, History Department, Georgia State University. A copy is also available at the office of the clerk, Atlanta City Council. For a description of the Gary plan which highlights the aspects that Atlantans feared, see Raymond E. Callahan, *Education and the Cult of Efficiency* (Chicago: University of Chicago Press, 1962), ch. 6. On Hoke Smith's earlier proposal for coeducation, see Board Minutes, April 25, 1901.
24. *Journal of Labor*, March 18, 1921; Board Minutes, January 28, 1926.
25. *Atlanta Constitution*, August 10, 1918, December 10, 1918.
26. Concerning the early unsuccessful attempts to obtain manual training for blacks, see Board Minutes, December 26, 1901, January 2, 1902, April 28, 1904, May 26, 1904, January 26, 1905.

27. Board Minutes, November 22, 1913.
28. Board Minutes, June 24, 1916, November 22, 1916.
29. Board Minutes, December 20, 1917, December 31, 1919.
30. Michael B. Katz, *The Irony of Early School Reform* (Cambridge: Harvard University Press, 1968), pp. 131–153.

Joseph W. Newman

Teacher Unionism and Racial Politics: The Atlanta Public School Teachers' Association

As school systems in the New South struggled with the problem of race relations, teachers and their organizations inevitably entered the controversy. The segregated Southern locals of the American Federation of Teachers (AFT) found the race issue particularly troublesome, for they were caught between the progressive stance of their national union and the provincial attitudes of their region. The national AFT was among the earliest advocates of equal educational opportunities for black students and equal salaries and working conditions for black teachers, yet most white Southerners regarded such policies as radical and threatening. How would teachers' unions in the New South resolve this fundamental conflict? How would members of an all-white AFT local, for example, react to black teachers' demands for higher salaries?[1]

This chapter explores the relationship between teacher unionism and race in Atlanta, "the original capital of the 'New South.'"[2] From 1919 through 1956, the Atlanta Public School Teachers' Association (APSTA) was the largest and most powerful teachers' union in the South. As Local 89 of the American Federation of Teachers, the APSTA practiced bread-and-butter unionism with great success, substantially increasing the economic security of its members. Local 89 worked its way into Atlanta's power structure, gradually building a power base that enabled it to elect friendly and sympathetic school board members. The association maintained good relations with local, state, and national labor organizations. Consistently ranked among the AFT's five largest locals, the APSTA furnished the national union a president and six vice-presidents.[3] As William Edward Eaton observes in his recent history of the federation, Local 89 was "the pride of the AFT for over three decades."[4]

It was also a segregated organization that restricted its membership to white teachers. The association always kept blacks at a social and economic distance. Early and late in its thirty-seven year career as an AFT local, the APSTA struggled against black teachers' demands for higher salaries. Members of Local 89 hurt themselves financially be perceiving black teachers as economic rivals rather than colleagues. Over the years, Atlanta's white teachers unwittingly took money from their own pockets by refusing to make short-term economic concessions to black teachers.

Although the history of teacher unionism in the South is only now being written, it already seems clear that the APSTA was in a better position than any other AFT local to play a major role in the rise of the New South.[5] Whereas the AFT organized only a minority of teachers in other Southern cities—and throughout most of the nation as well—more than 90 percent of Atlanta's white teachers were members of Local 89.[6] A close, cooperative relationship developed among teachers' union, school board, and school system management. When white teachers spoke collectively, the local press paid attention and citizens paused to listen. As Atlanta, like the rest of the South, attempted to come to grips with the difficult problem of race relations, the APSTA was strong and secure enough to provide badly needed leadership. Unfortunately, white teachers refused to take the lead on the race issue during the forties and fifties, arguing that they could move no faster than their community. This decision had tragic consequences for their local, the Atlanta public schools, and the American Federation of Teachers. With the AFT calling on its Southern locals to ease tensions between black and white teachers and aid the process of desegregation, the APSTA clung to the same spirit of segregation that had prevailed when the association affiliated with organized labor in 1919.

This chapter opens with a brief account of Local 89's first confrontation with black militancy in the post-World War I era, when black teachers pressed their case for higher salaries in the arena of municipal politics. The heart of this chapter, an analysis of the APSTA's race relations during the 1940s and 1950s, emphasizes the association's self-defeating attitude toward black teachers and its uphill fight against the progressive racial policies of the American Federation of Teachers.

A Missed Lesson: The White Response to Black Militancy, 1919–1921

One of the saddest aspects of Local 89's race relations is that its members did not learn from their early experiences with black teachers. In fact, the black militancy that swept Atlanta just after World War I was in many ways a dress rehearsal for the more serious racial conflicts of the World War II era. White teachers first encountered black militancy during the 1918–19 school year. The Atlanta Public School Teachers' Association, an independent teachers' organization founded in 1905, was gaining popularity among white teachers with its increasingly aggressive pursuit of a long-overdue salary increase. The cruel combination of postwar inflation and no pay raises had driven teachers, white and black, to the point of desperation. Nearly half of the entire teaching force had left the school system to find more profitable work elsewhere. Through the APSTA, white teachers turned to city politicians for relief. The mayor of Atlanta and members of the board of education were sympathetic and seemed willing to grant a salary increase, but they claimed that the city's revenues were insufficient. White teachers pinned their hopes for better pay on the mayor's proposal for a tax rate referendum that, if approved by Atlanta's voters, would generate enough new revenue to fund the raise. The APSTA lent its support to a campaign to raise the tax rate, only to see higher taxes fail at the polls in March, 1919, and again in April. It soon became clear that black voters had played a crucial role in defeating the two referenda, thereby denying teachers their first substantial pay raise in years.[7]

In 1919 Atlanta was a segregated city under the spell of Jim Crow. Just over 30 percent of the city's 200,000 residents were black, yet the school board's expenditures for black education had never even approached a comparable percentage of the total budget. Since the early 1900s black leaders had demanded better schools, looking to the ballot box as the best means of realizing their demands. To be sure, the white Democratic primary represented a formidable barrier, for it decided virtually all partisan contests in the one-party South. Urban blacks in cities like Atlanta, Charleston, and Memphis, however, were able to obtain a limited franchise unknown in rural areas. Blacks could participate in city politics by voting in nonpartisan municipal referenda, which offered the best opportunities for a black voice in urban affairs.[8]

After 1900 the board of education and city council relied heavily on bond issues to finance municipal improvements, including expansion of the school system. In 1903 and 1909 white politicians had promised blacks better schools in return for their support of municipal bonds. Black voters had come through at the polls, but members of board and council forgot their campaign rhetoric soon after the elections. When buildings and other educational improvements for blacks turned out to be cheap substitutes for what had been promised, or never materialized at all, black leaders realized that new tactics would be necessary to secure further educational opportunities.[9] The years after 1910 witnessed a new spirit of militancy among blacks in Atlanta, spurred by a new NAACP chapter, urged by the *Atlanta Independent*, a black weekly newspaper, and based on the power of black votes in nonpartisan municipal referenda.

By 1919 blacks were determined to block bond issues and tax increases for *all* purposes until the could obtain better public schools. Black leaders demanded a high school, improved elementary schools, and a pay raise for black teachers. For thirty years the maximum salary for black teachers had been less than the minimum for whites, and the raises sought by the APSTA would have done nothing to close the gap. When white city fathers declined to meet black demands, black voters registered their disapproval by tipping the balance toward the defeat of the tax rate referenda of March and April 1919, scoring two rare victories over Jim Crow.[10]

These victories for blacks were bitter defeats for white teachers, who had placed their hopes for better pay in the hands of Atlanta's voters only to suffer two stinging rebuffs at the polls. The APSTA was already considering affiliation with organized labor to gain outside support for the salary drive, and these events gave the association a final push. Nineteen days after the defeat of the April tax referendum, the APSTA became Local 89 of the American Federation of Teachers. In January, 1920, the new local joined the Atlanta Federation of Trades, the city's central labor council.[11]

When members of the APSTA met in November, 1919, to make plans for a new salary campaign, the white teachers' association considered the needs of black teachers for the first time in its history. Local 89 requested a $30 monthly raise for white elementary school teachers and administrators, a $20 increase for white high school teachers and administrators, and a $10 raise for black teachers and janitors. While APSTA members regarded this gesture as generous, black teachers took it as an insult. In November, 1919, and January, 1920, delegations of black teachers and community leaders appeared before the board of education in protest. Blacks seemed to know which arguments to use to sway the board. While one black teacher began by observing that the color of a person's skin had nothing to do with efficiency as a teacher, he concluded that black voters would not support school bonds unless board members treated black teachers equitably. Black community leaders, including Dr. John Hope, president of Morehouse College, relied on the same dual argument: an appeal to the board's sense of decency and good will followed by a direct economic threat.[12] The principal of a black elementary school summarized the case when she bluntly stated that if the board adopted the APSTA's salary recommendations, "not ten negroes would support a bond issue."[13] Blacks had learned that appealing to the board's sense of decency would carry them only so far. This militant stance deeply disturbed Atlanta's mayor, school board members, and other white politicians, for they were already planning another bond referendum to finance school construction and other municipal improvements.[14]

Blacks soon attracted a few whites to their side as delegations from a white ministers' association and the Atlanta Federation of Trades came before the board in January, 1920. Their arguments were similar to those advanced by blacks: both human dignity and political expediency, but particularly the latter, dictated better treatment for blacks.[15] The past-president of the city labor federation, a group that consistently supported white teachers in their quest for higher salaries, observed that "the colored people of the city had stood almost solidly against bond issues and other public improvement measures, and ... he believed this attitude would change if the negroes were shown a fair deal was intended for them."[16]

The board of education was in an uncomfortable position indeed. Its budget was so limited that giving black teachers a higher raise would necessitate reducing the raises for white teachers. Board members faced the painful choice of granting the demands of black teachers and thereby alienating the new white teachers' union or making white teachers happy and thereby losing black support for taxes and bond issues. After much deliberation, the board voted to reduce white elementary school raises from $30 to $28 per month and white high school raises from $20 to $18.50 in order to increase black raises from $10 to $15.[17] Blacks had won another victory over Jim Crow.

White politicians, ministers, and trade unionists had recognized the economic realities of the situation: unless they appeased blacks, bond issues and tax increases would likely fail at the polls. Full of "The Atlanta Spirit" (the city's booster slogan), these civic-minded leaders had learned their political lessons well: whites would have to compromise with blacks if Atlanta was to move forward. To secure black support for the next bond referendum in March 1921, the mayor willingly met black demands for a high school and several new elementary schools, promising to spend a full one-third of the $4,000,000 in bond revenue to improve black public education. This time the bonds passed.[18] By the same token, white teachers should have learned that they would have to make certain economic concessions to black teachers if Local 89 was to be an effective bread-and-butter union.

Instead, white teachers grew intransigent toward their black counterparts. When several black teachers voted to affiliate with the AFT in April, 1920, as the Gate City Teachers' Association, the white local refused to approve their charter.[19] The AFT proceeded to install the black local anyway, without the APSTA's support. Refusing to approve the charter was a needless, vindictive gesture that symbolized Local 89's attitude toward blacks. Even in the segregated capital of the New South, acknowledging the needs of black teachers under the banner of trade unionism could have helped reduce unnecessary and counterproductive economic competition between black and white employees in the same school system. More than twenty-five years would pass, however, before Local 89 and a group of black teachers established a limited working relationship. A myopic, conservative approach to race relations would characterize the APSTA throughout its career as an AFT local. Black teachers would hold their peace for another twenty years, but the decade of the forties would witness a renewal of militancy and an upsurge of demands for equalization of black and white teachers' salaries.

The APSTA at the Peak of its Strength:
The 1920s and 1930s

It is necessary to examine the APSTA's growth and maturation as a teachers' union during the 1920s and 1930s in order to understand the racial politics of the World War II era. Although the twenties and thirties were decades of financial crisis in the Atlanta public schools, Local 89 not only survived but increased its strength and influence. For several years during the late twenties, the Atlanta local was the largest in the entire federation. Mary C. Barker, one of the association's few liberals, served as national president of the AFT from 1925 through 1931. Allie Mann, a conservative on the opposite end of the social and political spectrum from Barker, lost a close election for the AFT's presidency in 1936. Organized teachers in other cities rightly came to regard the Atlanta local as one of the most successful in the federation.[20]

Ira Jarrell, the woman who served as the APSTA's president from 1936 through 1944, symbolized the local at the peak of its strength. Jarrell, an up-from-the-ranks elementary school teacher and principal, was the epitome of a bread-and-butter unionist. She helped restore the salary cuts that teachers had suffered during the Depression. A capable leader with a magnetic personality, Jarrell ruled the local with an iron hand. The APSTA had never been a model of participatory democracy—the association's officers and a board of directors had always dominated the rank and file—but under Ira Jarrell the membership of more than one thousand teachers became a rubber stamp for an inner circle of four or five executive board members. Few teachers complained, however, for President Jarrell delivered the economic benefits that teachers wanted.[21]

Jarrell knew how to use concentrated power to great advantage. She immersed the local in city politics with impressive and almost immediate success. Quite popular with local labor leaders, she cooperated with the Atlanta Federation of Trades to build a "political machine" with substantial clout in municipal elections. The teacher-labor alliance flexed its muscle in 1936 by helping to unseat a mayor who had been hostile toward municipal employees. Atlanta's new mayor was William B. Hartsfield, a "friend of the schools" and a powerful political ally of Jarrell and Local 89. Next, the machine determined to gain more leverage over the board of education. By 1941 white teachers were joking that Jarrell had the board in her pocket, for a board of six members, all approved by the APSTA, was in office. It is a testimony to the political power of the teachers' association and the labor federation that the same six members—all prominent business and professional men who represented Atlanta's "best"—retained their seats until the mid-fifties. APSTA members proudly (and accurately) came to refer to the six as "our board."

When Superintendent Willis Sutton announced his retirement during the 1943–44 school year, the board of education repaid its political debts by electing Ira Jarrell superintendent of the Atlanta public schools. Jarrell was already a well-known figure in municipal affairs, and the superintendency thrust her directly into the city's power structure. Atlanta, now an ambitious city of more than 300,000, was gradually being controlled by a small circle of business and professional leaders. As Floyd Hunter demonstrates in his classic *Community Power Structure*, a study of Atlanta under the pseudonym "Regional City," a group of approximately forty influential individuals at the vertex of a power pyramid was making decisions that would catapult the city into national prominence. Significantly, Hunter places Ira Jarrell (under the name "Mabel Gordon") within the inner circle of forty.[22] She was determined to find a secure place for the public schools in a closed, centralized political system.

Superintendent Jarrell viewed herself as pro-teacher, and in many ways she was. Teachers received an unprecedented series of raises during the late forties. However, Jarrell was unable to extricate herself from the internal affairs of the teachers' union after she joined management. She continued to play a dominant role in the small group of executive board members that ran the APSTA. Lines of demarcation between labor and management in the school system became blurred and indistinct as Local 89 became a quasi company union. Although few teachers knew enough about the principles of organized labor to sense the danger inherent in the situation, after 1944 the APSTA often seemed more responsive to the priorities of the superintendent and school board than to the best interests of its own rank and file.[23]

The local's hierarchical internal structure and its ties to the school board and the city's power structure became critical factors during the racially troubled forties and fifties. The APSTA would face its greatest challenge as black teachers renewed their demands for higher salaries. This time black militancy would seem even more threatening, and, to compound the problem, the AFT would soon pressure Local 89 to admit black teachers as members.

Resurgent Black Militancy: The 1940s

As C. Vann Woodward observes in *The Strange Career of Jim Crow*, racial tension in the United States subsided during the 1930s as blacks and whites alike struggled against the Depression. "Then, quite abruptly and unaccountably—or so it seemed to many Southern white people—" the 1940s ushered in an era of renewed demands for black rights.[24] The situation in Atlanta was no exception to this pattern. A precursor of resurgent militancy among

Atlanta's blacks came in the fall of 1938, when the city attempted to float a large bond issue in cooperation with the surrounding Fulton County. Angered that the bond commission had proposed to spend a mere $250,000 of the $15,000,000 in bonds for black education, blacks resurrected some of the tactics that had served them well almost two decades earlier. The *Atlanta Daily World*, at that time the nation's only daily black newspaper, and the Atlanta Urban League focused attention on miserable conditions in black schools, urging voter registration so that black citizens could make their anger felt at the polls. Black leaders believed that they could halt municipal progress at the ballot box until their demands for better schools were met, for the approval of bond issues required an affirmative vote by two-thirds of the city's registered voters. The 1938 bonds failed due to a low turnout on the part of both black and white Atlantans.[25]

The pattern repeated itself in 1940, when city fathers proposed another bond issue. Again blacks made educational improvements their critical demand. Their leaders had long insisted that since blacks constituted one-third of the city's population, they were entitled to approximately one-third of all monies spent for the schools. Tangible evidence to document their need was not difficult to find: every black school was on double sessions, most facilities were in deplorable condition, and black teachers were grossly underpaid. White leaders responded by promising to spend $100,000 of the proposed $1,800,000 in school bonds for black education—exactly one-eighteenth of the total. With the APSTA and the board of education cooperating in a campaign to pass the bonds, leaders of such groups as the NAACP, the Civic and Political League, and the Baptist Ministers' Union took to the pages of the *Daily World* to urge blacks to register to vote, then stay home on election day. Making the historical precedent explicit, the president of the NAACP called attention to the success of these tactics during the 1919–21 bond and tax campaigns. Blacks won another victory as the bond issue failed to pass, again due to a lower voter turnout.[26]

Winning two battles with Jim Crow within the span of two years encouraged Atlanta's blacks. They could also take heart in what they read in the news columns of the *Daily World*. In other cities blacks were pushing, often successfully, for equalization of black and white teachers' salaries. Within five months after the defeat of the 1940 bond issue, black teachers in the Atlanta public schools had adopted equalization as their goal. Significantly, members of the struggling black AFT local, the Gate City Teachers' Association, had initiated the drive for equalization that would cause a decade of trouble for the white teachers' union. Since 1920, the Gate City group had barely kept its head above water in an on-again, off-again relationship with the American Federation of Teachers, but now the black local had seized on a cause that commanded broad support among black leaders: narrowing the gap between the salaries of black and white teachers.[27]

Black teachers, who along with ministers, attorneys, dentists, and physicians enjoyed high status and respect in the black community by virtue of their formal education, felt insulted by the salary schedule under which they worked. A schedule won by the APSTA in 1926 was still in effect for white teachers, who were paid on the basis of both seniority and level of education. The board of education paid black teachers based on seniority alone, providing no recognition of educational attainment and no incentive to obtain advanced degrees. In 1926 the lowest-paid white teacher had earned more than the highest-paid black. The board had reduced the disparity somewhat through a series of small raises, but in the early forties glaring differences between black and white salaries remained. Black elementary school teachers earned between $800 and $1,800, white elementary school teachers between $1,200 and $2,400. Black high school teachers had salaries between $1,000 and $2,000 while their white counterparts earned from $1,600 to $2,800. With these issues on their minds, members of the Gate City Teachers' Association petitioned the school board for equal salaries in January, 1941.[28]

Superintendent Willis Sutton and the board took the petition seriously, realizing that the request was but one facet of a nationwide upsurge in black demands for better education. Sutton invited APSTA President Ira Jarrell and two other officers to meet with representatives of the black local. Black teachers carefully explained that they did not wish to lower the salaries of white teachers, nor did they want to take the matter to court. Equalization was nevertheless an expensive proposition. After calculating that approximately half a million dollars (between 10 and 15 percent of the annual budget) would be required to put black and white teachers' salaries on a parity, school board members and APSTA officers agreed that equalization was out of the question. The board informed black teachers of the decision by letter, acknowledging their petition and referring to a tight budget.[29]

Ira Jarrell explained the gravity of the situation to members of Local 89 in a general meeting. Suggesting that equalization would mean "a cutting down" of white teachers' salaries, Jarrell stated that the school board and the association had three options: (1) facing a lawsuit, "which we would try to talk them out of"; (2) equalizing salaries; (3) abolishing salary schedules and employing teachers on individual contracts.[30] Here it is important to notice that Jarrell, like Superintendent Sutton and the board, viewed options two and three as distinct: they regarded individual contracts as an alternative to equalization, not a means to the end of equalization. The difference between options two and three would play an important part in the events that followed.

Atlanta's black teachers were unwilling to abandon their goal of equal salaries, for black community leaders stood solidly behind them. Throughout 1941 the *Daily World* reflected a new spirit of activism. While the board of education was considering the Gate City petition, the NAACP launched a local membership drive. Roy Wilkins, editor of the NAACP's journal *Crisis*, came to Atlanta to give the drive momentum. News of campaigns for equalization in other Southern cities filled the pages of the *Daily World* alongside editorials that told black teachers they were "obligated to fight" for better salaries.[31] Soon an ad hoc group called the Atlanta Citizen's Committee on Equalization of Teachers' Salaries took up the black teachers' cause.

Rev. Martin Luther King, Sr., pastor of Ebenezer Baptist Church, headed the committee of black leaders that appeared before the school board in May, 1941. King played a prominent role in a variety of black civic organizations and was active as well in the Georgia State Teachers' Association, the black counterpart of the Georgia Education Association. King had helped elect C. L. Harper, principal of Atlanta's Booker T. Washington High School, president of the black teachers' association at its state convention in April, 1941. Harper's platform had included a demand for salary equalization. According to Harper, black teachers would raise their salaries only by fighting for their rights. The opposition to Harper had centered around a black normal school professor, an advocate of accommodation and gradualism, who had countered Harper's and King's call to arms with the promise that "our good white friends" would equalize salaries if only they were given a little more time. The majority of black teachers at the convention had rejected gradualism in favor of immediate action, representing a major change in strategy. A few days after the convention, King had called a mass meeting of concerned black citizens at the Ebenezer Baptist Church to mobilize support for C. L. Harper and salary equalization. One month later the Atlanta Board of Education came face to face with renewed black militancy in the form of another petition for equal salaries. Board members listened politely, thanked Rev. King's committee, filed the petition, and took no further action.[32]

At this point Superintendent Willis Sutton's attitude toward equalization of salaries became particularly important. By the early forties Atlanta's blacks had come to view Sutton with suspicion. Whereas two decades earlier the *Independent* had praised the superintendent's apparent desire for "equal opportunity in the public schools for all children," during the financial crises of the twenties and thirties blacks had grown tired of Sutton's willingness to economize by cutting expenditures for black education.[33] It probably surprised both blacks and whites, then, when Sutton took a positive stand on increasing educational opportunities for black students in May, 1941. Just after the King delegation left the board meeting, Sutton went on record in favor of a federal aid to education bill pending in the U. S. Senate. Having testified in Washington in support of the bill, Sutton told board members that federal aid would help promote "the equalization of education in America, particularly in the rural sections and as between Negroes and whites." Sutton termed federal aid "one of the most urgent needs . . . because of the requirements of recent Federal Court decisions interpreting the Fourteenth Amendment respecting equalization of educational opportunity."[34] Coming on the heels of the King petition, Sutton's remarks seemed to represent a small ray of hope for salary equalization. Thus far, the board had couched its opposition to equalization in strictly financial terms; Sutton's stand on federal aid offered a possible solution to the problem of a limited budget.

Unfortunately, Governor Eugene Talmadge injected his considerable influence into the situation to harden the board's stand on equalization. APSTA officers helped precipitate Talmadge's intervention. White teachers had grown increasingly concerned with equalization after learning of the King petition, and several of Local 89's leaders took the short walk from their downtown offices to the state capitol to seek Talmadge's assistance. The governor told white teachers what they wanted to hear: "Of course, he is opposed [to equalization] and promises that it will never happen while he is in office."[35] Talmadge did not stop with a verbal promise. Soon after the APSTA visit, he sent the board of education a curt letter that was highly critical of Superintendent Sutton. Had the board ever received money from the Rosenwald Fund, a philanthropy committed to improving black education in the South? Exactly what was Sutton's position on salary equalization? Hastily the board convened to formulate a response to Talmadge's questions. No, the board had never used Rosenwald monies. Furthermore, board members told the governor, "We do not contemplate any change in our salary schedule. . . . We have consulted with Dr. Sutton at this meeting and he has stated that he has never believed and does not now believe that equal salaries should be paid to white and negro teachers."[36] Political pressure from a segregationist governor, prompted at least in part by a visit from officers of the white teachers' union, had pushed Sutton and the board into a well-defined, hard-line position on salary equalization.

Blacks countered with a hard-line position of their own. The King petition had contained the thinly veiled threat that "the objectives of this petition . . . have been realized elsewhere by other methods and means."[37] In October, 1941, blacks made the threat explicit. C. L. Harper of the state's black teachers' association again requested better salaries for blacks, this time backing up his request with the promise of a court suit if the board failed to act.[38] Caught between the governor and the threat of litigation, Board President Ed Cook sent Harper a carefully worded reply. Once more Cook relied on the financial argument: if funds permitted, the board would consider "some increase . . . in the salary schedule of the colored teachers."[39]

That argument quickly lost credibility with blacks. One month after school board members used tight finances as an excuse not to equalize salaries, they acted favorably on a petition from the APSTA for a cost-of-living raise that would be almost as expensive as equalization. The board's immediate agreement to seek additional funds from the city council to finance the 10 percent raise made black teachers indignant enough, but their anger boiled over when they found out what white APSTA members already knew: the board would carry a surplus of almost $200,000 in 1942. This information shed new light on the situation: blacks now had evidence that the board's refusal to equalize salaries was based more on unwillingness than on inability. The board's financial argument against equalization was a distortion of the facts, and Ira Jarrell's suggestion to APSTA members that raising black salaries would necessitate lowering white salaries was clearly a scare tactic.[40]

After black teachers acquired this information, C. L. Harper made two more attempts to settle the matter out of court. Early in January, 1942, he wrote to Ira Jarrell requesting Local 89's support for "a substantial increase" in black teachers' salaries. As in his October 1941 letter to the board of education, Harper did not request immediate equalization, only a step in that direction. Emphasizing that black teachers did not wish to see the salaries of white teachers lowered, Harper called attention to the fact that both the APSTA and the Gate City Teachers' Association were "affiliated with the A F of L and therefore are pledged to support each other in any just contention."[41] He also wrote to the school board in February, 1942, pointing out that the 10 percent cost-of-living raise for all teachers would only "add to the grossness of an injustice which all of us want to remedy."[42] He received a favorable reply from neither Local 89 nor school board. Soon after Harper sent his final letter to the board, a black teacher at Howard Junior High School filed a suit for equal pay in federal district court.[43]

Superintendent, members of the board of education, and leaders of the white teachers' union drew together to meet the new threat. Already the board had asked the APSTA to retain an attorney to assist the board's legal counsel on the matter of equalization. Lawyers feared that the court would issue an injunction based on the *prima facie* evidence that separate and admittedly unequal salary schedules existed for the two races. Never giving serious consideration to actual equalization, the board accepted its counselors' advice to abolish both schedules and put teachers on individual contracts. This move would give the appearance of ending discrimination and thereby prevent an injunction.[44]

The board consulted the APSTA before implementing this drastic change. At stake was the seniority and education-based salary schedule that white teachers had won in 1926 after years of struggle. Many teachers regarded the schedule as Local 89's major victory of the twenties. Would white teachers be willing to return to the uncertain days when the board and superintendent had set salaries at will, rewarding their friends on the teaching staff and penalizing their enemies? Was resisting equalization worth that risk? Jarrell, Sutton, and the board made sure that white teachers would answer those questions affirmatively.

Members of Local 89 assembled in a called meeting on February 27, 1942 to discuss their response to the suit. President Jarrell set the tone of the meeting at the outset: "Beccause of the suit filed against the Board of Education and the Superintendent, the salary schedule must be abolished."[45] In her usual forceful style, Jarrell presented the matter as a foregone conclusion. Deliberations of the rank and file were mere formalities. She proceeded to introduce Superintendent Sutton, who spoke for several minutes urging white teachers to trust the school board and their leaders in the APSTA. Sutton claimed that the board had never "purposefully" discriminated on the basis of race or color; rather, the two schedules simply reflected the culture and tradition of the South. Indeed, noted the superintendent, salaries for black teachers in Atlanta were twice the average for all teachers in Georgia. He recounted the history of the white salary schedule, acknowledging "that the work of twenty-odd years is being disrupted and I am distressed, as you are." But, he reasoned, "why employ lawyers unless you are going to listen to their advice?" Sutton revealed himself as a gradualist with his remark that blacks were losing their best white friends and allies by taking the radical step of a lawsuit. Finally, he struck a chord that never failed to resonate in the APSTA: financial self-interest. "It is hard to keep all sorts of rumors out of circulation," he observed, ". . . when we talk about people's pocketbooks."[46]

Board President Ed Cook spoke next, underscoring briefly several of Sutton's points. He came down heavily on the notion that "compromising" with black teachers "would mean compromising out of white teachers' salaries because there [is] no money otherwise." Jarrell followed Cook to reiterate that the schedule had to be abolished to avoid an injunction.[47] After hearing the carefully orchestrated speeches of Sutton, Cook, and Jarrell, members of Local 89 passed two separate resolutions expressing confidence in the school board, paving the way for abolition of the salary schedules the next day.[48]

White teachers were all but unanimous in their support of the board. Only two teachers spoke against the resolutions. Mary Barker, the former president of both the APSTA and the American Federation of Teachers, made a brief speech that went to the heart of the matter. Regretting that the board had not acted to equalize salaries in January (before the suit had been filed and while the board still had a large surplus), Barker stated: "What we are doing is putting ourselves in the position of fighting the inevitable."[49] J. P. Barron, another former APSTA president who had served as vice-president of the AFT, took the floor at the end of the meeting to call attention to an article in a current issue of the AFT's journal, the *American Teacher*. The Louisville, Kentucky, schools had faced a similar situation, he noted, and members of the Louisville AFT local "went before the people and got the money to equalize the salaries." Couldn't Local 89 do the same? Ira Jarrell had a ready answer. "When the association instructed her to go out and raise the money, she would do it." On that disquieting note, the meeting adjourned.[50]

Abolishing the salary schedules blocked the injunction but failed to solve the basic problem. The black plaintiff recognized the subterfuge and refused to withdraw his suit. Motions by school board and APSTA attorneys to dismiss the suit failed as Thurgood Marshall of the NAACP cooperated with local black attorney A. T. Walden in piloting the litigation through the courts. The *Daily World* followed the matter closely, supplying news of related cases in other cities (many of the cases decided in the plaintiffs' favor) and answering repeated charges that black teachers wanted to lower white teachers' salaries. The litigation was tied up in federal district court until 1948, creating more than five years of financial uncertainty for white teachers.[51] Uncertainty resulted from their fears that the school board might actually have to pay black teachers on an equal basis, not merely appear to do so. Equalization of salaries would require more money and, as Jarrell and the board often reminded white APSTA members, that money might well come out of their own paychecks. A myopic financial imperative reigned supreme in Local 89.

Inequality Disguised: The 1944 Salary Schedule

With the demise of the salary schedules, the superintendent and school board had complete latitude in setting salaries. Sutton and board members asked teachers to trust them, promising that no teacher would be paid less than her former salary. From 1942 through 1944 the board worked to develop a unified schedule that, according to the board, would not discriminate by race. In June, 1944, five months after Ira Jarrell's election as superintendent, the board announced a new schedule. Its most prominent feature was that Superintendent Jarrell, subject to the board's approval, retained complete freedom in determining salaries. When a teacher was hired, the superintendent recommended a salary to the board. After evaluating the new teacher's first year on the job, the superintendent recommended which of four salary "tracks" the teacher would follow. A teacher could still attain tenure after three years, but at any point in the teacher's career the superintendent could recommend placement on a higher or lower track—or no further advancement on the schedule. After the seventh year of employment, the teacher could increase her salary by obtaining a master's degree, and after that by taking post-master's courses, but only if the superintendent approved her course of study. The superintendent considered seven factors in setting salaries: teaching efficiency, professional growth in service, special service to the school community, professional usefulness to the school system, special talent or skill, skill and success in pupil relations, and nature of assignment.[52]

The new schedule was, in short, a *merit* pay system—just the sort of system that AFT locals throughout the nation bitterly opposed. APSTA members themselves had suffered the hardships of merit pay under a capricious, efficiency-minded board president during the period from 1910 to 1920. Ironically, merit pay helped push Atlanta's teachers toward affiliation with organized labor in 1919, then returned twenty-five years later in the hands of a former president of the union. The irony continues. As president of Local 89, Ira Jarrell had been asked her opinion of the proposed schedule. First on her list of objections was "too much merit system."[53] Jarrell's perspective changed dramatically after she crossed the line into management. The merit-based schedule offered the new superintendent irresistible power, and she soon convinced herself that an appeals committee composed of the three assistant superintendents and two elected teachers would be able to minimize abuses of the system. Ira Jarrell was silent on the pitfalls of merit pay after she herself became the one who determined merit.

The nature of the schedule gave her yet another reason to keep silent on merit pay: it enabled the superintendent and board to pay black teachers lower salaries based on "objective" criteria other than race. Working papers used by the board in developing the schedule clearly indicate that actual equalization of salaries was not the board's goal: "This scale makes it possible to equalize salaries absolutely, on an automatic basis, *should the board ever desire to do so.*"[54] (Emphasis added.) In fact, the board set the new beginning salary for elementary school teachers assigned to the lowest track to correspond to the old beginning salary for black teachers. The new maximum salary for elementary school teachers on the lowest track was only slightly higher than the old maximum for black teachers. In other words, the old schedule for black teachers essentially became the lowest track on the new schedule, removing the appearance of discrimination based on race without drastically altering actual salaries for either black or white teachers. Board members themselves estimated that full equalization would cost about $400,000.[55] Their working papers for the new schedule, however, contain the crucial admission that while the new scale would "ultimately" necessitate an increase in the budget, "it should be possible . . . to introduce the scale with very little or no increase at all."[56] At best, the unified salary schedule held out the hope of equalization sometime in the future—subject to a change in the school board's disposition toward black teachers. It is obvious, then, why blacks pressed ahead with their lawsuit after the new schedule went into effect in 1944. The possibility that the suit might be decided in the plaintiffs' favor hung over the heads of the APSTA and the board of education for four more years.[57]

During the same period of time, Atlanta's blacks grew militant on other educational issues. With the salary schedule being fought in the courts, the

Atlanta Urban League turned its attention to securing more funds for black schools and published a detailed report on inadequacies in black education in December, 1944. The Urban League's goal was to secure for blacks at least 30 percent of the funds the school board had proposed to spend in a "post-war improvement plan." Throughout 1945 the League published leaflets and reports designed to marshal support for its campaign. With the support of Atlanta's black community, the league began a voter registration drive in the spring of 1946, just as the courts declared Georgia's white primary unconstitutional. With ten million dollars in school bonds at stake in a summer referendum, the board capitulated to black demands and agreed to spend approximately 30 percent of the bond revenue on black schools. The bonds passed by a large margin in August, 1946. This time the board kept its promise.[58]

In this atmosphere of black activism, Local 89 and the board of education treated black teachers with a new sense of caution and cordiality. In December, 1944, G. Y. Smith, a close friend of Ira Jarrell and her successor as APSTA president, reported that he had met with the black teachers' association and that better mutual understanding had resulted. Members of Local 89 sponsored a workshop for black teachers early in 1945. Smith, an AFT vice-president, helped reinstate the black teachers' association in the nearby Fulton County system as an AFT local.[59] Soon representatives of the Gate City Teachers' Association, the black local in Atlanta that had again fallen into bad standing with the national union, called on Smith for similar assistance. As he explained to the APSTA's directors and executive board, Smith carefully asked why the black teachers wanted back into the AFT. "The group asked for more money and seemingly, were not cognizant of the fact that we had employed legal aid to fight the negro case. . . . Mr. Smith asked them to submit to him a list of the prospective members and the salary of each. Three weeks have passed and no further word has been received."[60] In fact, four years would pass before a group of black teachers in the Atlanta public schools obtained an AFT charter. This new group, which disavowed any connections to the salary-conscious teachers who sought Smith's help in 1945, impressed him as moderate and nonmilitant. APSTA leaders were pleased to see such a group of black teachers organized as a new segregated local.[61]

While members of Local 89 perceived militant black teachers as economic threats, they overlooked the financial consequences of protracted litigation. One set of events in particular illustrates how shortsighted white teachers had been in opposing equalization. The salary schedule adopted in 1944 had "officially" put blacks and whites on the same scale but had continued the long-standing practice of paying high school teachers more than elementary school teachers. From 1946 through 1948 the issue of a "single salary schedule" for teachers at both levels threatened to split the association. In December, 1945, members of Local 89 went on record in favor of a single salary schedule, only to be told by Jarrell and the school board that the change was impossible for financial reasons. G. Y. Smith urged elementary school teachers to console themselves with the frequent across-the-board "bonuses" that were raising all salaries, but through 1946 and 1947 the disparity in salaries rankled a disgruntled minority of elementary school teachers. After Superintendent Jarrell stated that she and the board favored the single salary schedule, teachers wondered what stood in the way of its adoption.[62] The reason for delay finally came out: the board was reluctant to implement a single salary schedule because of the economic threat presented by the black lawsuit. As Smith explained to the association in December, 1947, just after the suit had been heard in federal district court, setting up the new schedule would require a financial "cushion," but that cushion might have to be used for another purpose. "Much depends on the decision in the Negro case," he pointed out. "We have to have some money in case the decision goes against us."[63] By cooperating with the board to avoid paying black teachers equal wages, white teachers had unwittingly worked against their own financial self-interest.

Tension mounted as the decision in the equalization case drew near. Federal District Court Judge E. Marvin Underwood heard the case late in 1947 and took his time weighing the evidence. APSTA members were encouraged by the fact that Underwood had served as the association's own attorney during the salary crisis of the late twenties. Now, Underwood was passing judgment on the 1944 salary schedule in one of his last major decisions before retirement. APSTA leaders expected a decision early in 1948, but when schools opened in September Underwood was still pondering the case. Blacks capitalized on the delay to put the board of education on the defensive once more. In September the board received a petition signed by black parents throughout the system protesting unequal educational opportunities for their children. Using statistics from the superintendent's annual reports, the parents documented the substantial gap between expenditures for black and white students. Not only were expenditures for whites more than twice as large as those for blacks, the gap had actually widened since Jarrell had become superintendent in 1944. The petition embarrassed Jarrell and the board, and in rebuttal they hurriedly assembled a booklet of facts on black education in Atlanta.[64]

Just as the board completed its work on the booklet in the fall of 1948, Judge Underwood announced his decision: the salary schedule did indeed discriminate against black teachers. Not misled by the argument that all teachers were on the same schedule and hence paid on an equal basis, Underwood fulfilled the worst fears of the APSTA and the board as he ordered adjustments in pay. For two months Underwood tried to hammer out a reasonable settlement. Blacks asked for equalization retroactive to September, 1948, a modest request in view of the fact that the schedule had been in operation for more than four years, but Underwood set the date at September, 1949, the start of the next school year. Attorneys for the school board and the APSTA rejected this compromise and appealed the case to the Fifth Circuit Court in New Orleans.[65] Uncertainty over the outcome of the equalization suit would haunt white teachers for several years to come.

Changes in Racial Politics: A New Interest in the NEA

Local 89 finally established a working relationship with a group of black teachers during the 1949-50 school year. Edward H. Lawson, a teacher at Booker T. Washington High School, cooperated with officers of the APSTA in organizing a group of moderate black teachers as a new AFT local. Lawson had serious reservations about reactivating the charter of the Gate City Teachers' Association, for that organization had acquired a radical reputation among some black teachers during the long drive for salary equalization.[66] Eschewing militancy, Lawson hoped that blacks could settle their "minor differences" with whites "without taking legal action which he considered ill advised and the result of certain pressure groups among the negroes who tried to keep an agitated condition by a series of court actions."[67] Lawson told Local 89's officers exactly what they wanted to hear. With the APSTA's blessings, in April, 1950, Lawson's group of fourteen black teachers became Local 1062, the Atlanta Federation of Teachers.[68]

If the desire to encourage nonmilitant black attitudes prompted the APSTA to help organize a new local for the AFT, racial politics also stimulated new interest among white teachers in the National Education Association (NEA). To be sure, the APSTA's relationship with the NEA had a long history. Unlike teacher unionists in other cities, members of Local 89 saw no conflict of interest in belonging to both the NEA and the AFT. Superintendent Willis Sutton, elected national president of the NEA in 1930, had encouraged APSTA members to join the "professional organization"; Allie Mann had done the same thing as president of the Georgia Education Association (GEA), the NEA's white state affiliate, during the thirties. In the early fifties Superintendent Ira Jarrell and APSTA officers pressured white teachers more than ever before to join the GEA-NEA. Blacks influenced this new policy in two ways. First, demands for integration were alienating the APSTA from the American Federation of Teachers; Jarrell and the association may have been anticipating the not-too-distant future when Local 89 would be told to admit black teachers or leave the union.[69] Second, APSTA President Dorothy Floyd, who succeeded G. Y. Smith in

1950, encouraged white teachers to become members of the GEA in order to counter the rapidly increasing strength of the NEA's black state affiliate. As Floyd explained to the APSTA's directors in March 1951, "Miss Jarrell is concerned over a current seeming lack of professional interest in G.E.A. and N.E.A. among our teachers. It behooves us to join both organizations and support them in other ways. The N.E.A. is organizing a large Negro group."[70]

Irving Fullington, a white AFT vice-president who organized for the federation in the South, substantiated Jarrell's and Floyd's concerns in his 1950–51 report to the AFT. Many black teachers preferred the NEA because of its superiority to the AFT in size and strength, he noted, and the NEA was organizing all-black chapters throughout the South, promising to work to end segregation.[71] The NEA's official stand on race was so vague that it was almost meaningless. Delegates to the 1954 convention declared that integration "is a process which affects every state and territory in our nation," urging citizens to approach the matter "with the spirit of fair play and good will which has always been the outstanding characteristic of the American people."[72] This policy would stand essentially unchanged until 1960.[73] With such an ambiguous position on race, the NEA could organize Southern blacks by claiming to be more interested in integration than the AFT's segregated locals in the South. Simultaneously, the NEA could attract Southern whites by claiming to be less radical on race than the national AFT. As Fullington saw first hand, this intentionally deceptive, circular reasoning enabled the NEA to play both ends against the middle in organizing Southern teachers, black and white.[74]

The strategy was highly successful in Georgia. The NEA's work among the state's black teachers had the ironic effect of pushing the South's strongest AFT local into the NEA's corner. Dorothy Floyd and Ira Jarrell readily agreed that the NEA's all-black state affiliate should not overshadow the all-white GEA. Superintendent Jarrell declared school holidays to coincide with the GEA's annual conventions, encouraging white teachers to become members and attend. Principals of schools in which more than half of the teaching staff were members could dismiss classes to allow teachers to attend district GEA meetings. Jarrell instructed principals to report to her the number of teachers who had joined the GEA and the NEA. To honor the APSTA's golden anniversary as a teachers' association in December, 1955, Jarrell sponsored a speech by the national president of the NEA—not, significantly, a speech by the president of the AFT. By the 1950s the APSTA was electing and paying the expenses of delegates to the NEA's annual conventions. White teachers heard increasingly favorable comments about the NEA and increasingly critical reviews of the AFT in their union meetings.[75] The stage was set for the APSTA's break with organized labor.

"We Are at Variance":
The APSTA and the AFT in the 1950s

After 1948 Local 89's leaders watched the tide of integration grow steadily stronger at the summer conventions of the American Federation of Teachers. The local's influence in AFT politics declined as Atlantans found themselves increasingly isolated from the federation's mainstream. The year 1948 was a turning point, for in that year the forces of gradualism in the AFT lost a major battle to teachers who demanded immediate action to end segregation. Changes in national leadership symbolized changes in the AFT's position on race relations. At the 1948 convention John M. Ecklund, a Denver teacher and a member of the Progressive Caucus, defeated incumbent president Joseph F. Landis of Cleveland. Landis was a moderate who counted Local 89's leaders among his supporters. G. Y. Smith had served as an AFT vice-president during Landis's administration, but Ecklund's election signaled the end of Smith's career as a national officer.[76] Throughout Landis's presidency Local 89 had maintained a positive image in the union, but the 1947 convention was the last from which Smith returned with the report that the Atlanta local "was called one of the best in the organization."[77] Already Smith could see signs of increasing interest in improving race relations in the aggressive work of the AFT's committee on cultural minorities.[78] In October, 1947, Smith ventured the prediction that southern locals might well "have to meet with colored people if they met at all."[79]

During Ecklund's four-term presidency the AFT took definite action to end racial discrimination in the federation. Delegates to the 1948 convention called on segregated locals to merge and integrate, citing a 1939 constitutional amendment that prohibited discrimination on the basis of race, religion, or political persuasion. The 1949 convention saw delegates instruct the executive council to hasten the process of integration by conferring with segregated locals and establishing joint boards to facilitate mergers. In 1951 gradualism lost further ground with passage of a resolution that prohibited the chartering of new segregated locals, and delegates to the 1952 convention added a ban on reinstating segregated locals in arrears or bad standing. In 1952 the national union resolved to take concrete action against discrimination by supervising the merger of three segregated locals in Washington, D. C., into one local for teachers of all races.[80]

Throughout this period APSTA leaders grew increasingly uncomfortable at the AFT's summer conventions. President Dorothy Floyd returned from the 1950 convention with nothing but criticism for what she had seen and heard. "We [are] at variance with many of the aims and methods of the majority of the Federation," she told the executive board. Scoring the "radical thinking" that had dominated the convention, Floyd noted that trends already underway might force Local 89 out of the union.[81] The AFT's financial and philosophical support of groups like the NAACP was particularly irksome to APSTA members; already the local had made known its dissatisfaction by withholding a portion of its national dues. Unswayed, the AFT continued its support of the NAACP and similar groups, filing *amicus curiae* briefs in school desegregation suits pending before the United States Supreme Court.[82] Floyd could only hope that the conservative wing of the AFT would regain power.

The 1952 convention offered the chance for a resurgence of conservative control. Throughout his presidency John Ecklund had faced opposition from the National Caucus of moderates and conservatives who had supported former president Joseph Landis. In 1952 the National Caucus nominated Carl J. Megel of Chicago in an attempt to unseat President Ecklund. Megel had lost to Ecklund the year before, but Megel's supporters believed that by rebuilding the old conservative alliance that included such locals as Chicago, Gary, and Atlanta, Megel could win in 1952. They were correct. When Megel was elected president by a close vote of 419 to 392, Dorothy Floyd believed that the AFT would take a more conservative approach to the race issue. She was mistaken.[83]

As a moderate, Megel did not move to end segregation as quickly as some progressive locals wished, but neither was he willing to fight the tide of integration that had gained strength for five years. The 1953 convention proved to be the most disappointing yet for Local 89. Former President George S. Counts set the tone for the meeting with his keynote address, "Let's Enter the Twentieth Century," in which he called on the Supreme Court to "consign [segregation] to the wastebasket of history."[84] The centerpiece of the convention was a resolution to declare void the charters of all locals that limited their membership by race or color. Predictably, furious politicking surrounded this proposed amendment to the constitution. APSTA delegates were encouraged when the amendments committee, chaired by a teacher from Landis's Cleveland local, recommended nonconcurrence, but the amendment passed on the floor of the convention by a vote of 219 to 80. Rather than immediately suspending the segregated locals, the convention encouraged them to set their houses in order and remain in the union.[85]

Back in Atlanta, Local 89's executive board debated how to respond to the resolution. The board decided that it would be only a matter of time before the AFT revoked the APSTA's charter. Officers spoke of "continu-[ing] our affiliation with Labor as long as possible" and staying in the union "until we are forced out." The board voted to reduce its financial support of the AFT once again by paying only token dues.[86] With eventual disaffiliation from the AFT a foregone conclusion, officers of Local 89 saw little need to bother the rank and file with the matter. One of the association's vice-presidents informed the membership in October, 1953, of the AFT's hard-line stand against segregation, and until May, 1956, the rank and file heard very little else about the national union. The executive board provided the membership so little information, in fact, that some teachers believed the association had left the federation during the summer of 1953![87]

What did concern both members and leaders was their pressing local political situation. Late in 1953 Governor Herman Talmadge and the Georgia legislature threatened to abolish the state's public schools in anticipation of a U.S. Supreme Court decision requiring integration. After the court handed down the *Brown* decision in May 1954, massive resistance swept the South. Georgians almost passed a constitutional amendment that would have closed the public schools and substituted the payment of public funds directly to citizens. In short, the local situation was so threatening that the AFT's policy on race received relatively little attention from either members or officers. Teachers who kept abreast of the issue concluded that disaffiliation was only a matter of time.[88]

The 1954 convention of the American Federation of Teachers, held just three months after the *Brown* decision, reflected the spirit of that ruling. Delegates passed a resolution praising the decision and pledging legal and financial assistance to promote integration. Step by step, the AFT moved to enforce integration of its own locals. The convention instructed all segregated locals to submit reports explaining why they had not lived up to the spirit of the union's constitution. President Megel and the executive committee took the responsibility of reviewing the reports and recommending suspension of locals making insufficient efforts to integrate.[89]

Megel visited Atlanta in February, 1955, to check on the progress of the four one-race locals in the vicinity: the white APSTA and the black Atlanta Federation of Teachers in the Atlanta public schools, and two segregated locals in the Fulton County system. The Fulton County locals were uncooperative and refused to submit reports. The Atlanta locals received Megel cordially. Megel gave the APSTA the benefit of every doubt in assessing its compliance with national directives. The long-standing political alliance between Megel's Chicago local and the APSTA may have influenced his evaluation; certainly he wished to avoid losing the AFT's strongest Southern local, still among the top five in the federation. Although there is no evidence in the APSTA's minutes and records to indicate that the association made any concessions, Megel left the city satisfied with the progress of the two Atlanta locals. He may have based his evaluation on the fact that Atlantans had elected their first black school board member, Dr. Rufus E. Clement, president of Atlanta University, late in 1953; that Superintendent Jarrell and the board, in contrast to Governor Talmadge and the state legislature, had said that they accepted *Brown* as the law of the land; and that there was no hostility between the APSTA and the Atlanta Federation of Teachers.

Megel returned to Chicago with a favorable report on the progress of the still-segregated AFT locals in the Atlanta public schools.[90]

The AFT's executive committee presented a surprisingly optimistic report at the 1955 convention. The two Atlanta locals, along with other segregated locals in New Orleans and Chattanooga, had shown the committee "evidences of satisfactory progress" toward integration.[91] A majority of delegates at the convention, however, was suspicious of the report. Exactly what constituted "satisfactory progress"? Delegates passed a resolution branding the executive committee "negligent" in carrying out the 1953 mandate for integration or charter revocation. At least one delegate was ready to suspend immediately the charters of segregated locals that had not submitted reports to the executive committee. His proposal did not pass, but Selma Borchardt, the AFT's legislative counsel, made certain that the executive committee would have more specific criteria to use in evaluating progress toward integration. Borchardt successfully moved that an attorney work with the executive committee in formulating a set of questions for segregated locals to answer by December 1, 1955. Delegates to the 1955 convention were in no mood to compromise on the issue of integration.[92]

During the fall of 1955 APSTA leaders made two parliamentary moves designed to demonstrate that they were dealing with the AFT in good faith. Taken at face value, these actions seemed to represent a significant change in policy. On October 31, 1955, the executive board recommended that the local rewrite the membership clause of its constitution to comply with the federation's constitution. The board sent this recommendation to the directors for consideration at their next meeting. On November 14 the directors endorsed the recommendation and sent it on for a vote by the general membership on December 12. The resolution did not reach the rank and file. After learning that a delegation of national officers would visit Atlanta on December 16, Local 89's leaders decided to postpone the vote by the membership until after the visit. This delay would allow them to present impressive evidence of progress toward integration—two affirmative votes by the local's leadership—without making the critical change in the membership clause.[93] At the meeting with the national officers, APSTA President Roger Derthick attempted to project the image of a local struggling in good faith against tremendous community pressures: the APSTA "could not move any faster than our community with the segregation issue." Derthick would continue to rely on the community standards rationale to justify the association's refusal to integrate, and other Southern locals would develop the theme as well. In this instance the strategy seemed to work. Derthick reported to the local's directors that the national officers "seemed anxious to keep our local affiliated with them and they were willing to go along with our progress now."[94]

For five months Derthick and the executive board let the matter rest, delaying the rank-and-file vote on the membership clause until the last meeting before the 1956 AFT convention. On May 14, 1956, an ad hoc constitution committee finally told the membership that the local would be subject to suspension at the convention if the word "white" remained in the membership clause.[95] During the discussion that followed it became clear that the two affirmative votes by the leadership had been nothing more than stalling tactics. Teachers spoke of striking the word "white" from the membership clause as simply a means of "gaining additional time." As the local's reporter admitted in the *Journal of Labor*, the association could show the AFT no genuine intention to integrate: "We cannot progress any faster than does the community in which we live."[96] Never giving serious consideration to admitting black teachers, members of Local 89 tabled the entire matter and awaited the inevitable at the summer convention.[97]

The question of what action to take against segregated locals dominated the 1956 convention of the American Federation of Teachers. Veronica Hill, a black AFT vice-president from New Orleans, presented the report of the executive committee. Officers of the four locals in Atlanta and Fulton County had treated the AFT's delegations cordially, Hill noted, but it seemed clear that they were unwilling to integrate. (More positive attitudes existed in the Chattanooga and New Orleans locals, where some officers and members were willing to give integration a chance.) Consequently, the AFT's executive committee recommended revoking the charters of its locals in Atlanta and Fulton County as of August 25, 1956, one day after the end of the convention.[98]

Before delegates voted on the recommendation, representatives of several segregated locals took the floor to present their case. Two teachers from Chattanooga, one black and one white, sounded the community standards theme. The Supreme Court's decision in the *Brown* case had been counterproductive in Chattanooga, they argued, for it had led to the formation of hate groups. Although the two Chattanooga locals had pledged to integrate, the two teachers concluded that a racially mixed local would be weak and ineffective. Local 89's Roger Derthick followed the Chattanooga teachers to present further evidence in support of the notion that teachers could not move ahead of their community. When the Atlanta League of Women Voters had tried to integrate in March, 1956, he pointed out, the group had split and lost its effectiveness. Derthick cited cooperation between Atlanta's two segregated locals and the fact that the school system now had a black area superintendent as well as a black board member as examples of progress in race relations.[99]

A representative of the Atlanta Federation of Teachers, the black local, spoke next. She agreed with Derthick that Atlantans had made racial progress, and parts of her speech seemed to defend black-white cooperation under the system of segregation. She probably surprised Derthick, however, with her conclusion that integration could occur "today or tomorrow" with "no problem." Veronica Hill of New Orleans quickly came to the podium to agree that integration was indeed feasible in the South. Hill forcefully stated that she would accept "nothing less than first-class citizenship" for herself and her son.[100]

As other delegates rose to present their views, two basic positions emerged. On the one hand, there were dire predictions that integration would make it impossible for AFT locals to carry on in the South. Delegates who argued this position defended segregation as a practical matter. On the other hand, there was the position that regardless of the practical consequences of integration, the union should stick to its principles. If segregation was morally wrong, it could not be rationalized and defended on practical grounds. The AFT faced the painful choice between keeping its segregated locals in the federation and keeping its principles intact. There was no middle ground.

At last the matter came to a vote. A series of compromises had rolled the date for compliance with the integration mandate forward to December 31, 1957. By a two-thirds majority, the American Federation of Teachers voted to allow its segregated locals in New Orleans, Chattanooga, Fulton County, and Atlanta sixteen more months to drop their racial barriers or forfeit their charters. The union had bent over backward to give segregated locals every opportunity to comply, but it was willing to cut them off rather than compromise the principle of integration.[101]

On December 10, 1956, members of the Atlanta Public School Teachers' Association voted unanimously to withdraw from the AFT. The resolution prepared by the constitution committee noted that the AFT had chartered the local in 1919 as a *white* teachers' association; that "the same State and local laws, mores, customs and traditions prevail[ed]" in 1956; and that "drastic changes" in the thinking of the national union now mandated integration or disaffiliation.[102] The APSTA had severed its ties to organized labor after a thirty-seven-year career as an AFT local. Already unofficially connected with the Georgia Education Association and the National Education Association, the APSTA eased into formal affiliation with no difficulty. There would be no pressure to merge with the NEA's black chapter in Atlanta until the mid-sixties. By then, white teachers were beginning to catch up with the times, and few could recall the day in 1956 when the Atlanta Public School Teachers' Association had left organized labor rather than integrate.

Prisoners of Their Culture? Southern Teachers and Community Standards on Race

The community standards rationale that the APSTA and other Southern locals developed to justify segregation deserves close analysis in conclusion.

In the 1950s Roger Derthick became the first APSTA president to articulate clearly the notion that teachers could not run ahead of their community on the issue of race relations, but that deterministic rationale seems to have influenced the local's earlier stand on salary equalization as well as its refusal to integrate. Superintendent Willis Sutton had spoken for most white teachers when he observed in 1942 that the school system was simply reflecting Southern tradition by paying lower wages to black teachers. To what extent, then, did the fact that Local 89 operated in a city in the New South dictate its attitude toward black teachers? Were Atlanta's teachers prisoners of their culture?

Certainly the belief in racial segregation was an article of faith for most Southern whites during the 1940s and 1950s. The research of historian C. Vann Woodward documents the long life of Jim Crow, who is in fact alive and well today with a new career. Governor Eugene Talmadge's stand against salary equalization in the early forties and his son's apparent willingness to abolish the public schools rather than integrate them in the fifties were serious threats and not to be taken lightly. There is additional evidence that Local 89's attitudes were in touch with the times. In 1949 black teachers lost their appeal for equalization to the Fifth Circuit Court in New Orleans, and the U. S. Supreme Court dismissed a subsequent appeal in 1951. In 1956 Georgia's state board of education threatened to fire any teacher who taught racially mixed classes. Black and white students would not attend school under the same roof in Atlanta until 1961, seven years after *Brown*.[103] Massive resistance was real. Operating in this climate, could the APSTA have acted other than it did? Had white teachers been willing to treat their black coworkers equitably, could they have done so?

The answer is a qualified "yes." During the forties and fifties black teachers were asking for economic, not social, concessions. Teacher unionism in Atlanta was almost exclusively economic. Without violating the Southern mores that prohibited blacks and whites from mixing socially, white teachers could have acknowledged that their economic interests were identical to those of black teachers. There was already a precedent for such action: As former APSTA President J. P. Barron told his association in 1942, the AFT local in Louisville had helped raise money to equalize salaries, and there were further precedents for equalization in Baltimore, Maryland, Norfolk, Virginia, and Escambia County, Florida.[104] Black leader C. L. Harper indicated that Atlanta's black teachers would have accepted step-by-step equalization presented in an honest and straightforward way. Ignoring these precedents, white teachers turned their backs on their black coworkers and worked against their own long-term economic interests by myopically endorsing the school board's subterfuge of a unified salary schedule.

To be sure, it would have taken courage to ask Superintendent Sutton and the board to equalize salaries, but the APSTA was a force to be reckoned with in city politics. Local 89 had considerable influence in school board elections. Atlantans paid attention when teachers spoke out. Had white teachers chosen to speak to the salary issue in strictly economic terms— equal pay for equal work—they might have helped ease the racial tensions that plagued Atlanta and its public schools for years to come.

By the mid-fifties there were scattered signs of changing attitudes on race to counter entrenched resistance to integration. Ralph McGill was bringing a liberal editorial policy to the *Atlanta Constitution.* James O. Moore, president of the Atlanta Federation of Trades, was praising organized labor's new interest in civil rights in the *Journal of Labor.* While the Georgia legislature and state board of education were staunchly defending segregation, a new day was already dawning in Atlanta. Superintendent Jarrell and the Atlanta board were on record as accepting the *Brown* decision. To their credit, they never publicly beat the drums of racism that echoed through the New South in the wake of *Brown.* One black man was on the Atlanta board and another served as area superintendent. If some of the city's most respected business and professional leaders could sit next to a black man on the school board, couldn't white teachers sit with blacks in union meetings? Local 89 could have identified itself with these positive signs of change, as it had done in 1954 when it joined organized labor in opposition to the amendment to abolish public schools in Georgia. That step defied Governor Talmadge, the state legislature, and other brokers of political power, but the local suffered no reprisals. It was possible, then, to buck community standards yet still survive.[105]

The situation in Atlanta offered an exceptional opportunity for constructive leadership on the urgent matter of race relations. Writing in 1952, Floyd Hunter predicted "increased community conflict" unless Atlantans could find some means of communicating the needs of blacks to the dominant white power structure. Since black leaders held educational improvements as their top priority, an integrated teachers' union could have served as one of the interracial links Hunter sought.[106] The APSTA was numerically strong, on good terms with management, and had direct ties to the city's power structure through Jarrell and the school board. Local 89, the largest and most successful teachers' union in the South, was in a position to take a risk and lead on the race issue. Instead, the APSTA's career as an AFT local ended in 1956 on a bitter, disappointing note. Its history of race relations is a tragedy of unrealized potential and bypassed opportunities for leadership.

Notes

1. The two standard histories of the AFT are William Edward Eaton, *The American Federation of Teachers, 1916–1961: A History of the Move-*

ment (Carbondale, Ill.: Southern Illinois University Press, 1975) (hereafter cited as *AFT*) and Commission on Educational Reconstruction of the AFT, *Organizing the Teaching Profession: The Story of the American Federation of Teachers* (Glencoe, Ill.: Free Press, 1955). Both works pay attention to the race issue, but both emphasize the official position of the national union rather than the dissenting views of segregated locals in the South.

Founded in 1916, the AFT had black members almost from the outset. Most black teachers were in segregated locals, to be sure, but a few locals were integrated as early as the 1920s. The federation's journal, the *American Teacher*, published articles and editorials supporting improvements in black education before 1920, several of them written by black teacher unionists. Delegates to the AFT's 1919 convention asked Congress to increase its financial support of Howard University in the District of Columbia; in 1928 convention delegates called for a more favorable treatment of black history in the public schools. The influential New York City local elected Layle Lane its first black vice-president in 1935, and in 1938 Doxey Wilkerson, a professor at Howard University, became the first black vice-president of the AFT. In 1940 the federation supported a federal circuit court decision equalizing black and white teachers' salaries in Norfolk, Virginia (see note 27). The national union was an early advocate of federal aid to education as a means of equalizing educational opportunities for children of all races. These actions are documented in Eaton, pp. 61–70, and in H. A. Callis, "The Negro Teacher and the A. F. T.," *Journal of Negro Education* 6 (April 1937): 188–190.

The AFT's white locals in the South often opposed the federation's policies on race. As Sterling D. Spero and Abram L. Harris point out in *The Black Worker: The Negro and the Labor Movement* (New York: Columbia University Press: 1931), pp. 70–71, delegates from white Southern locals went to work behind the scenes at the 1929 convention to block the passage of two significant resolutions. One resolution called for the abolition of Jim Crow schools and advocated equal work for equal pay, regardless of a teacher's race; the other called for a special campaign to organize black teachers and favored the chartering of more integrated locals.

Organizing the Teaching Profession is a house history published just before the AFT's showdown with its segregated locals at the 1956 convention. This volume should be used with caution, for it paints a somewhat misleading picture of the union's Southern locals, implying more interest in improving race relations than available evidence (particularly the AFT's convention proceedings)supports. Students of teacher unionism are just beginning to shift their focus from the national to the local level. Detailed studies of the locals in Birmingham, Chattanooga, Louisville, Memphis, and New Orleans will be a major step toward a better understanding of teacher unionism in the South.

2. George B. Tindall gives Atlanta this title in his classic *The Emergence of the New South, 1913-1945* (Baton Rouge, La.: Louisiana State University Press, 1967), p. 99. This massive work, volume 10 of *A History of the South* edited by Wendell Holmes Stephenson and E. Merton Coulter, contains several chapters that are pertinent to Southern teacher unionism and race.

3. Joseph W. Newman, "A History of the Atlanta Public School Teachers' Association, Local 89 of the American Federation of Teachers, 1919-1956" (Ph.D. diss., Georgia State University, 1978). This chapter on teacher unionism and race is based on Chapters 2 and 7 of the dissertation.

4. Eaton, AFT, p. 160.

5. The history of teacher organizations in the South, like the larger field of Southern labor history, is finally receiving scholarly attention. Wayne J. Urban has produced several key studies, including "Organized Teachers and Educational Reform During the Progressive Era: 1890-1920," *History of Education Quarterly* 16 (Spring 1976): 35-52 and "Progressive Education in the Urban South: The Reform of the Atlanta Schools, 1914-1918," in *The Age of Urban Reform: New Perspectives on the Progressive Era*, ed. Michael H. Ebner and Eugene M. Tobin (Port Washington, N.Y.: Kennikat Press, 1977), pp. 131-141. Both of these studies contain material on Atlanta's teachers and the APSTA. Urban is now at work on a book that will include a chapter on the early years of the APSTA, 1905-19. My dissertation carries the association's history from 1919 through 1956. There is an obvious need for detailed studies of other teacher organizations in the South (see note 1).

The standard treatise on Southern labor history is F. Ray Marshall, *Labor in the South* (Cambridge: Harvard University Press, 1967). George B. Tindall's *The Emergence of the New South* has two chapters on organized labor and an excellent bibliography. John Samuel Ezell, *The South Since 1865* (New York: Macmillan Co., 1963), contains a useful chapter on labor. Mercer G. Evans, "The History of the Organized Labor Movement in Georgia" (Ph.D. diss., University of Chicago, 1929), provides a valuable account of the early history of the Georgia Federation of Labor and the Atlanta Federation of Trades. The APSTA, as a member of both organizations, occupies a prominent place in Evans' work. Other state-level studies of the labor movement include Ruth A. Allen, *Chapters in the History of Organized Labor in Texas*, in *University of Texas Publications*, No. 4143 (Austin: University of Texas Press, 1941); George H. Haines, "A History of the Virginia State Federation of Labor" (Ph.D. diss., Clark University, 1946); Harley E. Jolley, "The Labor Movement in North Carolina, 1880-1922," *North Carolina Historical Review* 30 (July 1953): 354-375; Donald C. Mosley, "A History of Labor Unions in Mississippi" (Ph.D. diss., University of Alabama, 1967); and Philip Taft, *Labor in Alabama* (the late scholar's unfinished manuscript now being prepared for publication by Gary M. Fink). Georgia State University is the home of the Southern Labor Archives, a growing collection of primary source material. The Southern Labor Studies Association, based at the Southern Labor Archives, is sponsoring an ongoing series of conferences on Southern labor history. Several papers presented at the first conference (1976) have been published in Gary M. Fink and Merl E. Reed, eds., *Essays in Southern Labor History*, (Westport Conn.: Greenwood Press, 1977). A forthcoming volume will contain selected papers presented at the second conference (1978), including my essay, "Mary C. Barker and the Atlanta Teachers' Union."

6. As Eaton, *AFT*, p. 171, points out, "Most AFT locals were organized by a minority of teachers within the system." His next sentence, however, goes a bit too far: "Where the AFT locals were able to organize over one-half of a district's teachers, such as in Atlanta . . . , the locals were able to translate the national platform into local programs." While this statement may be accurate in a very general sense, this chapter shows that Atlanta's white teacher unionists resented the AFT's progressive stand on race and never seriously attempted to implement it.

7. *Atlanta Constitution*, January 24, March 6 and 8, April 24, 1919 (hereafter cited as *Constitution*). The Atlanta press followed these events quite closely during the winter and spring of 1919. See also Philip N. Racine, "Atlanta's Schools: A History of the Public School System, 1869–1955" (Ph.D. diss. Emory University, 1969), pp. 179–190 and Melvin W. Ecke, *From Ivy Street to Kennedy Center: Centennial History of the Atlanta Public School System* (Atlanta, Ga.: Atlanta Board of Education, 1972), pp. 126–128.

8. Paul Lewinson, *Race, Class, and Party: A History of Negro Suffrage and White Politics in the South*, 2nd ed. (New York: Grosset & Dunlap, 1965, pp. 132–152; C. Vann Woodward, *The Strange Career of Jim Crow*, 3rd ed. rev. (New York: Oxford University Press, 1974), pp. 82–93.

9. Racine, "Atlanta's Schools," pp. 120–121.

10. Tabulations published in the *Constitution*, March 6 and April 24, 1919, show that bloc voting against the taxes in the city's two predominantly black wards was the decisive factor in the defeats. For further information see Walter White, *A Man Called White: The Autobiography of Walter White* (New York: Viking Press, 1948), pp. 29, 32–33; *Atlanta Independent*, February 8 and 15, March 8 and 22, April 12, 19, 26, 1919; Ecke, *From Ivy Street*, p. 461. (*Atlanta Independent* will hereafter be cited as *Independent*.) Edgar A. Toppin analyzes these events in "Walter White and the Atlanta NAACP's Fight for Equal Schools," *History of Education Quarterly* 7 (Spring 1967): 3–21. A recent book that provides an excellent historical context is John Dittmer, *Black Georgia in the Progressive Era, 1900–1920* (Urbana, Ill.: University of Illinois Press, 1977).

11. Atlanta Public School Teachers' Association, Minutes, May 12 and December 18, 1919 and January 12, 1920, Atlanta Education Association Collection, Box 10, Southern Labor Archives, Georgia State University.

(Minutes of the Atlanta Public School Teachers' Association will hereafter be cited as APSTA Minutes.)

12. APSTA Minutes, November 10, 1919; *Journal of Labor* (official organ of the Atlanta Federation of Trades), December 5, 1919; *Constitution,* January 21, 1920; Atlanta Board of Education, Minutes, January 20, 1920. (Minutes of the Atlanta Board of Education will hereafter be cited as School Board Minutes.)

13. *Constitution*, January 21, 1920.

14. *Journal of Labor*, October 10, 17, 24, 31 and December 5, 1919. The Atlanta Federation of Trades initiated the proposal for a bond referendum, a plan that was quickly endorsed by civic clubs, business groups, and political leaders throughout the city.

15. School Board Minutes, January 29, 1920; *Constitution*, January 31, 1920; *Journal of Labor*, January 30, 1920.

16. *Journal of Labor*, January 30, 1920.

17. *Constitution*, February 1, 6, 15, 1920; School Board Minutes, January 31 and February 14, 1920. The APSTA stated that it had no objections to the board's adding to the raises for black teachers if the board could do so without cutting the raises for white teachers. "If we erred in making the minimum for the negro teachers too low it was not because we underestimated the value of their work, but because we felt that there might be a chance to secure $10 for them, but no more." See *Constitution*, February 3, 1920.

18. Racine, "Atlanta's Schools," p. 184; *Independent*, February 3, 1921; *Constitution*, March 9, 1921.

19. APSTA Minutes, April 12, 1920 (incorrectly designated April 12, 1919).

20. Barker was an exceptional woman, an activist whose social and political views disturbed and eventually alienated many of her Atlanta colleagues. A member of the American Civil Liberties Union, Urban League, and Commission on Interracial Cooperation, she was one of the few white teachers who maintained a cordial relationship with the Gate City Teachers' Association. It is ironic that Barker, a member of a conservative Southern local, helped move the AFT toward its advanced position on race. During her presidency the federation passed several resolutions in support of racial tolerance and better schools for blacks. I have analyzed some of her activities in Atlanta in my forthcoming essay "Mary C. Barker and the Atlanta Teachers' Union" (see note 5) and my paper "Grassroots Professionalism and Atlanta's Teachers, 1921–29," presented to Division F, American Educational Research Association, San Francisco, April 11, 1979.

Allie Mann, by contrast, was in the mainstream of teacher unionism in Atlanta. More popular than Barker within their own local, Mann was a bread-and-butter unionist who believed strongly in racial segregation. She played a key role in the AFT's bouts with communism and the Committee for Industrial Organization (CIO) during the thirties. See Newman, "A History of the Atlanta Public School Teachers' Association," Chapters 5 and 7.

21. Material on Ira Jarrell in this section is based on Newman, "A History of the Atlanta Public School Teachers' Association," Chapter 6. Charles Strickland has prepared a biography of Jarrell for a forthcoming volume of *Notable American Women*.

22. Floyd Hunter, *Community Power Structure: A Study of Decision Makers* (Chapel Hill, N.C.: University of North Carolina Press, 1953). See especially pp. 60–113. Hunter's study broke important new ground in the fields of political science and sociology.

23. I chose the term "quasi company union" to suggest the local's direct ties to management through Superintendent Jarrell. Since the APSTA was not *officially* sponsored and controlled by management, it does not meet the National Labor Relations Board's technical definition of a company union.

24. *Jim Crow*, Woodward, pp. 118–119.

25. Racine, "Atlanta's Schools," pp. 256–257.

26. *Atlanta Daily World*, August 31 and September 2, 4–6, 1940; APSTA Executive Board, Minutes, June 29, 1940, Atlanta Education Association Collection, Box 10, Southern Labor Archives, Georgia State University; Ecke, *AFT*, pp. 260–261; Racine, "Atlanta's Schools," p. 257. (*Atlanta Daily World* will hereafter be cited as *Daily World*. Minutes of the APSTA's Executive Board will hereafter be cited as Executive Board Minutes.)

27. See, for example, *Daily World*, February 7, 12, 15, 16, 18, 20, 23, 25, 1941; Ecke, *From Ivy Street*, p. 261. Tindall, *Emergence of the New South*, pp. 563–564, provides a general account of the quest for salary equalization. Black teachers in Maryland and Virginia led the way. In 1939 a federal district court ruled that minimum salaries for black teachers in Anne Arundel County, Maryland, should be no less than the minimum for white teachers. Other Maryland school systems settled out of court, and the state legislature passed an equalization law in 1941. A 1940 federal circuit court decision in favor of black teachers in Norfolk, Virginia, stimulated voluntary equalization plans in many school systems across the state. While Kentucky, Tennessee, Texas, and North Carolina moved toward equalization, Georgia and several other states in the Deep South lagged behind. For further information see Dewey Allen Stokes, Jr., "Negro Education and Federal Courts" (M.A. thesis, University of North Carolina, 1955) and Bernard H. Nelson, *The Fourteenth Amendment and the Negro Since 1920* (Washington, D.C.: Catholic University of America Press, 1946).

28. Racine, "Atlanta's Schools," p. 283, provides information on black-white salary disparities in the early forties. The board of education might have avoided some of these difficulties had it followed up on a much earlier sequence of events. During the 1920 confrontation over raises for black and white teachers (described in section 2 of this chapter), the board had instructed the superintendent to prepare a salary schedule for black teachers based on both seniority and education. Unfortunately, the board did not adopt such a schedule and continued to pay black

teachers on the basis of seniority alone. See School Board Minutes, February 14, 1920.

29. Executive Board Minutes, February 6, 1941; APSTA Minutes, February 10, 1941; School Board Minutes, February 11, 1941.

30. APSTA Minutes, February 10, 1941.

31. *Daily World*, February 5 and 16, 1941.

32. School Board Minutes, May 13, 1941; *Daily World*, April 10-13, 1941; Racine, "Atlanta's Schools," pp. 305-306; Ecke, *From Ivy Street*, pp. 194, 261-262. The Georgia State Teachers' Association, soon renamed the Georgia Teachers and Educational Association, had ties to the National Education Association (NEA). The NEA allowed black teachers' associations to affiliate indirectly, but black teachers held their own state conventions. The American Teachers Association, a national organization for black teachers, also maintained ties to the NEA although it was not allowed direct representation at NEA conventions until the 1950s. The two national organizations finally merged in 1966. See Eaton, *AFT*, pp. 64-66; Rolland L. Dewing, "Teacher Organizations and Desegregation, 1954-1964" (Ph.D. diss., Ball State University, 1967), pp. 61-62; and Michael John Schultz, Jr., *The National Education Association and the Black Teacher: The Integration of a Professional Organization* (Coral Gables, Fla.: University of Miami Press, 1970), pp. 57-65, 156-157, 174-175.

  The *Journal of Negro Education* is an excellent source of information on black teachers and their organizations. See, for example, H. A. Callis, "The Negro Teacher and the A. F. T.," *Journal of Negro Education* 6 (April 1937): 188-190; Walter G. Daniel and Marion T. Wright, "The Role of Educational Agencies in Maintaining Morale among Negroes," *Journal of Negro Education* 12 (Summer 1943): 490-501; and Layle Lane, "Report of the Committee on Cultural Minorities of the American Federation of Teachers," *Journal of Negro Education* 14 (Winter 1945): 109-112. News columns, articles, and editorials in the AFT's *American Teacher* are valuable as well. Some examples are Julian S. Hughson, "The Negro and Educational Reconstruction in the South," *American Teacher* 8 (April 1919): 82-85; Layle Lane, "Negro Teachers Win Fight for Equal Pay," *American Teacher* 25 (February 1941): 5-6; and Charles H. Thompson, "Needed—An Educational New Deal for the Negro," *American Teacher* 21 (March-April 937): 24-27.

33. *Independent*, April 10, 1925; Racine, "Atlanta's Schools," pp. 266-267. Sutton, who had been president of the APSTA in 1917-18, served as Atlanta's superintendent from 1921 through 1944. For a sympathetic treatment of Sutton's superintendency see Racine, "A Progressive Fights Efficiency: The Survival of Willis Sutton, School Superintendent," *South Atlantic Quarterly* 76 (Winter 1977): 103-116 and "Willis Anderson Sutton and Progressive Education, 1921-1943," *Atlanta Historical Bulletin* 20 (Spring 1976): 9-23.

34. School Board Minutes, May 13, 1941. See also Ecke, *From Ivy Street*, p. 264.

35. Executive Board Minutes, June 23, 1941.
36. School Board Minutes, July 17, 1941.
37. Quoted in Racine, "Atlanta's Schools," p. 306.
38. Ibid., p. 308.
39. Ibid., p. 309.
40. APSTA Minutes, December 8, 1941; School Board Minutes, December 9, 1941 and January 27, 1942; Racine, "Atlanta's Schools," p. 309.
41. Harper to Jarrell, January 9, 1942, Atlanta Education Associaton Collection, Box 24, Folder "Salary." (Atlanta Education Association Collection will hereafter be cited as AEA, specifying box and folder.)
42. Quoted in Racine, "Atlanta's Schools," p. 309.
43. *Daily World*, February 18, 1942.
44. APSTA Minutes, December 8, 1941 and February 27, 1942; Executive Board Minutes, December 5, 1941.
45. APSTA Minutes, February 27, 1942.
46. Verbatim transcripts of speeches made by Sutton, Board President Ed Cook, and Mary Barker have been preserved in AEA, Box 24, Folder "Salary."
47. Ibid.
48. APSTA Minutes, February 27, 1942; School Board Minutes, February 28, 1942.
49. See note 46.
50. APSTA Minutes, February 27, 1942. After Barron left the school system in 1942 and Barker retired in 1944, the local had no members who were willing to challenge Jarrell and the board of education on the race issue.
51. *Daily World*, February 18 through March 6, 1942; Racine, "Atlanta's Schools," pp. 310–311.
52. School Board Minutes, June 13, 1944.
53. Typed list on APSTA stationery headed "My Opinion—H. I. J.," AEA, Box 24, Folder "Salary."
54. The working papers are in AEA, Box 24, Folder "Salary."
55. Ibid.; APSTA Minutes, December 8, 1941.
56. See note 54. The school board's annual budgets during the 1940s show that the board's attitude toward black teachers, not its financial position, was the major obstacle to equalization. The board carried a surplus of $342,000 into 1944 (the year the unified salary schedule was adopted) and a surplus of $773,000 into 1947. See School Board Minutes, January 3, 1944 and January 10, 1947.
57. While the unified schedule fooled neither black nor white teachers as to its actual effect, it misled the authors of the two most comprehensive histories of the Atlanta public schools. Philip Racine describes the schedule as "equalization of salaries" and "the first major improvement in Negro education since 1872" in his study, "Atlanta's Schools," p. 311. Racine bases his conclusion, in part, on an interview with Ira Jarrell. Melvin Ecke is just as enthusiastic about the schedule in his detailed history of the school system: "Of course, the major signifi-

cance of the new schedule was its equalization of salaries for *all* teachers, white and black alike. Black teachers had been striving to attain that goal since 1872" (*From Ivy Street*, p. 276). Certainly the schedule was a step forward, for at least it placed black and white teachers on the same scale. But it obviously did not accomplish equalization of salaries, nor did the board intend it to.

58. Racine, "Atlanta's Schools," pp. 311–316; Ecke, *From Ivy Street,* pp. 281–288. Blacks had good reason to be wary of white promises, for the board had broken the promise to spend one-third of the 1921 bond issue to improve black schools. During the late twenties the board had added insult to injury by breaking yet another promise to blacks concerning the expenditure of bond revenues. See Racine, "Atlanta's Schools," pp. 254–255.

59. APSTA Minutes, December 11, 1944 and February 12, 1945; Irvin R. Kuenzli (secretary-treasurer of the AFT) to Smith, June 2, 1945 and Kuenzli to W. Paul Smartt (organizer for the Georgia Federation of Labor), June 13, 1945, AEA, Box 18, Folder "Capitol Co. Negro Local."

60. APSTA Minutes, November 12, 1945. See also Executive Board Minutes, November 10, 1945.

61. See AEA, Box 18, Folder "E. H. Lawson, Negro Organizer."

62. APSTA Minutes, December 10, 1945, May 13, 1946, May 12, 1947; Executive Board Minutes, February 9, 1946 and May 10, 1947.

63. APSTA Minutes, December 8, 1947. Early in 1947 the school board had deposited $500,000, enough money to close the gap between black and white teachers' salaries, in a local bank. See School Board Minutes, January 10, 1947.

64. APSTA Minutes, October 2, 11, 20, 1926, June 1 and October 13, 1927, December 8, 1947; School Board Minutes, September 14 and October 12, 1948; Racine, "Atlanta's Schools," pp. 316–318; Ecke, *From Ivy Street*, pp. 297–299. Ecke, p. 199, notes that Underwood was a former U. S. assistant attorney general who had graduated from Vanderbilt Law School and had practiced law in Atlanta since 1903.

65. APSTA Minutes, October 11, 1948 and January 10, 1949.

66. AEA, Box 18, Folder "E. H. Lawson, Negro Organizer" documents the close cooperation between Lawson and Local 89's officers.

67. Irving E. Fullington (a white AFT vice-president from Birmingham) to Kuenzli, March 28, 1950, AEA, Box 8, Folder "Areas Assigned to V. Pres American Federation of Teachers." Fullington's letter provides detailed information on organizing the new black local.

68. APSTA Minutes, April 17, 1950.

69. Sutton to B. W. Wells, January 23, 1934, AEA, Box 2, Folder "Sanders, Outgoing 1933–34"; form letter from Mann as GEA president, n.d. (evidently written during the 1934–35 school year), AEA, Box 4, Folder "Mann, Miss Allie B." G. Y. Smith predicted as early as October, 1947, that Southern locals would have to integrate if they wished to remain in the AFT. APSTA Minutes, October 13, 1947.

70. APSTA Minutes, March 12, 1951; Executive Board Minutes, March 8, 1951.

71. "Reports of Vice-Presidents to the American Federation of Teachers, July 1950 through June 1951," AEA, Box 8, Folder "Areas Assigned to V. Pres American Federation of Teachers."

72. Quoted in Schultz, *NEA and the Black Teacher*, p. 70.

73. See ibid., Chapters 3 and 4. For further analysis of the NEA's position on race see Lloyd P. Jorgenson, "The Social and Economic Orientation of the National Education Association," *Progressive Education* 34 (July 1957): 98–101; Myron Lieberman, "Segregation's Challenge to the NEA," *School and Society* 81 (May 28, 1955): 167–168 and "Civil Rights and the NEA," *School and Society* 85 (May 11, 1957): 166–169; and Edgar B. Wesley, *NEA: The First Hundred Years. The Building of the Teaching Profession* (New York: Harper & Bros., 1957).

74. "Reports of Vice Presidents to the American Federation of Teachers, July 1950 thru June 1951." Fullington predicted that the AFT's insistence on integration would cost it dearly in the South.

75. APSTA Minutes, March 12 and September 24, 1951, April 7, 1952; Jarrell to principals, February 26, 1951, AEA, Box 19, Folder "G. E. A."; *Journal of Labor*, December 16, 1955.

76. James Earl Clarke, "The American Federation of Teachers: Origins and History from 1870 to 1952" (Ph.D. diss., Cornell University, 1966), pp. 369–373; Eaton, *AFT*, pp. 128–129; APSTA Minutes, October 8, 1945 and February 10, 1947; Executive Board Minutes, January 11, 1947; O. H. Morris (a vice-president of the APSTA) to Annie Laurie Millsaps, September 17, 1953, AEA, Box 1, Folder "O. H. Morris, 1953–1954."

77. APSTA Minutes, October 13, 1947.

78. See Clarke, "AFT: Origins and History," pp. 368–369.

79. APSTA Minutes, October 13, 1947.

80. Clarke, "AFT: Origins and History," pp. 369–373.

81. Executive Board Minutes, August 31, 1950.

82. Fullington to Kuenzli, March 28, 1950; Eaton, *AFT*, p. 159.

83. Eaton, *AFT*, pp. 128–129, 174–175; Walter Werre (a member of the Chicago local) to Floyd, May 21, 1952, AEA, Box 1, Folder "1952–1953, President—Mrs. Dorothy Floyd"; American Federation of Teachers, *Report of the Proceedings of the Thirty-Fourth Annual Convention* (Chicago: published by the AFT, 1951), pp. 54, 73, and *Report of the Proceedings of the Thirty-Fifth Annual Convention* (Chicago: published by the AFT, 1952), pp. 102–103, 128. (Proceedings of the annual conventions will hereafter be cited as *AFT Convention Proceedings*, specifying year and pages.)

84. *AFT Convention Proceedings* (1953), p. 24.

85. Ibid., pp. 26–27, 45.

86. Executive Board Minutes, August 25, 1953 (see also September 16, 1953).

87. APSTA Minutes, October 12, 1953; Executive Board Minutes, September 16, 1953.

88. Executive Board Minutes, December 10, 1953; APSTA Minutes, December 14, 1953, September 29 and October 11, 1954; Woodward, *Jim Crow*, p. 158; *Journal of Labor*, October 29, 1954.

89. *AFT Convention Proceedings* (1954), pp. 142–147.

90. Executive Board Minutes, February 9, 1955; *AFT Convention Proceedings* (1955), pp. 129–130; Racine, "Atlanta's Schools," pp. 318–320; Ecke, *From Ivy Street*, pp. 316–317, 325–326. Clement received a large number of white votes throughout the city and easily won his seat. Eaton, *AFT*, pp. 174–175, analyzes the alliance between the Atlanta and Chicago locals, both successful bread-and-butter unions. Rolland Dewing, "The American Federation of Teachers and Desegregation," *Journal of Negro Education* 42 (Winter 1973): 82–87, documents Megel's desire to approach the integration of Southern locals with a policy of "patience without complacency."

91. *AFT Convention Proceedings* (1955), p. 129.

92. Ibid., pp. 141–145.

93. Executive Board Minutes, October 31, 1955; APSTA Minutes, November 14, 1955.

94. APSTA Minutes, January 9, 1956. Derthick succeeded Dorothy Floyd as president in 1955.

95. APSTA Minutes, May 14, 1956. See also Executive Board Minutes, May 7, 1956.

96. An account of the May 14 meeting appeared in the *Journal of Labor* on May 18, 1956.

97. APSTA Minutes, May 14, 1956.

98. *AFT Convention Proceedings* (1956), pp. 22–23; Dewing, "The American Federation of Teachers and Desegregation," p. 84.

99. *AFT Convention Proceedings* (1956), pp. 26–29.

100. Ibid., pp. 46–50.

101. Ibid., pp. 58–61.

102. Resolutions attached to APSTA Minutes, December 10, 1956. The AFT soon chartered an integrated local in the Atlanta public schools. After two decades as a minority movement, the local now appears to be challenging the NEA affiliate for the allegiance of Atlanta's teachers. The white locals in Fulton County and New Orleans voted to leave the federation in the fall of 1957. Chattanooga's white local appealed to the union to allow it to continue on a segregated basis, but delegates to the 1958 convention revoked the charter. The black locals in Fulton County, New Orleans, and Chattanooga agreed to integrate and remained in the federation. See Dewing, "The American Federation of Teachers and Desegregation," pp. 88–89.

103. APSTA Minutes, January 9, 1950 and November 12, 1951; Racine, "Atlanta's Schools," p. 311; Dewing, "The American Federation of Teachers and Desegregation," p. 83; Ecke, *From Ivy Street*, pp. 364–367.

104. Tindall, *Emergence of the New South*, pp. 563–564; *Daily World*, February 16 and May 22, 1941; February 19, 1942.
105. Woodward, *Jim Crow*, p. 126; *Journal of Labor*, February 4, 1955. Ray Marshall, *Labor in the South*, pp. 336–337, observes that "a forthright equalitarian racial position" helped some unions (for example, the Teamsters in Georgia) gain strength in the South during the fifties and sixties. See also Marshall, *The Negro and Organized Labor* (New York: John Wiley & Sons, 1965).
106. Hunter, *Community Power Structure*, p. 223.

William Bonds Thomas

Guidance and Testing: An Illusion of Reform in Southern Black Schools and Colleges

Introduction

The Southern drive for reform and modernization in the 1920s and 30s held significant consequences for the education of blacks in that region. Possibilities of mechanized agricultural and industrial production rivaling Northern advances[1] created new and alluring prospects of educational change. Interest in universal education as a mark of progress justified a tax-supported educational structure to serve the masses, especially those who had migrated from agrarian regions to urban centers.[2] Most importantly, reforms in educational organization and funding followed as growing educational bureaucracies at the state level sought to expand and centralize their powers over local systems in a major step toward modernizing educational programs to keep pace with social change.[3] At least implicitly, black schools now stood to gain a fairer share of their respective states' educational support for more differentiated, "progressive" curricula, new services from state supervisors, and scientific research on pupil personnel by expanding testing bureaus.

Lured by these new prospects, Southern black educators reiterated old but crucial questions regarding the ends for which black youth were to be educated. Would, for example, the adjustment problems of blacks, caused by social change and identified by researchers, require special attention within their schools?[4] Would young people now realize the benefits, previously denied in segregated schools, of a new and thriving Southern economy? Finally, there was the question of power and influence. To what extent, some asked, would blacks be able to direct their own educational programs to these ends?[5] Such questions were crucial, especially as prosperity gave way to a depression, which exacerbated the traditionally marginal status of black schools when they encountered educational retrenchment in the face of increased student enrollment and student-teacher ratios.[6] Considering (1) historical racial and social class antipathies, existing within the framework of an emerging New South; (2) state efforts to gain centralized control over local educational structures; (3) what seemed to be immense possibilities of new commitments to black education, implied in policy statements at state levels; and (4) the morass into which the Depression cast the national economy —this chapter will be concerned with how Southern black schools responded to social and economic conditions emerging from these circumstances.

One response to these exigencies was the use of intelligence testing and guidance as integral parts of the educational programs in Southern schools. The intricate and extensive network between guidance in Southern black schools and the realities of the South in the 1930s cannot be explored fully in a short essay. This chapter will therefore focus upon why intelligence testing, as an integral tool of guidance, became institutionalized in a number of black schools during the 1930s. Some of the rhetorical underpinnings of the testing movement will be explored to determine the goals of the guidance movement and how testing may have been used to foster these ends.

This essay contends that black educators adopted testing and guidance within their schools only partly as measures of modernization and progressive reform. More significantly, their adoption was largely a response to exigencies not unlike those confronting Northern urban centers in the late nineteenth and early twentieth centuries, when they, too, underwent similar social and economic transformations.[7] Guidance was an important consequence of a transforming social order,[8] and many educators, both black and white, viewed it as a viable means for *adjusting* black youths to Southern folkways and to the harsh realities of racism, elitism, and unemployment.

It is also important to understand that some black educators perceived the 1930s as a propitious era in which to build a black-controlled bureaucratic superstructure as a vehicle for increasing their influence.[9] This hope reflected a shift in the responsibility for the education of blacks, for there was, in fact, a "Southern Compromise" between the need for modernization and reform and a white hope that racist traditions of segregation would be preserved under the guise of new theories of "biracialism." Horace Mann Bond viewed this accommodation as allowing blacks to "handle their own affairs" within their educational communities.[10] One result was that blacks were drawn into a process of sorting and selecting black youths through intelligence testing and guidance. The inevitable outcome was the perpetuation of the status quo. Illusions of reform in social and economic relationships served social functions which were, at the least, paradoxical, and at most, tied tragically to the inherent contradictions in the region's political economy. Thus, the South, "a region theoretically the most democratic in its clamor for the rights of the common man,"[11] attempted to reconcile progressive reform and the continued status of blacks and poor whites. To understand these phenomena, it is important to look at the application of guidance and testing in the public secondary schools for blacks.

The Growth of Secondary Schools for Blacks

By the late 1930s the South had successfully built an extensive program of public education. The number of public secondary schools for blacks had increased from an estimated 91 in 1915 to a phenomenal 2,188.[12] Indeed, by as early as 1930, 79,388 black youths were already enrolled in public high schools in ten Southern states.[13] A number of factors contributed to this massive building program. In the first place, modernization provided greater access to resources of opportunity and status for the individual and the community. As whites upgraded their educational system on a regional basis, they could no longer justify denying education to blacks, especially since educational reform in the United States had been justified by "democratic" rhetoric. Sociologist Howard W. Odum, a leading spokesperson in the regionalization and modernization drive, asserted that

> The time has come to design events which should now set in motion
> processes which will result in the desired transformation of certain
> of the present regional unfair practices. . . , of race segregation, in
> economic and cultural relationships between the whites and Negroes
> of the South, in practices relating to the millions of farm tenants,
> or in the differentiated wage rate and standards of living and
> housing.[14]

As high schools became more available, increasing numbers of blacks maintained the traditional belief that education and individual achievement would yield greater benefits, diminishing emphasis on family status and race. Therefore, the dramatic increase in schools logically led to rising expectations.

The economic demands of World War I and the prosperity of the 1920s in industrial and agricultural communities had created a somewhat less impoverished class of blacks and whites. Thus, they could carry a greater portion of the tax burden.[15] This was accompanied by less white hostility to the indirect subsidy of black education.[16] A modernizing South had created more complex and subtle forms of public "support."

Finally, rising pupil enrollments were reassuring proof that large numbers of black youths were either returning to school for further educational training or were extending their schooling from elementary to secondary levels rather than joining the constricted Depression-era job market.[17] In the competition for remaining jobs in the Depression, black workers were being displaced in both the North and South in those occupational slots which had traditionally been labelled "Negro jobs."[18] The Depression forced vast numbers of disillusioned youth, who had sought employment in a world of economic collapse, to return to school for lack of any place to go or anything else to do.[19] Education was a safety valve against both economic and social conflict and was well worth its price.

These conditions, compounded by technological advancement and by the longstanding refusal of some labor unions to accept blacks into their ranks[20] affected not only blacks. The Conference on Fundamentals in the Education of Negroes at its 1934 meeting stated that "Unless we moderns can learn to use creatively the leisure—voluntary and enforced—that the machine is giving us, civilization as we know it will go to pieces.[21]

Problems from the Growth of Secondary Schools

Educators were challenged by the proliferation of schools and students. For example, how would a heterogeneous student population, continually entering secondary schools from agricultural and industrial working class families, affect the traditional mission of secondary schools? Formerly, black high schools were private and denominational academies, preparing youths for higher studies in such professions as teaching, medicine, law, and the ministry. Access to these schools had also been largely restricted to students who came from middle income families and had superior educational achievements.

Under the new massive building program, the traditional ladder of success from elementary school through college to the professions would no longer hold under the weight of the new demands being pressed upon the schools. Educators recognized that not all high school graduates could or would attend college and that there would not be room in the professions for the masses of potential college graduates who would soon engulf the job market.[22]

Moreover, schools had become overcrowded,[23] and student attrition was quite high at the secondary level.[24] A much higher percentage of students wanted to attend college in 1930 than in previous decades;[25] however, many of them did not finish high school. Educators worried about the better-than-average students from poor families who were unable to afford college but were pursuing college preparatory curricula which had little utilitarian function.[26] Tragically, they would not assume those leadership positions to which they had aspired.

Indeed, college entrance requirements continued to play an all-too-important role in the high school curriculum.[27] The relative smallness of the high schools often made adequate diversification of curriculum offerings impractical. Furthermore, the correlation between schooling and the rather circumscribed occupational levels at which blacks were finding jobs in the larger community was low.

A final set of problems stemmed from the growth of public high schools. The heterogeneous mixture of students introduced the school to many health problems, differing social attitudes, and the difficulties inherent in a wide range of mental aptitudes. These changes had a major impact upon high schools throughout the nation.[28] The Advisory Committee on Negro Schools in Virginia, calling for curricular adjustments to meet the social problems stemming from segregation, reported that black youths were compelled to live in the most unhealthful areas of the community.[29]

Black educators reassessed the role of their schools in light of new requirements for moral education. In fact, Gertrude H. Woodard, then Dean of Women at Miner Teacher's College in Washington, D.C., addressed the forty-fourth Annual Convention of the State Teachers Association for black educators in 1932 and asserted that

> Character education is a comparatively new thing in public schools. . . . Attempts have always been made to adjust the youth to the existing order, to the complexities of the present-day group life. It seems that the school, more than any other force, is being compelled to assume direct responsibility for the training that will accomplish this result. The home is no longer the training force that it used to be.[30]

The burdens facing the schools were immense. Since there were no special facilities for taking care of students who were labelled "mentally deranged" and "maladjusted," it also became the responsibility of the public school teacher to shape them into the people which society expected. The fact that blacks had shown a remarkable inclination toward extending their elementary education meant that secondary schools, traditionally steeped in academic formalism, would be required to revise their programs of study to meet current conditions.

Under these circumstances, the approach to education became one of stark realism. As Ambrose Caliver stated in 1933, it was a matter of "Negro educators acknowledging the situation, facing the facts, and devising ways and means of facilitating the personal and social integration of the race."[31] Such approaches were aimed primarily at adjusting black youth to a *Zeitgest*, and for many, guidance and testing were the best means to these ends.

Guidance for Economic and Social Adjustment

ECONOMIC ISSUES

Educational and vocational guidance on every educational level was a significant aid in assuring the satisfactory adjustment of black youths to the social and economic realities of the times. There was a dearth of guidance programs in the 1930s throughout the South,[32] although questions were being raised concerning the occupations to which black youths should be directed by teachers and counselors. An additional and interrelated issue was whether vocational guidance of blacks should be in terms of the status quo or whether it should seek to direct pupils toward new vocations.[33] Should vocational guidance of black youths assume that blacks provided certain professional services for other blacks more adequately than whites under a system of segregation?[34] Finally, black educators asked whether the education of rural black children in the South should seek deliberately to facilitate adaptation to urban life or be oriented to rural life.[35] This last question was particularly difficult in light of the continuing "push-pull" influences of the countryside and urban centers.[36]

The central philosophical issue was the extent to which education, vocational training, and guidance of blacks could and should serve as telic forces capable of changing the status of blacks in America. Some saw the role of guidance to be like that of the curriculum: as a means to improve the position of blacks living under the status quo. They had only to point with optimism to the 1930 Census Report for evidence that guidance could assist black youths in finding their niche in the segregated economic structure. The data showed that of 534 occupations listed, there were only four in which blacks were not found.[37] Under this assumption, black youths were told that "the individual was the principal arbiter of his fate" and that "merit, rather than influence, was an applicant's surest asset." Urging black youths to "crash the color line," the Urban League's Vocational Opportunity Campaign asserted, "What others have done, you too can do!"[38]

Howard Hale Long addressed the impact which artificially imposed social and economic restrictions were having upon black youths. As Assistant Superintendent for Research in the Washington D.C. public schools, he asserted that

> There must be a compromise of ambition, interest, and ability so long as the status quo [remains] in the American pattern. How gracefully to yield to the apparently inevitable without becoming off-guard for the escapes and vulnerable points of the status quo requires a technique and philosophy which need to be developed in the Negro. . . . [He] must learn how to yield only what he has to and in yielding not undergo a complete effacement.[39]

There were also those who rejected the status quo philosophy. For example, Horace Mann Bond recognized the immense potential for effective guidance and educational programs to lead the nation to a new and democratic order. Black youths could be taught to cope with larger problems of life that transcended economic uplift and survival on Southern terms. This philosophy addressed itself to how the total educational structure, both academic and vocational, might work toward goals of full citizenship for all Americans. It sought further to reexamine and reassess the role of guidance as a catalyst for change in a society which was hostile not only to blacks but to the economically dispossessed whites as well. Bond held that the school and its curriculum which maintained the status quo "presupposed an elastic, democratic social order in which there [were] no artificial barriers set against the social and economic mobility of the individual."[40]

Underlying the conflicting philosophies regarding the guidance of black youths was the certainty, as Charles H. Thompson, editor of the *Journal of Negro Education*, wrote in 1935, that "the occupational future of the Negro is inextricably bound up with that of all other workers in the country without consideration of race, and . . . only a policy of vocational guidance which recognizes this fact can be of a real value to Negroes."[41] This and the assertions of Doxey Wilkerson reached the very heart of the matter of caste and class in America. Writing in 1937 on "American Caste and the Social Studies Curriculum," Wilkerson contended that

> It is essential for the Negro to realize that his social proscriptions exist, not *merely because he is a Negro* [emphasis his]; but rather because he, in a system which affords a scarcity of jobs for all workers, happens to be the most "highly visible" economic competitor. [He is] a superstructure erected upon an economic base, a means of social control whose fundamental end is greater economic security for the white caste. So long as an economy of scarcity jeopardizes the welfare of the masses of white workers, just so long will strictly "racial" techniques of emergence remain impotent substantially to achieve their goal. . . . Both groups, the white and the Negro, respond to economic forces in exactly the same manner. Together do they advance in times of prosperity; together do they recede in times of depression. [The gap between whites and Negroes] can never be substantially closed until there is markedly increased economic security for all workers.[42]

SOCIAL ISSUES

In addition to the philosophical considerations over the economic adjustment of black youths, there were similar concerns over their social adaptation, bound inextricably to their economic status. The focus was on development of personality and character to survive in the South. Some black educators were in strategic positions to direct these ends. As members of such recommending bodies as the Advisory Committee on Negro Schools in Virginia and the Association of Colleges and Secondary Schools for Negroes, they were charged with defining and calling attention to *social* problems resulting from the biracial character of the South.[43] The process of adaptation to segregation placed an awesome burden upon blacks to adjust to situations which were neither of their own making, nor of their own wishes, nor in their own best interests.

For some educators teaching blacks, the solution lay in educational guidance and in applying the social sciences to practical life situations. These subjects could be used to foster biracial cooperation and understanding, good citizenship, and the development of good character and personality traits. For example, V. V. Oak,[44] speaking in 1938 before the North Carolina Negro Teachers Association, embraced the philosophy of continued emphasis on black capitalism, but only in those fields that were open to blacks. He called for black schools to delete from their economics curriculum courses emphasizing the history of economic thought and the economic theories of Marx and Veblen. Their ideas, Oak believed, were "too abstract and philosophic" for black students to digest. He recommended that blacks be steered into basic courses, stressing banking, business finance, insurance, real estate, and other subjects categorized as "applied economics." They were to be guided away from courses in cost accounting, investments, income tax, and corporation accounting, for such subjects were irrelevant to their needs.

Oak, who was born in India, took strong exception to those teachers who expounded too enthusiastically the doctrines of socialism. "Because of the Negro's social as well as economic oppression," he wrote, "our students are quite responsive to radical thoughts and ideas since these offer, at least in theory, both economic as well as social equality."

There were other educators, who, like Oak, believed accommodation to be the best means for adjusting black youths to Southern traditions. They suggested that blacks, being faced with the realities of caste and class, should take full advantage of what was available to them under the present system of segregation. Living within this social context, they might work toward its eventual transformation. For example, in 1936 Charles S. Johnson, Director of the National Urban League and later president of Fisk University, assumed that the present position of American blacks held certain strategic advantages. Since they were forced to live and compete in two worlds, they were "cultural hybrids." This situation, according to Johnson, presented a particular challenge to black education. While opposed to the idea of segregation, he believed, paradoxically, that education and guidance could fortify the black's personality against its insidious influences.[45] Frederick D. Patterson, president of Tuskegee Institute, wrote in 1938 on the necessity of blacks to capitalize upon the perpetual circumstances of economic marginality and low social caste under which they lived. He believed that a "hardy people is one that thrives on adversity, and in so doing will be capable of turning the apparent barreness of economic opportunity and the change of social expression to good account."[46]

One way to assure good citizenship and character in black youth was through recreational facilities. Given the scarceness of such facilities for blacks, black educators raised questions on how to curb problems of crime and juvenile delinquency among black youths.[47] Every kind of antisocial behavior was a further indication of the need for social adjustment. Gertrude Woodard noted as early as 1932 that

> No longer can we expect boys and girls to acquire habits of industry and thoroughness through regular home duties. The day is past when home pleasures and associations are the means of developing courtesy, kindness, and self-control; when there were time and opportunity for the development of parent-child relationships which resulted in loyalty, cooperation, reverence, and respect. Yet, these, and other desirable character traits *must* be developed if our boys and girls are to become good citizens.[48]

Actually, such concerns were beginning to generate research in black graduate schools. At Atlanta, Alabama State, Howard, Fisk, and Hampton, elementary and secondary school teachers pursued graduate degrees with theses correlating personality with the vocational interests, achievements, and intelligence of Southern black youth.[49] Such research was particularly significant since black youths had favored professional and semi-professional jobs, even though they could expect neither equal opportunity nor easy success in education, medicine, and law.

Black educators, including Charlotte Hawkins Brown, president of Palmer Memorial Institute in North Carolina, and W. W. Sanders, executive secretary of the National Association of Teachers in Colored Schools, knew that black graduates and nongraduates alike would face a "wall of concrete" in their social adjustment, particularly as they sought to enter the occupations.[50] They therefore called for black schools to stress "the activities of life so as to develop in students initiative, perseverance, optimism, and the destruction of the defeatist attitude."[51] Moreover, they felt, as did John J. Mullowney, president of Meharry Medical College, that the establishment of interracial good will, reliability, and honesty were "just as important as a thorough training in the educational field."[52] To assure these ends, adjustment and the integration of personality were essential to the successful education of black youth.

Ambrose Caliver, specialist in Negro Education in the federal government, viewed the personality as the key to an individual's success. He wrote that it was no longer knowledge, skill, or any other factors which would determine the successful life adjustment of youth. Instead, it was personality, and particularly certain personality factors including suitable desires, motives, and aspirations. He went on to suggest that the way in which an individual reacts to the positive and the negative elements in his daily experiences is the determining factor of his success or failure. He urged teachers to give more attention to the psychological forces governing students' behavior and to shift their emphasis from subject matter, drill, and techniques to the cultivation and guidance of personality.[53]

Black schools of the 1930s extended their roles beyond fostering the students' intellectual development. The role of vocational choices in the student's life, his physical health, his emotional life, and particularly his social attitudes and personality were increasingly emphasized. Positive attitudes and suitable vocational aspirations constituted a major part of the survival equipment for Southern black Americans. The intelligence test was a valuable tool for meeting these needs.

Institutionalization of Intelligence Testing

The motive for the institutionalization of intelligence testing in Southern black schools was the fact that these tests were perceived as a scientific, efficient, and modern mechanism for the adjustment of youth. This adjustment was to be accomplished through testing for curriculum differentiation, for predicting the probable success which the individual would meet in a given educational or vocational endeavor, and for identifying strengths and weaknesses of the student in suiting the curriculum to the individual student. As T. Arnold Hill, acting executive secretary of the Urban League's Social Services for Negroes, urged: "It [was] just as important that an individual discover[ed] what he [could] not do as it [was] that he discover[ed] the thing he [could] do."[54]

JUSTIFICATIONS FOR INTELLIGENCE TESTING

The justification for and employment of intelligence tests in the Southern educational setting of the 1930s were by no means confined to black schools. In fact, Margaret V. Cobb at the Institute of Educational Studies, Columbia University, had earlier voiced a similar concern over grouping, through testing, as applied to white and black Southern youth. Many of the white youths were of the same socioeconomic status as Southern blacks.

> It is obvious that large differences in the intelligence of the population in different states have very important implications for education. Since in some of the Southern states probably as many as 75 percent of the children cannot, or will not enter academic high

schools, the problem of providing other and perhaps new types of training for children from 14 to 18 years of age is most acute in this part of the country.[55]

As early as 1927, R. W. Gadsen promoted educational uses of intelligence testing in Southern black schools. As principal of a Savannah, Georgia, public school, Gadsen, praising the work of Binet, saw group tests as proving very valuable in education. He asserted that tests had "raised education to the level of science," by making grouping objective. Grouping on a scientific basis left no room for the influence of the child's family, his dress, his conduct, or his personality.[56]

Once a student decided to enter high school, it became the task of the school to assist him in making the appropriate course selection through the classification and adaptation of the curriculum to individual needs. Schools had to cope with more and more students from diverse and heterogeneous backgrounds, increasing the demand for scientific techniques of classification in secondary schools and colleges. Such factors, coupled with the requirements of state departments of education,[57] encouraged black educators to adopt a more efficient and sophisticated administration of student personnel programs.

In 1933, Ambrose Caliver, Senior Specialist in the Education of Negroes in the U. S. Department of Education, suggested that the application of science to education had progressed beyond the highest hopes of such earlier advocates of scientific education as Cattell, Rice, and Thorndike. He believed that science was moving toward the vanguard of social progress. Caliver further asserted that the results had led to a continual application and refinement of techniques and instruments until "finally we have what may be fairly called a science of education which finds its basis in education research." He went on to state that

> We are basing decision on facts. This can free us from educational
> moguls. Perhaps the most significant contribution which science
> has made to our educational thinking is the creation of the concept
> of the controlling power of facts. . . . It seems therefore, that our
> only escape from the educational morass in which we find ourselves
> is more religiously to apply scientific methods in our educational
> procedures.[58]

Caliver advocated "rigorously planned and scientifically executed long-range experimentation for the purpose of producing a body of scientifically derived principles for the guidance of Negroes."

Indeed, intelligence tests were "scientific" devices which, during the 1930s, were widely accepted in schools throughout the country,[59] even though they remained steeped in controversy.[60] In fact, Horace M. Bond,

then dean at Dillard University in Louisiana and once an outspoken opponent
of the early research by some white psychologists upon blacks, wrote that

> We may not be getting inferior students into our colleges, but it is
> time we recognized the fact that our entrants do differ widely in the
> kind of preparation and abilities represented by such a test as the
> American Council Psychological Examination. I do not think this is
> an occasion to develop a violent anger at intelligence testing, and to
> say that intelligence testing is "the bunk."[61]

Black colleges, more so than black secondary schools, were in the vanguard
of the mental testing movement. For example, in May, 1932, the College
Sophomore Testing Program was conducted under the auspices of the American Council of Education. The stated purpose of the tests, administered to
students representing 140 colleges and universities, was to "throw light upon
the capacities, needs, and problems of individuals." The tests were to provide
colleges with information on (1) the conditions for selecting students; (2) the
response of students to the formal and informal facilities for cultivation
offered by the college; (3) the effectiveness of instruction in departments;
and (4) the influence of age, home and social condition, previous school
training, scholastic and vocational aims, extracurricular interests, and faculty
counsel upon student performance. The participating black colleges in this
testing program were Bennett College for Women, Johnson C. Smith University, North Carolina College for Negroes, Wilberforce University, Claflin
College, Fisk University, and Storer College.[62]

Alphonso Elder, dean at North Carolina College for Negroes, used intelligence tests to improve academic work at his institution. He implemented
an instructional plan under which students were divided into two groups,
those who possessed limited ability and were capable of mastering only the
minimum essential of college work, and those capable of "constructive
thinking." He proposed further that under this plan each new student entering college be given an intelligence test and several placement tests. The
results, in conjunction with other data, were to be used by the advisors for
educational-vocational counseling of the students.[63]

The spirited interest of these blacks in mental testing was shared by
their counterparts in other schools and grew out of a desire to fit students
to what educators perceived to be their social and intellectual potentials. In
practice, this enabled educators to single out those superior students from
the heterogeneous mixing and "democratizing" of public schools. Herman G.
Canady, a psychologist at West Virginia State College, reporting the results
of his study of the academically talented student, suggested that, although
educators had always known that human beings differed, "it [was] only in
recent years that methods of precision in the measurement of the traits
involved [had] been developed. Recognition of the significance of these

findings [had] led to serious efforts on the part of the progressive school men to adapt better the curriculum [i.e., differentiation] to the abilities and needs of individual students."[64]

Revealing examples of black educators' approval of intelligence testing for educational efficiency are found in several essays by T. Roger Thompson, a mathematics teacher at Huntington High School in Newport News, Virginia. Teaching during the 1930s under Principal Lutrelle Palmer, an advocate of the progressive education movement, Thompson sought to justify testing from several standpoints. He perceived intelligence testing as a means to determine (1) the efficiency with which pupils had worked and teachers had taught and (2) the value of a given textbook and a given method of teaching. Testing also allowed comparisons between different schools. Thompson held that education was "a business, requiring frequent inventory." As the grocer, farmer, salesperson, and other business people had their standards for measurement, so the efficient teacher had educational tests as a standard by which to measure the results of teaching. In developing his analogy of education to business, he saw the teacher as the manufacturer, children as the raw material, and the textbook, physical facilities, and methodology as the machines. The finished products of education, then, were "boys and girls ready to do their part in society."[65]

In yet another essay, Thompson pointed to the changing parental attitudes toward aptitude testing. Parents saw tests as "miracle workers" which could help their children pick the right occupation. They therefore wanted to know these tests results. Thompson accepted the notion that these tests measured capacity to adjust to new situations. He held that despite varying interpretations, there was a "commonality of definition for all test designers," something that could not be imparted to the student and was independent of formal schooling. He further stated that since every child should be given the opportunity to develop to his highest, both socially and personally, every teacher should know something about intelligence tests. Such tests could be used to divide classes into fast, average, and slow groups. They might be used with aptitude and other educational tests in vocational guidance programs. Thompson believed that intelligence tests accurately showed the ability of the pupil to pursue higher education successfully.[66]

The introduction of the junior high school concept into black education contributed further to the enthusiasm of black educators for intelligence testing. In Kentucky, reorganized schools with separate junior and senior high divisions reported using tests in greater numbers than did the conventional schools. While the latter employed little psychological testing, junior high schools tested for determining pupil ability; for classifying, grouping, and placement; for diagnosing individual differences; and for grading and promoting. Reorganized high schools sought to determine pupil ability, improve instruction, and implement a research program.[67]

RAMIFICATIONS OF TEST USAGE

Well into the 1930s and 40s, black schools were still bound by the principles of utilitarian educational sociology, some of which had been a legacy of the educational theories of Booker T. Washington. These schools had been founded, like all American schools, upon national imperatives, inextricably linked to achievement and the American work ethic. They would help young people gain a "realistic" and "intelligent" assessment of their "abilities" and "capacities." These youths might then do better in school through self-control and ultimately find employment, a chain of events leading to an acceptance of their station in life.

Southern obsession for adjusting black youths to a "life situation commensurate with their capacities" and to the requisites of the social and economic order served mainly to accommodate a conservative sytem of caste and class. The use of standardized mental tests lent an air of objectivity to the process of sorting and selecting these students,[68] assuring their assignment to the proper situation. Thus, black youths might be made to accept their status as "natural," "logical," and "morally right."

It was indeed paradoxical that black educators spoke out so vehemently in the early testing movement against what they justifiably feared to be racist assumptions and inferences being generated and supported by mental tests. Even more impressive had been blacks' protest against possible test usage to relegate their racial group to unskilled agricultural and industrial labor. Yet, they unblushingly employed those very same instruments which had been designed for a Northern, urban, white middle-class milieu. Moreover, these tests had been used in the North to sustain pre-existing social and economic relationships as southern and eastern Europeans entered the United States just prior to and after World War I. Now they were being used to measure and gauge black students' progress as well as to determine black teachers' teaching effectiveness.

Data from these tests established only inferentially causative links between inadequate instructional and plant facilities and depressed intelligence test scores among poor whites and blacks. Yet, the enthusiasm over intelligence testing as a manifestation of progressive reform and scientific efficiency was both strong and pervasive, despite its tendency to both crystallize and standardize elitist and racist attitudes. Evidence of how these data from intelligence tests legitimized elitist attitudes to black teachers and their pupils may be found in the progressive thought of the period. For example, William A. Robinson, principal of the Atlanta University Laboratory School, was an educator who stood in the vanguard of progressive innovations in black education. In the 1920s and 30s he called for an educational environment which would discourage school staff from forcing students into submission by making direct reference to the failures of the race as an explanation of the pupils' conduct. Robinson was acutely aware of the results of the educators' attitudes toward lower and working class black youth. He wrote that

> These men, who are consciously or unconsciously establishing their
> ideas in the thinking of boys and girls, have very little faith in the
> possibilities of Negroes in industry or business or professions. They
> believe far more in the inherent inferiority and perversity of Negro
> people than in the fact that, as human beings, they normally act like
> all other people and are worthy of equal consideration with other
> human beings. In other words, too many of us in Negro schools are
> accepting without much inner protest a deterministic and defeatist
> philosophy about a group with which they are connected and
> willy-nilly, we are indoctrinating our charges with our professional
> belief.[69]

The distinct conservatism surrounding some black educators' responses to the social circumstances of their pupils indicated their acceptance, according to Bond, of "the tastes, ambitions, and viewpoints of the American middle class." Many, who themselves had risen from the ranks of the poor, had "lost their orientation with the masses of their race, . . . having no sympathy with the poor and the weak of their own people." He went on to note, "It is unfortunately true that there has been an immense amount of exploitation of the ignorant of their own people by college-trained, Negro professionals.[70]

They dynamics of the intraracial relationships and attitudes toward guidance and testing in black schools raise disturbing issues in the sociology of knowledge. While certain institutions may have at one time served the purposes of a rising black middle class, these same institutions were used for preventing further social change for a lower class of blacks striving for greater freedom. Concerning this type of relationship, John Dewey noted in his 1935 essay "The Future of Liberalism" that

> Even if the words remain the same, they mean something different
> when they are uttered by a minority struggling against repressive
> measures and when expressed by a group that having attained power
> then uses ideas that were once weapons of emancipation as instru-
> ments for keeping the power and wealth it has attained.[71]

The interest which black educators showed in intelligence testing as an explicit measurement tool and as an implicit tool of social class distinctions is an indication of the respectability such tests had gained in vocational and educational guidance. Some of the educators were seemingly impervious to the fact that this tool was counterproductive to the expressed ideas of education. Data gleaned from it aided in the rigid classification, labelling, and sorting out of the young people whom test users were supposedly assisting.[72]

More importantly, data from this battery of tests further legitimized a stratified, differentiated curriculum on four levels: academic, business, industrial/agricultural, and general. The academic track provided the greatest access to the resources of prestige and status. Youths from lower and working class homes, whom intelligence tests and teacher/counselors identified as unsuited for academic instruction, were directed into one of the other three tracks for "life adjustment." F. D. Beers, secretary of the Committee on Educational Testing in Georgia, expressed the notion that what the school should teach should be securely founded on what the child can learn. He perceived the role of democratic education to be primarily twofold. The first priority was to "protect society from shysters, charlatans, and quacks" by assuring "medicine, engineering, law, ministry, and teaching the best minds that the generation has produced." The second was to "give to youth who cannot attain to professional standards opportunities for developing along the lines of their God-given talents and their hereditary limitations, whatever those talents and limitations may be."[73]

School practices were in fact leading to an intellectual aristocracy, and intelligence testing was effectively fitting black students to what they were to continue to be in light of what other groups wanted them to remain. Roy K. Davenport claimed that "too often do we who term ourselves experts point out that pupils should pursue a specific course of instruction merely because a battery of tests have indicated an aptitude along that line and with never a consideration of what that student is to do in the way of earning a living."[74]

Conclusion

How guidance and testing for social and economic adjustment of black youth were optimistically employed as a sign of modernization must be seen against the background of Southern reform. In the larger arena, Southern reform was bankrupt by 1936 from both the ideological and the practical standpoint. In fact, Howard W. Odum noted in *Southern Regions of the United States* that

> [The] original proposals assumed the form and ideology of ambi-
> tous plans, sectional schemes, or outlets for personal expressions of
> leaders. ... So powerful [was] the "solid South" and the Civil War
> republican tradition that the old order continued unabated through
> the depression period, magnifying for the most part party and
> sectional acquisition over issues and men.[75]

Since initial plans and prospects for reform had held significant consequences for the education of blacks, the demise of these plans led to disillusionment.[76] The centralization of local schools under growing state

educational bureaucracies and the introduction of educational research through their testing bureaus did not eliminate provincialism, caste, and class.[77] Furthermore, in 1937 Albert L. Turner of Tuskegee Institute raised questions regarding Southern "commitments" to modern educational reform. He wrote that

> When Catherine the Great of Russia, who professed to be an enlightened despot, ordered schools built for the education of the common people of Russia, one of her ministers complained that she was doing a dangerous thing to educate her subjects. Catherine replied that the schools were not being built for Russia, but for the rest of Europe. In other words, establishing schools was considered an enlightened thing to do by the European countries, and Catherine wished to appear well in the eyes of her fellow sovereigns. She did not intend to educate the Russians.
>
> So it is with our improved standards for Negro teachers in the South. Many of them were instituted to avoid embarassment on the part of the Southern states in the face of more progressive policies of other sections generated by the successive wave of educational reform which swept the country a few years ago. Many officials of the State Department of Education in the Southern states do not have a genuine interest in these higher standards for Negro teachers.[78]

In what ostensibly was the acceptance of black schools as an integral part of the state educational structure, a number of supervisory programs for these schools focused their attention on three objectives: (1) improvement of instruction, (2) improvement of health, and (3) vocational adjustment of black youth. One such program in West Virginia devoted its energies to teaching black youths good manners in the home, school, church, theater, on the streets, and in other public places. Another sought to educate blacks to wage war against tuberculosis and other diseases which seemed common to blacks. Under this same state plan, black schools were to "emphasize the qualities and abilities which general education [was] supposed to provide, namely the qualities of accuracy, dependability, industry, and good manners, and the ability to perform well and speedily the fundamental process underlying the 3 R's, the surest road to satisfactory occupational adjustment in our changing technological age."[79]

Under the illusory terms of an agenda for modern educational reform and the adoption of guidance and intelligence testing as evidence of modernization, social boundaries within black communities and between black and white communities became more rigid than before. Moreover, such determinants also severely curtailed the possibilities of blacks from lower and working class homes of making their full contribution to society. The tragic result was a stifling of talents, not only for the black population[80] but for the entire nation.

Notes

Portions of this research were sponsored by a Faculty Research Grant, School of Education and a Buhl Fellowship with the Learning, Research, and Development Center, University of Pittsburgh.

1. For a comprehensive picture of the social and economic changes the South underwent and an analysis of the consequent plans for modernization and reform, see, for example, *The Annals of The American Academy of Political and Social Sciences*, vol. 153 (January 1931); George B. Tindall, *The Emergence of the New South, 1913-45* (Baton Rouge, La.: Louisiana State University Press, 1967); and Rupert B. Vance, *Regional Reconstruction: A Way Out for the South* (Chapel Hill, N.C.: University of North Carolina Press, 1935).

2. See H. Feldman, *Racial Factors in American Industry* (N.Y.: Harper, 1931), pp. 99, 296; and Charles S. Johnson, *The Negro in American Civilization* (New York: Holt, 1930), p. 103.

3. Later in the decade, Sidney B. Hall, Virginia State Superintendent of Public Instruction, addressed black supervisors and administrators at their Virginia State Teachers Association Conference. There he expressed his views on this decentralized arrangement: "If we are to have a hand in directing [educational] change, we must discover the movement in the making, [which is] usually difficult to apprehend due to the lack of centralized control over education." (Sidney B. Hall, "Trends in American Education," *Virginia Teachers Bulletin* 16 (January 1939: 6-9). Hall was alluding to the fact that historically the bulk of power and control over local school systems rested with sometimes partisan county superintendents and local school boards. Thus, the financial appropriations for black schools were almost entirely dependent upon the local sentiment of white Southerners, often resulting in blacks' receiving "less than two-fifths of their fair share of funds for common schools." (Reported in "The Harrison-Black-Fletcher Bill," *The Bulletin of the National Association of Teachers in Colored Schools* 15 (March 1937): 3-6 (hereafter referred to as *The Bulletin*).

4. See James W. Johnson, *Negro Americans, What Now?* (New York: Viking Press, 1934) pp. 42-54; and Carter G. Woodson, *Miseducation of the Negro* (Washington, D.C.: Associated Publishers, 1933) pp. 4-5, 46, 133.

5. Horace Mann Bond, *The Education of the Negro in the American Social Order* (New York: Octagon Press, 1966), pp. 391-412.

6. Ambrose Caliver, "Negro Education in the Depression," *School Life* 18, (February 1933): 111-112, 118.

7. Cf. David B. Tyack, *The One Best System: A History of American Urban History* (Cambridge: Harvard University Press, 1974).

8. N. C. Newbold, Director of Negro Education, State Department of Education in North Carolina, addressed the National Association of Teachers

in Colored Schools (NATCS). He contended that educational, vocational, and moral guidance was needed in the 1930s because of certain stark realities, namely, (1) our economic system had failed; (2) moral and spiritual values were being questioned; (3) education was not fitting students to current conditions; and (4) millions of people had lost their balance economically and were helpless. (N. C. Newbold, "Shall Guidance Programs be Established in High Schools for Negroes," *The Bulletin* 14 (November 1935): 35–37.

9. The 1931 report on resolutions by the NATCS asserted: "We favor the appointment of Negro supervisors over the separate schools in the county and district schools as rapidly as competent persons are found available." The Fourth resolution adopted at the 1934 annual conference of the NATCS in Baltimore read: "As long as certain states in this American Union legalize the operation of a dual system of schools, so long as this Association demands that the school for Negro youth be under the immediate control and supervision of members of the Negro race." ("Report of the Committee on Resolutions of the NATCS," *The Bulletin* 12 (October 1931): 9, 12, and "Resolutions," *The Bulletin* 13 (October 1934): 9. See also Ronald K. Goodenow, "Paradox in Progressive Educational Reform: The South and the Education of Blacks in the Depression Years," *Phylon* 39 (March 1978): 49–65.

10. Bond, *Education of the Negro*, pp. 3–36. This kind of compromise was crucial. In the first place, it seemed the most logical way for a Southern white power structure to proceed with plans for reform and to preserve, in the meantime the "racial integrity" (i.e., segregation) of the South. It was patently reminiscent of nineteenth century Southern tactics under which Booker T. Washington was catapulted into a position of political power as the overseer of Negro education. (See Booker T. Washington, *Up From Slavery* [New York: Bantam Books, 1970], especially chapters 13–15.) Secondly, Southern interest in preserving its racial integrity under an agenda for reform paved the way for the kind of rhetorical statements which emanated from leading white social scientists and politicians when they tried to reconcile the conflicts in Southern word and deed. For example, sociologist Guy B. Johnson applauded efforts by blacks to maintain a biracial society built upon interracial cooperation and good will. Citing W. E. B. DuBois's one-time advocacy of a "nation within a nation" concept, Johnson excused blacks' accommodation of biracialism as a boon to Negro leadership and racial solidarity. See Guy B. Johnson, "Education, Segregation, and Race Relations," *Quarterly Review of Higher Education Among Negroes* 3 (April 1935): 89–94 (hereafter referred to as *Quarterly Review*).

11. Howard W. Odum, *Southern Regions of the United States* (Chapel Hill, N.C.: University of North Carolina Press, 1936), p. 135.

12. Monroe Work (ed.), *Negro Year Book, 1937–38* (Tuskegee, Ala.: Tuskegee Institute Press, 1938), p. 166.

13. Bond, *Education of the Negro*, p. 206.

14. Odum, *Southern Regions of the U.S.,* p. 235.
15. Bond, *Education of the Negro,* p. 216.
16. Editorials and letters to the editor reflect a change in the attitude of some Mississipians toward the education of blacks. The *Jackson Daily News* stated: "Mississippi's Colored population constitutes one of the State's most valuable assets . . . that may and ought to be developed, mainly through education." ("Editorials and Letters from President Holmes," *The Bulletin* 10 [February 1930]: 19–20. For similar sentiments expressed by whites even earlier than the 1930s see Virginia Education Commission, *Virginia Public Schools: A Survey of a Southern State's Public School System* (New York: World Book Co., 1920), pp. 197–199.
17. The North Carolina Labor Department reported unemployment figures showing that "the greatest pressure for jobs [was] among the young." Out of 15,762 applicants for jobs, 42.5 percent were between 16 and 24. Of these 15,762 applicants, 7,088 were black, and of this number 1,932 were between 20 and 24. Therefore, 27.25 percent of the 7,088 had been in school during the Depression years (*See* Newbold, "Guidance Programs," p. 36).
18. See Charles S. Johnson, "The Negro's Status in the South," *Occupations* 14 (March 1936): 502–509.
19. Given the high unemployment figures, there was much concern over what Atlanta University sociologist Ira Reid termed "an accumulation of a new surplus occupational population" who seemed doomed to disappointment because of the depressed economic conditions. See Ira Read, "The Economic Situation and Occupational Opportunities for Negroes," *Quarterly Review* 4 (January 1936): 23–25. Such concerns were not unfounded, considering the earlier expression of Columbia University professors Samuel T. Dutton and David Snedden: "The occupationless class constitute a socially dangerous element, especially as it is felt that to some extent they are victims of social injustice." (S. Dutton and D. Snedden, *The Administration of Public Education in the United States* [New York: Macmillan Co., 1908] pp. 406–407.)
20. Phillip S. Foner, *Organized Labor and the Black Worker,* (New York: Praeger Press, 1974) and Ira Reid, *Negro Membership in American Labor Unions* (New York: National Urban League, 1930).
21. Ambrose Caliver (ed.), *Conference on Fundamentals in the Education of Negroes* May 9–12, 1934 (Washington, D.C.: United States Government Printing Office, 1934).
22. Homer Rainey of the American Youth Commission raised similar questions from a national perspective, noting: "If practically all American youth are to be sent to the high school, and if not more than 12 percent can be absorbed in the intellectual professions, and if it is true that 55–70 percent of all the jobs require little or no formal technical training, the conclusion is inescapable that a radical revision of our entire concept of high school education is essential. . . . Many high school graduates will be forced into common labor and dead-end jobs. When

this situation is reached, the purpose of high school education will have to be something more than 'preparation for a job.'" (Homer Rainey, "Social Factors Affecting General Education," *Thirty-eighth Yearbook of the National Society for the Study of Education* [Bloomington Ill.: Public School Publishing Co., 1939], p. 21.)

23. In her investigation of high schools in Georgia, Alabama, South Carolina, North Carolina, Florida, and Tennessee, Sara Bradley reported that of the schools she surveyed, 75 percent of the classes had at least 38 students enrolled, while 25 percent had from 40 to 80 students. See Sara Bradley, "Some Teaching Problems Peculiar to Negro Public Schools," *Quarterly Review* 6 (July 1938): 222–223. Edna Colson, Director of Education at Virginia State College, reported that in the face of a 36 percent increase of blacks in Virginia's secondary schools (1935–36), the student-teacher ratio had risen to 40:1. See Edna Colson, "The Status of Negro Education in Virginia," *Quarterly Review* 5 (October 1937): 191–197.

24. See Bond, *Education of the Negro*, pp. 164, 215, 289–293; and Doxey Wilkerson, "Some Aspects of Modern High School Education," *Virginia Teachers Bulletin* 7 (March 1930): 3–7.

25. In a survey of 1,833 black high school males, Bullock found that 1,601 or 87.6 percent planned to enter college upon high school completion and that the percentage expecting to go on to college greatly increased from the ninth through the twelfth grades. See R. W. Bullock, "A Study of Occupational Choices of Negro High School Boys," *Crisis* 37 (September 1930): 301–303.

26. G. W. Gore, "A Brief Survey of Secondary and Higher Education of Negroes in Tennessee," *Quarterly Review* 5 (October 1937): 186–190.

27. Cf. Dutton and Snedden, *Administration of Public Education, pp.* 406–407, for similar discussions on this subject relating to schools in the white community.

28. Sara Bradley reported that many lower and working class students entering high school did not have a suitable home environment for study. In many cases youths lived in homes without parents and were compelled to work at night to support younger siblings. See S. Bradley, "Some Teaching Problems," p. 222. For an example of an empirical study conducted in a Southern black secondary school, see William H. Robinson, "The Socio-Economic Composition of the 1938 Freshman Class of Huntington High School," (Master's Thesis, Hampton Institute, 1939).

29. Doxey Wilkerson, "A Determination of the Peculiar Problems of Negroes in Contemporary American Society," *Journal of Negro Education* 5 (July 1936): 315–350.

30. Gertrude Woodard, "The School's Responsibility for Character Education," *Virginia Teachers Bulletin* 9 (November 1932): 9; see also Edwin R. Embree, *Brown America* (New York: Viking Press, 1931), pp. 198–211.

31. See Ambrose Caliver, "The Negro Teacher and a Philosophy of Education," *Journal of Negro Education* 2 (July 1933): 432–447; and Robert

R. Moton (successor to Booker T. Washington as principal of Tuskegee Institute), "Negro Higher and Professional Education," *Journal of Negro Education* 2 (July 1933): 397–402.

32. In fact, as late as the early 1940s, a survey reported: "The need for guidance services is acute. . . . Evaluations of large urban schools [found] guidance services to be deplorably inadequate." (Virginia State Chamber of Commerce, *Opportunities for the Improvement of High School Education in Virginia* [Richmond, Va., 1944] pp. 56–57. Ambrose Caliver likewise of the U. S. Office of Education provided sobering statistics on the status of guidance in black secondary schools and colleges. Of the 2,578 institutions for blacks which he surveyed, only 602 offered guidance programs with only 159 high schools and 44 colleges reporting definite information concerning their programs. (Ambrose Caliver, *Vocational Education and Guidance of Negroes,* U. S. Office of Education, Bulletin no. 38, 1937 (Washington, D.C.: 1937), pp. 111–112.

33. See the entire issue "Vocational Guidance of Negroes," *Journal of Negro Education* 4 (January 1935) for a critical analysis and comprehensive discussion of underlying philosophies of guidance.

34. Charles H. Thompson, "The Vocational Guidance of Negroes," *Journal of Negro Education* 4 (January 1935): 1–4.

35. See Bond, *Education of the Negro*, pp. 200–201; and B. J. O. Schrieke, *Alien Americans* (New York: Viking Press, 1936), p. 191.

36. U. S. Commissioner of Education William J. Cooper, addressing the NATCS in 1931, noted that "our Negro citizens, most of whom were three-quarters of a century ago best prepared for agriculture [and] now failing in that field largely through ignorance, are migrating into cities and in large part satisfying themselves with menial services which require relatively little educational and special training." See William J. Cooper, "The Negro and Education," *The Bulletin* 12 (December 1931): 15–16.

37. Thompson, "Vocational Guidance of Negroes," pp. 2–3. Edith A. Lyons, principal of Morgan Demonstration School in Washington, D.C., pointing to these data, asked: "Are we satisfied to allow our children to yearly squander their rich educational opportunities through lack of understanding and guidance, when the doors of all types of occupations are opening to them today as never before?" Edith A. Lyons, "Contributions of the Elementary School to the Education of the Group," *The Bulletin* 14 (November 1935): 23–28. Lyons went on to suggest: "[One] element of our problem is the failure of members of our group to successfully avail themselves of the unrestricted, diversified occupational structure and opportunities now open to us." (p. 25). In contrast to positions advocating adaptation to the status quo, the National Education Association, meeting in Cleveland in 1934, called for long-term planning that would help the schools meet the challenge of the *changing* social, industrial, and economic order. Reported in "News Items," *Quarterly Review* 2 (April 1934): 141.

38. D. A. Wilkerson, "The Vocational Education and Guidance of Negroes," *Journal of Negro Education* 9 (March 1940): 259-266.

39. Howard Hale Long, "Guidance and Individual Difference Among Students," in *Problems in the Collegiate Education of Negroes*, ed. John W. Davis, West Virginia State College Bulletin no. 8, series 24, (June 1937), p. 37 (responses to questionnaire by Davis).

40. H. M. Bond, "The Curriculum and the Negro Child," *Journal of Negro Education* 4 (January 1935): 160-168.

41. C. H. Thompson, "Vocational Guidance of Negroes," p. 4.

42. Doxey Wilkerson, "American Caste and the Social Studies Curriculum," *Quarterly Review* 5 (April 1937): 67-74.

43. Doxey Wilkerson, "Statement of Advisory Commission on Negro Schools," *Virginia Journal of Education* 27 (January 1934): 204-207.

44. V. V. Oak, "Some Practical Aspects in the Teaching of Economics to Negro College Students," *Quarterly Review* 6 (October 1938): 283-286. For other curricular prescriptions for social control and for helping the individual "to balance or equilibrate himself inspite of baffling social forces," see: Thomas I. Brown, "Character Building Through the Teaching of Social Studies," *Quarterly Review* 7 (July 1939): 202-205; Warmoth T. Gibbs, "What Contributions Should the Colleges Make Toward Training for Good Citizenship," *Quarterly Review* 6 (October 1938): 279-282. The April 1934 issue, vol. 2, of the *Quarterly Review* is devoted entirely to the subject, "The Liberal Arts College Curriculum and the Development of Wholesome Interest and Vocations for Students."

45. Charles S. Johnson, "The Development of the Personality of the Students in Segregated Communities," *Quarterly Review* 4 (April 1936): 67-70.

46. Frederick D. Patterson, "Vocational Education and Guidance for the Negro," *Journal of Educational Sociology* 12 (January 1939): 298-307.

47. Some black educators contended that social problems of blacks stemmed from "the inability to adapt" due to "schools' failure to know intimately the interests, needs, and abilities of each child." See "Contributions of the Elementary School," Lyons, p. 27.

48. Woodard, "The School's Responsibility," p. 9.

49. For a comprehensive listing of theses and dissertations written in Northern and black Southern colleges during the 1930s on the educational and vocational guidance of black youths, see Doxey A. Wilkerson, "The Vocational Education and Guidance of Negroes," *Journal of Negro Education* 9 (January 1940): 123-130 and 9 (March 1940): 259-266. A number of monographs on guidance for the educational, vocational, and social adjustment of black youth were also written during this period. See, for example, Faye P. Everett, ed. *The Colored Situation*, (Boston: Meador Publishing Co., 1936); Ralph W. Bullock and W. R. Chivers, *Vocational Guidance for Negroes* (Atlanta, Ga.: National Youth Administration, 1937); George W. Crawford, *The Talladega Manual of Vocational Guidance* (Talladega, Ala.: Talladega College Press, 1937).

50. Charlotte H. Brown, "Student Initiative and Responsibility," in *Problems in the Collegiate Education of Negroes,* 34 (responses to questionnaire by Davis).

51. W. W. Sanders, *Ibid.*

52. J. J. Mulloney, *Ibid.*

53. Ambrose Caliver, "Education of Negroes for Leadership and for Work," *The Bulletin* 14 (November 1935): 15–21, 48.

54. T. Arnold Hill, "The Liberal Arts College Graduate–His Occupational Outlook," in *The Function of the Negro Liberal Arts College in the Social Process,* ed. J. T. Cater, (Talladega, Ala.: Talladega College Press, 1934).

55. Margaret V. Cobb, "The Limits Set to Educational Achievement by Limited Intelligence," *Journal of Educational Psychology* 13 (December 1922): 546–555.

56. R. W. Gadsen, "Some Observations on Mental Tests," *The Bulletin* 7 (February 1927): 26–28.

57. For examples of how state departments of education were influencing the use of testing in schools, see David Segel and Mardis M. Profitt, *Pupil Personnel Services as a Function of State Departments of Education,* U. S. Department of Education, Bulletin no. 6, (Washington, D.C.: 1940), p. 26.

58. Ambrose Caliver, "National Surveys and Education of Negroes," *The Bulletin* 12 (May 1933): 10–13.

59. As one example of how intelligence tests had been used in schools outside the South, see Virgil Dickson, "The Use of Group Mental Tests in the Guidance of Eighth Grade and High School Pupils, *Journal of Educational Research* 2 (October 1920): 601–610.

60. See William B. Thomas, "Black Educators and Intelligence Testing: The Case of the South and the Educational and Vocational Guidance of Blacks, 1920–50," (Doctoral diss., State University of New York at Buffalo, 1977). See also the July, 1934, issue of *Journal of Negro Education* 3:319–564, which is a comprehensive and critical analysis of the state of mental testing research on blacks.

61. H. M. Bond, "The Liberal Arts College for Negroes: A Social Force," in *A Century of Municipal Higher Education* (Chicago: Lincoln Printing Co., 1937) p. 361.

62. Editorial, "College Sophomore Testing Program," *Quarterly Review* 1 (January 1933): 43.

63. Alphonso Elder, "A Plan to Improve the Academic Work at the North Carolina College for Negroes," *Quarterly Review* 1 (January 1933): 33–34.

64. Herman G. Canady, "Individual Differences and Their Educational Significance in the Guidance of the Gifted and Talented Child," *Quarterly Review* 5 (October 1937): 202–205.

65. T. Roger Thompson, "Educational Tests as a Means of Increasing Efficiency in Teaching," *Virginia Teachers Bulletin* 10 (January 1933): 15–16.

66. T. Roger Thompson, "A Few Facts Every Teacher Should Know About Intelligence Tests," *Virginia Teachers Bulletin* 9 (May 1932): 23-24.

67. Reid E. Jackson, "Reorganized Secondary Schools in Kentucky," *Journal of Negro Education* 4 (October 1935): 506-509.

68. For example, candid discussions among black administrators of colleges and high schools and white state supervisors of black education over sorting and selecting black youths for college through testing and guidance are found in "Guidance in Our Colleges: A Panel Discussion" and "Guidance in Our Secondary Schools: A Panel Discussion," *Quarterly Review* (January 1935): 64-71.

69. William A. Robinson, "Vocational Guidance in the Negro Secondary School," *The Bulletin* 14 (November 1935): 32-35.

70. Bond, *Education of the Negro*, pp. 148-149.

71. John Dewey, "The Future of Liberalism," *Journal of Philosophy* 32 (April 1935): 225-230.

72. Such classification was contrary to a 1931 resolution by the NATCS stating: "Guidance does not mean *classifying* children and prescribing occupations, but is concerned with helping our youth to choose, prepare for, enter into, and make progress in occupations." ("Report of the Committee on Resolutions of the NATCS," *The Bulletin* 12 [October 1931]: 9.)

73. F. D. Beers, "What Tests Shall We Use?" *Occupations* 14 (March 1936): 528-530.

74. Roy K. Davenport, "Vocational Guidance and Educational Opportunities," *Quarterly Review* 2 (October 1934): 242-244.

75. Odum, *Southern Regions of the U. S.*, pp. 511-513.

76. Joseph H. Taylor, writing on education for democracy in 1940, articulated the extent to which blacks were feeling the disillusionment over their schools' failure to live up to their expectations. He wrote that "they took us at our word, and by the hundreds of thousands the mills have been grinding them out. But they have not found jobs. They are not becoming Booker T. Washingtons. They are not making money. They are on relief. Their collars are not white. They have not remade the world. Instead of interpreting the world, they stand in its midst— baffled and bewildered and embittered. They are skeptical. They are losing faith in both God and man. They are tramping the streets in search of work. They have taken to the road. They are furnishing a disproportionate percentage of law breakers. What are we going to do about it? What type of education should take the place of the old type that was supposed to prepare for life out in the world?" See J. H. Taylor, "Education for Democracy," *Quarterly Review* 8 (October 1940): 200-218.

77. In fact, British historian B. J. O. Schrieke contends that "so strong was the sentiment which recognized education as an enterprise which should be kept 'close to the people' that state departments on the whole were not adequately staffed to provide more than routine services to the school districts of the state. The granting of aid from state

funds to school districts was common practice in almost all states, but the county school boards were practically free to spend the money in the way they thought best." See Schrieke, *Alien Americans,* pp. 168–169.

78. Albert L. Turner, "Higher Education in Alabama," *Quarterly Review* 5 (October 1937): 153–159.

79. Cited in Ambrose Caliver, *Supervision of the Education of Negroes as a Function of the State Department of Education*, U. S. Office of Education, Bulletin no. 6 (Washington, D.C.: 1940), pp. 22–23.

80. Howard Odum referred to the "almost disgracefully negligible provision [of] trained Negro doctors, dentists, lawyers, and other professional folk" available to ten million blacks whose health and professional welfare were provided by this infinitesimally small percentage of professionals. See Odum, *Southern Regions of the U.S.,* p. 239.

Ronald K. Goodenow

Separate and Unequal Progressive Education: A Southern Case Study

Introduction

This chapter deals with the broad movement for progressive education in the Depression era South. A phenomenon generally overlooked by educational historians, Southern progressive education shared features with progressivism elsewhere. A list of these qualities would include child- and youth-centered curricular and cocurricular reform; new guidance, testing, and service endeavors; improved teacher education programs; conference and workship activities sponsored by the Progressive Education Association; and increasingly standardized and consolidated decision-making processes. Also present were complex and wide-ranging ideological rhetoric, increased professional and occupational self-consciousness, and philanthropic involvement in experimentation and in virtually all aspects of the movement's development.[1]

Southern progressive education was related as well to regional and national patterns of political change, economic development, and modernization. As such, it reflected evolving modes of governmental organization and reforms in the delivery of social and educational services, many of which were conducted through non-school agencies. But because they were in the South, afflicted by both the ravages of economic depression and the traditional attitudes toward the "place" of blacks in the regional political economy, so-called democratic reforms were laden with paradox and, more importantly, contradiction. When instituted by white-dominated public agencies and philanthropies, they were intended in part to maintain patterns of social control and stability. Progress toward a New South with its increased modernization and social planning seemingly required, particularly in a time of threatened social conflict, socialization processes which held out the promise of a better life. On the other side of the coin, it was also necessary that there be some social consensus on the need for progress within the confines of the existing political and economic modes. Such was the dilemma facing Southern educators, particularly those whites with a progressive orientation.

I have explored elsewhere broad ideological and policy questions raised by blacks who were concerned that progressive whites could use reform and

its language to downplay caste and class relationships which were exploita-
tive and probably not susceptible to progressive educational prescriptions for
social change.[2] The present study will look beyond argumentation and theory
to introduce the Secondary School Study of the Association of Colleges and
Secondary Schools for Negroes (ACSSN), a concrete black effort to gain
access to the broad progressive education movement, in part to develop some
influence over educational change processes in the South and partly to serve
other more direct racial interests. The study provides evidence of how influential black professional educators and their organizations perceived progressivism, what was happening in some black high schools, how segregation
might be used to black advantage, and what was the influence of a major
Northern foundation.

The Organizational and Professional Content
of the Secondary School Study

Southern blacks were not represented directly in the National Education
Association (NEA), which treated them as second-class citizens. The NEA
did, however, maintain relations with blacks through its Committee to
Cooperate with the National Association of Teachers in Colored Schools.
Established in 1926 to exchange "fraternal greetings" with the black organization, it accomplished little, aside from opening an avenue of communica-
tion and issuing occasional calls to produce motion pictures on blacks—one
such film was sponsored in 1941—and to reduce racial stereotypes in textbooks. And, although its membership grew from 4 to over 100 by 1940 and
it had the participation of Mabel Carney, the outspoken and pioneering
professor of rural sociology at Teachers College, Columbia University, black
sociologist Charles S. Johnson, and Ambrose Caliver, Senior Specialist for the
Education of Negroes in the U. S. Office of Education, as well as other whites
and blacks identified with both racial justice and progressive education, the
committee skirted most of the hard questions related to discrimination and
segregation. Indeed, while it flirted with certain broad issues, its views tended
to be dominated by its white Southern members, many of whom were associated with black education through state departments of education, philanthropies, or the George Peabody College for Teachers.[3]

As the 1930s unfolded, the National Association of Teachers in Colored
Schools (renamed the American Teachers Association in 1937) tried to serve
as the black equivalent of the NEA and assumed through its publications
and those of its segregated state affiliates the role of disseminating information on new educational methods and, at times, social reformist theories.
Its credo was that black schools must become less authoritarian, more pro-

fessional in orientation, and more attuned to the application of scientific principles in guidance, teaching, and school organization. Children must be taught more about "economic and social realities," including some of those associated with race, and encouraged to think about social change.

Founded in 1903 as the National Colored Teachers Association by J. R. E. Lee of Tuskegee Institute, the organization changed its name in 1907 to the National Association of Teachers in Colored Schools (NATCS) so that white teachers in black institutions might join. In 1923 it began publication of *The Bulletin* (retitled *The National Educational Outlook Among Negroes* in 1937). Its presidents were a Who's Who of black educators and included John Hope, Mary McCleod Bethune, and Mordecai Johnson. It remained the leading black professional education organization until the mid-1930s, attaining a paid membership of 1,000 of the estimated 60,000 black teachers in the country. The NATCS went into eclipse in the face of the Depression, a demise that was accelerated by the revitalization of the old Association of Colleges for Negro Youth (by the time of the Depression renamed the Association of Colleges and Secondary Schools for Negroes).[7]

Founded in 1914 to promote higher standards and professionalism in black colleges, this organization was in 1926 given the responsibility of rating black high schools by the white Southern Association of Colleges and Secondary Schools. The black group remained something of a segregated offshoot of the Southern Association until the 1933–1935 period, when it began to move beyond its accreditation functions to address more aggressively problems confronting black colleges beset by depression conditions. A reading of its literature and minutes shows that an informed body of opinion supported the notion that, through higher standards of accreditation uniformly applied, clearer articulation of the needs of secondary and higher education, improved guidance and counseling, and less authoritarian modes of administration, blacks could regionally systematize their separate educational system. From this would result a number of benefits, not the least of which would be more convincing claims for the equalization of expenditures.[5]

Complementing the efforts of these associations was the National Conference on Fundamental Problems in the Education of Negroes. Held in 1934 in Washington with the support of the U. S. Office of Education, it attracted over 1,000 delegates to a program planned and coordinated by Caliver, Carney, black historian Carter Woodson and others. Consultants included Grace Abbott, W. E. B. DuBois, Thomas Jesse-Jones, George S. Counts, William Heard Kilpatrick, Alain Locke, and many who were associated publicly with the Progressive Education Association and the broader movement for progressive education. Indeed, the national conference was replete with progressive talk and ideas. Caliver, who wrote widely on his social reconstructionist beliefs, claimed of himself and other blacks that

After economics, sociology, politics, technology, and religion failed
to offer satisfactory solutions to our vast and increasing number of
social ills we turned to education for a solution. As a result, there
are, at present, beginnings of a movement which is calculated to take
education out of its former state of lethargy and laissez faire, where it
has followed in the wake of all other types of progress and attempted
to adjust itself to demands growing out of an unplanned and un-
guided social order. The aim of this movement is to have education
assume its rightful place of leadership in social reconstruction.

The national conference, he claimed, was

a response to this educational movement, and was a conscious
effort to integrate the Negro into it. Scientific data must be developed, programs of publicity promoted, and the school must become
the center of all educative efforts for promoting education as "life
function," with all necessary overtones in areas of experiential
learnings and growth.[6]

The deliberations and recommendations of the conference were an inter-
esting mixture of this philosophy and other principles springing from the
ideology which afflicted blacks through "relevant" vocational training, industrial education, and other schemes inherited from Booker T. Washington and
his white philanthropic and political supporters. Some of the conference
committees, for example, fell into the trap of accepting the stereotype of
black unwillingness to work, perhaps, paradoxically, to demonstrate the need
for proposed reforms. However, it is apparent that as a whole this conference
legitimized discussion of much that was happening in progressive education.[7]
    The activities of the Progressive Education Association (PEA), the leading
proponent of progressive education in the United States, clearly influenced
the development of the Secondary School Study, its workshops, and the
involvement of many of its leading members in region-wide curricular reform.
The PEA, of course, upheld regional custom and did not directly integrate
blacks into its organizational activities in the South even if on at least one
occasion—at the University of Florida's P. K. Yonge Laboratory School—it
mistakenly invited blacks to participate in one of its workshops. This being
said, a number of prominent blacks, including Mordecai Johnson, Charles S.
Johnson, Alain Locke, Charles Thompson, and William A. Robinson belonged
and in some cases served in official capacities on national advisory boards
and published in PEA journals. A reading of the organizational minutes
suggests that national PEA officials were interested in organizing regionally
and becoming far more active in the South. But it was unsuccessful in its
efforts to raise the necessary funds from the General Education Board (GEB)
because of the board's policy to support existing organizations in the South

and not to encourage intrusions from other parts of the country; it worried over what one of its officials called an "attack" on the region by this organization which ahd something of a radical image. The PEA in the South was thus far less active than some of its leaders desired.[8] Its highly publicized Eight-Year Study of curricular experimentation and evaluation, however, was to provide a stimulus for blacks looking for a practical program to enact on a region-wide basis. What made this PEA program respectable in the South was a GEB-funded equivalent study developed by the white Southern Association of Colleges and Secondary Schools.

The Southern Association Study is the last development to be considered because its exclusion of blacks and its GEB funding made it ultimately impossible for blacks to be kept out of an important aspect of the progressive education movement in the United States. An outgrowth of several years of discussion, as well as a workshop at Sarah Lawrence College and an Atlantic City conference in 1937, both of which included PEA participation and GEB support, the Southern Association Study, which was directed by Frank Jenkins, duplicated some of the essential features of the Eight-Year Study.[9] Although blacks were able to participate in the Sarah Lawrence workshop, it is apparent that the Southern Association had no place for them in its Study despite the best efforts of the ACSSN. A separate program would have to be created.

The Secondary School Study

The futile attempts of blacks to be included in the Southern Association study demonstrates something of the Catch-22 situation in which they found themselves. In December, 1937, shortly after the Atlantic City conference, the Commission on Secondary Schools of the ACSSN wrote to the Southern Association requesting the inclusion of several black schools in the Southern Association Study. There was no response. William A. Robinson, the principal of the Atlanta University Laboratory School and later the director of the Secondary School Study, called on Leo Favrot, the powerful field agent of the General Education Board, to discuss direct board sponsorship of a black program. In the course of their conversation, Robinson mentioned that the Southern Association had not replied to the ACSSN letter. Favrot's internal board memorandum notes that

> It was explained to Mr. Robinson that since participating secondary
> schools in the Southern experiment now in progress were restricted
> to actual members of the Association, it was probably impossible for
> [the] . . . Commission to include Negro secondary schools in that
> experiment.

The way in, Favrot continued, would possibly be a *separate* program for black schools which, in his words, "might well be operated under the direction and auspices of the white Commission. This might call for a special supervisor to help select and organize a limited number of Negro schools for experimental work."[10]

The GEB continued to press for white supervision of a separate black program, with Favrot noting at one point that the board would feel "safer" if the Southern Association maintained a position to give "advice and guidance."[11] The board also wished to scale down a black request for $10,000 (the amount initially provided to the Southern Association) because it was "disproportionately large in view of the smaller number of Negro high schools in the South than of white high schools," an odd argument, given that both programs were to include only a handful of institutions. Further, board officials held that Robinson, who seemed to be the likely director of a separate black study because he chaired the ACSSN Commission on Secondary Schools, would be a poor choice. Perhaps the cooperation of state agents could be enlisted. In any case, Favrot and other GEB officials bluntly advised Rufus Clement, president of the ACSSN, in 1939 that "the white association determines the standards that Negro high schools have to meet."[12]

Its concerns stated, the GEB provided $40,000 for a three-year project to be developed and directed by Robinson; another $36,000 was to be awarded for a three-year program extension. This compared quite unfavorably to the total of over $135,000 awarded the Southern Association. Robinson was given a small black control committee, and two whites from the Southern Association were put on as consultants.

It is not evident why the board agreed to appoint Robinson. In all likelihood, it was unavoidable, and he most certainly knew of reservations regarding himself and the entire project. His appointment may also have been due to pressure from progressive whites. For example, in 1937 Wilfred Aiken of the Eight-Year Study, reacting to Robinson's expressed interest in having blacks included in the Southern Association study, wrote to Robert Havighurst, Director of Education for the GEB, that "obviously Robinson is an intelligent fellow. If there are many like him, the negro schools could do something worthwhile."[13]

Robinson was not only intelligent but quite outspoken. He is deserving of study, in part because of his directorship of the Secondary School Study, but also because he and his educational philosophy were probably a bit "uppity" for many of his Southern white contemporaries. Perhaps more than any other black in the Depression years, he came to represent a progressivism which included child-centered pedagogy, racial uplift, and the desire to develop regional organizational structures for reform. A 1913 graduate of Atlanta University and holder of an M.A. from Teachers College, Columbia University (1924), Robinson was president of the NATCS in 1926-27, served as State Supervisor of High Schools and Teacher Training, Division of Negro Education, in North Carolina from 1921 to 1928, became principal of Atlanta University's Laboratory School shortly thereafter, and in 1935 was elected the first schoolman president of the ACSSN. His extensive publications reflect his personal experience and a firm knowledge of progressive educational thought and practice. He spoke in favor of nonauthoritarian boarding schools, sex education, the progressive science curriculum, new guidance programs to strengthen racial pride and combat personal feelings of inferiority, the use of intelligence testing to prove black equality, and improved means of regional accreditation to overcome local efforts to maintain separate and unequal conditions in black schools.

Most of Robinson's writing on the progressive education movement came after his fierce 1936 attack in a *Journal of Negro Education* article on black powerlessness in the Southern curriculum revision movement. Here he wrote that there could be no equality for blacks in an educational system which only pretended to provide for separate but equal programs and facilities, even if it used democratic rhetoric to describe what it was doing in the area of curriculum change. But pointing to hypocrisy was one thing and developing a program to combat it yet another, and thus it may have been his 1937 address to the ACSSN which made the GEB nervous.

In this talk, Robinson linked the anti-authoritarianism of progressive education to a national liberal movement which he characterized as desiring to establish a truly American educational ideology and practice in accordance with "America's political and social philosophy." As such, it provided blacks with a golden opportunity to associate with true progressives, as opposed to those who simply used liberal and radical rhetoric for conservative purposes. Progressivism offered this chance precisely because it had become a popular element of conventional educational philosophy. "The liberals," Robinson informed association members,

> are now able in the accepted language of progressive education to formulate statements which previously would have brought upon them the active antagonism of the traditionalists, but the most rabid of the traditionalists are, in theory at least, accepting these statements as their guiding aims because under the banner of progressive education, they are somewhat too respectable to be challenged. In other words, progressive education has already begun the task of reemphasizing and reinterpreting the democratic way of life even in those parts of America where the democratic way of life has been most seriously challenged and it has frankly set up the tenets of democracy as the guiding principles of the education of all the people. What this implies for all the submerged groups in America is at least the source of a new hope for a better day in social thinking.

Robinson contended that to deny blacks the opportunity to be evaluated by scientifically based and professionally determined standards in accord with the most modern educational methods and theories would force recognition that whites in the South who used democratic rhetoric were at best insincere. With this in mind, he advocated that the ACSSN create programs that would make education a "joyous experience" for blacks, conduct "a serious study of the progressive movement in education," and have its Commission on Secondary Schools develop an appropriate program "for experimentation with and evaluation of progressive school practices."[14]

In subsequent publications and speeches, Robinson attacked conservative textbook publishers, educational businessmen, and even architecture which supported traditional schooling.[15] He called for progressive education to be protected from the domination of private schools and for blacks to join the PEA.[16] In a 1940 *Progressive Education* article, he criticized the segregation of black progressives from the mainstream progressive education movement and informed his readers that, while it was all well and good to advocate the equality of facilities and spending, they should understand that existing inequalities "have come to represent . . . a visible measure of the extent to which we are politically exploited because of our political helplessness." This crucial point was virtually always absent from the commentaries of white progressive educators who claimed sympathy for the poor in the Depression years. Robinson concluded his article with a reference to the secondary school study as a means of breaking into the progressive movement.[17]

In the course of its development, the Secondary School Study did its best to be identified with mainstream progressive education. Robinson and his assistant, William O. Brown, brought in Hilda Taba, H. H. Giles, and other well-known white progressives as consultants to work with the sixteen co-operating schools from eleven Southern states identified to take part in the study. The first major conference held under its auspices was patterned directly on techniques devised by the PEA.

This gathering, which met at Fisk University in April, 1940, provides insight into the broad concerns and scope of the study. Those in attendance studied new classroom and administrative procedures, ways in which teacher isolation could be overcome, techniques for involving community members in matters of policy and practice, the nature of evaluation, and the application of technology to schooling.[18] It is probably fair to say, in part on the basis of the documentary evidence, that just below the surface of the conference ran a broad social consciousness. In this respect it resembled black state teachers' association journals which showed, far more than their white counterparts, social concerns. Only further research will demonstrate conclusively if the Secondary School Study was more advanced in this regard than the Southern Association Study and the Eight-Year Study. It does seem to have been, since in the Southern setting progressive educational theory and the obviously racist attitudes of the region in the Depression years were a volatile combination. To be progressive and black at that time involved risks, especially as it became evident that this new progressivism was not necessarily the warmed over "practical education" of the Booker T. Washington accommodationist type.

What did the Secondary School Study accomplish over its six-year span? *Serving Negro Schools,* its final report, provides considerable information regarding the implementation of its philosophy, as do numerous documents in the files of the GEB and reports published in the ACSSN's *Quarterly Review of Higher Education Among Negroes.* This material shows that black teachers obtained support to attend conferences and workshops at Columbia University's Teachers College, the University of Chicago, and Ohio State University. Numerous black institutions hosted study-supported workshops and conferences. Schools were encouraged to produce their own evaluation criteria and, indeed, literature developed by schools taking part in the study indicates that, if fundamental changes did not come about in terms of the ultimate control of schools, black educators in these institutions (most of which were loosely supervised at local and state levels) were less dependent upon the white power structure for information regarding educational change. When whites were consulted, as noted above, they were often those associated with the PEA in the North.[19]

The Secondary School Study, moreover, provided blacks with some opportunities to implement new state guidelines on curricular reform on the basis of information generated by blacks.[20] When World War II broke out, study-produced publications seized the opportunity to emphasize the value of participatory democracy *and* black pride. Study literature and local school publications did not overtly emphasize black history and culture, but reading lists generated by member schools did move appreciably in that direction. Most significantly, the study provided blacks, in the words of *Serving Negro Schools,* with "a regional organization which they might turn to for extended consultant services on matters pertaining to school curricula and region-wide educational problems" that was far in advance of any previous efforts. Obviously, one of the latent functions of progressive educational reform in a segregated context was this extremely valuable opportunity.[21]

Motivated by a desire to avoid unnecesary and divisive comparisons and competition, the study did not develop comparative data on participating schools. Thus, there is little empirical evidence on the nature of changes actually induced by the study. As has been the case with much progressive experimentation and change, longitudinal data is not readily available. For some idea of what was accomplished, it is helpful to refer to a report by Flora M. Rhind of the GEB that was circulated internally to her colleagues. In addition to providing information on the Secondary School Study's impact, it shows some Board priorities.

Rhind reported that in March, 1943, she visited several high schools, including Huntington High School in Newport News, Virginia, Booker T. Washington High School in Rocky Mount, North Carolina, the Laboratory High School at State Teachers College, Montgomery, Alabama, and Drewery Practice High School at Talladega College in Alabama. She wrote that

> There can be little question that participation in the Study has made administrators and teachers in the member schools sharply aware of the need to study and appraise their activities in terms of existing conditions and the needs of their students. It has shaken them out of complacency and done much to make them alert to educational trends. They have a sense of pride in belonging to a South-wide study and most of them show some sense of obligation for leadership in the development of higher standards. . . . Probably the area where most change has been effected is that of improved administrative techniques and better teacher-student relationships. In almost all of the schools visited there was evidence of democratic procedures in administration, and students appeared at ease and happy. Discipline problems were at least not obvious. . . . Another important achievement is increased interest in school-community relationships which takes the form of teacher-parent meetings to discuss problems, community surveys to find what students can do about health and housing problems, and, in a few cases, community recreation programs. There is also considerable evidence of increased reading of educational literature on the part of teachers. . . . Curriculum reconstruction is moving slowly and with varying degrees of success.

Rhind also pointed to the value of workshops as "the Study's most important form of assistance" and cited the use of consultants and the circulation of educational materials as valuable. The major problem, and one which will be discussed below, was that "not much has been accomplished in the development of increased cooooperation between schools and colleges." She also noted that many schools found it difficult to use the services of the study fully—some moved too fast and others too slow—and that guidance, evaluation, reading, recreation, health, and the general cooperation of colleges were all areas which needed strengthening.[22]

This latter area, cooperation between the secondary schools in the study with the black colleges, was essential to the success of the study and seems to be the one with the most difficulties. Unlike the Eight-Year Study, there was virtually no effort to evaluate empirically the impact of the Secondary School Study upon college attendance and performance. This may be explained partially by the intervening war and by the obvious need for blacks to deal with educational problems of a much more basic nature. It also appears that there were other reasons. A July, 1943, GEB internal memorandum by Rhind reports on a meeting held by the Control Committee at Virginia Union University in which better coordination between high schools and colleges was a major item on the agenda. "Just how this should be done," she reported,

> was the subject of somewhat acrimonious debate, and FMR was disturbed by some evidence of Mr. Robinson's inability to work tactfully with his committee. He appeared to react defensively to any suggestion made by a representative of higher education, and especially by President Clement. This same attitude is also present, but to a lesser degree, in Mr. Palmer, Chairman of the Control Committee and formerly Principal of Huntington H. S. at Newport News. It probably stems from a tendency on the part of the college people to resist changes in the high schools that imply adjustments at the college level. But certainly Robinson could get more help from his control committee if he showed less antagonism to the college representatives. It is too bad that his able mind, broad understanding of secondary school problems, and intense desire to serve his race, are not combined with poise and tact.

Palmer's testiness was explained in one of those brief passages that serves to remind us of the indignities which faced even one of the most respected black educators. Rhind's explanation was that "he has recently been discharged by the Newport News School Board [according to rumor because of his fight for equalization of salaries]."[23]

Robinson's behavior, assuming the accuracy of this report, is less easy to explain. Some of it was doubtless related to his drive and outspokenness. Another explanation emerges from an October 1943 letter he wrote to Rhind. With reference to the Virginia Union University meeting, he said that

> You will remember that the principals . . . indicated that guidance efforts in the schools are at present almost without any effective help from the colleges of the region and is one of the pressing needs of the schools. . . . As far as I have seen what the colleges are prepared to do for teachers-in-service or prospective teachers, there is little help to schools that can be expected of them until some college people in the region are trained to give some realistic help to teachers and to schools. In some of the colleges teachers of "education" have had courses in guidance and teach these courses to students of education. These courses, as I have seen them, are textbook courses and are highly academic and theoretical but is about all that the colleges are prepared to do at this time.[24]

These, of course, are the perpetual frustrations of school people who look askance at the relevancy of much of what goes on in colleges of education.

They irritated Robinson, the dreamer who had such high hopes for his work and that of the study. In mid-1945, as the Secondary School Study moved into its final phases (attempts to obtain further having failed), Robinson visited Rhind to inform her that he had accepted the principalship of a small Phoenix, Arizona, high school for blacks, where he believed conditions would be less frustrating than in Atlanta.[25] Obviously, however, his frustrations were with far more than Atlanta. In a 1946 handwritten letter to Fred McCuiston of the GEB, Robinson seemed to admit that his earlier expectations had been disappointed, at least as far as higher education was concerned. Black colleges, he wrote, were "little tyrannies, some more benevolent than others, and they are so abstract in their teaching that few teachers could tell anyone what their goals, other than academic, are." There must be a place, he mused, for black young people to come of age. And what of the General Education Board? This man who endured the suspicion of board officials for many years wrote that

> the General Education Board has done more to remake American
> education than any other influence. . . . I must say that the Board
> has not indoctrinated, a phenomenon I shall never understand
> knowing the source of the funds. I know I would have been sensi-
> tive to any such effort and would have rebelled strongly against
> it personally.[26]

With that note of appreciation, Robinson disappeared from the files of the General Education Board and American educational history. He was to live but a few more years.

Conclusion

Robinson's departure coincided with the decline of his brand of progressive education as a movement in the new postwar world and, not insignificantly, with the deterioration of the segregated system of education of which the Secondary School Study, the NATCS, the ACSSN, and other separate black organizations were a part. Within twenty years it would be hard to speak of "black" progressive education. It is difficult at this point to assess the long-range impact of the Secondary School Study on subsequent events in the South, particularly on the black consciousness which exploded throughout the region and ultimately ended regional segregation. Until much more is known about the intersection of what went on in black schools and the development of this consciousness, the question will go unanswered. As it is, historians have yet to explore in any detail the place of black educators in reform movements and the nature of curricular innovation and change in schools which, in their daily operation, were largely controlled by the people who worked in them. The hidden and, as in the case of the Secondary School Study, the not-so-hidden agendas of these institutions must be studied and understood.

It does seem likely that the study, possibly more than any other event in the history of black public schooling in the South, represented a coming of age and an attempt to introduce progressive forms of education which would lighten some of the burdens imposed by a patently racist educational super-structure. Robinson and his colleagues must therefore be seen as part of the black movement for justice in the South; their progressivism broke with that of the past in critical respects. They must be included in future histories of the progressive education movement.

The study also provides a glimpse into some of the functions of progressive education. Many historians have argued that in important respects progressivism has been a conservative phenomenon, something that is masked by its apparent concern for the child and its democratic rhetoric. The Secondary School Study and its leaders recognized this clearly almost fifty years ago. But they also believed that progressivism provided an avenue to liberal if not radical reform. It may be argued that Robinson and his fellow black professional educators who tried to climb on the progressive bandwagon were interested primarily in self-serving professional agendas, like many of their white counterparts. They did, after all, support measures which are now looked upon with some suspicion by those who are critical of the historical development and use of testing, guidance, and many of the other reforms supported by the study. This being said, these black educators, even if ultimately dependent on white funding and political control, showed courage in arguing for a *black* application of progressive education which would not serve these conservative functions. They recognized some of the contradictions inherent in progressivism's pluralistic nature and were willing to consider progressivism per se, independent of those progressives who would consciously or unconsciously victimize them. Given progressivism's democratic philosophy, they knew that it would be impossible to deny them access to *some* resources for the implementation of a program which, in its essential features, appeared similar to white progressive programs. Hence, through judicious imitation, they were able to launch a small attack on educational practices which oppressed them and their children. A study of their actions increases our understanding of some of the functions of progressive educational reform and underscores the need for historians to explore the relationship between progressive reform, ethnic and racial minorities, the modernization process, and specific regional, national, and perhaps international contexts.

Notes

This paper was presented in slightly different versions at the University of
Florida and at a meeting of the History of Education Society in 1978.
Financial support from the Regents of the University of Florida, the
Research Foundation of the State University of New York, and Trinity
College contributed to its development. I would also like to acknowl-
edge the assistance of the staff of the Schomburg Collection of the New
York Public Library, the Archives of the University of Illinois, the
Special Collections Department of the Teachers College, Columbia
University Library, and the Rockefeller Archives Center in Pocantico
Hills, New York. Walter Feinberg, David Tyack, Arthur O. White, and
James Anderson shared materials and insights. I, of course, am respon-
sible for the essay's main ideas.

1. Several books provide helpful introductions to the progressive education
   movement in the years covered by this paper although they do not deal
   with Southern progressive education per se. The most thorough and
   comprehensive history is Lawrence A. Cremin, *The Transformation of
   the School: Progressivism in American Education, 1876–1957* (New
   York: Vintage Books, 1961). Patricia A. Graham, *Progressive Education: From Arcady to Academe* (New York: Teachers College Press,
   1967) discusses the organizational history of the Progressive Education
   Association. Differing views of the social reconstructionist wing of the
   progressive movement are offered in C. A. Bowers, *The Progressive
   Educator and the Depression: The Radical Years* (New York: Random
   House, 1969) and Walter Feinberg, *Reason and Rhetoric: The Intellectual Foundations of Twentieth Century Educational Policy* (New York:
   John Wiley & Sons, 1975). Of the above, only Feinberg examines the
   reactions of progressive educators to problems related to race and
   ethnicity. There is very little general literature on the history of South-
   ern black education in the Depression. A helpful introduction is Horace
   Mann Bond, *The Education of the Negro in the American Social
   Order* (New York, Octagon, [1934] 1966). For additional information
   on these topics, see other essays in this book and Ronald K. Goodenow,
   "Paradox in Progressive Educational Reform: The South and the
   Education of Blacks in the Depression Years," *Phylon*, 39 (March
   1978): 49–65; and William H. Martin, "Unique Contributions of Negro
   Educators," Ch. 2 in *Negro Education in America: Its Adequacy,
   Problems and Needs,* ed. A. Clift, Archibald W. Anderson, and H. Gordon Hullfish, Sixteenth Yearbook of the John Dewey Society (New
   York: Harper & Bros., 1962).
2. See Goodenow, "Paradox"; also "The Progressive Educator, Race and
   Ethnicity in the Depression Years: An Overview," *History of Education Quarterly* 15 (Winter 1975): 365–395; "The Progressive Educator
   on Race, Ethnicity, Creativity and Planning: Harold Rugg in the
   1930's," *Review Journal of Philosophy and Social Science* 1 (Winter

1977): 105–128; and "Buell Gallagher as President of Talladega College: An Educational Reconstructionist in Action," *Cutting Edge: Journal of the Society for Educational Reconstruction* 8 (Winter 1977): 9–19. I have provided other relevant information on the progressive education movement and race in the 1930s in Ronald K. Goodenow, "Racial and Ethnic Tolerance in John Dewey's Educational and Social Thought: The Depression Years," *Educational Theory* 26 (Winter 1977): 48–64; "The Progressive Educator as Radical or Conservative: George S. Counts and Race," *History of Education* 7 (Winter 1977): 45–57; and "The Progressive Educator and Native Americans," *History of Education Quarterly* 20 (Summer 1980): 207–216.

3. The annual committee reports published in *NEA Addresses and Proceedings* provide the best insight into the committee's activities. See especially pp. 876–887 for 1939. Also helpful are Edgar B. Wesley, *NEA: The First Hundred Years: The Building of the Teaching Profession* (New York: Harper & Bros., 1957), pp. 317–320 and the general background information in Michael John Schultz, *The National Education Association and the Black Teacher: The Integration of a Professional Organization* (Coral Gables, Fla.: University of Miami Press, 1970). See W. W. Sanders, "The Problem of Negro Education Presented to the Department of Superintendence of the NEA," *The Bulletin* 12 (January 1934): 9, and "Current Events of Importance in Negro Education," *Journal of Negro Education* 3 (October 1934): 648.

   The national constitution of the competing American Federation of Teachers forbade discrimination, although custom in the South generally made integrated activity difficult. Blacks did, however, occupy positions on national committees, including the AFT Executive Council. Doxey Wilkerson, for example, was a national vice-president in the late 1930s. For a brief but helpful discussion see H. A. Callis, "The Negro Teacher and the A. F. T.," *Journal of Negro Education* 6 (April 1937): 188–190 and Joseph Newman's essay in this book. For a look at a black chapter in Virginia which enjoyed considerable support see *Virginia Teachers Bulletin* 3 (October 1939): 648.

4. For a general history see J. R. E. Lee, "Report of Committee to Compile History of N. A. T. C. S.," *Bulletin* 14 (November 1935): 54–55, 101. Lee noted that as of 1935 organizational records were virtually nonexistent. For the estimate of its minimal membership see Ambrose Caliver, "The Role of the Teacher in the Reorganization and the Redirection of Negro Education," *Journal of Negro Education* 5 (July 1936): 513. Valuable background material may be found in the following articles in the *National Educational Outlook Among Negroes:* "Report of the Committee on Resolutions of the American Teachers Association," 18 (September 1937): 24–25; Editorial, "A Message and a Challenge," 18 (September 1937): 4–5; Carrington L. Davis, "Basic Program of the American Teachers Association," 19 (December 1938): 28–31; and Carrington L. Davis, "Statement of the President," 17 (June 1936): 38.

5. For a detailed discussion of this organization and its continued efforts to avoid the smothering embraces of the Southern Association, see W. A. Robinson, "The Association of Colleges for Negro Youth Organizes," *High School Quarterly* 18 (April 1935): 181–185, and Joseph Arthur Payne, Jr., "An Analysis of the Role of the Association of Colleges and Secondary Schools for Negroes from 1934 to 1954," (Ed.D. Diss., University of Indiana, 1957). While this generally uncritical history makes the role of the organization rather clear with reference to the issue of professionalism and the reform of black schooling, it is absolutely silent on the Secondary School Study, perhaps the major effort of the ACSSN in the late 1930s and early World War II years.

6. Ambrose Caliver, "Outcomes of the National Conference on Fundamental Problems in the Education of Negroes," *Quarterly Review of Higher Education Among Negroes* 2 (October 1934): 230–239 (hereafter cited as *Quarterly Review*). I have purposely avoided a discussion of the blacks who constituted the "Social Reconstructionist" wing of the Progressive Education Movement. For brief discussions of this topic see Goodenow, "Paradox," and "The Progressive Educator."

7. Its proceedings are included in Ambrose Caliver (ed.), *Fundamentals in the Education of Negroes*, U. S. Office of Education, Bulletin no. 6 (Washington, D.C.: U. S. Government Printing Office, 1935).

8. PEA work in the South warrants separate study and will only be touched upon in this essay. For information on its activities see Goodenow, "Paradox;" "Minutes of Board of Directors, Progressive Education Association," April 7, 1935, PEA Mss., Teachers College, Columbia University, New York, N.Y. and various requests for funding to the General Education Board, located in the manuscript collections of the Rockefeller Foundation Archive Center, Pocantino Hills, N.Y. For these requests (which often included reports on its Southern work) and the GEB's response see especially "Field Work in the South Sponsored by the Progressive Education Association," Southern Conference of the Progressive Education Association: Education and Southern Problems, Greensboro, N.C., December 2–3, 1938; interview, Frank C. Jenkins by Leo M. Favrot of the GEB, March 27, 1939; interview, Favrot of Frederick L. Redefer of the PEA, April 17, 1939; Redefer to Favrot, April 18, 1939; notes on a telephone conversation between Fred McCuiston of the GEB and Dean K. J. Hoke of the College of William and Mary, August 11, 1939; and Robert J. Havighurst's internal GEB memorandum, "Conference with PEA Committee on Workshops and Field Service concerning Workshops in the South," August 2–21, 1939, GEB Mss. Of a total PEA membership of 8,635 in 1936, 743 Southerners belonged. See "Comparative Membership Breakdown, PEA." PEA Mss., University of Illinois, Champaign-Urbana, Illinois. Aside from the fact that by the late 1930s PEA committees and commissions were openly addressing racial matters, the PEA was beset by a radical image. Its files and those of the GEB evidence fears that this image would hinder the progress of gradual education (and presumably

social) reform. See, for example, W. A. Robinson to N. C. Newbold, August 14, 1942 (GEB Mss.), and J. G. Umstattd to V. H. Tibbetts, January 24, 1944. PEA Mss.

For a comprehensive review of Southern GEB policies through the mid-Depression years, see the work of James D. Anderson, especially "Northern foundations and the shaping of Southern black rural education, 1902–1935," *History of Education Quarterly* 18 (Winter 1978): 371–396. Anderson's citations provide information on relevant secondary materials. The reader is also referred to the serially published *Annual Report of the General Education Board* for valuable statements of board philosophy which was supportive of economic and educational modernization, the maintenance of an appropriately trained and compliant labor force, and, in the Depression years, peace in the region. Also see Goodenow, "The Progressive Educator."

9. See Frank Jenkins, *The Southern Association Study, A Report of the Work with the Thirty-Three Cooperating Secondary Schools* (The Committees on Curricular Problems and Research of the Southern Association of Colleges and Secondary Schools: 1941). The PEA's study is discussed in Wilfred Aiken, *The Eight-Year Study: With Conclusions and Recommendations* (New York: Harper & Row, 1942).

10. Favrot, interview with W. A. Robinson, July 14, 1938. GEB Mss.

11. Favrot to Frank Jenkins, October 21, 1938. GEB Mss.

12. Interview, Leo Favrot and Fred McCuiston with Rufus E. Clement, July 19, 1939. GEB Mss.

13. Wilfren Aiken to Robert Havighurst, December 16, 1937. PEA Mss.

14. W. A. Robinson, "Progressive Education and the Negro," *Proceedings, Association of Colleges and Secondary Schools for Negroes*, 1937, pp. 57–64. The progressive pedagogy of Robinson's Atlanta University Laboratory School is described in Homer H. Howard, "Look in Your Own Backyard," *Progressive Education* 12 (January 1935): 24–29.

15. W. A. Robinson, "What is Progressive Education?" *Virginia Teachers Bulletin* 14 (February 1937): 23–26.

16. W. A. Robinson, "The Challenge of Progressive Education," *Virginia Teachers Bulletin* 16 (May 1939): 15–16. Robinson claims here that "the Progressive Education Association . . . invites all of us to join and share with them their conferences, workshops and their magazines and other publications." I have found no evidence of such a call to *blacks*.

17. W. A. Robinson, "A New Era for Negro Schools," *Progressive Education* 17 (December 1940): 541–544.

18. See W. H. Brown, "A Partial Evaluation of the Secondary Schools Study—Implications for Schools and Colleges," *Proceedings, Association of Colleges and Secondary Schools for Negroes*, 1945, p. 48. The single most helpful guide to study programs is William H. Brown and William A. Robinson, *Serving Negro Schools: A Report on the Secondary School Study, Its Purposes, Working Techniques and Findings*, Secondary School Study of the Association of Colleges and Secondary Schools for Negroes (Atlanta, Ga.: 1946). See p. 71 for a listing of

workshop publications. For details on techniques developed and used by
the study see William H. Brown, "An Experimental Study of Workshop
Type Professional Education for Negro Teachers," *Journal of Negro
Education* 14 (Winter 1945): 48–58. There is considerable black litera-
ture on the influence of PEA-developed workshop techniques. See, for
example, William H. Martin, "Providing Non-School Experiences in
Teacher Education," *Quarterly Review* 10 (April 1942): 106–108;
George N. Redd, "Experimenting with the Workshop and Seminar in
the Education of Teachers," *Quarterly Review* 9 (January 1941): 10–
15; and George N. Redd, "An Analysis of Teacher Education Trends in
Negro Colleges," *Educational Administration and Supervision* 35
(December 1949): 461–474. A product of Teachers College, Columbia
University. Redd, like many leading black progressives, was deeply influenced by his graduate training at this center of progressive thought.
Also influential was Teachers College's short-lived New College, a demonstration teachers' college which featured field work and experimentation in its curriculum, and a social reconstructionist philosophy. It operated from 1932 until 1939 when it was closed down, ostensibly for
financial reasons. Attractive to radical students and left-leaning faculty,
it offered community-based courses and even the opportunity to study
in rural Georgia, where it operated out of an abandoned black school.
This latter undertaking was conducted with the understanding, dictated
by the local superintendent of schools, that "no one of Negro extrac-
tion shall come to the proposed institution as either student or teacher
or administrator; although it is understood New College may engage in
educational work for the negroes of this county." See Claude L. Purcell
to the director of New College, December 7, 1935, William Russell
Mss., Teachers College, Columbia University, New York, N.Y. For a full
description of the work of New College, see *New College for the Education of Teachers, Teachers College Bulletin,* twenty-seventh series, no. 2
(New York: December 1935). See also Lawrence Cremin, David Shannon, and Mary Evelyn Townsend, *A History of Teachers College, Columbia University* (New York: Teachers College Press, 1954), pp. 221–229.
19. See Brown, "A Partial Evaluation," and "Serving Negro Schools." Some
leading whites approached the Study with offers of help. See, for
example, V. T. Thayer to W. A. Robinson, November 26, 1940, GEB
Mss. Other whites volunteered to help, often without compensation. One such case was W. R. Wunsch of Black Mountain College, a
progressive North Carolina institution which was concerned about racial
issues in the early 1940s. See W. R. Wunsch to Robinson, February 3,
1941, and Robinson to Fred McCuiston, March 20, 1941, GEB Mss.
For a valuable look at Black Mountain College and the tragic career of
the brilliant Wunsch, see Martin Duberman, *Black Mountain: An Exploration in Community* (New York: Dutton, 1972).
20. For information on the Southern curriculum reform movement, its progressive theoretical base and the black response, see Goodenow,
"Paradox."

21. Robinson, *Serving Negro Schools*, p. 12. Study literature included some emphasis on civics, minority group problems, black economic conditions, and the meanings of democracy. See, for example "Report of Conference on Planning the High School Social Studies Curriculum around Wartime and Postwar Needs," held by The Secondary School Study of ACSSN at Fisk University, Atlanta, Ga., April 2–5, 1943 (GEB Mss.), and W. H. Brown, "Report of Two Years of Activity of the Secondary School Study of the Association of Colleges and Secondary Schools for Negroes," *The Virginia Teachers Bulletin* 21 (November 1942): 8–9. Brown wrote that study efforts to develop resources to improve the quality of instructional materials on civics and other social studies areas were limited. For a picture of study influence on one participating school, see *The Evolution of Susan Prim*, Lincoln High and Elementary School Faculties (Tallahassee, Fla., 1944). Prim, according to the booklet, developed a progressive educational philosophy, attended workshops, and taught her students about socio-economic conditions among blacks. Other helpful materials in the GEB files include *High School Was Like This*, Booker T. Washington High School Faculty (Rocky Mount, N.C., 1946); "Cooperative Planning for School Development: A Conference Report Developed Jointly by the Lincoln-Grant School and the Secondary School Study" (Covington, Ky., March 8–12, 1943); and "Report of Conference on Planning the High School Social Studies Curriculum Around Wartime and Post-War Needs held by the Secondary School Study of the ACSSN at Fisk University, Atlanta, Ga., April 2–5, 1943. The concerns expressed in these papers, of course, were not unique to the Secondary School Study. A partial listing of periodical publications on the need for progressive social studies in black schools would include H. Theo Tatum, "Education for Democratic Living," *National Educational Outlook Among Negroes* 19 (March 1938): 21–23; A. Ogden Porter, "How to Make the Social Studies More Practical," *Quarterly Review* 3 (October 1935): 201–206; George H. Binford, "The Contemporary American Social Situation and the Social Function of the School," *Virginia Teachers Bulletin* 8 (May 1936): 16–17; Luther P. Jackson, "Citizenship and Government," *Virginia Teachers Bulletin* 14 (March 1937): 18–19; and Fred Alexander, "The Social Basis for Integrating Experience," *Virginia Teachers Bulletin* 16 (May 1939): 2–13. There is also considerable literature on the need for a new approach to the social sciences at the college level. See, for example, Charles H. Wesley, "Guiding Principles in the Teaching of Social Sciences in the Negro Colleges," *Quarterly Review* 3 (October 1935): 180–188. Wesley was influenced by the work of James Harvey Robinson, Harry Elmer Barnes, Charles Beard, and the Commission on the School Studies of the American Historical Studies. For a review of his publications and influence see Earl E. Thorpe, *Black Historians: A Critique* (New York: Morrow & Co., 1971), pp. 134–137.
22. Flora M. Rhind, memorandum. Report on Negro Secondary School Study, March 15, 1943, GEB Mss. Literature generated by participants in the

Study provides excellent glimpses of black schools. See, for example,
W. A. Robinson, "Report on a Visit to the Schools of Savannah and
Chatham County, March 6–10, 1945," GEB Mss. The GEB files also
contain considerable correspondence from school principals and others
who had reason to communicate with the board. The actual study files
seem to have been destroyed in a post-World War II fire at Atlanta
University.

23. Flora M. Rhind, memorandum. "Meeting of Control Committee, Negro
Secondary School Study, Virginia Union University, July 29, 1943,"
GEB Mss. Palmer, one of the most outspoken and courageous of black
principals in the Depression years, was deeply influenced by progres-
sive theory and practice. See Lutrelle Palmer, "Cooperation Versus
Competition," *Virginia Teachers Bulletin* 12 (May 1935): 13; and "The
Negro in the High School Curriculum," *Virginia Teachers Bulletin* 4
(February 1937): 30–31. For a general description of his work and his
influence on Robinson and others see Clift, Anderson, and Hullfish,
Negro Education in America.

24. Robinson to Flora M. Rhind, October 26, 1943, GEB Mss.

25. Flora M. Rhind, internal memorandum, July 26, 1945, GEB Mss.

26. Robinson to Fred McCuiston, July 10, 1946, GEB Mss. For similar
sentiments, see also Robinson to Fred McCuiston, October 15, 1945,
GEB Mss.

Nancy L. Grant

Government Social Planning and Education for Blacks: The TVA Experience 1933-1945

The 1930s was a decade of social planning in many parts of the world, including the United States. New Deal planners labeled their form of social planning as "democratic" to dissociate themselves from the negative connotations of planning in totalitarian regimes. Planners assumed the responsibility for assuring the rights and fair treatment not only of the powerful majority but also of economically and politically marginal groups.

The largest unassimilated and powerless group in the United States were American blacks, particularly those who lived in the segregated South. Planners were caught between the intransigent attitudes of many whites who were against any form of racial equality and the increased pressure from civil rights groups and the federal courts to end racial discrimination.

The Tennessee Valley Authority (TVA) was the one institutionalized example of social planning in the New Deal. The TVA was located in a seven-state area encompassing parts of Kentucky, Tennessee, Alabama, Georgia, Mississippi, North Carolina, and Virginia. The topography ranged from the sparsely populated mountains of eastern Tennessee with its poor whites and Indians to the rolling hills of northern Alabama with its forty-percent black, sharecropper population. Despite the immense obstacles before it, TVA promised not only to "foster an orderly and proper physical and social development of the Tennessee Valley area, to provide jobs for the unemployed, to raise the standard of living through cheap electricity and income from improved farming methods," but also "to use a policy of racial non-discrimination in its hiring and training programs."[1]

An important ingredient in the TVA social development plan was the creation of educational opportunities to train valley inhabitants for the technologically skilled jobs of a modern society. Through its educational program, TVA sought to reshape the lives of inhabitants by providing a "ready and uncostly access to necessary knowledge and strength." TVA attempted to create educational opportunities in four ways: through vocational training directed by craft unions, through adult education programs in cooperation with local social service agencies, through experimental schools, and through supplementary funding of valley schools. Although most programs were provided for "the proud and inherently able Anglo-Saxon stock found in the southeastern region," blacks and other minorities were included in the TVA educational programs, albeit in a segregated position.[2]

The TVA educational programs for blacks between 1933 and 1945 illustrated several issues concerning the possibilities and limitations inherent in TVA social planning for all valley inhabitants. Among these issues were the conflicting and sometimes confusing roles of TVA educators in changing the economic aspirations and social mores of valley blacks and whites, the relationship between labor unions and TVA concerning the separate training programs for blacks and whites, the influence of local political and civic interest groups on the scope and impact of educational opportunities. Perhaps the most important issue was the dilemma within TVA caused by the need to reconcile its promise as a federal agency to avoid racial discrimination in hiring and training programs with its principles of social planning that provided for a retention of local customs and a sensitivity to racial mores, which in the Tennessee Valley meant separate and unequal schools, few accredited black colleges, and the exclusion of blacks from most skilled trades and professional positions.[3]

The social and planning sections of the TVA Act of 1933 were the basis for the educational programs and policies. This act was a product of compromise between the Congress and President Franklin Roosevelt. From the congressional initiative came the authorization for TVA to build dams for power production and to use the old Muscle Shoals nitrate plants for fertilizer production. From the presidential initiative came the supervision and authorization for TVA "to plan for the proper use of conservation and development of the natural resources of the Tennessee River Drainage Basin . . . for the general social and economic welfare of the nation.[4]

Although the TVA Act empowered the agency to establish a program for regional planning and development, TVA preferred to justify any developmental activity through its "action program" which consisted of whatever supportive activity was necessary to implement TVA's program of flood control, power production, and fertilizer manufacture. TVA promised to maintain a practical and fiscally responsible social planning program without any "harmful visionary or socialistic aspects." The decidedly pragmatic approach to problem-solving was championed by Arthur Morgan, the first chairman of the TVA board of directors. He believed that, "in taking any issue that may require attention, there is an effort to meet that particular issue so as to achieve good and enduring results by whatever methods will work best in that case."[5]

The action program served as the justification for the wide-ranging educational activities. A job-training program was necessary to produce more efficient employees. TVA also offered leadership training in order that "a more productive group of foremen, and personnel administrators be made available." TVA held adult education classes to stimulate the workers culturally and intellectually. A better informed employee was more satisfied and alert. To insure a ready pool of technologically trained employees for the future, TVA formed cooperative programs with Tennessee Valley colleges and vocational schools. In order to develop a prosperous and informed farming community better able to utilize TVA fertilizer and nitrate products, TVA formed cooperative programs with local farmers and agricultural colleges. The influx of TVA personnel involved in the construction and maintenance of dams put a strain on local facilities, particularly school systems; consequently, TVA made agreements with local school boards to help expand in order to meet the needs of the children of TVA employees. In addition, TVA built and maintained schools for several years in isolated dam sites where no other schools were available.[6]

TVA administrators promised that all employees would have access to a wide variety of skill-enhancing courses and programs. The programs were widely publicized in the local and national press. According to early newspaper and journal articles, TVA would bring wealth and prosperity to a valley that was economically depressed and would gently shove the people of the valley into the twentieth century.[7]

The task of implementing and supervising all forms of educational activities was given to the training section within the Division of Personnel. The staff was divided along functional lines. Separate staffs worked in the three major areas of TVA activities: the construction camps near the dam sites, the reservoir clearance areas where buildings and foliage were cleared away before the flooding, and the cities where TVA headquarters and regional offices were located. The demands and circumstances in each area were distinctly different. Training programs in reservoir clearance areas had to appeal to employees who lived close to their jobs and could easily scatter to their homes instead of taking vocational training. Here, the training staff served as community liaison aides rather than educational supervisors. A partial impetus for offering training programs at reservoir clearance areas came from TVA's need to improve its public relations efforts in those areas. For example, large numbers of people were relocated from the flood plain of Douglas Dam and were dissatisfied with TVA's efforts at resettlement. The training staff was reminded that "the problem of population readjustment in this reservoir is more difficult than any other project so far constructed and special efforts will be made to alleviate the conditions that will arise through this necessary readjustment. All assistance possible in building and maintaining employee morale and in securing ... friendly and cooperative relationships with the general public in these areas appears to be desirable."[8]

The construction villages presented a second set of circumstances. The workers were isolated from their home communities and had considerable leisure time; consequently, they were more willing to attend evening classes. The TVA staff in cooperation with the craft unions offered many classes in building trades and office skills. The cities presented a third set of circumstances. The educational facilities of the cities of Chattanooga and Knoxville, Tennessee, were rather extensive. Since most employees were professional or semiprofessional, the training staff placed an emphasis on career development classes. Classes in management skills and leadership training were well attended. The training staff also cooperated with the University of Tennessee and the University of Chattanooga in offering courses for employees through the university extensions. TVA also recruited students from local colleges as interns, assistants, and student engineers under arrangements that provided for practical work experience.[9]

The training staff was divided not only along functional lines but also along racial lines. The black training staff supervised all job training programs for black employees. In 1933, much to the interest of civil rights groups, the TVA board announced that it intended to give all the valley inhabitants an equal consideration for jobs and promotions. The promise of job equality was particularly significant in light of TVA's Southern location. TVA operated in states that practiced many forms of racial discrimination. Civil rights groups were also interested in the publication of the TVA Employee Relationship Policy which stated, "Appointments, . . . promotion, demotion, transfer, and retention in or termination of service with TVA will be made on the basis of merit and efficiency." More importantly it stated, "no discrimination in occupational classification or in rates of pay shall be made on the basis of sex or race."[10]

In order to insure that blacks received a proportionate share of employment opportunities, TVA initiated a quota system "to maintain the same proportion in the work force as the total population." Approximately eleven percent of the valley population was black. TVA managed to keep its percentage of blacks in the work force at eleven percent between 1933 and 1945. The quota was maintained through careful attention to the racial background of each TVA worker.[11]

The promise of nondiscrimination in TVA, if kept, could have signalled the beginning of the end to federally supported racial discrimination in the South. However, the reality of TVA was that of a government agency unable or unwilling to live up to its public promises for equality of treatment. In reality, the quota system produced a situation that continued the practice of hiring blacks in only the lowest, most temporary positions. TVA felt it could best meet its percentage objectives with the minimum disturbance to local custom or political pressures by confining its racial quota system to blacks employed in the reservoir clearance stage of the TVA. Most reservoir clearance work was unskilled and temporary in nature, with the average employment lasting only six months. TVA did not use racial quotas to fill skilled positions, insisting that "relatively few applicants of the Negro race have competed successfully with white applicants in training, experience, and examination requirements." Yet there was considerable evidence to show that eligible and qualified blacks were available for skilled work.[12] The meeting of the quota through unskilled positions gave no incentive for the personnel department to hire black skilled workers or to break down job barriers.[13]

The job training programs for white workers in construction villages, reservoir clearance areas, and cities appeared to be well implemented and have a positive impact, particularly in comparison with the limited program available to blacks. Yet these programs for whites had significant weaknesses and limitations. The job training program had little formal structure or overall plan. The courses of study were geared to interest a population that had little classroom experience and exhibited a "nonbookish" inclination. The TVA program lacked a basic curricular focus, primarily due to the policy of TVA to organize or arrange courses only around interested groups. A significant number of employees had to request a course for it to be included in the program. While employees were allowed to help shape their program, their imput also created a haphazard offering of courses.

The most popular courses were those specializing in the skilled construction trades. These courses were conducted in cooperation with the training staff and trade union representatives. Apprenticeship training was an important part of the program. The Joint Advisory Committee, comprised of representatives from the personnel department and the trade unions, set the standards for credit in the training courses. The stormy relationship with its trade unions was a major problem that plagued the TVA. Although union members served as instructors in the apprenticeship program, union representatives criticized TVA's efforts to provide instruction for a greater number of workers in the white community. Union representatives were very concerned when TVA circumvented the apprenticeship programs by recommending for advancement several employees who had not been approved by the Joint Committee. The unions fought to retain the final approval of hiring, firing, promotion in the TVA skilled trades. Yet the personnel department justified the retention of final approval by stating, "the eligibility standards for positions included in the established and prospective joint training programs were not sufficiently precise and comprehensive . . . to remove all questions of doubt . . . with respect to qualifications of prospective candidates for promotion."[14]

The unions also resisted efforts of the training staff to give prospective supervisors temporary job experience in the various crafts. The unions wished to promote members from their ranks and resented efforts to recruit supervisors from graduate schools and technical colleges. The unions wanted to guarantee that all skilled positions in TVA, even on a temporary basis, would be filled by union members. TVA compromised and hired a limited number of graduate students who were assigned temporarily to grades below foreman. The training programs were also hindered by jurisdictional battles between rival unions over which was more qualified to conduct the training sections. Approval for an operator training program for whites was delayed by claims from both the International Brotherhood of Electrical Workers and the International Union of Operation Engineers.[15]

Despite the difficulties with the unions, the apprenticeship training programs offered a wide variety of courses. White TVA employees could take classes to be trained as machinists, carpenters, electricians, pipefitters, and steelworkers, among other positions. Skills useful in a trade, such as the principles of blueprint reading and the essentials of alternating current, were also taught. Enrollment remained flexible and an employee could enter the course at any time of the year. Unfortunately, by necessity, many courses began at a basic level of instruction and enrollment for a period of three to six years was necessary to become a skilled craftsman. Most employees were hired only for the duration of a dam construction project which lasted at most two years. A terminated employee had no equivalent courses available in his or her resident community. TVA acknowledged that job training in the communities "has not been well-developed." Consequently, former employees who had been introduced to the basic skills necessary for apprenticeship could not continue in their community unless they followed the traditional route and worked under a skilled tradesman. The numbers that could be accommodated in the traditional system were far less than had been enrolled in the TVA courses.[16]

The problems in the training programs for whites were small compared with the enormous difficulties that beset the training programs for blacks. These programs were hindered by a combined unwillingness of TVA officials, trade unions, local inhabitants, and national politicians to allow an equal training opportunity for blacks. These programs were both separate and unequal. Adhering to the social mores of the region, TVA held segregated classes. Classes were available in all three areas, construction sites, reservoir clearance areas, and in the cities of Knoxville and Chattanooga, Tennessee, and Muscle Shoals, Alabama, but the number and variety were far less than that available to whites.

There were three basic types of courses open to black employees. The most widely available was instruction in janitorial services. This course emphasized the maintenance and care of modern electric tools, such as floor waxers and vacuum cleaners. Basic instruction in electrical wiring, meter reading, and plumbing repair were also included in the course. Another category of job training was instruction in catering and basic cooking skills that would be most useful for future domestics. A third category was instruction in gardening, poultry raising, the care of livestock, and other practical agricultural skills. In addition, there was instruction in the traditional

"Negro" semi-skilled trades for powermen, jackhammer operators, and wagon drill operators.[17]

The major training program in semi-skilled work for blacks before 1943 was the chemical operators program in the fertilizer plants at Muscle Shoals. Civil rights groups criticized TVA for having a large concentration of blacks in the fertilizer plants. The work force was over forty percent black, and most of the workers were laborers. Work at the fertilizer plants was considered one of the most undesirable positions available in TVA.[18]

There were no other types of courses available to black employees until 1942 when labor shortages caused by World War II forced TVA to offer apprenticeship training for electricians and line technicians on a limited basis. The Fair Employment Practices Committee (FEPC) also forced TVA to eliminate the most overt signs of discrimination, such as the exclusion of black workers from isolated dam sites. Established in 1941, the FEPC had little impact on racial practices in TVA. The FEPC used no punitive measures, and TVA chose to ignore the many warnings to end discrimination.[19]

TVA attempted to recruit black college students to work part-time or during the summer. Yet, unlike white college students who were made assistants in technological areas and worked as student engineers, black college students were given positions as student janitors. In 1936, TVA decided to upgrade its janitorial and charwoman staff. Citing new cleaning methods that utilized complicated washing and waxing machinery, TVA officials suggested that black students be employed as replacements for older employees. Unlike white students who eagerly sought TVA internships, very few black students responded to the recruitment efforts. Many black civic leaders expressed disappointment that TVA offered only janitorial work and not more professional positions.[20]

Partially in response to such criticism, TVA established an intern training program for blacks. Yet the training experience was social-service–oriented rather than technological. Students from Atlanta University, Fisk University, and Alabama Agricultural and Mechanical College were sent under TVA supervision into the black rural communities to act as recreational aides, librarians, and teacher aides. This program provided relatively inexpensive assistance to the black staff and extra income for the student interns. TVA also hoped to provide "real-life experience" and training in community relations. However, the program was discontinued after one summer due to inadequate supervision and direction by TVA personnel and the inability of some black students from urban areas to adjust to a rural environment.

The programs for blacks emphasized the status quo while programs for whites emphasized future positions in an increasingly modern society. Blacks were trained by TVA for positions that they had held traditionally in the valley. Indeed TVA acknowledged "that the educational need of Negro workers in the Authority arise from the environment in which they are placed and the occupations that are open to them."[22]

TVA officials contributed to the inferiority of the job training programs for blacks. Members of the first board of directors, Arthur Morgan, Harcourt Morgan, and David Lilienthal, did not believe that blacks were capable of filling skilled or professional positions in TVA, nor did they envisage a society that would allow equality of opportunity. Blacks had to institute self-help programs because, "TVA can only do so much for the Negroes." The TVA board considered the existence of the quota system and a limited training program to be more than adequate to satisfy the needs of blacks.[23]

Managers and supervisors also resisted an expansion of the job training program. The training staff interpreted the unfavorable response of black employees to the basic training courses as an example of poor motivation and lack of desire for self-improvement. The black training staff, on the other hand, noted that interest was high among blacks for courses in the skilled trades, yet none were offered, despite the TVA policy of selecting courses from requests made by workers. Low morale and discouragement were important factors that led to a small attendance. The black staff also noted that "workers who took part in the training program were seemingly the first ones to be laid off when the cuts came." Some supervisors resented black workers who participated in the training programs and openly discouraged workers from enrolling.[24]

Skilled trade unions were another obstacle. Already concerned about jurisdictional rights and control of apprenticeship training for white workers, the unions were not sympathetic to the prospect of black skilled labor. In 1940, TVA signed an agreement with the Tennessee Valley Trades and Labor Council, a body of sixteen unions affiliated with the American Federation of Labor. There was no mention of race in the agreement, although most participating unions excluded blacks from membership. The International Brotherhood of Electrical Workers and the United Association of Plumbers and Steam Fitters, among others, excluded blacks. Despite its problems with unions, TVA placed a high premium on cooperation. Although it denied allegations that blacks could not be hired unless the unions agreed, TVA did acknowledge that the representation of its employees by unions "is indispensible to the accomplishment of the public purposes for which the Authority has been established." TVA kept a "hands off" policy in regard to the discriminatory practices of the unions. During World War II, TVA did hire Negro linemen but forestalled significant protest from the unions by strictly segregating the crew.[25]

Political pressure was also exerted to maintain the racial status quo. Congressmen John Sparkman of Alabama and John Rankin of Mississippi protested that TVA was too liberal in its racial policies. Rankin warned that any increase in economic opportunities for blacks would "engender more

bitterness among southern representatives and southern senators than anything else I could mention and I do not want to see you [Lilienthal] hurt
by it." Rankin described himself as "a true friend of the TVA." The TVA,
troubled by congressional investigations and several lawsuits that threatened
the existence of the agency, did not wish to institute policies that could lose
its vital, Southern Democratic support.[26]

The adult education program, which was closely linked to the job training
program, had a similar disparity in treatment between blacks and whites.
General adult education was designed to bring the culturally isolated valley
society into the mainstream of American life. Educational and recreational
films were the main teaching aids. Many employees, both black and white,
had minimal reading skills and could understand visual images more easily.
TVA also used the radio to stimulate discussions about news and public
information programs.[27]

TVA established an extensive lending library system where popular and
scholarly books were available to the white workers and their families.
Classes were held to acquaint white employees on the virtues of good citizenship and the need to vote and participate in local government. Community
leadership classes were held to prepare TVA employees for the role of cultural
and social missionaries in spreading new methods of living throughout the
Southeast. TVA sponsored lecture series on such subjects as the value of
regular school attendance and the need for community cooperation in planning projects.[28]

Adult education for blacks was aimed at removing illiteracy and improving
basic hygiene. The workers were given instruction in basic English and social
workers visited their homes and taught the women ways of improving health
standards. While there were similar basic classes for whites, the more educated
blacks did not have the additional choices that whites had of such activities
as science club, applied psychology classes, and the TVA lecture series.[29]

TVA did atttempt to give black workers a degree of pride in their community and a sense of self-sufficiency. TVA clubs were organized to discuss
serious problems in the black community such as high infant mortality,
inadequate housing, crime, and irresponsibility. Although social issues were
discussed in the clubs, criticism of the larger society was not encouraged.
Criticism was directed at the black community's inability to take advantage
of existing opportunities within a segregated society. For example, there were
discussions on how better to develop dependable work habits to offset a
negative image of blacks within the white community. Through its leadership
program, TVA sought to develop leaders from the black community who were
good organizers, uncritical of existing inequalities, and grateful for assistance
and guidance by the TVA.[30]

In addition to job training and adult classes, the TVA educational program
included cooperative efforts between TVA and the land-grant colleges and

universities in the valley. TVA had cooperative programs with the Universities of Virginia, Alabama, Tennessee, Georgia, Mississippi, Kentucky, and North Carolina. Virginia Polytechnic Institute and Alabama Polytechnic Institute also participated. Harcourt Morgan had been the president of the University of Tennessee before his appointment to the TVA board of directors and was a well-known expert in the field of agricultural education. He assured the valley associations of higher learning that TVA did not intend to duplicate the efforts and programs already established in the colleges. Rather, TVA promised to pool available knowledge and use university experts as consultants.[31]

TVA signed contracts with the colleges to provide specific services and personnel. University laboratories were contracted to do research, primarily in phosphates for fertilizers. Engineering departments were charged with the development of new and better-adapted forms of farm machinery. The agricultural extension services of the land grant colleges were used to promote agricultural education on the farms through farm demonstration projects. TVA also employed university faculty and staff for periods of up to a year to conduct surveys and studies on land use, regional planning, and resettlement adjustment problems.[32]

The colleges and universities received various forms of support from TVA in order to expand and improve those departments and fields most vital to the long-range development of the Tennessee Valley. An arrangement between the University of Tennessee and the TVA for the provision of training in public administration resulted in the formation of the political science department at the university. The TVA training division employed a supervisor of training in public administration. TVA recommended this supervisor to the individual who hired him as a teacher of political science. He was soon promoted to lecturer, then assistant professor, and later became an associate professor in the expanded department.[33]

The relationship between the TVA and the valley colleges remained positive throughout the early years, although there were serious complaints from both sides. The colleges were concerned that contracts with TVA were too short in duration to allow successful completion of experiments and research and did not allow enough time for follow-up studies. On the other hand, TVA administrators considered themselves to be practical and realistic planners and complained that academics were impractical, politically naive, occasionally irrational, and consequently, could not be trusted with policy decisions.[34]

Despite misgivings about the practicality of university professors, TVA did establish ties with white land-grant colleges. For a variety of reasons, TVA chose not to establish a similar cooperative program with the few black land-grant colleges in the valley. TVA did have some contact with black colleges in the area, including Knoxville College, Fisk University, Alabama Agricultural and Mechanical College, and Tuskegee Institute. TVA contacted Knoxville College in order to recruit college interns for its janitorial trainee program. Fisk University had a more academic relationship with TVA, although on a limited scale. TVA and Fisk University exchanged speakers. Floyd Reeves, the first director of personnel, was a frequent lecturer at Fisk, and Charles Johnson, a Fisk sociologist, was a frequent visitor to TVA. Johnson conducted several studies for TVA. One study was entitled, "The Negro Personality Changes under Conditions of Race and Culture in the Tennessee Valley area." Fisk also participated in the adult education program of TVA and offered college credit for some courses in the TVA extension program.[35]

Fisk professors occasionally sought advice from TVA on courses and exams. Fisk sent Masters examinations to Reeves, a former professor at the University of Chicago. Students were asked to write essays on, "the married woman as school teacher," "the depression and education," and "the over-supply of teachers." Reeves replied, "the objective and subjective scores would differ but I would pass six without question if they were at University of Chicago—fail one and conditionally pass three." By sending exams, Fisk was able to establish an early relationship with the director of personnel and to obtain written legitimization of standards and the quality of students, although the college was unable to translate approval of standards and quality into TVA employment for many Fisk students.[36]

TVA also formed a cooperative relationship with Alabama Agricultural and Mechanical College, although the relationship involved participation in TVA's adult training program. In 1938, TVA encouraged Alabama A&M to rent and remodel a dwelling in the city of Huntsville in order to conduct classes for TVA. TVA sought to obtain money to facilitate the renovation. It attempted to gain financial support from the Alabama Department of Education as well as the Julius Rosenwald Fund. Yet TVA itself did not give financial support and stated, "we are not justified in withholding funds in order to assist with that project." The A&M project was not funded, primarily due to resistance from the state department of education. Traditionally, Alabama A&M had diffi-culty securing an operating budget. In 1938, the appropriation for A&M was $17,000 while the appropriation for white institutions of like rank and size was $35,000. The chief reason for the small budget was "the opposition of the legislators from this region. [T]hey are definitely not in favor of much Negro education." TVA elected to place the cooperation with local and state institu-tions above the need to build a strong adult educational program in Alabama and did not press for further cooperative projects with Alabama A&M.[37]

Tuskegee Institute was the only black college with which TVA made an effort to establish cooperation in research. TVA did not consider other insti-tutions to be worthy of cooperation. One TVA official stated, "so far as we are able to determine at this time the Tuskegee Institute is the only Negro institution with which we may cooperate." Schools such as Alabama A&M College were considered to be advanced high schools that sent their best stu-dents to either Fisk or Tuskegee to finish their undergraduate degrees.[38]

TVA sought to arrange a cooperative relationship with the laboratories of Dr. George Washington Carver, a well-known black chemist at Tuskegee. From 1933 through 1939, it attempted to contact Carver about a series of experiments Carver was conducting on outdoor paint. Carver, an extremely cautious individual, questioned TVA's interest in his research projects. Educators were divided over the wisdom of cooperating with Carver. Some TVA educators noted Carver's lack of cooperation and questioned the legitimacy of Carver's scientific credentials. One skeptical TVA administrator wrote, "from sources of information we understand the chemist is somewhat of an eccentric genius whatever that might be and that he has hit on several things that have possibilities of being developed into industries with commercial value."[39]

To offset the negative image of Carver within TVA, letters of support for his scientific contributions were written by non-TVA academics. One such academic, Ernest Seeman of Duke University wrote:

> Personally I think there is a great misunderstanding about this man
> Carver in that he is "said to be an eccentric genius" and "has hit
> upon several things." . . . He has worked industriously long hours
> for long years and if his skin had been white he would now have a
> high place in the annals of science. . . . He is the same kind of eccen-
> tric genius as were Galileo, Langley and Edison.

Seeman also sent clippings from Carver's biography in *Who's Who*. As a way to pressure Carver, Seeman suggested that the president of Tuskegee be contacted.[40]

TVA followed Seeman's advice and used a variety of intermediaries to finally succeed in establishing a small cooperative research project for the development of low-cost paints. TVA hoped that through its rural electrification program, more homes in poorer cotton-belt regions would use electric power and electric equipment and appliances. There would also be a growing need for low-cost paint for interior use to improve lighting. Through cooperation with Carver's laboratory, which had developed an organic paint, TVA hoped to develop a market for low-cost paint which would result in a new industry of paint manufacture.[41]

TVA and Tuskegee conducted the research project from 1939 through 1941. TVA contributed approximately $4,000 to the project. Yet TVA retrieved all equipment purchased for the research project and reserved control over any invention or new processes developed during the period of cooperation.[42] After 1941 TVA did not have another cooperative program with a black college until 1949, when it concluded an agreement with Tuskegee to provide a study of the effects of rapidly changing economic conditions upon six black communities in northern Alabama.[43]

Black schools including Tuskegee were virtually ignored in comparison with money spent and energy expended on white colleges. In connection with TVA's announced program of agricultural development and watershed protection through improved fertilization, Tuskegee asked for a carload of TVA fertilizer for experimental purposes. TVA replied that it could not comply with Tuskegee's request for several reasons. TVA noted that all requests for experimental work had to be cleared with the state-controlled Alabama Experimental Station and no guarantee could be given that Tuskegee would be accepted. In addition, Tuskegee had requested nitrate fertilizer and, at the time of the request, TVA was manufacturing only phosphate fertilizers.[44] Finally, TVA chose to interpret Tuskegee's request as being more suitable as a demonstration farm project than an experimental project. A demonstration farm project consisted of several chosen farmers being given fertilizers and instruction in growing techniques, while an experimental project involved academic departments and brought thousands of dollars along with the latest research techniques and equipment to the college.[45]

The fourth part of the TVA education program and the most important in terms of impact on future generations was the elementary and secondary school program. TVA built and operated schools in isolated areas and made contracts with school boards in more established communities. The TVA-operated schools were laboratories in which new teaching methods and experimental curricula were introduced into the very conservative region of the Scottsboro and Scopes trials. Norris School, located in the TVA model community of Norris, Tennessee, was the first and most ambitious laboratory project. The town of Norris was built by TVA for the workers engaged in the construction of Norris Dam in eastern Tennessee. Instead of building a temporary camp or construction village, TVA decided to plan and build a model community with spacious homes, recreational facilities, and a permanent, well-equiped school for the children. Originally, only those employed by TVA were allowed to live in Norris; however, after the dam was completed in 1936 and the work force decreased, TVA decided to open the town to all white inhabitants of the region.[46]

The secondary school at Norris attempted an innovative approach to education and hoped to attract students who ordinarily would not have continued in school. TVA educators were very concerned with the widespread apathy toward high school and consequently placed considerable emphasis on the practical nature of high school education and its usefulness in later life. Science students were taken on field trips to learn about weather forecasts and physical geography. Math classes were taken to banks where bookkeeping systems, financial contracts, and investments were explained. Younger children in junior high school were given courses in home living, emphasizing, "the duties in a modern home including home management, budgeting, repair, cooking, sewing, and child care instead of traditional courses in home economics and woodworking." Students were encouraged to talk freely in classroom discussions. Total participation was encouraged in recreational activities as well. TVA educators felt that too much emphasis had been placed on the competitive aspect of school sports. Athletic activities at Norris School were intramural, and every student had an opportunity to participate.[47]

TVA educators were concerned that Tennessee Valley children had been raised in an atmosphere of failure and inferiority for many years. They attempted to create a comfortable, noncompetitive atmosphere. There were no written grades or report cards. The parents received letters from the school indicating the progress or lack of progress of the child. The child never repeated a grade. Grade levels were sufficiently flexible to allow various levels of proficiency in each classroom. Educators also believed that chronological age and similar physiological development were factors significant enough to prevent unusually bright pupils from skipping ahead several grades.[48]

The innovative programs of Norris School lasted eight to ten years. After the completion of the Norris Dam, TVA gradually divested itself of the primary responsibility and support of the school. As the local institutions, particularly the Tennessee Department of Education and the Anderson County School Board, took control, the more "nonessential" features of the school were eliminated. Staff hired by TVA were replaced by local school-teachers. All art and music teachers were fired. Expenditures for the upkeep of the physical plant, particularly the landscaping and janitorial services, were cut. Library services were curtailed. The school returned to a grading system and the practice of failing poor students. The school year was shortened from ten months to eight months. By 1945, Norris School began to resemble the neighboring county schools.[49]

The reduction of services and standards at Norris School caused considerable disappointment among the Norris parents who were supportive of the innovative program. Parents protested the change to local control with the resultant deterioration of academic standards, yet they had little impact on the TVA decision. TVA asserted that it had no legal responsibility to educate the children of workers. It had built schools to help local school boards adjust to the sudden influx of students in an isolated and poor region. After the number of students in the region decreased, TVA felt the local school boards could provide for TVA children. Norris School was turned over to the Anderson School Board in 1945.[50]

Protests were also heard from black TVA workers concerning the Norris area. They protested the racial exclusion practiced by TVA at Norris. TVA contended that it did not exclude blacks from the model community and only wished to minimalize racial tension by keeping the black population small. Protests from the Knoxville Civic Committee, a group comprised of local black leaders, and the NAACP did not end the exclusionary practices.

No blacks lived or attended school in Norris, although a few worked at the dam, between 1933 and 1945.[51]

TVA operated two other experimental schools for workers' children, one at Wilson Dam for whites and one at Joe Wheeler Dam for blacks. The Wilson Dam school was similar to Norris in its overall educational philosophy, yet the Wilson School was even more pronounced in its advocacy for the rights of the child. The interests, problems, and desires of the child came before the need to conform to a standard curriculum. Different ways to encourage interest in learning were tried, including reading "Alley Oop" comic books to stimulate reading skills. Despite protests from parents, TVA decided to discontinue the Wilson School in 1942 and send the workers' children to the inferior Sheffield, Alabama, county schools.[52]

TVA provided an elementary school for blacks during the height of construction of Joe Wheeler Dam, located near Muscle Shoals. The school had one room where one teacher taught grades one through six. The school was established only after the parents in the community requested a school for their children. The black workers at first obtained the services of three volunteer teachers and held classes in their homes. A teacher was hired for 1935. The Wheeler School attempted to introduce black children to modern teaching methods on a limited scale.

The school had a small library, a nature museum, and an arts and crafts shop. The curriculum of the Wheeler Dam School reflected the perceived special needs of black children. Although the standard elementary subjects were taught, hygiene and music classes were stressed. A special emphasis was placed on music appreciation and the playing of the piano. The teacher observed that "music plays an important role in the daily life of the people. . . . [F]or this reason there is a high correlation between leadership and the ability to play the piano. . . . I therefore decided to provide free instructions to those students who were interested."[53]

In addition to new definitions of leadership abilities, the teacher relied on standardized test scores and IQ tests to evaluate her pupils. Although most of the students at the Wheeler School were judged as capable or above average in school assignments, most tested between 76 and 90 on the Binet-Simon intelligence tests. The teacher noted that one boy had been found to have an IQ of only 76. He had been considered a very bright boy who did excellent work and was the school leader. Regretting the mistaken and inexact appraisal, the teacher welcomed the "more exact measure . . . of the Binet-Simon intelligence test."[54]

A program that used the questionable pedagogic concepts of one teacher for one year could not compare with the two extensive programs for white children at Wilson and Norris dams. When questioned about the lack of TVA-run schools for blacks, TVA officials stated that they preferred to form contracts with local school boards for the education of black TVA employees.[55]

Indeed, it was the policy of TVA to enter into a contract with local school boards to educate most children of TVA employees. To offset the problem of increased attendance in local schools, TVA provided tuition vouchers on a per pupil basis. Many schools did not meet TVA minimum standards for elementary education in the number of days in session and the number of books per pupil. There were many schools for whites that had one teacher for all six grades. Many schools were heated with a single wood burning stove and did not have janitorial service. In order to raise the standards of the local schools, TVA provided additional money for supplies and persuaded many school districts to lengthen their school terms to at least 156 days. Each school district was assigned a TVA education consultant who worked closely with the boards of education to lessen educational deficiencies in the district. The consultant offered advice on qualification examinations for schoolteachers and the selection of proper and useful textbooks.[56]

Contracts with local school boards for the education of black children presented special problems for TVA. While local white schools were considered substandard by TVA, most black schools were much worse. The school boards in the seven Tennessee Valley states traditionally spent less on black schools, and the facilities and level of instruction reflected this disparity in funding. TVA signed contracts for the education of black children with school boards who promised to use the TVA money to upgrade their instruction. For example, Rhea County, Tennessee, promised to provide adequate materials and keep their schools for blacks open at least 156 days. The school board also provided transportation in TVA-approved metal school buses. In return, TVA agreed to pay $60 for each pupil assigned. The school board was free to use any money above the actual expenses per child for purchasing additional books, equipment, and training materials. TVA entered into an agreement with the city of Benton, Kentucky, to take black and white children of employees working at Kentucky Dam. TVA agreed to pay a sum of $80 for each white pupil and $135 for each black pupil. The higher cost per pupil for black children was due to the unavailability of black schools in Benton; consequently, other communities, particularly Paducah, Kentucky, were paid extra money by Benton to take the children. On the other hand, in keeping with local practices, TVA paid the school board of Sheffield, Alabama, the sum of $55 for each white child and only $30 for each black child.[57]

The additional expense of educating black children was used as a partial excuse to argue against hiring blacks at certain work sites, particularly Hiwassee and Douglas Dams. Hiwassee Dam was located in an area where there were few blacks. TVA argued that the number of black children would not be enough to warrant a TVA-operated school and there were no schools for blacks in the vicinity of the dam site. TVA decided to solve the problem by not hiring any blacks.[58]

All contracts between TVA and school districts were terminated by 1945 and the subsidies were eliminated from TVA's expenditures. Contract terminations caused some hardships for school boards. Some board members questioned the equity of the discontinuance. They complained that they had not been given adequate notice and consequently did not have enough money appropriated to educate the unsubsidized TVA children. TVA consistently replied that it had no legal responsibility to continue the subsidies.[59]

The period of TVA participation in elementary and secondary school education and to a large extent in adult education ended in 1945. Cooperation with colleges and the job training program continued to be supported but in a much less publicized manner. The year 1945 represented the end of many social planning programs that had started with such fanfare and hope in 1933. The TVA educational programs were not supported long enough to change significantly the economic aspirations and cultural mores of valley blacks and whites. Most schools were supported for much fewer than ten years which was not enough for even one child to have a completely TVA-run or TVA-assisted public school education. Students and their parents were exposed to the possibilities of well-supplied and innovative school programs only to be suddenly thrown back into inadequate local schools. Many parents reacted angrily, accusing TVA of "kicking us in the face with a dirty boot." Parents noted that their children were disappointed and disoriented by the shift in schools. The time factor also disturbed university professors who complained they were not given enough time to complete their projects and carefully analyze the results.[60]

The TVA education program, despite its 1933 promises, was limited in scope. TVA preferred to justify its social programs on the basis of necessity. It did not build programs on the basis of duty or legal commitment. By basing its social programs on need and expediency and not on legal responsibility, TVA could more easily dismantle the programs without fear of law suits or organized opposition when it was faced with pressure to shift to power production during World War II and with increased opposition from conservative congressmen.

TVA educational efforts were inadequate to fill the great need for reform and change in the Tennessee Valley. The wishes and desires of many white inhabitants for better funded and more progressive education were thwarted to a certain degree. Yet, the TVA education programs were particularly inadequate in the face of the even more desperate plight of blacks in the valley. TVA educators and planners who developed educational programs for blacks were limited by their belief that blacks were best suited to be janitors, servants, or small farmers. TVA planning also reflected the belief that the position of blacks would remain essentially unchanged in future generations. Consequently, there was not much need to offer skilled job training, cooperative programs with black colleges, sophisticated adult education, or progressive schooling for the elementary and secondary grades. In addition, TVA planners, in their efforts to appear sensitive to the racial mores of the region, did not press for economic opportunities for blacks. Rather than risk opposition, TVA chose to exclude blacks from dam sites if the presence of blacks constituted a departure from the past.

TVA chose virtually to ignore the criticisms and threats of civil rights groups and fended off the relatively innocuous queries by the federal government. TVA preferred to align itself with the more powerful interest groups of skilled labor unions, state educational officials, and racially conservative politicians who demanded and received an adherence to discriminatory educational policies from TVA.

Notes

1. Franklin D. Roosevelt, "Message to Congress on Muscle Shoals Development," *House Journal*, doc. 15, 73rd Cong., 1st sess., April 10, 1933, p. 7; Tennessee Valley Authority, *Employee Relationship Policy* (Knoxville, Tenn.: Tennessee Valley Authority, 1940), p. 4.

2. John Chancellor, "TVA Objectives and the Education Scheme," *The Library in TVA Adult Education,* (Chicago: American Library Association, 1937), p. 18.

3. For a more complete discussion of the racial climate in the Tennessee Valley see Nancy L. Grant, "Blacks, Regional Planning, and the TVA," (Ph.D. diss., University of Chicago, 1978), pp. 205–261.

4. C. Herman Pritchett, *The Tennessee Valley Authority: A Study in Public Administration,* (Chapel Hill, N.C.: University of North Carolina Press, 1943), p. 29; Clarence Hodge, *The Tennessee Valley Authority* (Washington, D.C. American University Press, 1938), p. 47; U.S. Congress, *House Journal,* Rec. 2282, 73rd Cong., 1933.

5. Phillip Selznick, *TVA and the Grass Roots* (New York: Harper & Row, 1966), p. 6: Pritchett, *The TVA*, p. 122; Arthur Morgan, "Social Planning in the TVA," *New York Times*, March 25, 1933; Tennessee Valley Authority, *Annual Report 1933–1934,* (Knoxville, Tenn.: Tennessee Valley Authority, 1935), p. 16.

6. Chancellor, "TVA Objectives," pp. 18–22. Also see Floyd W. Reeves, "TVA Training," *Journal of Adult Education* 7 (January 1935): 48–52; Reeves, "Adult Education in the Tennessee Valley Authority Program," *Bulletin of the Bureau of School Service, College of Education, University of Kentucky* 8 (December 1935): 26–38.

7. R. L. Duffas, "A Dream Takes Form on the Tennessee," *New York Times*, April 19, 1936. Arthur Morgan, "Social Planning in the TVA," *New York Times*, March 25, 1933. Clippings of the Morgan article along with many pro- and anti-TVA newspaper articles are compiled in

a collection, "Pamphlets and Articles on the TVA." TVA Files, Knoxville, Tennessee.

8. Malcolm Little to Ira N. Chiles, Memorandum, March 9, 1942, TVA Files; also see Gordon Clapp to John Blandford, Memorandum, June 8, 1938, pp. 16–21, TVA Files.

9. Clapp to Blandford, Memorandum, June 8, 1938, pp. 16, 17, 18, TVA Files.

10. Tennessee Valley Authority, *Employee Relationship Policy* (Knoxville, Tenn.: Tennessee Valley Authority, 1935), p. 4; U. S. Congress, Tennessee Valley Authority Act, 48 Stat. 58 (May 18, 1933): 9.

11. Tennessee Valley Authority, *Annual Report 1933–1934,* p. 48; B. M. Haskin, Documentation, "TVA's Employment of Negroes 1933–1964," February 25, 1965, pp. 10–12, Appendix A, Table 1, TVA Files.

12. Clapp to Marguerite Owen, Memorandum, August 3, 1939, TVA Files; *New York Times,* August 30, 1938. In 1938 TVA hired a highly qualified electrician named Francis Steele. When he reported for work, TVA discovered its racial mistake and fired him.

13. Clapp to Owen, August 3, 1939, TVA Files; John P. Davis, Ex. Sec. Joint Committee on National Recovery, "Report of Chief Social and Economic Problems of Negroes in the TVA," August 1935, p. 5, TVA Files.

14. L. L. Huntington to M. G. Little, Memorandum, June 8, 1943, TVA Files.

15. Josiah Work to Arthur Miller, Memorandum, November 17, 1942, TVA Files; E. B. Schultz to E. M. Reed, Memorandum, September 23, 1940, TVA Files.

16. Chiles to George Gant, Memorandum, November 4, 1937, pp. 5, 6, TVA Files.

17. Staff Memorandum, "Negro Employment in the TVA," January 1941, TVA Files; W. M. Thomas, Staff Report, "The Negro Training Program," n.d., pp. 16–22, TVA Files; Gant to J. Max Bond, Memorandum, July 7, 1938, TVA Files. J. Max Bond was the highest paid black in TVA from 1933–1938. He was the supervisor of negro training.

18. Haskin, "TVA's Employment of Negroes," p. 31.

19. U. S. Government, Executive Order 8802, June 25, 1941; Lawrence Cramer, Ex. Sec. FEPC to Gant, October 1941; Gant to Cramer, December 5, 1941; Cramer to Gant, April 17, 1942; David Lilienthal to George Johnson, Asst. Ex. Sec., FEPC, May 11, 1942, TVA Files.

20. Schultz to George Slover, Memorandum, May 19, 1936, TVA Files; Louis McDade to George Benjamin, Memorandum, February 17, 1939, TVA Files.

21. J. Max Bond, Report, "Negro Intern Training Program," October 1936, pp. 1–10, TVA Files.

22. Bond to Gant, Memorandum, July 7, 1938, p. 2, TVA Files.

23. Arthur Morgan, "On the Future of the Colored Race," address delivered at Knoxville College, Knoxville, Tenn., June 12, 1934, p. 4, TVA Files; Arthur Morgan, "Bench Marks in the Tennessee Valley," *Survey*

234 Education and the Rise of the New South

Graphic 13 (November 1934): 551; Harcourt Morgan, "Considerations to be Given in Carrying Out Objectives of TVA," April 20, 1939, H. A. Morgan Papers, University of Tennessee, Knoxville, Tenn.: David Lilienthal, *The Journal of David Lilienthal: The TVA Years,* (New York: Harper & Row, 1964), pp. 446, 447, 516.

24. Chiles to Gant, Memorandum, November 4, 1937, TVA Files; Bond to Gant, Report, July 7, 1938, pp. 15–17, TVA Files; W. T. Thomas, Report, n.d., pp. 16–22, TVA Files.

25. A. Phillip Randolph, "The Trade Union Movement and the Negro," *Journal of Negro Education* 5 (January 1936): 54–58; Gant to Cramer, December 5, 1941, p. 5, TVA Files; A. S. Jandrey to S. E. Roper, President Tennessee Valley Trades and Labor Council, August 18, 1941, TVA Files.

26. John Rankin to Lilienthal, May 29, 1943, TVA Files; John Sparkman to Lilienthal, April 8, 1943, TVA Files. The most famous court case was *Tennessee Electric Power Company* v. *Tennessee Valley Authority,* which was part of a campaign against TVA led by private utilities. There was also an extensive investigation of the TVA by a Joint Congressional Committee in 1938.

27. Floyd Reeves, "Adult Education as related to the TVA," *School and Society* 44 (August 29, 1936): 257–266.

28. Clifford Seeber to Gant, Memorandum, February 23, 1938, TVA Files; Chancellor, "TVA Objectives," pp. 27–29, TVA Files.

29. Little to Ed Campbell, Memorandum, February 4, 1942, TVA Files; J. Max Bond, "The Educational Programs for Negroes in the TVA," *Journal of Negro Education* 6 (April 1937): 147, 151; Chancellor, "TVA Objectives," pp. 28, 29.

30. J. Max Bond, "TVA Educational Programs," p. 151.

31. Carleton R. Ball, Report, "A Study of Work of Land Grant Colleges in the Tennessee Valley Area in Cooperation with the Tennessee Valley Authority," October 1938, pp. 12–15, TVA Files.

32. Ibid., pp. 17–22.

33. Ibid., pp. 33–34.

34. T. Levron Howard, "Minutes of the University of North Carolina Institute on Regional Development," Session 13, June 17, 1936, Howard Odum Papers, Southern Historical Collection University of North Carolina, Chapel Hill, N. C.; Ball, "Land Grant Colleges," pp. 33–34.

35. TVA Announcement, October 23, 1934, TVA Files; Ralph Martin to Charles Johnson, April 27, 1938, TVA Files; Little to Charles Johnson, November 8, 1937, TVA Files.

36. Floyd Reeves to Harold Smith, Director of Summer Quarter, Fisk University, June 7, 1934, TVA Files.

37. Chiles to Gant, January 10, 1938, TVA Files.

38. R. Brooks Taylor to John P. Ferris, Memorandum, July 27, 1939, TVA Files.

39. L. Campbell to Ernest Seeman, Professor, Duke University, February 12, 1934, TVA Files.

40. Seeman to Campbell, March 27, 1934, TVA Files; Seeman to Campbell, March 31, 1934, TVA Files. There is considerable controversy surrounding the scientific contribution of George Washington Carver. One writer maintains that Carver's reputation "depended less on these supposed achievements than on his psychological and social utility to both blacks and whites." The writer states that Carver did not produce any original work and refused to itemize his findings for future research. The writer does not mention the reasons for Carver's refusal to document experiments—the legitimate fear of losing credit for discoveries—nor does he question the possible prejudiced assessments of Carver's white contemporaries. Barry Mackintosh, "George Washington Carver: The Making of a Myth," *Journal of Southern History* 42 (November 1976): 509–528.

41. Contract, Tuskegee Institute and the Tennessee Valley Authority, October 1939, TVA Files.

42. Contract, Tuskegee Institute and the Tennessee Valley Authority, July 1940, TVA Files. The control of inventions and research is not an unusual condition in cooperative research projects with government agencies.

43. Haskin, "TVA Employment of Negroes," p. 24.

44. J. R. Otis, Tuskegee, to Department of Agriculture, November 12, 1935, TVA Files; George Rommel to M. J. Funchese, Director, Alabama Experimental Station, November 12, 1935, TVA Files. TVA was criticized for its decision to use phosphate fertilizer instead of the less expensive and easier-to-use nitrates. In addition, poor farmers could only use nitrates because phosphates involved sophisticated farming methods of crop rotation and nitrogen mixing. See Selznick, pp. 98–99.

45. Selznick, pp. 110–113.

46. Gant to Clapp, Memorandum, November 4, 1937, TVA Files.

47. An Observer, "The School of Norris, Tennessee," *The School Executive,* (October 1935), p. 55.

48. Ibid.

49. J. W. Bradmer, Town Manager, Norris, to Maurice Seay, July 14, 1936, TVA Files.

50. Mildred Kranock to John Jennings, House of Representatives, Tennessee, February 21, 1946, TVA Files; Clapp to Jennings, April 3, 1946, TVA Files; Chiles to W. J. McGlothlin, Memorandum, November 1, 1943, TVA Files.

51. Robert Weaver, Assistant to the Sec. of Interior, to A. Morgan, Report, "Racial Discrimination in the TVA," November 12, 1935, TVA Files; W. C. Sturdevant to A. Morgan, Memorandum, July 5, 1935, TVA Files; John P. Davis, "The Plight of the Negro in the TVA," *Crisis* 42 (October 1935): 294, 314–315.

52. Tennessee Valley Authority, Notice to Residents of Villages, February 1, 2, 3, 19, 1941, TVA Files; Frank Grove, Alabama Education Association, to Virginia James, Principal, Wilson School, April 8, 1941, TVA Files; A. S. Jandrey to Clapp, Memorandum, January 27, 1941, TVA Files.

53. Mattie L. Gilchrist, Report, "A Description of School for Negroes at Joe Wheeler Dam," July 1936, pp. 3–6, TVA Files.

54. Ibid. In 1905, two Frenchmen, Alfred Binet and Theophile Simon, developed the first "intelligence test" in order to detect mentally deficient children in the French public schools. The test was subsequently used to test black and white children in the American public schools and to screen out "feebleminded" immigrants arriving in the United States. In 1916, the test was revised and standardized for American society by Lewis Terman of Stanford University. This Stanford-Binet test remained the popular and accepted measurement of intelligence throughout the 1930s. TVA's use of the older French test showed either a lack of knowledge or a lack of acceptance of the newer, though still questionable, American test. For further discussion of intelligence testing see Vincent Franklin, "Black Social Scientists and the Mental Testing Movement, 1920–1940," in *Journal of Black Psychology*, 2nd ed. (New York: Harper & Row, forthcoming 1980); Clarence Karier, ed., *Shaping the American Educational State, 1900 to the Present*, (New York: Free Press, 1975).

55. Contract, Board of Education, Benton, Kentucky, and TVA, July 5, 1941, TVA Files; Contract, Board of Education of Rhea County, Tennessee, and TVA, August 28, 1943, TVA Files; Contract, Board of Education of Sheffield, Alabama, and TVA, September 21, 1942, TVA Files.

56. Mrs. L. B. Murray, President, Hales Bar PTA, to L. N. Allen, November 20, 1940, TVA Files.

57. Contract, Benton, Kentucky, July 5, 1941; Contract, Rhea County, Tennessee, August 28, 1943; Contract, Sheffield, Alabama, September 21, 1942, TVA Files.

58. Allen to Blandford, Memorandum, January 19, 1937, TVA Files; Clapp to C. A. Bock, Memorandum, November 28, 1936, TVA Files.

59. McGlothlin to Campbell, Memorandum, October 4, 1943, TVA Files.

60. L. R. Reynolds to C. L. Richey, October 3, 1936, TVA Files; Krannock to Jennings, February 21, 1946, TVA Files; Gant to Clapp, April 14, 1945, TVA Files.

Arthur O. White

State Leadership and Public Education in Florida: The Evolution of a System

A public school system figured prominently in Radical Republican plans for reconstruction in Florida. Owing to extreme white hostility to the new "carpet bag" government, the radicals designed the school system particularly to educate the freedmen who constituted three-sevenths of Florida's population. They hoped that by manipulation of this population, they would attain the votes necessary for decades of political control and the workers necessary for economic prosperity.[1]

Because planter-aristocrats kept education a private affair, reserved mostly for the well-born, the new government had to start at the beginning when building the public school system. From the federally subsidized Freedmen's Bureau came funds to build hundreds of schoolhouses and from state and local taxes came funds to pay salaries of teachers recruited mainly from Northern patriotic, religious, and political societies. Though officials attributed the use of Northern teachers to a lack of qualified Floridians, it was generally known that such teachers taught republicanism and unionism along with the three Rs.[2]

The Illinois public school plan was used as the basis of the school clause in Florida's 1868 constitution and the resulting 1869 school law. The law stipulated that the State Superintendent of Public Instruction, the Attorney General, and the Secretary of State form a State Board of Education to administer federal land grants to public schools, regulate state schools, set policy to implement school laws, appoint county school board members, and arbitrate appeal cases sent up from county school districts. The county district plan guaranteed a well-defined area with sufficient population to support schools. A county school superintendent administered policies passed by the county school board. The school board appointed trustees for each school from among the taxpaying residents of the attendance district and had to meet the approval of those trustees before locating a schoolhouse, employing a teacher, and setting up the academic program. For their part, trustees collected the funds from local residents for the schoolhouse. The county school board levied taxes not to exceed five mills of assessed valuation which supplemented state funds accrued from a one-mill property tax and other revenues distributed to counties according to the number of school-age residents.[3]

Schoolmen grappled with monumental problems. In a population of 187,748 in 1870, over 50 percent of the people reported themselves illiterate. Schools were within commuting distance for only one in four children. Where available, schools averaged only a few hours per day of class time for a term of eighty days or less in a rented room or dilapidated one-room log building, often lacking water and privies. Everywhere, carpetbag public school promoters met with hostility from Floridians indignant at the "hateful imports" for allowing blacks, "the recent denizens of the cotton patch," into the public schools. They registered their indignation through school boycotts and taxpayer strikes.[4]

When Southern white Democrats "redeemed" the state under the banner of gubernatorial candidate George Drew, many foresaw the end of the public schools. Quite the contrary, Drew from Massachusetts launched a new era in Florida government by pledging to increase the "general diffusion of knowledge as a principle in a representative form of government based on universal suffrage." He thought it "cheaper to build schoolhouses than to build poor houses and jails to support paupers and criminals." "Only through the schools," Drew asserted, "could the colored race become fit to exercise the privileges of voting intelligently, to perform all the sacred rights of freedmen, to enjoy their liberty, to become wise and good citizens."[5]

Inspired by such rhetoric, the State Superintendent of Public Instruction toured the schools of every county by September, 1878. He concluded that the schools should be consolidated into larger units, that teachers should be given professional training and higher wages, and that the state should develop a course of study and a uniform series of textbooks, guarantee a four-month school term, and concentrate revenues on elementary education. To meet the objections of racist whites while soothing politically active blacks, the State Superintendent encouraged development of a dual school system based on the separate but equal principle. The newspaper took up the cause of public education, and by 1877 attendance of school-age children rose above 50 percent.[6]

The appointment in 1884 of "Colonel" Albert J. Russell, the first Confederate veteran to hold the office of State Superintendent of Public Instruction, indicated problems for black education. By the process of biased legislative apportionment and intimidation, "white Democrats" had driven nearly all blacks from state government. As to be expected of such politicians, Russell sought to undermine black leadership. When declaring blacks ineligible for seats on county school boards, he falsely accused them of nonpayment of their poll taxes. He ignored accusations that the black school system had become a "miserable farce," characterized by "sham schools and mock teachers" and perpetuating illiteracy among students and graduates.[7]

Rural schools for whites, however, were not much better. Widely scattered and housed in dilapidated one-room buildings, these schools suffered from poor administration and poor teaching. Trustees, bickering among themselves or with school board members, often showed more concern for the convenience of their own children than for the needs of the community when locating a school. Sometimes feuding trustees went to the expense of erecting two schoolhouses when one would have been sufficient or angrily refused to erect any schoolhouse at all.

The teacher, typically a city-bred young woman in her late teens, seldom had more than primary schooling. Paid $1 per month for each student recruited but not more than $15 total, she taught for a three-month period, provided that she could retain at least ten students. Parents resentful of her youth, sex, and urban origins, sometimes closed a school by withholding their children. One child, expecting discipline, threatened to tell his father, who would then withdraw his several children, thus causing the school to close.

Discipline problems were great in rural schools. The long school hours and the absence of physical activity caused boys in particular to challenge the teacher. One young woman remembers looking down the barrel of a horse pistol held by a twelve-year-old boy, who vowed to pull the trigger if she whipped him again. When superintendents sought to place male teachers in tough rural schools, these teachers sometimes manipulated the trustees in order to secure places in town schools instead. Then, too, the appearance of a male teacher in a rural school could incite the largest farm boys to try to "turn the teacher out" and close the school.

A teacher's success could be enhanced by a willingness to socialize with the "Crackers." Social activities for women included quilting and snuff dipping, and for men comprised, hunting, fishing, storytelling, moonshine drinking, and spitting streams of tobacco juice at sleeping "cur" dogs. Once a month the schoolhouse was transformed into a church where "hard shell" or "primitive" Baptists or "shouting" Methodists held forth. Few teachers could tolerate these activities and in general they had so little regard for their rural environs that Crackers described them as "too particular."[8]

Nevertheless, in some ways the schools did progress. Alachua County School Superintendent William N. Sheats led a debate in 1885 resulting in the Florida Constitution guaranteeing a minimum local school millage and allowing residents to constitute themselves as a special tax district for an additional tax levy. Other clauses set up normal schools, one for each race, guaranteed support of black schools, and called for an elective superintendent of public institutions, elective county superintendent, and elective county school boards. The *Jacksonville Herald* labeled Sheats "the school crank trying to confiscate the property of the state to educate negroes with." That same year the *New York Post* cited Florida for having nearly 93 percent of 67,000 eligible children in school and averaging 73 percent daily attendance, a record equal to that of any state in the Union. The next year 500 teachers chartered the Florida Teachers Association, and 3 years later 30 black leaders started a similar organization for teachers of their race.[9]

Taking office as Florida's first elective state superintendent of public instruction, Sheats sought to revamp the entire school system. He announced revocation of teaching licenses and reexamination at the county and state level. The examination, consisting of hundreds of questions answered over a several-day period, covered teaching methods and subject matter. Teachers could either be denied certification or certified for one, two, three, or five years, depending on their scores. The purpose of this test was that teachers, in awe of the examination system, would keep abreast in their fields. Though many teachers threatened to boycott the examinations, enough took the exam and passed at the county level to staff every school. "As is the teacher so is the school," believed Sheats.[10]

The issue of textbooks next drew Sheats's attention. Seldom did any two children possess the same books, while textbook agents took advantage of ignorant parents to sell overpriced and useless merchandise. Typical abuses of textbook agents included differential pricing in different counties for the same books and the infiltration of county school systems where they disguised themselves as ministers, school board members or teachers and bribed school personnel. On Sheats's insistence a committee of several educators recommended a list of sixty books for adoption based on an approved curriculum. Accompanying the list was Sheats's controversial demand that textbook companies send sample books but "keep their agents out of Florida."[11]

Sheats also advocated rural school consolidation. By pooling the resources of several communities, he expected that well-designed multiroom schoolhouses could be built for rural children. Moreover, the increased resources would employ more teachers at higher salaries and would offer a more diverse curriculum. Blocking such reform were the trustees, either concerned about the abolition of their positions or chagrined at losing such an important community facility as the one-room schoolhouse. In addition, teachers noted that rural children brought by wagon to town schools complained of feeling "lost" and "out of place."[12]

Apparently Sheats's zeal helped encourage progress. Between 1892 and 1904, the schools absorbed 32,000 additional children while increasing the school term from 96 to 108 days. He seemed proud of a decrease in the number of schools which indicated the effects of consolidation. The state school fund in 1903 for the first time exceeded one million dollars and 500 schools were included in special tax districts. "Just think," wrote Sheats to a member of the Southern Education Board, "of such appropriations for education in a state with only about 500,000 inhabitants. There is no parallel among southern states in educational liberality."[13]

Unfortunately, however, Sheats violated his own dictum, "Never force the prejudice of any people, especially a Florida cracker."[14] A firm believer in the separate but equal doctrine, Sheats worked hard to equalize the dual school system. His policies of appointing only black teachers and trustees for black schools increased the economic and social status of these people within their community. In 1900 the *National Independent* cited his bravery when he publicly castigated the state for spending so little on black education that black taxpayers were actually subsidizing white education. However, his downfall came when an interest in industrial education prompted him to invite Booker T. Washington to speak in Gainesville. Forgery and intrigue by supporters of Alachua County Superintendent William Holloway convinced many voters that Sheats had insulted Southern whites by scheduling the speech at the white high school. A large majority of voters rejected Sheats at the polls in favor of Holloway.[15]

In 1905 state leaders debated the prospects of consolidating several small state colleges into a university for men and a college for women. By zealous lobbying, these small colleges had obtained state monies and were becoming a tremendous financial burden. One legislator suggested ending state support of higher education because his backwoods constitutents had little prospect of attending college. The legislature instead consolidated these schools into the two recommended institutions under a citizens' Board of Control. This board also supervised a public college for blacks and a small industrial school for deaf and blind children.[16]

Institution of state uniformity in textbooks in 1911 ended decades of debate. The success of this measure in other states convinced the Florida legislature that a properly drawn law could encourage sufficient competition to keep prices low. The law set up a textbook commission of the State Board of Education to choose books for grades one through eight from a list recommended by a subcommission of public school teachers and administrators. The posting of large bonds by successful bidders assured that textbook companies complied with contract provisions.[17]

Not until 1919 did Florida achieve a workable compulsory school attendance law. The legislature was swayed by arguments that compulsory school attendance would reduce the state's 14 percent illiteracy rate, lessen teacher concern over insufficient attendance, cut down on petty crime by truant children, and reduce the number of black failures on intelligence tests for military service. By law all children aged six to fourteen attended school, except for those judged physically or emotionally unfit or employed in occupations exempt from child labor laws.[18]

In the 1920s the Florida Education Association (FEA) emerged as a powerful statewide school lobby. Rapidly increasing in membership, the organization in 1926 hired an executive secretary and published a journal.

The FEA sought to attain better training for teachers and administrators, a code of ethics, a pension plan, tenure, salary schedules, and state equalization of school funding between rich and poor counties. Under the guidance of school principals, the organization began to acquire allies among business and civic organizations concerned about the state's national image as a progressive place for industrial development.[19]

However, before achieving these goals, the "school lobby" had to struggle for the survival of the public schools during the Depression. Squaring off against the school lobby were vested interests including large land companies and businesses which wanted the lowest possible tax rates and certain divisions of state government, especially the State Road Department, which wanted an ever-larger share of public money. These groups considered any schooling beyond basic literacy-training as "wasteful frills." The school lobby rallied behind the efforts of State Superintendent of Public Instruction J. Colon English, FEA Executive Secretary James Riekerts, and the Continuing Education Council set up by the FEA to coordinate the efforts of dozens of citizens' organizations interested in education. The combined efforts not only kept the schools open but also extended the term to eight months, established an instruction unit of one certified teacher for every 36 students, and, except for the governor's veto, would have gained a teacher tenure law. Such victories prompted the House Speaker to label the school lobby "the most powerful and most vicious [lobby] in Florida."[20]

These qualities worked well for the school lobby during its successful effort to obtain the Minimum Foundation Program (MFP) in 1947. Indeed, the lobby's aggressive advertising campaign caused legislators to complain that it had become politically dangerous for them to oppose any of the MFP's many provisions. Essentially, the MFP distributed state money for most school operations on the basis of each county school district's tax-paying ability relative to the value of railroad and telegraph property, farm products, auto license tag sales, real estate, and retail sales. The program required each county to levy at least six mills for schools, hold school for 180 days per year, establish teacher salary schedules, guarantee degree-holding teachers a salary of at least $2,550 per year, and employ "master teachers to supervise instruction." During the MFP's initial two years, the per pupil expenditures increased from $114 to $158. These funds provided Florida with the eighteenth best teacher salary schedule in the nation, a school year ten days longer than the national average, and an instruction unit reduced to 27 pupils per teacher. In 1949 the state legislature enacted a 3 percent sales tax to help finance the MFP. Within the decade, Florida's nationally acclaimed MFP had become a model for similar programs in most other states.[21]

Nonetheless, Florida's boom-or-bust economy, consumer tax base, and volatile political atmosphere kept the school lobby busy working to maintain an adequately funded school system. Through speeches, pamphlets, and newspaper dispatches, lobby leaders endeavored to inform Floridians that the public schools were not receiving their fair share of tax revenues. In 1950 the school lobby began to popularize the National Advertising Council's slogan, "Better schools make better communities." The slogan appeared on letter-heads, postmarks, editorial captions, and auto tags. By March, 1954, the auto tag had become a national sensation with 20,000 cars in Florida and 100,000 in the nation displaying the "Florida school tag."[22]

Subsequently, the school lobby's policies reflected the influence of teachers recently migrated from Northern states to Florida's southern and coastal counties. When, for instance, news of the 1954 school desegregation decision broke in Florida, the school lobby strongly backed state leaders who counseled a moderate "wait and see" attitude. The 20,000 member FEA and its 500,000 member citizen affiliate, the Continuing Educational Council, were given much credit for preventing school closing provisions and other "ultrasegregationist" legislation typical of Southern states. In 1955 Floridians took pride that the intent of Florida's friend-of-the-court brief, the only one received from a Southern state, seemed embodied in the "all deliberate speed" language of the Supreme Court's enforcement decree. In 1959 Dade County, heavily settled by Northern immigrants, placed a black child in a white elementary school, giving Florida the distinction of being first in the South to voluntarily break the color barrier in public education.[23]

Northern influence could also be detected in teacher militancy. Beginning in 1956, FEA affiliates in urban counties demanded a state-guaranteed $4,200 minimum teacher salary. Dominated by teacher migrants from Northern cities who were accustomed to labor tactics, some of these CTAs threatened to strike. To rally public opinion for the teachers, the school lobby pointed to teacher moonlighting, the teaching of double sessions, and high rates of teacher turnover. That the legislature not only voted the appro-priation for the salary raises but also provided funds for rural classroom construction, driver education, exceptional education, vocational education, adult education, and junior college construction prompted the *New York Times* to cite Florida for being the state with the nation's greatest improve-ment in public education in the nation.[24]

Unfortunately, such successes bred resentment. A recessional economy and persistent public hostility to school desegregation caused many Floridians in 1959 to label the schools dangerous bastions of racial liberalism that wasted the taxpayers' money on educational "frills." While preventing drastic cuts in the MFP, school lobby leaders described the 1959 legislative session as "the roughest in memory."[25]

Only higher education escaped unscathed. Beginning in 1957 and con-tinuing through 1975, the state implemented the nation's most ambitious "master plan" for community college development. The program eventually established 28 community colleges, thus placing higher educational opportunity within commuting distance of nearly every Floridian; in addition, it included the nation's only upper division universities. In explaining their strong commitment to the colleges, legislators pointed to constituent's demands for a school in their vicinity and a belief that such a program enhanced industrial development.[26]

Nonetheless, tight fiscal policies continued to undermine funding for public education. By 1967, after several governors had pledged "no new taxes," Florida's per capita expenditure on education and teacher salary schedules had fallen to twenty-ninth nationally. Unable to obtain necessary funds from any level of government, the FEA on February 29, 1968, issued an order prompting 25,000 to 30,000 teachers to leave their classrooms, some for almost three weeks, in the nation's first state-wide teachers' strike.

Public opinion ran strongly against the teachers. Early in 1968, FEA strike threats had pressured Governor Claude Kirk to recall the legislature for an educational finance session, the first such session in the state's history. While the legislature appropriated enough additional money to raise Florida's public school salary schedule to the fourteenth highest in the nation, the FEA nevertheless called a strike to force the legislature back into yet another session for the purpose of removing a ten mill limit on local property taxes for education. However, the teachers, having just been granted a raise, were condemned by the media for breaking their contracts to strike illegally against the public interest. Confusion over goals, financial hardships, threats of reprisals, and, most of all, a hostile public opinion, sent the teachers back to work without substantial gains.

This outcome destroyed the school lobby. Early in the strike, the Continuing Education Council repudiated the teachers' action. After the strike, teachers by the thousands, disillusioned and threatened by school board reprisals, discontinued their FEA memberships. At their first post-strike convention, public school administrators voted themselves out of the FEA.[27]

These significant setbacks ushered in the 1970s, an era characterized by waning faith in public education. The public school problem could be traced to popular dissatisfaction over desegregation, student militancy, and teacher militancy. On the first issue, people resented federal officials intruding on what they believed to be local prerogatives in order to force the races together in the public schools. In regard to student militancy, people were angered over what they believed to be permissive and inappropriate public school methods which were turning youths into a "bunch of longhairs" rioting on college campuses. On the third issue, people resented teachers for abandoning their posts in order to obtain more money through an illegal strike.

State offices have sought to rekindle faith in the public schools. In 1971 the legislature launched the Florida Accountability in Education Program.

By law public school educators must now demonstrate to the public through standardized tests the "cost effectiveness" of their methods for attaining prescribed academic goals. Since test technology and public demand have directed most of this effort at verbal and mathematical skills, the Florida program is representative of the "back to basics" movement. Strong points of the Florida Program include promotion of students contingent upon their satisfactory performance on standardized tests, high school diplomas contingent upon passage of a functional literacy test, and an extensive remedial education program.

The Florida approach seeks more public involvement in the schools and a more realistic funding formula. After abolishing millage elections and school trustees as undermining the authority of school boards, the legislatures took into account taxpayers' reluctance to pay for a school system over which they had little direct influence. Consequently, they mandated that each public school have citizen advisory boards elected from among the taxpaying citizens of the attendance district. Meeting frequently, the board of each school advises the principal on all phases of the school program while preparing a final progress report for the school board.

In 1973 the lawmakers combined a revolutionary concept in state funding equalization with the highest possible levels of local initiative in the Florida Education Finance Program (FEFP). This program is responsible for each district's number of full-time students, type of instruction programs, cost-of-living factors, and millage yields. Its intent is to achieve a level of equalization in Florida surpassing every state but Hawaii and to guarantee to "every public school student [kindergarten through twelfth grade] programs and services appropriate to his educational needs, which are substantially equal to those available to any similar student regardless of geographic location or local economic factors."

The new fiscal arrangement emphasizes flexibility in district-level planning. In place of the MFP's dependence on instructional units and average daily attendance records as distribution factors, the FEFP incorporates a formulation based on full-time equivalent students (FTEs) into its distribution index. More than merely a reflection of the number of public school students registered in a district, FTEs are determined in terms of programs needed, yielding values as low as unity (1 FTE) for a student in basic (1–12) programs to fifteen (15 FTEs) for students in certain exceptional education programs. Promoting flexibility in staffing procedures, the new arrangement transfers to the districts the responsibility for employing supervisory personnel, for setting teaching load guidelines, and for establishing minimum salaries at each instructional level. The districts in turn, as part of a "school-based management" scheme, have transferred to school principals considerable authority over curriculum, budget, and staff employment. These latter provisions, combined with a statute requiring district school boards to provide incentives for efficient service, should enable district level planners to relate competency of school personnel to educational achievements as measured on standardized tests.[28]

Innovations also have affected teacher education. As of 1980, those seeking teacher certification in Florida must demonstrate their skills in a 23-area competency test covering such fields as philosophy, classroom discipline, learning theory, and boardmanship and must fulfill a "full year internship" in the public schools. Since 1973, in-service teachers have had the benefit of state-funded teacher centers where they can obtain expert help with any classroom-related problem.[29]

The Florida strategy has not been without its detractors. The accountability plan has been criticized for requiring expensive and time-consuming testing that is beginning to limit the education program to testable literacy skills. There are complaints about money being drawn away from physical education, the social sciences, civics, languages, and vocational subjects to pay for state-mandated remedial programs. Having organized most Florida teachers at the county level, teacher unions deplore Florida's plunge to near bottom among the states in its financial efforts on behalf of public education. They further argue that a 30 to 1 basic classroom unit, with 3 students more than in the 1947 instruction unit, is unrealistic, given the nature of today's student and the complicated instruction strategies required. For their part, Civil Rights groups have begun scrutinizing Florida testing programs for racial bias. Thus far, their 1977 legal action brought to a federal circuit court has delayed for four years the functional literacy requirement for a high school diploma on the grounds that because black students were restricted to segregated schools, they did not have equal educational opportunity. In answer to all these criticisms, the department of education points to the rising standardized test scores of Florida pupils in contrast to national trends toward lowered scores.[30]

Because they live in a rural state, Floridians have depended on state leadership for development of their public school program. Their leaders designed the public schools to provide citizenship training, literacy, and a disciplined work force capable of serving industry. These goals were pursued in the face of such typically Southern obstacles as a scattered rural population, virulent racism causing the wasteful dual school system, and "boosterism" for industry resulting in a regressive and unstable tax base. Florida leaders, however, obtained recognition by emphasizing innovative programs while "holding the line" on spending. These innovations have included such outstanding programs as the Minimum Foundation Program, the growth of community colleges and upper division universities, and the implementation of the nation's most advanced accountability in education program. Notwithstanding the attitudes of special interest groups and political leaders toward school finance, Florida teachers generated one of the nation's most agressive and effective school lobbies, culminating in the calling of the nation's first state-wide teacher strike. In view of these apparent contradictions, Florida's public school system may be considered as "the best of the worst"—ahead of other Southern states, but behind the rest of the nation.

Notes

1. Bruce Rosen, "The Education of the Negro During Reconstruction in Florida 1866–1876" (Ph.D. diss., University of Florida, 1974), pp. 214–228.
2. William N. Sheats, *Biennial Report of the Superintendent of Public Instruction of the State of Florida for the Two Years Ending June 30, 1894,* State of Florida, Department of Education, p. 18.
3. Thomas Everette Cochran, *History of Public School Education in Florida* (Lancaster, Pa.: New Era Printing Co., 1921), pp. 36–37.
4. *Sixth Annual Report of the Commissioner of Lands and Immigration of the State of Florida for 1874,* p. 38; Sheats, *Biennial Report 1894,* pp. 24–25.
5. Sheats, *Biennial Report 1894,* pp. 24–25; *A Journal of the Proceedings of the Assembly of the State of Florida at Its Ninth Session 1877,* p. 47.
6. Sheats, *Biennial Report 1894,* pp. 23–27; William P. Haisley, *Biennial Report of the Superintendent of Public Instruction for the School Years 1876–1877 and 1877–1878,* pp. 24–27.
7. Sheats, *Biennial Report 1894,* pp. 28–29; *Florida Times Union,* April 5, 1889.
8. *Florida Times Union,* October 10, 1890; Maude Shuttee, "School Teacher in the Backwoods of Florida," and M. Etta Cubberly, "A Pioneer School," in *History of Alachua County 1824–1969,* ed. Jesse G. Davis (Gainesville, 1970), pp. 48–51.
9. *Journal of the Proceedings of the Constitutional Convention of the State of Florida 1885; Jacksonville Herald* as cited in *Florida Times Union,* July 2, 1885; *History of the Florida Education Association 1886–1887 to 1956–1957* (Tallahassee, Fla.: Florida Education Association, 1958), p. 272; *Florida Times Union,* July 18, 28, 1886.
10. Sheats, *Biennial Report 1894,* pp. 77–80, 103.
11. Sheats, *Biennial Report for the Two Years Ending June 30, 1898,* pp. 465–470; *State of Florida Action on the Textbook Committee, June 25, 1898.*
12. Sheats, *Biennial Report for the Two Years Ending June 30, 1904,* pp. 85–87, 106. Sheats to C. D. McIver, May 23, 1903, Letterbook, May 13 to September 2, 1903 (State of Florida Department of Education Files), p. 63.
13. Sheats, *Biennial Report for the Two Years Ending June 30, 1904,* pp. 85–87, 106; Sheats to C. D. McIver, May 23, 1903 (State of Florida Department of Education Files) p. 163.

14. Sheats, *Biennial Report for the Two Years Ending June 30, 1894*, p. 15.
15. Arthur O. White, "Race, Politics and Education: The Sheats-Holloway Election Controversy, 1903–1904," *Florida Historical Quarterly* 53 (January 1975): 253–272.
16. Samuel Proctor, "The University of Florida: Its Early History 1835–1906" (Ph.D. diss., University of Florida, 1953) pp. 465–513.
17. *Florida Times Union*, May 14, 1911; Regular Session 1911: Acts and Resolutions Adopted by the Legislature of Florida: 1911, Chapter 6178.
18. *Florida Times Union*, April 7, 23, 1919; Sheats, *Biennial Report for the Two Years Ending June 30, 1920*, p. 32.
19. Arthur O. White, "The Florida School Lobby" (Paper delivered before the Southern History of Education Society, Atlanta, Ga., October 22, 1976).
20. *History FEA*, pp. 25, 86–93, 102–103.
21. *Tampa Morning Tribune*, May 21, June 6, 1947; *The Nation's Schools* (July 1947) as cited in *Tampa Morning Tribune*, July 22, 1947; *NEA Bulletin* as cited in *Florida Times Union*, August 4, 1947; *Ladies Home Journal* as cited in *Pensacola News*, August 26, 1947.
22. Thomas D. Bailey, *Are the Public Schools Bankrupting the State?* (Tallahassee. Fla.: State of Florida Department of Education, 1950); *Miami Herald*, September 22, 1950; *Florida Times Union*, November 23, 1952; *Lakeland Ledger*, April 22, 1953; *Deland Sun News*, March 28, 1954.
23. Arthur O. White, *One Hundred Years of State Leadership in Florida Public Education* (Tallahassee, Fla.: University Presses of Florida, 1979).
24. *New York Times* as cited in Howard J. Friedman, *Summary of Legislative Action Pertaining to Education* (June 29, 1957), in author's private file.
25. Arthur O. White, *Florida's Crisis in Public Education: Changing Patterns of Leadership* (Tallahassee, Fla.: University Presses of Florida, 1975), pp. 6–11.
26. Ibid., 10; Arthur O. White, "A Thirty Year History of Florida's State System of Community Colleges 1947–1977" Report, State of Florida Department of Education, September 1978.
27. White, *Crisis in Public Education*, pp. 25–80.
28. Ibid., pp. 90–109; Florida Department of Education, *Minimum Student Performance Standards for Florida Schools: 1977–78, 1978–79, 1979–80, Grades 8 and 11, Reading, Writing and Mathematics* (Tallahassee, Fla., 1977).
29. Council on Teacher Education, "COTE's Working Draft," mimeograph, State of Florida Department of Education, May 1979; *The Teacher Certification Examination—Bulletin I* (Tallahassee, Fla.: 1980); Zohra Setranjiwala, "Teacher Centers in Florida" (Ph.D. diss., University of Florida, 1979); Zohra Setranjiwala and William H. Drummond, "Cri-

teria for Evaluating Teacher Education Center Programs" (State of Florida Department of Education, April 1979).

30. *Gainesville Sun,* January 31, March 16, 1976, May 5, 1977, October 4, 1978; *The United Teacher,* vol. 6 (October 1977), vol. 8, (May 1979); Arthur White, Interview with Linda Ramsey, Coordinator of Special Services, Alachua County Schools, November 16, 1979; Sarah W. I. Pell, "Legal Challenges to Testing Programs: Guidelines for Educational Researcher" (Paper delivered to Florida Educational Research Association, February 1980, St. Petersburg, Fla.); George C. Carr, Memorandum Opinion, *Debra P.* v. *Turlington* (U. S. District Court, July 17, 1979); Arthur O. White, *Debra P.* v. *Turlington* (Paper delivered at Southern History of Education Society Annual Meeting, Atlanta, Ga., October 13, 1980; Florida Department of Education, *Statewide Assessment Program, A Guide to 1977–1978 Statewide Assessment Results* (Tallahassee, Fla., 1978); Ralph Turlington, "Remarks at the Dedication of Norman Hall Annex, October 12, 1979," *Edugator* (Fall 1979), p. 6.

Harvey Neufeldt and Clinton Allison

Education and the Rise of the New South: An Historiographical Essay

Over the past generation there has been a renaissance in the history of education, with educational historians selfconsciously reexamining their discipline. As Sol Cohen points out, this renaissance "has witnessed a surge of writing on the history of American education, broadly conceived, closely allied with the fields of social and intellectual history, imaginative and mature in its use of the tools and apparatus of historical scholarship."[1] The result has been the development of vigorous history of education societies, the transformation of the homely *History of Education Journal* into the nationally recognized, scholarly *History of Education Quarterly*, and a new richness in published scholarship. Yet, with the exception of the history of black education, the history of Southern education has not shared in the wealth.

Such neglect was not the case before World War II. At that time, copious material was produced on the history of education in the South, much of it written by the survivors of earlier educational battles, and much of it still worthy of study today. Certainly it would be a major mistake for students of the history of Southern education to conclude as a result of the criticisms of revisionists over the past two decades that earlier histories of Southern education had nothing of value to say. At the very least, these older works should form the foundation for further research and interpretation.

As far as recent historical scholarship is concerned, Southern educational history has suffered less from misinterpretation or bias than from omission. For example, James Anderson's 1978 article in *The History of Education Quarterly* was one of the first papers to be published since 1970 which dealt primarily with some aspect of education in the South.[2]

The purpose of the present essay is to describe and analyze selected works on the historiography of educational developments in the South since the Civil War. In addition, attention will be given to treatments of the interrelationship between education and modernization in the emerging New South. However, this presents several difficulties. First, what is meant by the term, "New South"? As Paul Gaston points out, the term has often been used to designate a particular ideology or mark off a chronological period, "the South since 1865, since 1877, from 1877 to 1913; since 1900, or simply the

South to the present."[3] The term "New South" in this essay will be used as Gaston has done, namely, as an adjective rather than as a noun, and will refer not only to an ideology but also to social, economic, political, and educational developemnts which served to modernize the South and resulted in the diminishing of distinctive differences between the South and the rest of the nation. Furthermore, no attempt will be made to define the South in precise geographic terms; generally, "the South" will refer to the south-eastern states, with Maryland, West Virginia, and Kentucky forming the northern boundary and Arkansas and Louisiana, the western boundary. The term "modernization" as used by historians and social scientists is usually linked with such aspects as "the growth of industry, cities, secularization, democratization, and a mass bureaucratic society."[4] In addition, it has often been associated with the decline of regional distinctions or differences in values and institutions.[5]

Civil War and Modernization

Although the focus of this paper will be on the historiography of Southern educational developments after 1865, a few comments should be made relative to the Civil War and its impact on the emergence of a new, modern South. At the risk of resurrecting the simplistic notion that one can neatly divide American history into two epochs, before and after the Civil War, it must be kept in mind that the Civil War does indeed serve as a watershed in Southern history, as scholars like Raimondo Luroghi and Richard Brown have attested. According to Luroghi, slavery had served as an obstacle to the rise of "wage labor" and the accumulation of capital for industry. But the Civil War forced the South to embark on an ambitious program designed to "create an industrially efficient apparatus of its own." What it was able to accomplish was "astounding."[6]

The creation of an efficient industrial apparatus was not without implications for Southern society. According to Robert Brown, it brought with it the demise of traditional society. The surrender of the Confederate army "stood for the final surrender of traditional society." This traditional society had received "powerful support" from "plantation agriculture and slave labor." It had been characterized by such aspects as the veneration of "hier-archy and the ethic of aristocratic paternalism" and a "highly personalized politics, heavily based on family, country and traditional loyalties."[7] A similar note is struck by Ann Firor Scott. The Civil War, she argues, "passed over the South like a giant tidal wave, cracking many structures so fatally that it was only a matter of time before they fell to pieces."[8]

Although the Civil War itself had little positive effect on Southern educational institutions, nevertheless it set the stage for the emergence of the New

South. It brought with it an end to slavery but left unresolved the issues of black rights and black education. It also made possible the intervention of the federal government in Southern institutions and paved the way for Northern investments in Southern agriculture, transportation, natural resources, and industry as well as Northern philanthropists' "investments" in Southern education.

Writings on Southern Educational History

Many educators and historians have argued that Southern education took a new direction after the Civil War. However, before considering individual studies of particular topics and developments, a word is necessary on our orientation to this material. First, we have restricted this essay to secondary sources dealing with education per se rather than with the general history of the period. No attempt has been made to analyze the primary sources on Southern and black education; notes on such sources are available in many of the works cited.[9] Secondly, it should be emphasized that this is a selective rather than exhaustive list. When dealing with the pre-World War II writers, for example, we have generally limited the material to book-length studies, and, in several cases, we have omitted well-known works in favor of lesser known but more revealing studies.

Southern educational writers of the early twentieth century are a mixed group. Not more than four of the twenty-four writers whose work is reviewed could be classified as trained, professional historians, and two of these professionals, Merle Curti and Holland Thompson, devoted some attention to education in the South in works devoted primarily to broader topics.[10] Books by trained historians devoted exclusively to education in the New South were often outgrowths of doctoral dissertations; included in this group are Edgar Wallace Knight's *The Influence of Reconstruction on Education in the South*, Stewart Grayson Noble's *Forty Years of the Public Schools in Mississippi*, Ullin Whitney Leavell's *Philanthropy in Negro Education*, Horace Mann Bond's valuable study, *Negro Education in Alabama: A Study in Cotton and Steel*, and Henry Lee Swint's *The Northern Teacher in the South*.[11]

Some of the material included, especially certain texts by black writers, belong to the field of sociology rather than social history. Certain of the DuBois essays are a case in point.[12] Only a third of Horace Mann Bond's *The Education of the Negro in the American Social Order* is historical; these last 300 pages are an excellent primary source of information on black education in the early decades of the twentieth century.[13] Charles S. Johnson's classic study of 600 black rural Alabama families, *Shadow of the Plantation*, is also sociological rather than historical.[14] However, using

Bernard Bailyn's now famous definition of education as "the entire process by which a culture transmits itself across the generations,"[15] no better source for the education of the rural black Southerner can be found, for Johnson devotes chapters to the family, the economy of the community, the school, religion, and the church. The largest group of writers were participants in the movements and events which they describe. Edwin A. Alderman, J. L. M. Curry, Charles Dabney, and Walter Hines Page were among the most influential leaders of the Southern Education Movement.[16] *Investment in People: The Story of the Julius Rosenwald Fund, A Short History of Colleges and Secondary Schools,* and *The General Education Board, 1902-1914,* were official histories written by the officers of particular organizations.[17] Similarly, one of the biographies of Booker T. Washington was written by Emmett J. Scott, Washington's long-time secretary, with assistance from Lyman Beecher Stowe, grandson of Harriet. The writings of Booker T. Washington and W. E. B. DuBois, extremely personal accounts of people and events, are particularly valuable as primary sources for the development of more sophisticated histories.[18]

The only book-length comprehensive histories of Southern education are Edgar Wallace Knight's survey, *Public Education in the South*[19] and Charles W. Dabney's two-volume *Universal Education in the South.*[20] Knight was for many years a professor of the history of education at the University of North Carolina. Unfortunately, his textbook is still often listed in bibliographies and other reading lists as a standard work on the history of Southern education. It is actually too dated to be useful today. It lacks in-depth analyses and makes many over-generalizations. In this white person's history of education, blacks are seldom mentioned except as an impediment to white educational progress. The organization of Knight's book by states is disjointed and often repetitive. Another major problem is that this text has been used to serve purposes for which it was not intended. Lacking scholarly surveys of the history of Southern education, educators often substituted Knight's work, which was written as a pedagogy textbook for undergraduates, often in normal schools. Except as a valuable primary source on the spirit of the times in which it was written, *Public Education in the South* should be laid to rest.

Less well-known but far more useful for the serious student of Southern education is Charles William Dabney's *Universal Education in the South.* Dabney, descended from a distinguished Virginia family and holding a German Ph.D. in chemistry, was elected president of the University of Tennessee when he was 31 years of age. He was a charter member of the Southern Education Board and a leader in most of the numerous activities of the Southern Education Movement. His study is in two volumes. The first quickly sketches the colonial period, stressing the influences of Jeffersonian thought on all that was good in Southern education. Most of this volume is devoted to the struggles for tax-supported schools in the nineteenth century. The second volume is a history of the Southern Education Movement, including summaries of each of the seventeen Conferences for Education in the South. It describes the activities of the various boards and commissions related to the movement. There are chapters on education and sanitation, health, and tenancy; Dabney gives a detailed account of school campaigns in Southern states, with individual chapters devoted to Virginia, North Carolina, Kentucky, Tennessee, and Alabama. He called his book a biographical history, and much of it is organized around accounts of individual leaders; most of these accounts are replete with hyperbolic praise for the workers in the movement. Special attention is given to Robert Ogden as the "Richard Coeur de Lion of the crusade for universal education in the South."[21] Dabney was not one to hide his light under a bushel and often quotes tributes to himself. Basically, this book remains extremely useful in determining who was who and what was what. While some of Dabney's readers may well be cautious about his generalizations concerning the always disinterested motives of school reformers, they should recognize that he was much more evenhanded and sensitive in his treatment of blacks than many of his contemporaries, including Knight. He condemned the state of black workers and was not hesitant in documenting and condemning inequalities in both black and white schools.

Those who wrote on the history of Southern education were usually self-consciously progressive, promoting the kind of schooling they believed would aid the modernization process. Traditional historians saw the victory of the common school crusade as the climax of American educational history, and historians of Southern education saw the success of the Southern Education Movement prior to World War I in the same way. The victories of this movement settled the most important issues, including legislative requirements for schooling, dual school systems, and mandatory industrial and agricultural education programs.

It is true that these early historians viewed the New South from a relatively narrow perspective. There were radicals of the period who looked contemptuously at the South as the land of chain gangs, lynch mobs, boll weevils, and hookworms, but they, generally did not write histories of education. Likewise, little was heard from the defenders of the virtues of the traditional agrarian Old South, at least until a group of conservative Southern writers, the Fugitives, went on the offensive against the advocates of modernism in 1930 with the publication of *I'll Take My Stand.*[22]

Contemporary historians and educators are still addressing themselves to the same topics raised by the Knight-Dabney school. The focus has remained on the Reconstruction era, the New South, the Southern Educational Movement, and Northern philanthropy. Today, however, the interpretations are often quite different. Studies by Abbott, Bullock, Rose, Vaughn, and

Williamson have challenged former conclusions relative to the Reconstruction era and the educational activities of the Freedman's Bureau.[23] Other scholars like Woodward, Tindall, Gaston, and Sellers have turned their attention to analyzing the New South ideology, including its proponents' insensitivity to economic exploitation and racial discrimination and their overtly negative evaluation of the populists.[24] The Southern Educational Movement, including its directors and philanthropists, has had its halo tarnished by writers such as Harlan and Anderson.[25] The meaning of Southern progressivism has also been explored, particularly in biographies of political statesmen and educators like Hoke Smith, Charles Aycock, Andrew Montague, Charles McIver, and Eugene Brooks.[26] But once one moves beyond the 1920s to the periods of the Depression and the New Deal, and if one is interested in the impact of national foreign policy on education or in the history of vocational and industrial education in the South, the material is still limited.

However, the 1960s and 1970s have witnessed the growth of a greater sensitivity toward racism and its impact on Southern education. Thus, not surprisingly, historical research of the past two decades has shown a much greater interest in black education than was the case prior to World War II.[27] Not only have writers like Vaughn, McPherson, and Anderson reexamined the motives and behavior of white missionaries, radical governments, and philanthropists in promoting or inhibiting black education; others like Harlan, Meier, and Bullock have begun to look past what George Tindall has called "the static image" of the black and have attempted to consider black life and education from the perspective of the black community and its leaders.[28]

Major Topics in Southern Educational History

Few topics have received more attention from historians than the Reconstruction era. For the pre-World War II generation of educational historians, the reconstruction experience was the rocky foundation upon which educational policy in the South would forever be based. C. Vann Woodward, in discussing the loss of those myths which had given a separate identity to the South, writes of "the consoling security of reconstruction as the common historic grievance, the infallible mystique of unity. . . ."[29] According to the interpretation of the white educational historians of the period, Southerners' bitter memories of Congressional Reconstruction were continuing obstacles to the growth of widespread support for quality schooling. With only black scholars dissenting, these historians accept uncritically a William A. Dunning-type interpretation of a sordid period in which cynical Radical Republicans in Congress punished the South by imposing on it governments run by ignorant brutes, worthless vagabonds, and drunken knaves. Knight argues that Congressional Reconstruction was "the explanation of the South's

educational backwardness," because it created distrust of government expenditures for public welfare programs:

> In fact, the so-called restoration period proved more destructive
> than the war itself. It robbed the South of what the war had spared,
> and by looting treasuries of public funds, by imposing enormous
> taxes, by practicing faud and extravagance, and by piling up colossal
> bonded debts it succeeded in running its corrupt fingers deep "into
> the pockets of posterity" and left in those States, already reduced
> to penury by the terrors of war, a debt of more than $300,000,000.
> Thus many of the richest portions of the South were wasted and
> shorn of their prosperity; industry was checked in its development;
> idleness and fraud were widely encouraged; local justice was
> thwarted and put in contempt; the people were ruled by corrupt
> and reckless officials, and almost all tendencies to good government
> were stifled.[30]

This description was, of course, consistent with that of the broader historical community. Holland Thompson, in *The Chronicles of America Series*
written during the same period as Knight's textbook, makes the same generalizations, summarizing that "the schools were neither honest nor judiciously
administered." "Much money was deliberately stolen," he charges, "and
much more was wasted." And, in a common complaint of these historians,
he further reports that many leaders seem more interested in the idea of
educating black children with white children than in the real process of
education. Even in white schools, he complains, teachers were often carpetbaggers who insisted that children "yield assent to the proposition that
all Southerners were barbarian traitors who deserved hanging."[31] Basil
Matthews, a black biographer of Booker T. Washington, not only agrees
that reconstruction governments under the control of blacks and carpetbaggers "were probably the worst that had ever been known in any English
speaking land," but further argues that among the trends "that drove back
the evil forces of reconstruction was that the Negro majority came gradually
to loathe playing the part of the tool of corrupt industrialists and politicians
of the North."[32]

This "tragic era" interpretation of reconstruction was challenged only by
the black historians. DuBois, of course, wrote the seminal Marxist revisionist
work on reconstruction, *Black Reconstruction*. Bond argues with Knight
regarding the excesses of reconstruction, calling Knight's statements "exaggerated and incorrect."[33] He is particularly unhappy with Knight's assertion
that Alabama schools were backward because black Republican regimes had
left immense debts and had wasted the economic resources of the state.
Bond responds that there had been no "Negro" government, that "no such
debts were left after Reconstruction; and what debts were created resulted

from the activities of various capitalists working through both Republican and Democratic Party channels."[34]

While most historians saw the Northerners in the South as fanatics and zealots, a few recognized the complexity of motives of the carpetbaggers. Among those who did was Henry Lee Swint:

> Some of the men were motivated by abolitionist zeal. Others were moved by pity for the helpless treatment. Some saw the necessity of educating the Negro if he was to be made a citizen of the republic. Others, perhaps, realized the economic implications of their actions, or it may be that they merely regarded the anticipated profits as the just reward of the righteous. Others may have recognized several or all of these factors.[35]

The chief character in Swint's book, the Yankee teacher, was motivated largely by religion. Bond asserts that "practically all were religious to the point of fanaticism,"[36] although he does recognize that broader humanitarian interests, as well as economics, health, and love of adventure were other reasons for going South. Whatever the reasons for making the trip, Bond sees these teachers' tenure as a disaster; they aroused the suspicion, contempt, and hatred of the Southern whites by their behavior. In contrast, the Northern businessmen conducted themselves in such a way that they were generally welcomed.[37]

Not only were the motives and behavior of the carpetbaggers deleterious, but, according to the white historians, Reconstruction made few significant contributions to education in the South. Knight asserts that "it is clear that the direct influence of the period was much less than is popularly supposed," whereas a good deal of progress in schooling had been made before the war. Using his home state of North Carolina as an example, he argues that teachers' salaries were higher, the percentage of children enrolled in school was greater (omitting blacks, of course), and provisions for local school organization and supervision were better before than after reconstruction.[38] He concludes that "evidence is strong that had the native conservative element of the State been free to act without unwholesome influences from outside a safer and more adequate educational plan than that supplied by reconstruction would have been outlined and promoted."[39] DuBois dismisses such arguments as nonsense. There were no state systems of public schools in the South until the blacks, during Reconstruction, furnished them, he declares; "the public school system of the whole South is the gift of black folk."[40]

DuBois has not remained alone in challenging the Dunning-Knight account of the Reconstruction era. Daniel Whitner, in his study of North Carolina, credits the Republican legislature and Governor William Holden with establishing the legal basis for North Carolina's public school system. Governor

Holden, despite his shortcomings including his opposition to integrated schools, did provide strong support for the education of all children. Whatever mistakes the Republican Party made during Reconstruction, concludes Whitner, "public education was not one of them."[41] A similar note is struck by Louis Harlan and Thomas Clark. The introduction of state-supported schools, asserts Harlan, was a "revolutionary" act and "ranks as one of the few constructive and permanently popular achievements of Radical Reconstruction."[42] Furthermore, the concept of public schooling was so firmly established by 1876 that no Redeemer government "dared repudiate its obligations to public education."[43]

Although the Harlan-Whitner account differs substantially from the interpretation of Dunning and Knight, it does agree on one point—Reconstruction was a radical experiment. This theme has been rejected by Rush Welter and modified by Robert Church. Both Welter and Church view Reconstruction from the standpoint of Northern aims and stress its impact on the freedmen. They see Reconstruction as a program designed to eradicate Southern distinctions and to bring about social stability and harmony. For Welter, the tragedy of post-Civil War education was that it became a tool of conservative spokesmen who cut it loose from its moorings in Jacksonian liberalism. And while Church admits that many Northern educators hoped to aid blacks to become at least partially self-sufficient and independent, these wishes were overshadowed by their search for social unity, stability, and cultural homogeneity. Furthermore, both Welter and Church question the wisdom of relying solely on education to effect any far-reaching changes in the South. Thus, according to this interpretation, regardless of the goals of the reformers, the tragedy of Reconstruction lay not in its radicalness, but in its conservatism.[44]

A review of the literature from Dunning to Church suggests that the yardstick by which many historians measured the success or failure of Reconstruction was the black himself. For Dunning, Reconstruction was a failure because it sought to artificially exalt the freedman; for Church and Welter it was a failure in that it ultimately doomed the black to disappointment. Grady McWhiney rejects these interpretations. Northerners and Southerners, he argues, shared similar viewpoints; both assumed black inferiority, and both ranked material progress over democracy. Once Northerners found that former Confederates would defend Yankee interests in the South, the importance of black votes diminished. By the time Reconstruction ended, argues McWhiney, "Southerners were thoroughly Americanized. Every Southern state was controlled by businessmen or friends of business. The dream of an industrial millenium captivated nearly every mind."[45] If this were indeed desirable, the period of Civil War and Reconstruction was not a tragedy; it was a success and served to modernize the South.

The decades between the end of Reconstruction and the rise of the Southern Educational Movement appear to be barren ones as far as education is concerned. This conclusion is aptly summarized in Clark's and Irwin's assertion that the "basic history of educational accomplishments in the Southern states, 1876-1910, can be written in a few terse statements;" namely, insufficient funds and lack of "long-range plans and clearly defined objectives for a system of public education," including a lack of "clearly defined answers as to what the elementary goals of education should be."[46]

Yet this period saw the rise of a New South ideology, proclaimed by men like Henry Woodfine Grady, Walter Hines Page, and Bishop Atticus Haygood and reflected in the writings of Booker T. Washington. Central to the New South creed, according to Paul Gaston, were several concepts. First, there was a call for economic regeneration to be achieved through a diversified economy, urbanization, and industrialization. Secondly, there was a call for national reconciliation, shifting the blame for Southern poverty from the Civil War to the characteristics of the Old South which brought on the war, namely, slavery, anti-industrialism, and anti-urbanism. In addition, the New South ideology called for the resolution of the race question by advocating a middle-of-the-road policy between outright racism and social equality. New South spokesmen expressed a willingness to accept enfranchisement of blacks but not black domination; they talked of separate and equal provisions but also assumed white supremacy.[47]

Although he wrote in a later era and could be classified as a Southern progressive, nevertheless Edwin Mims's writings incorporate much of the New South ideology. His book, *The Advancing South: Stories of Progress and Reaction*, published in 1926, is an excellent source for becoming acquainted with an ideology shared by many of his contemporaries who wrote educational history. For Mims, industrialization was the salvation of the South, not only economically but esthetically as well. He insists that modern industrialization was humane and enlightened. He is full of praise for the social welfare programs for the workers in the larger Southern industries and expresses no fears of paternalism inherent in the social programs of the industrialists. Obviously, to enjoy the virtues of industrialization, technical and industrial education needed to be fostered. In addition, he supports the other major principles of the Southern progressive educators: a Booker T. Washington-style education for blacks (although he was willing to listen to criticism of Southern culture and education from more radical thinkers—even blacks like W. E. B. DuBois and Walter F. White), progressive state universities, efforts of schools to avoid or escape ecclesiastical control, and increased educational opportunities and social roles for women.[48]

Mims's vision of the New South owes much to Walter Hines Page, to whom he devotes the second chapter of his book. Page, one of the most prominent leaders of the Southern Educational Movement, was also one of its most articulate voices. No more straightforward statement of the relationship between schooling and the modernization of the South may be found than in his *The Rebuilding of Old Commonwealths: Being Essays Towards the Training of the Forgotten Man in the Southern States.* The three essays which make up the book amount to a polemic in behalf of tax-supported public schools for "wealth creation." An unequivocal proponent of modernization, he insists that all resources must be developed and that the most important undeveloped resource in the South was its people. "The right training of men," he writes, "is a better thing than the bounty of nature itself."[49] Page here as elsewhere in his speeches and writings makes clear that industrial training rather than literary schooling is the ideal education for all Southerners, blacks and whites alike.

Implicit in the New South creed was the need for a regeneration of values. The work ethic was promoted in contrast to the concept of the gentleman of leisure, materialism was proclaimed as a positive good, and failure was attributed to personal shortcomings. Booker T. Washington's writings with their emphasis on the gospel of work, thrift, cleanliness, and practicality echo much of the New South creed.[50]

Such an ideology obviously had relevance for schooling in the modernization of the South. However, despite leaders such as J. L. M. Curry who "sought to make education the South's number one concern" and spokesmen like Page who stressed the importance of literacy, especially for the poor whites, according to Gaston, "education remained a relatively minor part of the New South Creed." Instead, spokesmen held up industrialization and scientific agriculture as the keys to regional salavation.[51] Irving Gershenberg, on the other hand, attributes the dismal educational statistics of the turn-of-the-century South to the opposition of that "group which controlled the region's political institutions, namely the plantation owners, industrialists, merchants, and bankers."[52]

Nevertheless, the first two decades of the twentieth century witnessed an educational renaissance unparalled in Southern history. For many writers, this educational crusade incorporated the best in Southern liberalism, philanthropy, and humanitarianism. To pre-World War II historians, the crowning glory of education in the South was the Southern Educational Movement—a constellation of activities and organizations aimed at bringing to the South state systems of public schools equivalent to those in other parts of the country. It was a multi-faceted movement, and its historians have had to direct their attention to a number of different but related topics: political crusades, Southern progressivism in educational practice, industrial training, Northern philanthropy, and black education. Its beginnings may be found in the Peabody fund established in 1867; it reached the height of its propaganda efforts with the Conference for Education in the South and the Southern

Education Board in the first decade of the twentieth century, and it received its greatest financial support from the General Education Board and the Rosenwald Fund after World War I.

As was the case with education and reconstruction, there were differences in the interpretations of the movement by black and white writers, with blacks also badly divided among themselves. Generally, however, it has received enthusiastic praise from historians. Dabney's hyberbole is not uncommon:

> Surely there never was, in modern times a movement grounded in a higher purpose, or, as it turned out, conducted on a better plan, and carried forward with nobler zeal than the movement aimed to make this people, so stricken, so impoverished, and so burdened, an integral, prosperous, and happy part of the nation their fathers had helped to build.[53]

A similar note is struck by Thomas Clark in the mid-sixties in describing the first meeting of the organization which was to produce the Southern Education Movement:

> In the long-range of southern history those altruistic men who met on June 30, 1898, at Captain William H. Sale's Capon Springs Hotel in West Virginia were greater heroes than were the soldiers who struggled away from the battlefields at the end of the war.

These men are credited by Clark not only "with the mere matter of organizing and the gradual uplifting of schools" but also with reaching "deeper in the fabric of southern life to correct the handicaps of employment" through such measures as vocational training and preventive medicine.[54]

The reformers tried to buy support for public schools by stressing a powerful, if somewhat mystical, relationship between schooling and prosperity. For example, Thompson informs his readers that a major reason why Southerners failed to support public schools adequately, in addition to their religious, racial, and political values, was simply crushing poverty—even after they "began to feel the thrill of growing industrialism."[55] Southerners were told that a lack of education was a chief cause of their poverty and that they would have to go against their natural instincts to oppose increased taxes during hard times and spend their way to prosperity by investing in schools. "Poverty is the inevitable result of ignorance," Curry warns and adds, "capital follows the school house."[56] But, lest this sound like a complete capitulation to materialism, Dabney reminds his audience that the ultimate goal of the movement "was the inspiration of the people to a higher and fuller realization of their duty to all their fellow men and to their nation."[57] Citizenship and prosperity could march hand in hand.

Despite many positive evaluations, the Southern Educational Movement has not escaped criticism. Various historians have pointed out its economic blindspots. Horace Mann Bond rejects the notion that more and better schools would necessarily follow industrialization. He argues that a study of Alabama demonstrates "that the economic penetration of Alabama by capital ... not only failed to furnish that necessary foundation but, in fact, ended by protecting its failure by hamstringing educational progress."[58] Others like Charles Sellers and C. Vann Woodward have underscored the Southern leaders' inability to see poverty in institutional terms. Like the Northern millionaire philanthropists of the time, they saw no need for a "basic alteration of social, racial, and economic arrangements."[59]

The second area of dispute has centered around the philanthropists and their funds—especially insofar as the funds affected black education. Many of the pre-World War II writers are in full agreement with Hoke Smith who, in his address to the Conference for Education in the South in 1902, calls the leaders of the conference, "big hearted philanthropists."[60] The majority of these writers were unabashed admirers of the philanthropists, giving them credit for almost everything worthwhile that happened in Southern education for a generation. They particularly admired the restraint and willingness to defer to Southern opinions by these Northern leaders, especially in contrast to the zealots of the Reconstruction era. Comparing Barnas Sears to his predecessor Horace Mann as secretary of the Massachusetts Board of Education, Curry records the traits considered most worthy by the leaders of the Southern Education Movement: Sears was "less aggressive, less iconoclastic [and] less obstrusive. . . ."[61]

The motives of the philanthropists, currently the subject of vigorous dispute, were not subject to much critical examination in the first half of the twentieth century. Most of the writers (Leavell is a good example) uncritically accept the official statements of fund reports on the aims and motives of the funds, which suggested that the philanthropists were motivated by Christian or, at least in the case of Julius Rosenwald, religious idealism. The historians recognize that many of the philanthropists had interests, direct or indirect, in the Southern economy, but, as mentioned above, economic development and improvement in all aspects of Southern life were considered indivisible. As an example, in his biography of Seaman Knapp, Joseph Cannon Bailey stresses that much of Knapp's work in Southern agriculture under the auspices of the General Education Board was based on the faith that greater prosperity leads to higher civilization; his ultimate goal in organizing corn and tomato clubs was to advance the social and cultural life of Southerners.[62] Dabney's gingerly treatment of William Henry Baldwin, Jr., Southern railway mogul and prominent leader of Southern education causes, is likewise illustrative. Although Baldwin "descended from a line of abolitionists, he did not share their prejudices." Little is said about his interests in profits for his railways; rather, "his chief interest was in the education and training of neglected men."[63]

With more detachment, Merle Curti suggests that the work of the philanthropists "was not, at least directly and consciously, motivated by economic
considerations."[64] He is able to see some spots on the robes of the philanthropists and crusaders—George Peabody's fortune, as an example, was
acquired "by somewhat questionable means."[65] He includes a particularly
good sketch of Curry, showing the old confederate as a complex mix of
idealism, racism, nationalism, and naivete. However, for Robert Curtis Ogden,
long-term president of the Conference of Education in the South, Curti,
like the other historians can find no base motives: "If Ogden was motivated
by economic considerations in his work for Southern education, his private
papers do not reveal any such interest. In part he was motivated by a sense
of the successful businessman's *noblesse oblige*."[66]

Bond, almost as much as his white counterparts, finds the work of the
funds praiseworthy. He acknowledges that blacks were divided; some feared
that the large foundations might attempt to gain control of the "thought
and opinion" of blacks for their own selfish interests and sought to remind
the blacks "to fear the Greeks, bearing gifts," while others quoted the contrary maxim, "Don't look a gift-horse in the mouth."[67] But after summarizing the work of the funds, Bond concludes that much of the progress of
contemporary blacks could "be traced back to the friendly intermediation of
philanthropic persons of both races."[68] The opportunity for spiritual and
physical growth and development of leadership ability, he insists, would not
have come without the aid of the large foundations.[69]

Examples of institutionalized racism are often ignored by the earlier
writers. Most of them matter-of-factly notice that those funds not devoted
exclusively to black education provided disproportionately more for white
than black schools. Generally, only toward the end of the period are writers
such as Embree and Waxman critical of the inequities. Indeed, as might be
expected, treatment of racial issues, more than other factors, changed with
the passage of time. In 1898 Curry insists that blacks shared in the largesse
of the Peabody Fund, "according to numbers or the prospects of usefulness."[70] In 1911 Alderman unselfconsciously and uncritically quotes Curry:
"If there were any way of bleaching the negro, our land would be at
peace."[71]

Prior to 1960, few historians see much reason to question these overall
evaluations. While there are some like Embree and Waxman who already in
the late 1940s insist that the Rosenwald Fund direct "its attention squarely
to the problem of segregation,"[72] there are others like S. Alexander Rippa,[73]
Franklin Parker,[74] Martin Watkins Black,[75] and Earl West[76] who continue
through the 1960s and into the 1970s to give the philanthropists a clean bill
of conduct. West, for example, argues that Barnas Sears's support of the
private white schools in Louisiana during the experiment with mixed schools
in the 1870s and his opposition to portions of the Civil Rights Bill in the

same decade were in keeping with his assumption that social progress required universal education and that the educational systems must be a natural outgrowth of popular sentiment. To accomplish this Sears felt he had to gain the support of the white leadership class. Temporary discrimination, as far as Sears was concerned, was not too high a price to pay for "long range justice."[77]

Unlike the Dabneys and Currys, post-World War II historians of the philanthropic funds could no longer ignore the issue of racism. A good example is Raymond Fosdick's in-house history of the General Education Board. Fosdick admits that men like Ogden built their program for black education on the base of white supremacy. They were men who were "dreaming dreams of a new future, but in many respects they were prisoners of their times." They sought to allay fears of Northern imperialism by stressing the fact that schools were built by and for Southerners and in keeping with Southern traditions. They did what they could to salvage black education in the face of white opposition. The General Education Board accepted segregation "because at that moment there was nothing else to do if education for the Negroes was to be developed." They acted wisely in proceeding with "caution and modesty," in realizing "that nothing but an indigenous development of Southern education was feasible." He defends the board's emphasis on industrial training for blacks on two grounds: (1) industrial training in its origins was not linked to race and (2) any education for blacks was an improvement. Fosdick concludes by taking a swipe at presentism in history; one "cannot demand that an earlier generation should have fought the battle we are fighting now."[78] A similar note is struck by Louis Rubin relative to the activities of the Slater Fund. Its efforts in black education must be evaluated against the backdrop of worsening conditions for blacks. At best, the Slater Fund helped keep matters from becoming worse.[79]

Some historians have found the salvaging thesis to be an insufficient defense.[80] William Vaughn, for example, admits that white attitudes made it impractical for Barnas Sears to work actively for integrated schools. But in his refusal to aid the mixed schools in Louisiana, in his curtailment of funds to the integrated University of South Carolina, and in his active opposition to Summers' Civil Rights Bill, Sears "lent his own considerable energies and the resources of the Peabody Fund to perpetuating a policy of racial segregation in Southern schools."[81] Church is willing to admit that the philanthropists began their work with "some limited commitment to providing equal educational opportunity for the blacks." However, they found it impossible to fulfill this commitment and to expand public schools in the South at the same time. In the end, they opted "to sacrifice equality for the blacks in order to achieve better school systems for the southern white." But everyone would presumably benefit since better schools would increase prosperity, reduce corruption in government, improve public services, and help curtail child labor.[82]

Thus far, the debate has revolved around the issue of racism. Anderson, however, has recast the debate around economics as well as race. In so doing, he rejects the salvaging thesis presented by both the defenders and critics of the philanthropists. Anderson asserts that the problem with many histories is that they focus solely on quantitative differences between black and white schools. In addition, these interpretations assume a monolithic opposition on the part of Southern whites to black education. According to Anderson, Southern industrialists, unlike their agrarian counterparts, did not oppose education for blacks per se. They supported public schooling for blacks because it fit into their concept of an industrialized South. The question was not whether there should be schooling for blacks, but rather what kind of schooling and for what purposes. The philanthropists called for an education which would replace the former control exercised by slavery, substituting "the internalization of social and psychological values" for physical coercion. The goal was to create a cheap and efficient labor force which would aid in guarding the South from a "more organized working class." They found the proper kind of black education to be the Tuskegee model of industrial and moral training. Industrial education was not a program designed to salvage something of black education in the face of white opposition, nor was it a program for "negro uplift." Quite simply, it was a program designed to control and repress the blacks while safeguarding the nation "against the seeds of labor disruption and social instability."[83]

In an article published in 1978, Anderson applies this economic interpretation to the programs for rural black education. The Northern philanthropists' policies and programs for the rural blacks, he argues, "were designed primarily to develop an economically efficient and politically stable Southern agricultural economy by training efficient and contented black labor while leaving the Southern racial hierarchy intact."[84]

Few writers have analyzed the relationship between the nascent progressive movement and educational reform in the twentieth-century South. This is in striking contrast to the number of general social and political histories. As Grantham has pointed out: "The most substantial contribution that historians have made to a greater understanding of the twentieth-century South has been their work in the first two decades of the century. Much of this writing has dealt with one aspect or another of southern progressivism. . . ."[85] However, political and social historians have not, as a rule, made education their primary concern. And educational historians have only begun to look beyond the surface meaning of reforms, having concentrated primarily on providing descriptions of educational crusades and organizational and administrative reforms and on citing statistics relative to educational expenditures, length of school terms, literacy rates, and school attendance patterns.[86]

Consequently, the starting place for a study of Southern progressivism and education must be in social, political, and intellectual histories. C. Vann

Woodward[87] and Dewey Grantham[88] have emphasized the color line—Southern progressivism was for whites only. Hugh Bailey has explored the ideology of Southern liberalism, including its faith in education as a powerful instrument for solving social problems including the race problem.[89] Using the biographies of several Southern statesmen, he has analyzed the meaning of Southern progressivism and political reform. However, although educational reforms are mentioned in these biographies, they are never the focus of attention.[90]

The meaning of progressivism per se is seldom discussed by the older generation of historians. However, a "Progressive spirit," as Noble calls it, does permeate their works.[91] They vigorously support major tenets of the progressives, including the necessity of having appointed rather than elected school officials ("It is an established principle in political science that expert and skilled leaders cannot be selected by popular election"),[92] professionally trained teachers, graded classrooms, and school consolidation. Similarly, studies of educational leaders such as Charles McIver,[93] James Joyner,[94] and Eugene Brooks[95] seldom make mention of progressivism. They do agree however, that (1) an educational revival took place in the early twentieth century marked by increased school expenditures, improved teacher training programs, longer school terms, improvement in county school administration, improved school facilities, and some movement towards consolidation of small rural schools; (2) blacks as well as whites and rural as well as urban areas shared in the educational crusade; and (3) this educational crusade was unique in the South's history.

Was Southern progressivism as reflected in the educational revival for whites only? Here the post-World War II writers present a mixed picture. Gatewood, and especially Holder, attempt to portray their subjects as friends of black education. (Holder writes her biography in the Dunning-Knight tradition and does not question the legitimacy of white supremacy.)[96] The school leaders, according to this interpretation, were products of their day, accepting without question segregation in the schools but opposing the expansion of white schools at the expense of black education.[97] A different version, however is presented by Harlan and Gershenberg. The dual educational systems were not a significant factor, they argue, in retarding the growth of white schools after 1900. In fact, discrimination in school funds often aided white schools at the expense of black institutions; it was the basis of the compromise between the "tax payer" and the "tax layer." In this respect, the Southern Education Board's "sympathetic and gentle approach to the race issue" was a failure.[98]

The conservative side of Southern progressivism in education has received attention from several writers. Goodenow points out that while progressivism was not a monolithic movement during the 1930s, its "rhetoric was used by whites to justify and tolerate the continuation of segregation and economic exploitation of blacks."[99] Urban's study of Atlanta's public schools from 1914 to 1918 led him to conclude that the "predominant reform goals" which emerged were "social efficiency and business efficiency" despite "democratic rhetoric." Urban's article thus constitutes one more attack on the assumption of the pre-World War II writers that the Southern Educational Movement had been a liberating, humane crusade. Harlan and Woodward have assailed that assumption as it concerned blacks; now Urban questions it as far as educational reform in Atlanta for whites was concerned.[100]

A major emphasis of progressivism in education was the drive for industrial and vocational education, not only in the South but in the urban centers of the North as well. Useful studies of the nation-wide industrial training and vocational education movements have been provided by Lazerson and Grubb,[101] Church,[102] and Violas.[103] However, except for their treatment of Booker T. Washington, these studies have largely neglected the South.

Discussion to date of industrial training in the South has focused primarily on black education. An excellent overview of the rise of industrial education in black institutions is provided by Meier, who reminds his readers that industrial education was not invented by nor restricted to Booker T. Washington and his schools,[104] a point underscored by McPherson as well.[105] Bullock[106] and Anderson[107] present a negative appraisal of the role of Booker T. Washington and the philanthropists in promoting industrial training as the panacea for problems related to black education. Anderson, in particular, indicts the philanthropists for attempting to relegate blacks to a separate, inferior position in American society by limiting their schooling to industrial education. Such a generalization would not have been acceptable to the earlier generation of writers, with the exception of DuBois. Some of these writers, like Washington, do advocate industrial training as the proper kind of education for "backward or weak races" such as blacks because of their "relative stage of racial development."[108] And most of the other earlier historians agree with Knight that progress for both the South and the blacks depended on Negro industrial education.[109] But all insist that the purpose of industrial education is to enhance black development, not to limit it.

When one proceeds from industrial training for blacks to industrial training for whites, one finds little material in the literature. Yet these earlier writers assume that industrial training is an ideal education for anyone desiring to capitalize on opportunities offered by the new industrial society. As early as 1898, Curry advocates a reorganization of schooling for the modern world:

> One of the most remarkable phases of educational thought and action of modern times is the fixed conviction that manual training, because of its educational and economic value, should be established and sustained as an inseparable part of our public schools. It has long been felt that instruction in school and college has been too much

restricted to literature, or to purely mental development and culture. Pupils are educated away from productive industry and the ranks of labor; and deplorable consequence, trained skill and high compensation are monopolized largely by the foreign-born, who owe their success to the practical and better-rounded education obtained abroad.[110]

Whether such a reorganization was ever realized in the South for whites is debatable. Nowhere does one find a study that penetrates beneath the surface in analyzing the rise of vocational and industrial education for whites. Grantham's biography of Hoke Smith concentrates on the politics of getting the Smith-Hughes Act through Congress.[111] The drive to promote vocational education in North Carolina in general is noted by Gatewood,[112] while Pannell and Wyatt,[113] as well as Holder,[114] describe the introduction of vocational education for females. In addition, Saloutos's study of farmer organizations concentrates on vocational education at the college level.[115] In short, it appears that while the history of industrial training for blacks may suffer at times from the authors' preoccupation with class and race, the history of industrial education for whites suffers from omission.

Aside from the Reconstruction era and the Southern Educational Movement, no topic in Southern education has received such extensive attention as black education. Yet, despite this emphasis, George Tindall concludes in the mid-sixties: "In the general American or southern historical studies, Negroes seldom appear as actors with vital roles or collectively as a positive social force. They appear as an undifferentiated background, as subjects to be acted upon, but not as people whose affairs have innate significance."[116] Part of this problem, as Tindall points out, stems from the fact that blacks "are seen largely through white man's eyes."[117] Until recently, most available sources of black history were of white origin and reflected the determination of whites that the South should remain a white man's country. Fortunately, Negro sources are becoming increasingly available. Among these sources are: the Carter Godwin Woodson collection of black manuscripts at the Library of Congress, the W. E. B. DuBois papers at Fisk University, printed materials on black history and life at Harvard, Fisk, Yale, and Atlanta universities, Hampton and Tuskegee Institutes, and the Schomburg Collection at the New York Public Library.[118] Extensive bibliographic references on this topic are provided in *Blacks in America: Bibliographical Essays.*[119]

Traditional historical scholarship often ignores examples of institutionalized racism while at the same time reflecting the racial stereotypes of Southern whites of the period under study. Curry and his biographer, Alderman, have no qualms about stressing a lifelong friendship for blacks ("dusky negro playmates") and an advocacy of their needs along with a most insensitive description of them. Stereotypes of a "childlike race" abound, and pronouncements such as the following are matter-of-factly included in Alderman's book: "It is a characteristic of the negro race, familiar to those who have associated with them in more than one of the Southern states, that the further south they live, and the nearer to the equator, the more amenable they appear to the impressions of superstitions."[120]

Knight's acceptance of racial stereotypes is obvious in many ways, including his illustrating the freedmen's ignorance by "quoting" them in dialect. The following, supposedly a statement by a black member of the Virginia Constitutional Convention opposed to an amendment against integrated schools, lacks documentation of any kind (no source, date, or names): "He didn't want to see no such claws in the constitution, and the first thing we knew, der would be similar claws regards waship. Ex fer dis, dere was worser company of white children dan he wised his children to be wid, and dese was secesh children."[121] Bond, as part of his continuing campaign to "correct" Knight, comments on the passage: "One would hardly expect a truly illiterate Negro to use such straight-forward grammar with such marked adherence to the pronounciations suggested by the spelling of his words, nor to spell [in a speech] 'clause' as 'claws' while spelling 'similar' [again in a speech] . . . correctly."[122]

The problem of the Northern missionaries, from the viewpoint of traditional historians, was that they came with false conceptions of the black. Holland Thompson writes that "they went with an ideal negro in their minds," and, "in order to prove their sincerity in the brotherhood of mankind, they entered into the most intimate associations with their pupils and their families. Some . . .were compelled to struggle hard to overcome their instinctive repugnance to such intimacy."[123] Northern enthusiasts, according to Knight, "made the mistake of believing that the chief difference between the white man and the negro was the enforced ignorance of the latter."[124] Swint, the historian of the Northern teacher, pictures him as generally unaware and ignorant of the primitive state of the black, intellectually, morally, and aesthetically. He also tends to soft-pedal Southern racism and brutality.[125]

According to the traditional historians, in contrast to the false notions and unwise behavior of the Northern missionaries were the wise actions of the philanthropists. These men were the true friends of the black. The Jeanes, Slater, Phelps-Stokes, and Rosenwald Funds and the General Education Board, according to Knight, "seemed to develop a better sentiment for the education of the negro."[126] Dabney agrees, writing that there was "nothing finer in the history of education than this story" of the work of the funds on behalf of blacks.[127] Dabney, who was one of the strongest supporters of blacks and frequently comments on their strength of character and intelligence, reveals a good deal about the racial attitudes of Southern progressives in the following comment:

> In one of those simple brick houses with green shutters and white
> marble steps, so characteristic of old Philadelphia, Robert Curtis
> Ogden was born on June 20, 1836, and delivered into the kind arms
> of an old Negro nurse. Did the love bestowed by the black mammy
> upon her white child have any influence in implanting in him that
> interest in her race which made him one of the truest friends it
> ever had?[128]

Needless to say, the traditional story of black education has not stood the
test of time. One line of attack has centered on quantitative differences in
schooling for blacks and whites, especially in expenditures. Harlan[129] and
Gershenberg[130] have focused on discriminatory funding in the public schools,
while Johnson[131] has pointed to the limited contribution of the Peabody
Fund to rural and black education in Alabama. Others have taken up the
segregation-integration debate. Harlan,[132] and Vaughn,[133] and McPherson[134]
have provided the best comprehensive accounts of the "mixed schools"
experiments in New Orleans, the University of South Carolina, and in the
Northern missionary schools such as Berea College, and Hollis[135] has presented a negative evaluation of the impact of the integration experiment
on the University of South Carolina. The concept of industrial training as
the solution for black education has also come under scrutiny. Carnoy[136]
and Anderson[137] have gone beyond the quantitative difference–segregation
debate. They have placed black education in the context of the industrialists'
attempt to educate an efficient black labor force without raising their social
and political aspirations.

The story of the activities of the Freedman's Bureau and Northern mis-
sionaries in promoting education for social equality has also been rewritten.
Writers such as Abbott,[138] Aldersen,[139] Alexander,[140] Howard,[141] and
Low[142] all provide a basically positive portrayal of the activities of the
Freedman's Bureau and Northern missionaries in educating the ex-slave.
The most comprehensive account of the Northern missionaries' activities is
provided in James McPherson's study of the abolitionists after the Civil
War. In his provocative account, McPherson takes issue not so much with
traditional accounts as with the bulk of recent scholarship in black education;
in so doing, he often agrees with the older historians. McPherson rejects
the view that most abolitionists gave up the struggle for equal rights after
1870. Abolitionist teachers did not melt away as Reconstruction collapsed,
nor did they give in to segregation without opposition. He agrees with the
early historians that these Northern missionaries were radicals who took the
notion of social equality seriously.[143]

Although McPherson's focus is on white missionary societies rather than
on blacks, nevertheless the study provides much pertinent, and often overlooked, information on black schools, especially colleges. He highlights the

activities of foundations founded by the missionary societies, such as the Daniel Hand Fund, rather than those of the General Education Board, the Slater, Rosenwald, and Anna T. Jeanes Fund. His interest is in black institutions founded by the Congregationalists, Methodists, Presbyterians, and Baptists and not in industrial schools such as Tuskegee and Hampton. He recognizes the existence of a white paternalism and an emphasis upon cultural assimilation but argues that the latter was viewed as the road to equality, not subordination. Similarly, industrial values and training were viewed as having relevance for social uplift and mobility. Once segregation closed in on the South, the debate was less over curriculum than over black control in Negro institutions.[144]

The symbol of black industrial education, Booker T. Washington, presents a continuing problem of interpretation for educational historians. Early works including Washington's *Up From Slavery* and *Working With the Hands*[145] and biographies of Matthews[146] and by Scott and Stowe[147] offer noncritical success stories of Washington. After reading of his successes in enhancing the rights of blacks, one would almost think that the civil rights movement of the 1950s and 1960s was unnecessary. Reading his works, even those already informed of Washington's dislike for a dirty collar or of his insistence that the toothbrush was the major tool for civilizing a society will be struck anew at his obsession with cleanliness, neatness, and order. "Wherever you may go in the shops," he assures his readers proudly, "you will find someone busy with a broom most of the time."[148] He seems to have been driven by a desperate need to help blacks escape the epithet "shiftless."

He does not attempt, nor do his biographers, to conceal his antiintellectual bias and his disregard for academic freedom. He always stressed "the practical usefulness of the Academic Department,"[149] and when his teachers in that department began backsliding toward the theoretical, he sent them nasty notes on how unsatisfactory their work was. He ruled Tuskegee with an iron fist and an eye for minute detail. His constant prying was, his biographers hint, the source of a good deal of animosity and anxiety on the part of his faculty and staff. Both biographers picture him as bigger than life; his human qualities are hidden. Matthews writes on his "racy wisdom" and "salty humor," but the reader gets no taste of these qualities. The closest suggestion of a human weakness is Scott's confession that Washington had a particular fondness "for the picturesque ne'er-do-wells of his race," particularly if they were elderly, giving them both money and time.[150]

There is little comment in the biographies on criticisms that Washington accommodated himself to Jim Crow. The effects of segregation are downplayed to the extent that the reader is left with the impression that Washington considered segregationist practices as merely customs to be observed by blacks in the South with a sort of "when in Rome do as the Romans do" attitude. Moreover, according to these studies, he was continually at work behind the scenes to improve the lot of blacks. "He always preferred private influences to public declamation," writes Matthews.[151] Of the three biographers, only Matthews gives a hint of criticism of Washington's belief that character, skill, and hard work were all that a black needed for economic success. "He did not bring into his discussion," Matthews writes, "the fact that so many Negro men of intelligence, high character and industry, because of the inequitable pressures of their environment, are frustrated by unjust discrimination from ever rising."[152]

Although Knight, incredibly, manages to write his survey textbook on Southern education without mentioning Washington and Tuskegee, or DuBois and Fisk for that matter, most of the other pre-World War II writers reviewed in this essay are as laudatory of Washington as his biographers. Alderman, for example, calls him "the most farseeing man of his race."[153] Bond agrees that he was the "greatest of Negro leaders," but goes further, referring to him as "without doubt" the greatest Southerner of the post-Civil War period and one of the "most distinguished" Americans of his time.[154] Curti, as usual, is the most analytical; engaging in neither praise nor censure, he analyzes Washington's social philosophy and activities in terms of an ideology more middle-class white American than black. "The limitations of his social thinking were not," Curti writes, "primarily those of a Negro—they were those of the class which, on the whole, determined American values and governed American life."[155] Regardless of an author's attitudes toward him, the reader is left with the conclusion that Washington found it impossible to be critical of a rich man.

Modern scholarship has attempted to separate Booker T. Washington the man from Booker T. Washington the myth. Louis Harlan has provided what one authority describes as "the fullest and most incisive study of Washington's life and career."[156] Harlan takes the reader behind the public image to the private Booker T. Washington. What emerges is not a philosopher but a power broker—"Ideas he cared little for. Power was his game, and he used ideas simply as instruments to gain power."[157] Church and Meier have provided excellent interpretive studies of Washington's concept of industrial training. Both agree that industrial training did not begin as an education calculated to produce black inferiority and subordination.[158] With the reversal of the gains from Reconstruction, some blacks began to shift their attention from political to economic strategies "as the primary instrument of racial leverage." Don Kelly briefly discusses the interrelationship between economic action and industrial training in Booker T. Washington's philosophy.[159]

Unlike Booker T. Washington, W. E. B. DuBois has received little attention from the pre-World War II educational historians. Merle Curti provides an excellent, balanced, classic presentation of the Washington/DuBois controversy.[160] Matthews delineates in an evenhanded but incisive manner their fundamental differences. Keeping Washington's image untarnished, he concludes by stressing DuBois's "genuine respect for and admiration of Booker T. Washington."[161] Scott and Stowe, however, denounce the "carping and sometimes bitter criticisms" of Washington by DuBois, who is not mentioned by name but referred to as part of that "'talented-tenth' element of Northern negroes."[162] Of course, it was DuBois himself who started the controversy in 1903 with the publication of *The Souls of Black Folks* which included the offending chapter, "Of Booker T. Washington and Others."[163]

Recent scholarship on DuBois has been hampered due to the fact that DuBois's private papers were inaccessible to scholars. Francis L. Broderick's study of DuBois as a leader provides a mixed picture, stating that his leadership was more apparent than real, and that his published works demanded attention but few were "first class."[164] Eliott M. Rudwick has examined the paradox in DuBois's philosophy, the emphasis on racial pride and black nationalism as well as an insistence on the black's right to participate fully in the common political, social, and spiritual life.[165] DuBois's debate with Washington concerned more than curriculum; it concerned tactics of accommodation or protest, a point discussed in Meier and Rudwick.[166] It also concerned the role of an educated black elite in charting the blacks' future course. Rutledge Dennis's article notes the shift in DuBois's own thinking on the concept of "the talented tenth" from a race to a class analysis.[167]

The last two decades have witnessed an increasing attempt on the part of historians to explore black education from a black viewpoint. The freedmen's enthusiasm for schooling and the high expectations which blacks had for schooling have been underscored by Robert G. Newby and David Tyack.[168] Black life in a segregated world is explored by Bullock in his study on Negro education. He points out that the protest tradition was never eradicated and that one of the unintended by-products of black schooling was the education of a black leadership which would eventually lead the assault on segregation.[169] Scholars such as Dittmer, Gray, and Sherer have also explored the problems of surviving in a hostile racist environment.[170] John Dittmer's focus is on higher education in the private sector, especially at Atlanta Univeristy. Dorothy A. Gray paints a rather bleak picture, describing the Negro community's inability to oganize effectively for collective action and its tendency to place a "naive faith in education as the key to social development." Robert G. Sherer's study of nineteenth century Alabama describes the diverse strategies black educators used in their attempt to escape the web of subordination. Although blacks were often more acted upon than acting and although they were disenfranchised throughout much of the South by the early twentieth century, this did not preclude some opportunity for local victories. One example is given by Toppin in his account of the Atlanta NAACP's successful fight for more equal educational funding in 1916-1917.[171]

Judging from the number of publications, it would be safe to say that few issues have sparked more interest than the desegregation movement. Of special importance in this movement is the role of the federal government and the federal courts in shaping the direction of Southern education. C. Vann Woodward has provided the classic study of the segregation movement in the South. In his book, *The Strange Career of Jim Crow*, Woodward argues that, except for segregated schools and churches, physical segregation of the races was not the norm in Southern practice prior to the late nineteenth and early twentieth centuries. In tracing the "strange career" of segregation, Woodward not only places its rise in the "broader political and economic currents of southern history" but also depicts the national and international developments which served eventually to undermine de jure segregation in the mid-twentieth century.[172]

The legal bases for segregation and desegregation and the response of Southern whites to the Civil Rights Movement have been adequately covered. John Garraty has edited an excellent series of readings describing and analyzing key Supreme Court decisions that have helped shape American history. Of special interest here are Alan F. Westin's treatment of *The United States* v. *Singleton*, C. Vann Woodward's treatise on *Plessy* v. *Ferguson*, and Alfred Kelly's discussion of *Brown* v. *The Board of Education of the City of Topeka*. These articles place the cases in their historical context, linking them to the political currents and racial ideologies of their day.[173] In addition, Blaustein and Ferguson have provided a comprehensive study on the background and significance of the landmark 1954 Supreme Court decision, examining it in its legal context.[174] Billington,[175] Smith,[176] and Gates,[177] have treated the rise of white opposition in the South to civil rights legislation and Supreme Court decisions. Smith's study of Prince Edward County, Virginia, highlights the human element involved in the struggle.

It has become increasingly evident that desegregation was linked somehow to the broader domestic and foreign policies of the federal government. This relationship is touched upon in Woodward's study, *The Strange Career of Jim Crow*, and is made explicit in Joel Spring's study of national educational policy since 1945. Spring analyzes the *Brown* v. *The Board of Education* case, the enforcement of that decision in 1957, and the Civil Rights Act of 1964 in light of America's foreign policy. Spring argues that blacks were finally admitted into Little Rock's Central High School, "not because of Eisenhower's devotion to civil rights but because of his devotion to winning the cold war against the Soviet Union." Title VI of the Civil Rights Act of 1964 was important because it set the precedent for future national regulation of education to implement other policies."[178]

Neglected Topics in Southern Educational History

It would appear that, aside from increased attention to black education, those topics raised by the pre-World War II historians and educators still dominate the field. Revisionism may have challenged traditional interpretations, but it has been reluctant to look at new areas or topics. Thus, Reconstruction, the Southern Educational Movement, and the philanthropists and their funds still hold the major share of attention. The purpose of this section is to suggest some hitherto neglected research topics.

One of the distinctive hallmarks of the South has been its commitment to a militant, fundamentalist Protestantism. According to scholars such as Francis Simkins, William B. Hesseltine, and David L. Smiley, "conservatism in religion" ranks close to "white supremacy" as a significant factor in explaining the South's distinctiveness. It has served as an "intellectual blockade" to isolate the Southern mind and churches from "prevailing trends of American Christianity and society."[179] Its impact was also felt in education, especially in the opposition of church schools to the expansion of public higher education, in the militant anti-Catholicism of the 1920s, and in the evolution debates.

In Southern education there has long been a close relationship between the pulpit and the desk, the church and the schoolhouse. The dividing line between private and public schooling has not always been clearly marked, as Nelms's study of Selma, Alabama, has shown.[180] Nor is it clear to what extent the church promoted or retarded educational expansion in the South. A substantial and well-written study of this issue and others, including changing conceptions of the phrase "separation of church and state" may be found in Sadie Bell's work, *The Church, the State, and Education in Virginia*, published in 1930. Bell analyzes (and approves of) the common compromise by which school and public officials encouraged religious activities in public schools without giving such activities official recognition or approval.[181] Griffith Hamlin's article suggests that church leaders were strong proponents of schooling, including public schooling. However, Holder presents a somewhat different appraisal. She argues that churchmen used their support of the common school as a strategy to argue against increased state aid and involvement at the college level.[182]

The religious solidarity of the South was based not on a denominational loyalty, but rather on a conservative Protestant theological unity. This Protestant solidarity was evident in urban as well as rural areas and united with the increasingly popular Klu Klux Klan in an anti-Catholic drive in cities such as Atlanta and Memphis.[183] Aside from its influence on the firing of Atlanta teacher Julia Riordin in the 1920s, little is known of its impact on

Southern schools. In their discussion of the Julia Riordin incident, both Racine[184] and Newman[185] point out that there were limits to the Klan's ability to effect a wholesale purge of Catholic teachers.

The clash between traditionalism and modernism in religion and science erupted in the anti-evolution campaigns of the 1920s. As Tindall points out, H. L. Mencken's stinging barbs and the Clarence Darrow–William Jennings Bryan clash at the John Scopes trial in Dayton, Tennessee, saddled the South with the image of a benighted region devoid of culture and intelligence.[186] The Scopes Trial is graphically retold by Ray Ginger who focuses on the personalities and legal skirmishes involved.[187] The evolution controversy in North Carolina has been analyzed by Willard Gatewood. He argues that the anti-evolution laws were defeated, in part, due to the effective opposition of university spokesmen.[188] Gatewood also interprets the evolution controversy as being, to some extent a rural-urban conflict, a view rejected by Paul Carter.[189]

The role of higher education in the emergence of the New South deserves more attention. Horace Cunningham includes a brief overview of the historiography in his essay, "The Southern Mind Since the Civil War," focusing primarily on histories of colleges and college administrators, including presidents of black colleges.[190]

Of special interest for the educational historian is the work of social scientists like Howard Odum. According to Grantham, the growth of sociology and other social sciences in the South during the 1920s and 1930s "reflected the widespread conviction . . . that the region's problems could be solved through science and education."[191] Odum's work at Chapel Hill thrust the University of North Carolina into a leadership role in the promotion of and research on Southern regionalism. Wilson's study of the University of North Carolina, despite its provocative subtitle, *The Making of a Modern University*, and chapter title, "Training Experts for the South's Rebuilding," provides little for the social historian beyond a description of programs and a listing of faculties. A much more critical analysis of Odum's work is provided by Michael O'Brien in his recent study of the concept of the New South. He leaves one with the conclusion that Odum's studies on Southern regionalism never quite achieved "theoretical respectability."[192]

The drive for regional planning in Southern higher education after World War II merits more study. Sugg and Jones have provided a useful history of the rise and development of the Southern Regional Education Board from 1949 to 1959.[193] Noteworthy in their study is the description of the Board's attempt to link higher education to such off-campus centers and agencies as the Oak Ridge center for atomic research, the Tennessee Valley Authority, and defense agencies in order to expand graduate and professional training opportunities and to attract funds. What is lacking here, however, is an analysis of the implications of integrating higher education with industry and the military. Another point mentioned but meriting further research is the relationship between racially segregated colleges and a regional approach to education. The Southern Regional Education Board followed the policy of the General Education Board in promoting regional rather than state centers of higher education. This approach had special relevance for black education since it assumed that equal education need not be provided at the state level. Sugg and Jones defend the regional board on the grounds that its arrangements "concerned the strengthening of higher education and not discriminatory treatment of students."[194]

The history of the junior college–community college movement in the South has yet to be written. Much of the history of state community college systems lies buried in dissertations. Furthermore, little is known as to whether black and white junior and community colleges had similar or different histories. The growth of state-wide community college systems along with the expansion of four-year colleges and universities gave rise to state master plans in higher education. A study would be useful to determine to what extent these master plans were designed for and led to a tracking system at the postsecondary level in the South.

Because of the existence of a plethora of Southern state histories of education, it may appear strange to include such histories in a discussion of neglected topics. However, they suffer more than most sources from the cardinal sins of educational historians as enumerated by Bernard Bailyn: anachronism, parochialism, evangelism, and isolation from general American historiography.[195] Several Southern states have been included in *Contributions to American Educational History*, edited by Herbert Baxter Adams and published by the Bureau of Education between 1887 and 1903: North Carolina, South Carolina, Georgia, Florida, Louisiana, Alabama, Mississippi, and Arkansas.[196] However, these studies are not very useful for one pursuing the history of education in the New South, in part because they were written too early and in part because they are generally little more than compilations with heavy emphasis on the founding of specific schools and on short biographies of prominent schoolmen. Most other Southern state histories of education are also in-house and suffer from an overabundance of statistics and statutes given in isolation from the main currents of social history. Detailed summaries of reports and commissions often make these books more like reports of state superintendents than histories. Examples of this genre include the works on Florida by Thomas Cochran in 1921, Boyce Fowler Ezell in 1932, and Vita Katharine Pyburn in 1954.[197] More substantial and scholarly are Dorothy Orr's 1950 work on Georgia and J. L. Blair Buck's history of education in Virginia.[198] A 1916 study of Virginia by Cornelius Heatwole is an early attempt to give adequate treatment to black education. Heatwole was a warm supporter of the Southern Education Movement.[199] Knight's 1916 study of public schooling in North Carolina contains the same attitudes as those found in his other works: Reconstruction was the greatest tragedy in the modern world and the work of Peabody Fund the most wholesome and beneficial remedy. Marcus C. S. Noble's study of North Carolina, although written in 1930, deals with events only until the early 1890s and does not discuss the Southern Education Movement.[200] Andrew Holt's *The Struggle for a State System of Public Schools in Tennessee, 1903-1936*, chronicles the political campaigns in support of improved schooling.[201] Frank L. McVey, the former president of the University of Kentucky, tells much the same story for his state in *The Gates Open Slowly.*[202] Minns Sledge Robertson's study of education in Louisiana after 1898 is an in-house history, and his occasional attempts to relate his state's story to larger movements leave something to be desired, as in his one remark on progressive education: "As is usually the case in a reactionary movement, the emphasis swings far to the progressive point of view in the late thirties."[203]

Educational historians have largely overlooked the role of the Tennessee Valley Authority as an educating agency. Yet, as Lilienthal, Artman, Allbaugh, and Derryberry have shown, motivated by its belief in regional planning and its desire to revitalize a depressed area, the TVA cooperated with the land grant colleges in promoting phosphate research and farm demonstration programs, it worked with the Civilian Conservation Corps and county agricultural agents in reforestation programs, and it promoted research in preventive medicine.[204]

TVA's role in economic planning and revitalization has come under scrutiny. Gilbert Banner criticizes TVA for its failure to recognize "the possibility of structured unemployment and depressed areas in a full-employment economy." It assumed that flood control, electrification, navigation, and fertilizer programs would "automatically improve the region" and it made no special provisions for instituting educational programs which would "create a labor force from rural people."[205] Raymond Wolters pointed to the TVA's neglect of blacks. It discriminated against blacks in "housing, employment and training," thinking of them only as "unskilled and semi-skilled laborers."[206]

The impact of the Depression of the 1930s and the New Deal on Southern education has received little attention from educational historians. Those few studies which have dealt with the Depression era and education have not had the South as their primary focus. C.A. Bowers's monograph on the progressive educator during the Depression years does not treat the South.[207] Edward A. Krug's analysis of the high school in the Depression era does include a brief description of Virginia's state-wide program in curriculum planning.[208]

Occasional mention of the impact of the Depression and the New Deal on Southern education can be found in various studies. Tindall provides a brief overview of the depressed state of education and its revival after 1933 due, in part, to federal relief.[209] John Robert Moore's case study of Louisiana underscores the far-reaching impact of Huey Long's policies and the New Deal on teachers, students, and other professionals.[210] Elaine Von Oesen describes the beneficial role of the WPA in aiding North Carolina's public libraries and in instituting a bookmobile program for the rural areas.[211] Paul Conkin's study of the New Deal community programs includes brief descriptions of the attempts by professional planners to implement progressive educational programs in communities such as Pine Mountain Valley, Georgia, and the Pendula Homesteads in North Carolina.[212]

Many of the New Deal's educational programs took place outside the schoolhouse. Of key importance here were the programs of the National Youth Administration and Civilian Conservation Corps. John Salmond's article on Aubrey Williams includes a brief note on the shift in focus from relief to vocational training in Arkansas.[213] Salmond's comprehensive study of the Civilian Conservation Corps provides a generally positive evaluation of the Corps' educational efforts, especially in the area of remedial education. However, he makes no attempt to breakdown the Corps' activities by regions.[214]

Historians of the last two decades have begun to look at the New Deal's impact on blacks. As mentioned previously, Raymond Wolters understood the discriminatory role of the TVA in dealing with blacks. John Salmond highlights the discriminatory practices of the CCC in the enrollment and placement of blacks and points to the racial attitudes of its director, Robert Fechner, as part of the problem.[215] Fishel, however, concludes that, despite the discriminatory practices, blacks gained overall, both materially and psychologically, from the New Deal.[216]

The preoccupation of contemporary educational historians with urban education tends to give a misleading picture as far as the South is concerned. For the majority of Southerners, both white and black, educational experience well into the twentieth century remained rural, and as yet the story of rural education remains to be written. Descriptions of the support of farmers' organizations for public, agricultural, and vocational education may be found in Saloutos's study.[217] Histories of Southern educational crusades make mention of educators' attempts to improve teacher salaries, teacher training, school facilities, and curricular offerings in rural schools as well as of drives to establish rural high schools and to consolidate small districts. What is lacking are case studies analyzing the impact of these crusades on rural education.

Until World War I, the majority of American blacks lived in the South, and the majority of these Southern blacks lived in rural areas. One of the problems in dealing with educational statistics is that one must consider not only white v. black but also rural v. urban differences.[218] Fosdick and Anderson both look at the efforts of Northern philanthropists in promoting education for blacks in the rural South. Their evaluations, however, are very different.

Anderson sees little evidence of a humanitarian crusade; rather he views Northern efforts as an attempt to develop an economically efficient and politically stable Southern agricultural conomy.[219] One of the striking phenomena of the twentieth century South has been the decline of the black landowner, the focus of a recent publication by McGee and Boone.[220]

The impact of modernization upon the Southern family and the Southern woman in particular has been largely overlooked by historians. One exception is Anne Scott's study of the Southern woman from 1830 to 1930. Scott highlights the importance of the Civil War and Reconstruction in undermining the traditional female role and "foreshadowing ... a new style of woman." This foreshadowing became a reality in the early twentieth century as new educational opportunities, most notably in the normal schools, opened training possibilities and concomitant professional advancement for women. Scott's study leaves one with the impression, however, that the new woman she describes was more the exception than the norm.[221] Julia Tutwiler's biographers have provided an overly sentimental and nonanalytical account of her efforts in promoting higher education for Alabama's women.[222] Holder's study of McIver, although it includes much useful information on the establishment of the Normal and Industrial School for Women in North Carolina, suffers from a similar defect.[223]

Except for the Northern missionaries, teachers in the South have remained, until recently, conspicuously absent in historical scholarship. Wayne Urban and Joseph Newman have begun to look at the Atlanta teacher and especially the white Atlanta Public School Teachers Association. What is most striking in their studies is the conservative orientation of the APSTA despite its affiliation with the American Federation of Labor.[224] Newman has also analyzed the socio-economic background of Atlanta's teachers in 1881, 1896, and 1922.[225]

Conclusion

When Church wrote his excellent interpretive history of American education, he entitled one of his chapters, "The Failure of the Common Schools (1): The South." Such a chapter title would have been incomprehensible to pre-World War II historians such as Dabney and Knight. They had lived through the public school crusade of the early twentieth century and had given it their unqualified support. They had a dream of a new South where schools and industries would push back the walls of poverty for all and thereby diminish some of the Southern separateness. The story they told reflected their dreams as well as their racial and economic biases. But it was a thrilling story.

Unfortunately, this thrilling tale has too many limitations to serve as a conclusive history for the historian of Southern education. But, as the present essay has demonstrated, an acceptable revised version has yet to be written. Historians have pointed to errors in various sections of the old account, but they have not yet provided a comprehensive history. Perhaps such a history must wait until more case studies are done and more monographs on individual topics are available. One thing seems certain; the historian need not worry that everything worth saying on Southern education has already been said.

Notes

1. Sol Cohen, ed. *Education in the United States: A Documentary History*, vol. 1 (New York: Random House, 1974), Preface.
2. James Anderson, "Northern Foundations and the Shaping of Southern Black Rural Education, 1902–1935," *History of Education Quarterly* 18 (Winter 1978): 371–396. Wayne Urban's study on teacher organizations published in 1976 included but was not restricted to teacher organizations in the South. See Urban, "Organized Teachers and Educational Reform during the Progressive Era: 1890–1902," *History of Education Quarterly* 16 (Spring 1976): 35–52.
3. Paul M. Gaston, "The New South," in *Writing Southern History: Essays in Historiography in Honor of Fletcher M. Green*, ed. Arthur S. Link and Rembert W. Patrick (Baton Rouge, La.: Louisiana State University Press, 1965), p. 316.
4. Michael O'Brien, *The Idea of the American South, 1920–1940* (Baltimore and London: Johns Hopkins University Press, 1979), p. xvii.
5. H. Dudley Plunkett, "Modernization Reappraised: The Kentucky Mountains Revisited and Confrontational Politics Reassessed," *Comparative Education Review* 22 (February 1978): 136.
6. Raimondo Luraghi, "The Civil War and the Modernization of American Society: Social Structure and Industrial Revolution in the Old South Before and During the War," *Civil War History* 18 (September 1972): 234–240.
7. Richard D. Brown, *Modernization: The Transformation of American Life, 1600–1865* (New York: Hill & Wang, 1976), pp. 143, 181, 186.
8. Anne Firor Scott, *The Southern Lady: From Pedestal to Politics, 1830–1930* (Chicago: University of Chicago Press, 1970), p. 71.
9. On manuscript sources, see the materials in Louis R. Harlan, *Separate and Unequal: Public School Campaigns and Racism in the Southern Seaboard States, 1901–1915* (Chapel Hill, N.C.: University of North Carolina Press, 1958), pp. 270–272.
10. Merle Curti, *The Social Ideas of American Educators* (New York: Charles Scribners' Sons, 1935); Holland Thompson, *The New South* (New Haven: Yale University Press, 1921).

11. Edgar Wallace Knight, *The Influence of Reconstruction on Education in the South,* Contributions to Education no. 60 (New York: Teachers College, Columbia University, 1913); Stewart Grayson Noble, *Forty Years of the Public Schools in Mississippi,* Contributions to Education no. 94 (New York: Teachers College, Columbia University, 1918); Ullin Whitney Leavell, *Philanthropy in Negro Education* (Nashville, Tenn.: George Peabody College for Teachers, 1930); Horace Mann Bond, *Negro Education in Alabama: A Study in Cotton and Steel* (New York: Octagon Books, [1939] 1969); Henry Lee Swint, *The Northern Teacher in the South* (New York: Octagon Books, [1941] 1967).

12. W. E. B. DuBois, *The Education of Black People: Ten Critiques 1906–1960,* ed. Herbert Aptheker (Amherst, Mass.: University of Massachusetts Press, 1973).

13. Horace Mann Bond, *The Education of the Negro in the American Social Order* (New York: Prentice-Hall, 1934).

14. Charles S. Johnson, *Shadow of the Plantation* (Chicago: University of Chicago Press, 1934).

15. Bernard Bailyn, *Education in the Forming of American Society* (Chapel Hill, N.C.: University of North Carolina Press, 1960), p. 14.

16. Edwin A. Alderman and Armistead Churchill Gordon, *J. L. M. Curry* (New York: Macmillan Co., 1911); J. L. M. Curry, *A Brief Sketch of George Peabody, and a History of the Peabody Education Fund Through Thirty Years* (Cambridge: University Press; John Wilson & Son, 1898); Charles William Dabney, *Universal Education in the South,* 2 vols. (Chapel Hills, N.C.: University of North Carolina Press, 1936); Walter Hines Page, *The Rebuilding of Old Commonwealths: Being Essays Towards the Training of the Forgotten Man in the Southern States* (Garden City, N.Y.: Doubleday, Page, & Co., 1902).

17. Edwin R. Embree and Julia Waxman, *Investment in People: The Story of the Julius Rosenwald Fund* (New York: Harper & Bros., 1949); *The General Education Board: An Account of its Activities, 1902–1914* (New York: General Education Board, 1915); Guy E. Snavely, *A Short History of the Southern Association of Colleges and Secondary Schools* (The Southern Association of Colleges and Secondary Schools, 1946?).

18. Emmett J. Scott and Lyman Beecher Stowe, *Booker T. Washington: Builder of a Civilization* (Garden City, N.Y.: Doubleday, Page, & Co., 1917); Booker T. Washington, *Working With the Hands* (Garden City, N.Y.: Doubleday, Page, & Co., 1904); DuBois, *The Education of Black People.*

19. Edgar Wallace Knight, *Public Education in the South* (Boston: Ginn & Co., 1922).

20. Dabney, *Universal Education in the South.*

21. Ibid., p. 12.

22. Twelve Southerners, eds., *I'll Take My Stand* (New York: Harper & Bros., 1930).

23. Martin Abbott, *The Freedman's Bureau in South Carolina, 1865–1872* (Chapel Hill, N.C.: University of North Carolina Press, 1967); Henry Allen Bullock, *A History of Negro Education in the South: From 1619 to Present* (Cambridge: Harvard University Press, 1967); William P. Vaughn, *Schools for All: The Blacks and Public Education in the South, 1865–1877* (Lexington, Ky.: University of Kentucky Press, 1974); Joel Williamson, *After Slavery: The Negro in South Carolina During Reconstruction, 1861–1877* (Chapel Hill, N.C.: University of North Carolina Press, 1965).

24. C. Vann Woodward, *Origins of the New South, 1877–1913*, vol. 9 of *A History of the South*, ed. Wendell H. Stephenson and E. Merton Coulter (Baton Rouge, La.: Louisiana State University Press, 1951); George B. Tindall, *The Emergence of the New South, 1913–1945*, vol. 10 of *A History of the South* (Baton Rouge, La.: Louisiana State University Press, 1967); Paul Gaston, *The New South Creed: A Study in Southern Mythmaking* (New York: Alfred A. Knopf, 1970); Charles Greer Sellers, Jr., "Walter Hines Page and the Spirit of the New South," *The North Carolina Historical Review* 29 (October 1952): 481–499; Michael O'Brien, "C. Vann Woodward and the Burden of Southern Liberalism," *American Historical Review* 78 (June 1973): 589–604.

25. Harlan, *Separate and Unequal*; Anderson, "Northern Foundations"; James Anderson, "Education for Servitude: The Social Purposes of Schooling in the Black South, 1870–1930" (Ph.D. diss., University of Illinois, 1973).

26. Dewey Grantham, Jr., *Hoke Smith and the Politics of the New South* (Baton Rouge, La.: Louisiana State University Press, 1958); Oliver H. Orr, Jr., *Charles Brantley Aycock* (Chapel Hill, N.C.: University of North Carolina Press, 1961); William Larsen, *Montague of Virginia: The Making of a Southern Progressive* (Baton Rouge, La.: Louisiana State University Press, 1965); Rose Howell Holder, *McIver of North Carolina* (Chapel Hill, N.C.: University of North Carolina Press, 1957); Willard B. Gatewood, Jr., *Eugene Clyde Brooks: Educator and Public Servant* (Durham, N.C.: Duke University Press, 1960).

27. For bibliographies on black education see James M. McPherson, Laurence B. Holland, James M. Banner, Jr., Nancy J. Weiss, and Michael D. Bell, *Blacks in America: Bibliographical Essays* (Garden City, N.Y.: Doubleday & Co., 1971).

28. Vaughn, *Schools for All*; Anderson, "Education for Servitude"; Anderson, "Northern Foundations"; James M. McPherson, *The Abolitionist Legacy: From Reconstruction to the NAACP* (Princeton, N.J.: Princeton University Press, 1975), see esp. part 2, pp. 143–295; Louis Harlan, *Booker T. Washington: The Making of a Black Leader, 1865–1901* (New York: Oxford University Press, 1972); August Meier, *Negro Thought in America, 1880–1915* (Ann Arbor, Mich.: University of Michigan Press, 1963); Bullock, *A History of Negro Education in the South*; George Tindall, "Southern Negroes Since Reconstruction: Dissolving the Static Image," in *Writing Southern History*, ed. Link and Patrick, p. 338.

29. C. Vann Woodward, *The Burden of Southern History* (Baton Rouge, La.: Louisiana State University Press, 1960), p. 13.
30. Knight, *Public Education in the South*, p. 307.
31. Thompson, *The New South*, pp. 160–161.
32. Basil Mathews, *Booker T. Washington: Educator and Interracial Interpreter* (Cambridge: Harvard University Press, 1948), p. 29.
33. W. E. B. DuBois, *Black Reconstruction in America* (New York: Russell & Russell, [1935] 1962); Bond, *Negro Education in Alabama*, p. 59.
34. Bond, *Negro Education in Alabama*, p. 59.
35. Swint, *The Northern Teacher in the South*, p. 26.
36. Ibid., p. 36.
37. Ibid., p. 141.
38. Knight, *Influence of Reconstruction*, p. 99; *Public Education in the South*, p. 370.
39. Ibid.
40. DuBois, *The Education of Black People*, p. 129.
41. Daniel J. Whitner, "The Republican Party and Public Education in North Carolina, 1867–1900," *North Carolina Historical Review* 37 (July 1960): 382–395.
42. Harlan, *Separate and Unequal*, p. 4.
43. Thomas Clark, *Three Paths to the Modern South: Education, Agriculture and Conservation* (Athens, Ga.: University of Georgia Press, 1965), p. 4.
44. Rush Welter, *Popular Education and Democratic Thought in America* (New York: Columbia University Press, 1962), pp. 142–158; Robert S. Church and Michael W. Sedlack, *Education in the United States: An Interpretive History* (New York: Free Press, 1976), pp. 124–140.
45. Grady McWhiney, "Reconstruction: Index of Americanism," in *The Southerner as American*, ed., Charles Sellers (Chapel Hill, N.C.: University of North Carolina Press, 1960), p. 101.
46. Thomas Clark and Albert Kirwin, *The South Since Appomatox* (New York: Oxford University Press, 1967), p. 169.
47. Gaston, "The New South," pp. 314–320; Gaston, *The New South Creed*, pp. 57, 63, 100–103, 131–133.
48. Edwin Mims, *The Advancing South: Stories of Progress and Reaction* (Garden City, N.Y.: Doubleday, Page, & Co., 1926).
49. Page, *The Rebuilding of Old Commonwealths*, p. 94.
50. Gaston, *The New South Creed*, pp. 207–221; Booker T. Washington, *Up From Slavery: An Autobiography* (Cambridge: Houghton Mifflin Co., 1928); Washington, ed., *Tuskegee and Its People: Their Ideals and Achievements* (reprinted, New York: Negro University Press, 1969).
51. Gaston, *The New South Creed*, pp. 102–106.
52. Irving Gershenberg, "Southern Values and Public Education: A Revision," *History of Education Quarterly*, 10 (Winter 1970): 413–422.
53. Dabney, *Universal Education in the South*, p. 52.

54. Clark, *Three Paths to the Modern South*, pp. 9-12. For a similar positive note see S. Alexander Rippa, *Education in a Free Society: An American History*, 3rd ed. (New York: David McKay Co., 1976), pp. 137-153.

55. Thompson, *The New South*, p. 70.

56. Alderman, *J. L. M. Curry*, p. 416.

57. Dabney, *Universal Education in the South*, vol. 2, p. 67.

58. Bond, *Negro Education in Alabama*, p. 62.

59. Woodward, *Origins of the New South*, p. 397, and Sellers, "Walter Hines Page and the Spirit of the New South," p. 494.

60. Hoke Smith, "Popular Education as the Primary Policy of the South," *Proceedings of the Fifth Conference for Education in the South*, (1902), p. 43.

61. Curry, *A Brief Sketch of George Peabody*, p. 69.

62. Joseph Cannon Bailey, *Seaman A. Knapp: Schoolmaster of American Agriculture* (New York: Columbia University Press, 1945).

63. Dabney, *Universal Education in the South*, p. 149.

64. Curti, *The Social Ideas of American Educators*, p. 263.

65. Ibid., p. 262.

66. Ibid., pp. 284-285.

67. Bond, *The Education of the Negro*, p. 148.

68. Ibid., p. 150.

69. Ibid.

70. Curry, *A Brief Sketch of George Peabody*, p. 83.

71. Alderman, *J. L. M. Curry*, p. 332.

72. Embree and Waxman, *Investment in People*, p. 180.

73. Rippa, *Education in a Free Society*, pp. 137-153.

74. Franklin Parker, *George Peabody: A Biography* (Nashville, Tenn.: Vanderbilt University Press, 1971), see especially pp. 160-167.

75. Martin Watkins, "Private Aid to Public Schools: The Peabody Fund in Florida, 1867-1880," *History of Education Quarterly* 1 (September 1961).

76. Earl West, "The Peabody Education Fund and Negro Education, 1867-1880," *History of Education Quarterly* 6 (Summer 1966): 3-21.

77. Ibid, p. 21.

78. Raymond B. Fosdick, *Adventure in Giving: The Story of the General Education Board: A Foundation Established by John D. Rockefeller* (New York: Harper & Row, 1962), pp. 11, 13-24, 320-324.

79. Louis D. Rubin, ed., *Teach the Freeman: The Correspondence of Rutherford B. Hayes and the Slater Fund for Negro Education, 1881-1887*. vol. 1 (Baton Rouge, La.: Louisiana State University Press, 1959), pp. xlii-xliii.

80. Bullock, *History of Negro Education in the South*, p. 89. A similar note is struck by Harlan in *Separate and Unequal*, pp. 77-97.

81. William P. Vaughn, "Partners in Segregation: Barnas Sears and the Peabody Fund," *Civil War History* 10 (September 1964): 260-274 and Vaughn, *Schools for All*, pp. 119-158.

82. Church, *Education in the United States*, pp. 149–150; see also Bullock, *A History of Negro Education in the South*, pp. 89–121. On the efforts to curtail child labor see Hugh C. Bailey, "Edgar Gardner Murphy and the Child Labor Movement," *Alabama Review* 18 (January 1965): 47–59.

83. Anderson, "Education for Servitude," pp. 1–2, 35–36, 44–46, 62–63, 119; Anderson, "Education as a Vehicle for the Manipulation of Black Workers," in *Work, Technology and Education: Dissenting Essays in the Intellectual Foundations of American Education*, ed. Walter Feinberg and Henry Rosemont, Jr. (Urbana, Ill.: University of Illinois Press, 1975), pp. 15–40.

84. Anderson, "Northern Foundations," p. 392.

85. Dewey Grantham, Jr., "The Twentieth-Century South," in *Writing Southern History*, ed. Link and Patrick, pp. 415, 422–424.

86. Ibid., p. 422.

87. Woodward, *Origins of the New South*, pp. 321–388, 404–440.

88. Dewey Grantham, "The Progressive Movement and the Negro," in *The Negro in the South since 1865: Selected Essays in American Negro History*, ed. Charles E. Wynes (University, Ala.: University of Alabama Press, 1965), pp. 62–82.

89. Huch C. Bailey, *Liberalism in the New South: Southern Social Reformers and the Progressive Movement* (Coral Gables, Fla.: University of Miami Press, 1969), see especially pp. 131–152.

90. Examples of biographies include Grantham, *Hoke Smith*, Larsen, *Montague of Virginia*, and Orr, *Charles Bentley Aycock*.

91. Bailey and Curti observed that the learning-by-doing work supported by the movement anticipated the progressives.

92. Knight, *Public Education in the South*, p. 451.

93. Holder, *McIver of North Carolina*.

94. Elmer D. Johnson, "James Yadkin Joyner: Educational Statesman," *North Carolina Historical Review* 33 (July 1956): 359–383.

95. Gatewood, *Eugene Clyde Brooks*.

96. Ibid., pp. 26–27, 162–171; Holder, *McIver of North Carolina*, pp. 34–45, 75–77, 200, 228; see also William E. King, "Charles McIver Fights for the Tarheel Negroes' Right to an Education," *North Carolina Historical Review* 41 (Summer 1964): 360–369.

97. Ibid.

98. Harlan, *Separate and Unequal*, pp. 268–269; Louis Harlan, "The Southern Education Board and the Race Issue," in *The Negro in The South Since 1865* ed. Wynes, p. 218; Irving Gershenberg, "The Negro and the Development of White Public Education in the South: Alabama, 1880–1930," *Journal of Negro Education* 39 (Winter 1970): 50–59.

99. Ronald Goodenow, "The Progressive Educator, Race and Ethnicity in the Depression Years: An Overview" *History of Education Quarterly* 15 (Winter 1975): 365–394.

100. Wayne Urban, "Progressive Education in the Urban South: The Reform of the Atlanta Schools, 1914–1918," in *The Age of Urban Reform:*

New Perspectives on the Progressive Era, ed. Michael Ebner and Eugene Tobin (Port Washington, N.Y.: Kennikat Press, 1977), pp. 131–141. On business efficiency and Southern progressivism in the 1920s, see Tindall, *The Emergence of the New South*, pp. 219–253. Philip Racine also notes the business efficiency movement in Atlanta schools during the 1920s and early 1930s but sees this as a movement separate from and in opposition to progressivism. See Racine, "A Progressive Fights Efficiency: The Survival of Willis Sutton, School Superintendent," *South Atlantic Quarterly* 76 (Winter 1976): 103–116.

101. Marvin Lazerson and W. Norton Grubb, eds., *American Education and Vocationalism: A Documentary History, 1870–1970*, Classics in Education no. 48, (New York: Teachers College Press, 1974), pp. 1–50.

102. Church, *Education in the United States*, pp. 192–226.

103. Paul C. Violas, *The Training of the Urban Working Class: A History of Twentieth-Century American Education* (Chicago: Rand McNalley College Publishing Co., 1978), pp. 124–228.

104. Meier, *Negro Thought in America*, pp. 85–99.

105. McPherson, *The Abolitionist Legacy*, pp. 203–222.

106. Bullock, *History of Negro Education*, pp. 74–85.

107. Anderson, "Education for Servitude," pp. 62–67, 119, 148–151.

108. Washington, *Working With the Hands*, p. 64.

109. Knight, *Public Education in the South*, pp. 456–457.

110. Curry, *A Brief Sketch of George Peabody*, p. 110.

111. Grantham, *Hoke Smith*, pp. 118–124, 254–267.

112. Gatewood, *Eugene Clyde Brooks*, p. 121.

113. Anne Gary Pannell and Dorothea Wyatt, *Julia J. Tutwiler and Social Progress in Alabama* (University, Ala.: University of Alabama Press, 1961).

114. Holder, *McIver of North Carolina*, pp. 110–126.

115. Theodore Saloutos, *Farmer Movements in the South, 1865–1933* (Lincoln, Nebr.: University of Nebraska Press, 1960), pp. 33–46, 86.

116. Tindall, "Southern Negroes Since Reconstruction," p. 338.

117. Ibid., p. 359.

118. Ibid., p. 360.

119. McPherson, et al., *Blacks in America*, pp. 119–120, 162–165, 212–218, 331–340.

120. Alderman, *J. L. M. Curry*, p. 28

121. Knight, *Public Education in the South*, p. 321.

122. Bond, *The Education of the Negro*, p. 52.

123. Thompson, *The New South*, pp. 162–163.

124. Knight, *Public Education in the South*, p. 309.

125. Swint, *The Northern Teacher in the South*.

126. Knight, *Public Education in the South*, p. 456.

127. Dabney, *Universal Education in the South*, vol. 2, pp. 432–433.

128. Ibid., p. 21.

129. Harlan, *Separate and Unequal*.

130. Gershenberg, "The Negro and the Development of White Public Education," pp. 50–59.
131. Kenneth R. Johnson, "The Peabody Fund: Its Role and Influence in Alabama," *The Alabama Review* 27 (April 1974): 101–126.
132. Louis Harlan, "Desegregation in New Orleans Public Schools During Reconstruction," *American Historical Review* 67 (April 1962): 663–675.
133. Vaughn, *Schools for All*.
134. McPherson, *The Abolitionist Legacy*, see especially pp. 224–261.
135. Daniel W. Hollis, *University of South Carolina*, vol. 2, *College to University* (Columbia, S.C.: University of South Carolina Press, 1956), pp. 61–79.
136. Martin Carnoy, *Education as Cultural Imperialism* (New York: David McKay Co., 1974), pp. 270–305.
137. Anderson, "Education for Servitude."
138. Abbott, *The Freedman's Bureau in South Carolina, 1865–1872*, pp. 82–98.
139. William T. Aldersen, Jr., "The Freedman's Bureau and Negro Education in Virginia," *North Carolina Historical Review* 29 (January 1952): 64–90.
140. Roberta S. Alexander, "Hostility and Hope: Black Education in North Carolina During Presidential Reconstruction, 1865–1867," *North Carolina Historical Review* 53 (Spring 1976): 113–132.
141. Victor B. Howard, "The Struggle for Equal Education in Kentucky, 1866–1884," *Journal of Negro Education* 46 (Summer 1977): 305–328.
142. W. A. Low, "The Freedman's Bureau in the Border States," in *Radicalism, Racism, and Party Realignment: The Border States During Reconstruction*, ed. Richard Curry (Baltimore and London: Johns Hopkins University Press, 1969), pp. 245–264.
143. McPherson, *The Abolitionist Legacy*, pp. 3–10, 143–297.
144. Ibid. This struggle for black control was also evident in urban public schools prior to 1890. See Howard Rabinowitz, "Half a Loaf: The Shift From White to Black Teachers in the Negro Schools of the Urban South, 1865–1890," *Journal of Southern History* 60 (November 1974): 565–594.
145. Washington, *Up from Slavery; Working with the Hands*.
146. Mathews, *Booker T. Washington: Educator and Interracial Interpreter*.
147. Scott and Stowe, *Booker T. Washington: Builder of a Civilization*.
148. Washington, *Working with the Hands*, p. 67.
149. Ibid., p. 97.
150. Scott and Stowe, *Booker T. Washington: Builder of a Civilization*, p. 144.
151. Mathews, *Booker T. Washington: Educator and Interracial Interpreter*, p. 240.
152. Ibid., p. 184.
153. Alderman, *J. L. M. Curry*, p. 334.
154. Bond, *The Negro in the American Social Order*, p. 122.

155. Curti, *The Social Ideas of American Educators*, p. 309.
156. In addition to Louis R. Harlan, *Booker T. Washington*, see also Harlan, "Booker T. Washington in Biographical Perspective," *American Historical Review* 75 (October 1970): 1581–1599; "The Secret Life of Booker T. Washington," *Journal of Southern History* 37 (August 1971): 393–416; and McPhearson, et al., *Blacks in America*, p. 150.
157. Harlan, *Booker T. Washington*, p. viii.
158. Church, *Education in the United States*, pp. 204–217; Meier, *Negro Thought in America*, pp. 85–99.
159. Don Quinn Kelley, "The Political Economy of Booker T. Washington: A Bibliographic Essay," *Journal of Negro Education* 46 (Fall 1977): 403–418.
160. Curti, *The Social Ideas of American Educators*, pp. 304–309.
161. Mathews, *Booker T. Washington: Educator and Interracial Interpreter*, p. 279.
162. Scott and Stowe, *Booker T. Washington: Builder of a Civilization*, pp. 24, 314.
163. W. E. B. DuBois, *The Souls of Black Folk* (New York: New American Library, [1903] 1969).
164. Francis L. Broderick, *W. E. B. DuBois: Negro Leader in a Time of Crisis* (Stanford, Ca.: Stanford University Press, 1959), pp. 291–312.
165. Eliott M. Rudwick, *W. E. B. DuBois: A Study in Minority Group Leadership* (Philadelphia, Pa.: University of Pennsylvania Press, 1960).
166. Ibid.; Meier, *Negro Thought in America*.
167. Rutledge M. Dennis, "DuBois and the Role of the Educated Elite," *Journal of Negro Education* 46 (Fall 1977): 388–402.
168. Robert G. Newby and David Tyack, "Victims Without Crimes: Some Historical Perspectives on Black Education," *Journal of Negro Education* 40 (Summer 1971): 192–206; David Tyack, "Growing Up Black: The Education of the Negro," in *Turning Points in American Educational History*, ed. David Tyack (Waltham, Mass.: Blaisdell Publishing Co., 1967), pp. 264–275; Timothy L. Smith, "Native Blacks and Foreign Whites: Responses to Educational Opportunity in America, 1880–1950," *Perspectives in American History* 6, ed. Donald Fleming and Bernard Bailyn (Cambridge, Mass.: Harvard University Press, 1972): 309–335.
169. Bullock, *A History of Negro Education in the South*.
170. John Dittmer, *Black Georgia in the Progressive Era, 1900–1920* (Urbana, Ill.: University of Illinois Press, 1977), pp. 141–162; Dorothy A. Gray, "Crisis in Identity: The Negro Community in Raleigh, 1890–1900," *North Carolina Historical Review* 50 (Spring 1973): 121–140; Robert G. Sherer, *Subordination or Liberation? The Development and Conflicting Theories of Black Education in Nineteenth Century Alabama* (University, Ala.: University of Alabama Press, 1977).
171. Edgar A. Toppin, "Walter White and the Atlanta NAACP's Fight for Equal Schools, 1916–1917," *History of Education Quarterly* 7 (Spring 1967): 3–21.

172. C. Vann Woodward, *The Strange Career of Jim Crow* 2nd ed. rev. (New York: Oxford University Press, 1966); Tindall, "Southern Negroes Since Reconstruction," p. 315.

173. John A. Garraty, ed., *Quarrels that have Shaped the Constitution* (New York: Harper & Row, 1962). See Alan F. Westin, "The Case of the Prejudiced Doorkeeper," pp. 128–144; C. Vann Woodward, "The Case of the Louisiana Traveler," pp. 145–158; and Alfred Kelley, "The School Desegregation Case," pp. 243–268.

174. Albert P. Blaustein and Clarence C. Ferguson, Jr., *Desegregation and the Law: The Meaning and Effect of the School Desegregation Cases* (New Brunswick, N.J.: Rutgers University Press, 1957).

175. Monroe Billington, "Civil Rights, President Truman and the South," *Journal of Negro History* 58 (April 1973): 127–139.

176. Bob Smith, *They Closed Their Schools: Prince Edward County, Virginia, 1951–1964* (Chapel Hill, N.C.: University of North Carolina Press, 1965).

177. Robbin L. Gates, *The Making of Massive Resistance: Virginia's Politics of Public School Desegregation, 1954–1956* (Chapel Hill, N.C.: University of North Carolina Press, 1962).

178. Joel Spring, *The Sorting Machine: National Educational Policy Since 1945* (New York: David McKay Co., 1976), pp. 160–185.

179. Horace H. Cunningham, "The Southern Mind Since the Civil War," pp. 386–387 in *Writing Southern History*, ed. Link and Patrick.

180. Jack Nelms, "The Dallas Academy: Backbone of the Permanent School System of Selma," *Alabama Review* 29 (April 1976): 113–123.

181. Sadie Bell, *The Church, the State, and Education in Virginia* (Philadelphia, Pa.: The University of Pennsylvania, 1930).

182. Griffin A. Hamlin, "Educational Activities of the Disciples of Christ in North Carolina, 1852–1902," *North Carolina Historical Review* 33 (July 1956): 310–331; Holder, *McIver of North Carolina*, pp. 143–161.

183. Woodward, *Origins of the New South*, p. 448; Kenneth T. Jackson, *The Ku Klux Klan in the City, 1915–1930* (New York: Oxford University Press, 1967), pp. 33, 48.

184. Philip N. Racine, "The Ku Klux Klan, Anti Catholicism and Atlanta's Board of Education, 1916–1917," *The Georgia Historical Quarterly* 57 (Spring 1973): 63–75.

185. Joseph W. Neuman, "A History of the Atlanta Public School Teachers' Association, Local 89 of the American Federation of Teachers, 1919–1956" (Ph.D. diss., Georgia State University, 1978), pp. 67–94.

186. Tindall, *The Emergence of the New South*, pp. 196–203.

187. Ray Ginger, *Six Days or Forever? Tennessee v. John Thomas Scopes* (Boston, Mass.: Beacon Press, 1958).

188. Willard Gatewood, "Politics and Piety in North Carolina: The Fundamentalist Crusade at High Tide, 1925–1927," *The North Carolina Historical Review* 42 (Summer 1965): 275–290; Gatewood, *Preachers, Pedagogues and Politicians: The Evolution Controversy in North Carolina, 1920–1927* (Chapel Hill, N.C.: University of North Carolina

Press, 1966). Gatewood has also edited documents relating to the anti-evolution debates in *Controversy in the Twenties: Fundamentalism, Modernism and Evolution* (Nashville, Tenn.: Vanderbilt University Press, 1969).

189. Paul Carter, "The Fundamentalist Defense of the Faith" in *Change and Continuity in Twentieth-Century America: The 1920's*, ed. John Broeman, Robert Bremner, and David Brody (Columbus, Ohio: Ohio State University Press, 1968), pp. 179–214.

190. Horace Cunningham, "The Southern Mind Since the Civil War," in *Writing Southern History*, ed. Lind and Patrick, pp. 395–400.

191. Grantham, "The Twentieth Century South," in *Writing Southern History*, ed. Link and Patrick, p. 412.

192. Louis R. Wilson, *The University of North Carolina, 1900–1930: The Making of a Modern University* (Chapel Hill, N.C.: University of North Carolina Press, 1957), pp. 457–471; O'Brien, *The Idea of the American South, 1920–1940*, pp. 31–93.

193. Reading S. Sugg, Jr., and George Hilton Jones, *The Southern Regional Education Board: Ten Years of Regional Cooperation in Higher Education* (Baton Rouge, La.: Louisiana State University Press, 1960).

194. Ibid., pp. 46–48.

195. Bernard Bailyn, *Education in the Forming of American Society* (Chapel Hill, N.C.: University of North Carolina Press, 1960).

196. Herbert Baxter Adams, ed., *Contributions to American Educational History* (Washington, D.C.: United States Bureau of Education, 1887–1903). Each state history was published as a *Circular of Information*.

197. Thomas Everett Cochran, *History of Public-School Education in Florida* (Lancaster, Pa.: Press of the New Era Printing Co., 1921); Boyce Fowler Ezell, *The Development of Secondary Education in Florida: with Special Reference to the Public White High School* (DeLand, Fla., privately printed, 1932); Nita Katharine Pyburn, *The History of the Development of a Single System of Education in Florida* (Tallahassee, Fla.: Florida State University, 1954).

198. Dorothy Orr, *A History of Education in Georgia* (Chapel Hill, N.C.: University of North Carolina Press, 1950); J. L. Blair Buck, *The Development of Public Schools in Virginia, 1907–1952* (Richmond, Va.: Commonwealth of Virginia State Board of Education, 1952).

199. Cornelius J. Heatwole, *A History of Education in Virginia* (New York: Macmillan Co., 1916).

200. Edgar W. Knight, *Public School Education in North Carolina* (Chapel Hill, N.C.: University of North Carolina Press, 1930).

201. Andrew David Holt, *The Struggle for a State System of Public Schools in Tennessee, 1903–1936*, Contributions to Education, no. 753, (New York: Teachers College, Columbia University, 1938).

202. Frank L. McVey, *The Gates Open Slowly: A History of Education in Kentucky* (Lexington, Ky.: University of Kentucky Press, 1949).

203. Mimns Sledge Robertson, *Public Education in Louisiana after 1898* (Baton Rouge, La.: Louisiana State University, 1952), p. 98.

204. David E. Lilienthal, *TVA: Democracy on the March* (New York: Harper & Bros., 1953), pp. 26–32, 79–89; Roscoe Martin, ed., *TVA: The First Twenty Years: A Staff Report* (University, Ala., and Knoxville, Tenn.: University of Alabama and University of Tennessee Presses, 1956), see J. O. Artman, "Forestry," pp. 177–192; O. M. Derryberry, "Health," pp. 193–205; and L. G. Allbaugh, "Fertilizer–Munitions and Agriculture," pp. 152–176.

205. Gilbert Banner, "Toward More Realistic Assumptions in Regional Economic Development," in *The Economic Impact of TVA*, ed. John R. Moore (Knoxville, Tenn.: University of Tennessee Press, 1967), pp. 121–143.

206. Raymond Wolters, "The New Deal and the Negro," in *The New Deal*, ed., John Braeman, Robert Bremner, and David Brody, vol. 1, *The National Level* (Columbus, Ohio: Ohio State University Press, 1975), pp. 191–200.

207. C. A. Bowers, *The Progressive Educator and the Depression: The Radical Years* (New York: Random House, 1969).

208. Edward A. Krug, *The Shaping of the American High School, 1920–1941*, vol. 2, (Madison, Wisc.: University of Wisconsin Press, 1972), pp. 201–327; see especially p. 277.

209. Tindall, *The Emergence of the New South*, pp. 483–504.

210. John Robert Moore, "The New Deal in Louisiana," in *The New Deal*, vol. 2, ed. Braemen, Bremner, and Brody, *The State and Local Levels*, pp. 137–165.

211. Elaine Von Oesen, "Public Library Extension in North Carolina and the WPA," *North Carolina Historical Review* 29 (July 1952): 379–399.

212. Paul Conkin, *Tomorrow a New World: The New Deal Community Program* (Ithaca, N.Y.: Cornell University Press, 1959), pp. 138–144, 192–205.

213. John A. Salmond, "Aubrey Williams, 'A Typical New Dealer,'" in *The New Deal*, vol. 1, ed. Braemen, Bremner, and Brody, pp. 227–229.

214. John A. Salmond, *The Civilian Conservation Corps, 1933–1942: A New Deal Case Study* (Durham, N.C.: Duke University Press, 1967), pp. 46–54.

215. John A. Salmond, "The Civilian Conservation Corps and the Negro," *Journal of American History* 52 (June 1965): 75–88.

216. Leslie H. Fishel, Jr., "The Negro in the New Deal Era," in *The Negro in Depression and War: Prelude to Revolution, 1930–1945*, ed. Bernard Sternsher (Chicago: Quadrangle Books, 1969), pp. 7–28.

217. Saloutos, *Farmer Movements in the South*.

218. See for example, Patricia Graham, *Community and Class in American Education, 1865–1918* (New York: John Wiley & Sons, 1974), pp. 101–141.

219. Fosdick, *Adventure in Giving*, pp. 39–114; Anderson, "Northern Foundations," pp. 371–396.

220. Leo McGee and Robert Boone, eds., *The Black Rural Landowner– Endangered Species: Social, Political and Economic Implications*

(Westport, Conn.: Greenwood Press, 1979); see especially the article by Manning Marble, "The Land Question in Historical Perspective: The Economics of Poverty in the Blackbelt South, 1865–1920," pp. 3–24.

221. Scott, *The Southern Lady*, p. 102.

222. Pannel and Wyatt, *Julia J. Tutwiler*.

223. Holder, *McIver of North Carolina*.

224. Newman, "A History of the Atlanta Public School Teachers Association;" Wayne Urban, "The Origins of Teacher Unionism: Atlanta, 1905–1919" (Paper presented at the Southern History of Education Society Meeting, Atlanta, Ga., October, 1978); and Urban, "Organized Teachers and Educational Reform," pp. 35–52.

225. Joseph Newman, "The Social Origins of Atlanta Teachers, 1881, 1896, 1922," *Urban Education* 11 (April 1976): 115–122.

About the Authors

JAMES D. ANDERSON   teaches history of education in the College of Education at the University of Illinois.

JENNINGS L. WAGONER, JR.   teaches history of education and is Director of the Center for the Study of Higher Education at the Curry Memorial School of Education at the University of Virginia.

SPENCER J. MAXCY   teaches history of education in the College of Education at Louisiana State University.

AMY FRIEDLANDER   is Historian for the Earth Systems Division of Soil Systems, Inc., in Marietta, Georgia.

MARK K. BAUMAN   is a member of the Social Sciences Division of the Atlanta Junior College in Atlanta, Georgia.

WAYNE J. URBAN   teaches history of education in the Department of Educational Foundations at Georgia State University, and is President of the History of Education Society.

JOSEPH W. NEWMAN   is a member of the Educational Foundations Department at the University of South Alabama.

WILLIAM BONDS THOMAS   teaches courses on the history and politics of education in the School of Education at the University of Pittsburgh.

RONALD K. GOODENOW   is a member of the Department of Education at Trinity College, Hartfort, Connecticut, and a Fellow of the Institute of Philosophy and Politics of Education at Teachers College, Columbia University.

NANCY L. GRANT is a member of the Department of History at Northwestern University.

ARTHUR O. WHITE teaches history of education in the College of Education at the University of Florida.

HARVEY NEUFELDT teaches in the Department of Secondary Education and Foundations at Tennessee Technological University.

CLINTON ALLISON teaches history of education in the College of Education at the University of Tennessee.

Index